P9-BJR-242

Ancient Near Eastern
Thought and the
Old Testament

Ancient Near Eastern Thought and the Old Testament

Introducing the Conceptual World of the Hebrew Bible

John H. Walton

Baker Academic
Grand Rapids, Michigan

I would like to acknowledge the important roles played by my student assistants over the years that this book was in process: Caryn Reeder, Liz Klassen, Melissa Moore, and Alyssa Walker. This book would have been poorer without their able assistance in editing at various levels.

© 2006 by John H. Walton

Published by Baker Academic
a division of Baker Publishing Group
P.O. Box 6287, Grand Rapids, MI 49516-6287
www.bakeracademic.com

Printed in the United States of America

All rights reserved. No part of this publication may be reproduced, stored in a retrieval system, or transmitted in any form or by any means—for example, electronic, photocopy, recording—without the prior written permission of the publisher. The only exception is brief quotations in printed reviews.

Library of Congress Cataloging-in-Publication Data
Walton, John H., 1952–
    Ancient Near Eastern thought and the Old Testament : introducing the conceptual world of the Hebrew Bible / John H. Walton.
        p.   cm.
    Includes bibliographical references and indexes.
    ISBN 10: 0-8010-2750-0 (pbk.)
    ISBN 978-0-8010-2750-5 (pbk.)
    1. Middle Eastern literature—Relation to the Old Testament. 2. Bible. O.T.—Criticism, interpretation, etc. 3. Bible. O.T.—Comparative studies. 4. Bible. O.T.—Extra-canonical parallels. I. Title.
    BS1171.3.W35 2006
    221.6′7—dc22   2006022891

Photos supplied by Zev Radovan, Land of the Bible Photo Archive, Jerusalem.

10   11   12   13   14   15   16   10   9   8   7   6   5   4

Contents

Contents

Illustrations

Tables

Sidebars

Abbreviations

AB	Anchor Bible
ABD	*Anchor Bible Dictionary*, ed. D. N. Freedman. 6 vols. New York: Doubleday, 1992
AEL	*Ancient Egyptian Literature*, M. Lichttheim. 3 vols. Berkeley: Univ. of California, 1973–80
AfO	*Archiv für Orientforschung*
ANET	*Ancient Near Eastern Texts Relating to the Old Testament*, ed. J. B. Pritchard. 3rd ed. with supplement. Princeton: Princeton University Press, 1969
AOAT	Alter Orient und Altes Testament
ARM	Archives royales de Mari
ASOR	American Schools of Oriental Research
BBR	*Bulletin for Biblical Research*
Bib	*Biblica*
BibOr	Biblica et orientalia
BM	B. Foster, *Before the Muses*. 3rd ed. Bethesda, MD: CDL, 2005
BRev	*Biblical Review*
BSac	*Bibliotheca sacra*
BWL	W. G. Lambert, *Babylonian Wisdom Literature*. Oxford: Clarendon, 1960
CAD	*The Assyrian Dictionary of the Oriental Institute of the University of Chicago*
CANE	*Civilizations of the Ancient Near East,* ed. J. Sasson. 4 vols. New York: Scribner's, 1995
CBQ	*Catholic Biblical Quarterly*
CBQMS	Catholic Biblical Quarterly Monograph Series

CC	Continental Commentaries
ConBOT	Coniectanea Biblica, Old Testament
COS	*Context of Scripture*, ed. W. W. Hallo and K. L. Younger. 3 vols. Leiden: Brill, 1996–2002
DDD	*Dictionary of Demons and Deities*, ed. K. van der Toorn. 2nd ed. Leiden: Brill, 1999
EI	*Eretz Israel*
FAT	Forschungen zum Alten Testament
FDD	B. R. Foster, *From Distant Days*. Bethesda, MD: CDL, 1995
HSM	Harvard Semitic Monographs
HSS	Harvard Semitic Studies
HTO	T. Jacobsen, *The Harps That Once—Sumerian Poetry in Translation*. New Haven: Yale University Press, 1987
HTR	*Harvard Theological Review*
HUCA	*Hebrew Union College Annual*
IEJ	*Israel Exploration Journal*
JANES	*Journal of the Ancient Near Eastern Society*
JAOS	*Journal of the American Oriental Society*
JBL	*Journal of Biblical Literature*
JCS	*Journal of Cuneiform Studies*
JEOL	*Jaarbericht van het Vooraziatisch-Egyptisch Gezelschap Ex oriente lux*
JETS	*Journal of the Evangelical Theological Society*
JNES	*Journal of Near Eastern Studies*
JNSL	*Journal of Northwest Semitic Languages*
JR	*Journal of Religion*
JRitSt	*Journal of Ritual Studies*
JSOT	*Journal for the Study of the Old Testament*
JSOTSup	Journal for the Study of the Old Testament, Supplements
KAR	*Keilschrifttexte aus Assur religiösen Inhalts*
LABS	*Letters from Assyrian and Babylonian Scholars*
LXX	Septuagint
MARI	*Mari: Annales de recherches interdisciplinaires*
MFM	S. Dalley, *Myths from Mesopotamia*. Repr. Oxford: Oxford University Press, 1991
NICOT	New International Commentary on the Old Testament
NIDOTTE	*New International Dictionary of Old Testament Theology and Exegesis*, ed. W. A. VanGemeren. 5 vols. Grand Rapids: Zondervan, 1997
NIV	New International Version
NIVAC	New International Version Application Commentary

OEAE	*Oxford Encyclopedia of Ancient Egypt*, ed. D. B. Redford. 3 vols. New York: Oxford University Press, 2001
OEANE	*Oxford Encyclopedia of Archaeology in the Near East*, ed. E. M. Meyers. 4 vols. New York: Oxford University Press, 1997
Or	*Orientalia*
OTL	Old Testament Library
OTP	V. H. Matthews and D. J. Benjamin, *Old Testament Parallels: Laws and Stories from the Ancient Near East*. 2nd ed. New York: Paulist Press, 1997
OtSt	*Oudtestamentische Studiën*
RA	*Revue d'assyriologie et d'archéologie orientale*
RAI	Rencontre assyriologique internationale
RANE	B. T. Arnold and B. Beyer, *Readings from the Ancient Near East*. Grand Rapids: Baker, 2002
RB	*Revue biblique*
RIMA	Royal Inscriptions of Mesopotamia, Assyrian Periods
RIME	Royal Inscriptions of Mesopotamia, Early Periods
SAA	State Archives of Assyria
SAALT	State Archives of Assyria Literary Texts
SAAS	State Archives of Assyria Studies
SBLDS	Society of Biblical Literature Dissertation Series
SBLMS	Society of Biblical Literature Monograph Series
SBLWAW	Society of Biblical Literature Writings from the Ancient World
SBTS	Sources for Biblical and Theological Study
SJOT	*Scandinavian Journal of the Old Testament*
TCS	Texts from Cuneiform Sources
TDOT	*Theological Dictionary of the Old Testament*, ed. G. J. Botterweck et al. Trans. D. E. Green et al. Grand Rapids: Eerdmans, 1974–
TynBul	*Tyndale Bulletin*
UBL	Ugaritisch-biblische Literatur
VAT	Vorderasiatische Abteilung Tontafel
VT	*Vetus Testamentum*
VTSup	Vetus Testamentum, Supplements
WBC	Word Biblical Commentary
WTJ	*Westminster Theological Journal*
YOS	Yale Oriental Series
ZA	*Zeitschrift für Assyriologie*

Part 1

Comparative Studies

1

History and Methods

History

The rediscovery of Egypt began in earnest in the eighteenth century AD and of Mesopotamia in the mid-nineteenth century AD. With the decipherment of the ancient languages, the tens of thousands of texts that were being unearthed began to be translated and analyzed. In many cases the motives of the adventurers and scholars represented a strange combination of politics, interest in antiquities (or treasures), and biblical apologetics. Initial studies were inclined to be defensive of the Bible, even if such a stance required the dismissal or distortion of the cuneiform texts. The flurry of activity in connection with the relationship of these texts to the Bible had reached a critical mass of sorts by the turn of the century; and, consequently, widespread attention was attracted by the series of lectures presented in 1902 under the auspices of the German Oriental Society and attended by Kaiser Wilhelm II. What the Scopes trial was to the discussion of evolution, these lectures were to comparative studies. The lecturer was the noted Assyriologist, Friedrich Delitzsch, son of the famous conservative biblical commentator, Franz Delitzsch.

Delitzsch's lectures, entitled "Babel und Bibel," brought a more focused attention to the impact of Assyriology on the understanding of the Bible. More controversial, however, was his claim that the literature of the Bible was dependent on, and even borrowed from, the literature of the dominant culture represented in the region of the Tigris and Euphrates

Photo 1
Cuneiform Writer

rivers. His contention was: "The Mesopotamian evidence shows us not just parallels to Old Testament customs and ideas, but genuine evidence regarding their origin."[1] The inevitable conclusion would therefore be that the origin of the Old Testament was human, not divine, and that the Christian faith therefore had its roots in pagan mythology. Two more lectures elaborating on this thesis came over the next two years. In the second, more objectionable than the first, he questioned the appropriateness of the traditional theological terminology used to describe the Bible (e.g., revelation, inspiration) in light of its now evident dependency. As H. Huffmon observes, "Delitzsch had moved from Babylonia as interpreter and illustrator of the Old Testament to a general attack on the religious value of the Old Testament for the modern German."[2] At this time, many Assyriologists were people of faith, with the result that Delitzsch was criticized vehemently in their written responses to his lectures. Over the following decades, however, as Assyriology became increasingly secular and its scholars, if concerned with the Bible at all, had embraced the tenets of critical scholarship, Delitzsch's lectures became recognized as a watershed in comparative studies.

1. M. T. Larsen, "The 'Babel/Bible' Controversy and Its Aftermath," *CANE* 1:95–106, quotation on 99.
2. H. B. Huffmon, "Babel und Bibel: The Encounter Between Babylon and the Bible," in *The Bible and Its Traditions*, ed. M. P. O'Connor and D. N. Freedman (Ann Arbor: University of Michigan Press, 1983), 309–20, quotation on 315.

The result was a growing ideological divide between those who viewed comparative studies from a confessional standpoint seeking to use Assyriology in their apologetics, and those who viewed it from a scientific or secular standpoint viewing the Bible as a latecomer in world literature filled with what were little more than adaptations from the mythology of the ancient Near East. Critical scholars considered their opponents to be naïve traditionalists. Confessional scholars considered their opponents to be godless heretics.[3] As evidence emerged that did not fit easily with a desire to vindicate the Bible, the critics became more strident, and many came to agree with Delitzsch's contention that "the Old Testament was no book of Christian religion and should be excluded from Christian theology."[4] In response confessional scholars became more entrenched and defensive. The cycle of division drove its wedges deeper and deeper.

The space of a century allows current scholars to recognize that Delitzsch's lectures were not motivated solely by a sense of scientific objectivity. He was a child of his culture as we all are, and his obvious nationalism can now be seen to have been encumbered with not only anti-Christian but also anti-Semitic sentiment.[5] Huffmon summarizes the regression well: "In dealing with Assyriological matters, as Delitzsch did in his first two lectures, he combined scholarship with special pleading; in dealing with Old Testament materials, Delitzsch mixed learning with considerable naiveté; in dealing with the New Testament, or, more specifically Jesus, Delitzsch displayed naiveté and perfidy."[6]

Delitzsch's work spawned a movement, never widely popular but remarkable for its excesses, called "Pan-Babylonianism," which argued that all world myths and all Christian Scriptures (Old and New Testament alike) were simply versions of Babylonian mythology. For instance, the stories of Jesus in the Gospels were based on the *Gilgamesh Epic*, and the passion of Christ was based on Marduk mythology.[7]

Even as Assyriology and Egyptology (and also Hittitology) emerged as serious, autonomous, academic disciplines, the attention of many remained focused on the Bible. As discoveries of major archives followed one after

3. There is no question that confessional scholars can use critical methodologies or that critical scholars may have confessional convictions. I am using the terms as generalizations to represent relative positions on a spectrum. They refer to those with a strong critical or confessional inclination.

4. Huffmon, "Babel und Bibel," 319.

5. B. T. Arnold and D. B. Weisberg, "A Centennial Review of Friedrich Delitzsch's 'Babel und Bibel' Lectures," *JBL* 121 (2002): 441–57, esp. 442–43.

6. Huffmon, "Babel und Bibel," 319.

7. M. W. Chavalas, "Assyriology and Biblical Studies: A Century of Tension," in *Mesopotamia and the Bible*, ed. M. W. Chavalas and K. L. Younger Jr. (Grand Rapids: Baker, 2002), 21–67, esp. 34.

another from the 1920s to the 1970s, each was greeted with initial excitement as scholars made great claims for the impact of the archive on the Bible. In most cases, time and more careful attention resulted in many, if not all, of the initial claims being rejected. Methodological maturity began to be displayed in the careful work of W. W. Hallo, who promoted a balanced approach called the "contextual approach," which seeks to identify and discuss both similarities and differences that can be observed between the Bible and the texts from the ancient Near East. "Hallo's goal, 'is not to find the key to every biblical phenomenon in some ancient Near Eastern precedent, but rather to silhouette the biblical text against its wider literary and cultural environment.' Thus we must not succumb either to 'parallelomania' or to 'parallelophobia.'"[8] It is Hallo's work that has provided the foundation for the following discussion of methodology.

Methodology

What Is Comparative Study?

Just as it would be foolish to think that all Europeans share the same culture, it would be a mistake to suppose that Babylonians, Hittites, Egyptians, Israelites, and Sumerians all shared the same culture. There would even be noticeable differences between the second-millennium Babylonians of Hammurabi's time and the first-millennium Babylonians at the time of Nebuchadnezzar. Nevertheless, there were some elements that many of the cultures of the ancient Near East held in common, and certainly many areas in which they shared more commonality with one another than they do with our modern culture.

Ultimately the goal of *background* studies is to examine the literature and archaeology of the ancient Near East in order to reconstruct the behavior, beliefs, culture, values, and worldview of the people. These could alternatively be called *cultural* studies. *Comparative* studies constitutes a branch of cultural studies in that it attempts to draw data from different segments of the broader culture (in time and/or space) into juxtaposition with one another in order to assess what might be learned from one to enhance the understanding of another. The range of this understanding can include behavior and belief within the culture, or the ways in which a culture is represented in art or literature. Within the literary category, areas for research include the larger issues of literary genre, the analysis of specific traditions and texts, and the use of individual metaphors, idioms, and words.

8. Ibid., 43.

Development of Sound Methodology for Comparative Study

As one can infer from the history related at the beginning of the chapter, early practitioners were distracted from this larger task by curiosity or by axes to grind. Whether defending or critiquing the Bible or defending the ancient Near East, some scholars became enmeshed in using cultural and comparative studies as a means to a polemical end. As is often the case in polemics of any stripe, techniques such as selectivity and special pleading can create distortion. This polemical application resulted in the abuse of comparative studies from scholars at either end of the spectrum. Consequently some confessional scholars concluded that comparative studies posed a danger to the biblical text when they saw it wielded as a weapon of skepticism and unbelief. At the same time some critical scholars openly ridiculed what they saw as feeble attempts by apologists to use comparative studies to prove that the Bible was true.

It took some generations for correctives to be put in place that served to establish an appropriate methodology for background and comparative study, which will be introduced below. Even as these have been put into place over the last several decades, abuse and misunderstanding persist in pockets. These methodological correctives have exposed the dangers inherent in research that ignores either similarities or differences between the Bible and the ancient Near East.

One of the earliest and most significant correctives was the insistence that neither biblical studies nor ancient Near Eastern studies should be subordinated to the other. Both represent autonomous disciplines, though they can mutually benefit from cross-fertilization. Even as comparative studies are important for those seeking to understand the Bible, study of the ancient Near East is not merely a subservient field to biblical studies. Assyriology, Egyptology, and the like are disciplines in themselves and valid academic, cultural, and linguistic pursuits. Comparative study by Bible students is just one application of the findings from those fields.

Why Do Bible Students Need Comparative Study?

Cultural Dimension of Language and Literature

When I first began teaching in the early 1980s, I could refer in passing to "the incident at Kent State" and feel assured that students would know what I was talking about. By the 1990s that was no longer the case. As another example, I can still refer to the "Berlin Wall" or to the "Iron Curtain" and assume that students need no further explanation. Within a decade, that may no longer be true. Effective communication requires a body of agreed-upon words, terms, and ideas.

19

Since communication requires a common ground of understanding, both speaker and audience must do what they can to enter that common ground. For the speaker this often requires accommodation to the audience. One uses words (representing ideas) that the audience will understand, thus, by definition, accommodating to the target audience.

When that common core of understanding exists, the author will not bother to explain him- or herself to the understanding audience against the chance that an uninformed person might be listening. This is where the work of the audience comes in if they are not native to the language/culture matrix, because reaching this common ground may require seeking out additional information or explanation. If someone outside the language/culture matrix wants to take advantage of information that is communicated within the language/culture matrix, cultural education is required—the individual has to adapt to the unfamiliar language/culture matrix.

For example, twice every year in most of the United States and in many other places around the world we encounter the phenomenon known as "daylight savings time." If someone from another culture came to the United States and heard the phrase "daylight savings time," no study of the individual words would alert them to its meaning. They would need information that would enable them to adapt to the culture. These are issues that go beyond language to culture. In the same way, if we are going to comprehend communication that took place between members of an ancient culture, we are going to have to adjust our thinking to be able to sit in the circle of communication with the ancient audience. The Bible has plenty of examples like "Iron Curtain" and "daylight savings time" that are not explained, and we do not intrinsically understand. But in many cases the key to understanding can be found in other ancient Near Eastern literature.

When we study an ancient text, we cannot make words mean whatever we want them to, or assume that they meant the same to the ancient audience that they do to a modern audience. Language itself is a cultural convention, and since the Bible and other ancient documents use language to communicate, they are bound to a culture. As interpreters, then, we must adapt to the language/culture matrix of the ancient world as we study the Old Testament. But as P. Michalowski has pointed out, "It is one thing to state banalities about 'the Other,' or about the inapplicability of western concepts to non-western modes of thought; it is something quite different actually to step outside one's frame of reference and attempt a proper analysis."[9]

9. P. Michalowski, "Commemoration, Writing, and Genre in Ancient Mesopotamia," in *Limits of Historiography*, ed. C. S. Kraus (Leiden: Brill, 1999), 69–90, quotation on 72.

This awareness of the integration of language and culture (and ultimately, worldview) moves us well beyond the sorts of research that were alluded to at the beginning of this chapter. Here we are no longer talking about trying to figure out whose religion is better, who was more ethical, who copied what literature from whom, or what should be considered Scripture and what should not. Methodology need not be tailored to detect literary borrowing or govern polemical agendas. When comparative studies are done at the cognitive environment level, trying to understand how people thought about themselves and their world, a broader methodology can be used. For instance, when literary pieces are compared to consider the question of dependency, the burden of proof is appropriately on the researcher to consider the issues of propinquity and transmission—that is, would the peoples involved have come into contact with one another's literature, and is there a mechanism to transmit said literature from one culture to the other? Literary questions of genre, structure, and context would all be investigated as well as geographical, chronological, and ethnic dimensions.[10] When considering larger cultural concepts or worldviews, however, such demands would not be as stringent, though they could not be ignored altogether. When we see evidence in the biblical text of a three-tiered cosmos, we have only to ask, Does the concept of a three-tiered cosmos exist in the ancient Near East? Once it is ascertained that it does, our task becomes to try to identify how Israel's perception of the cosmos might have been the same or different from what we find elsewhere. We need not figure out how Israel would have gotten such a concept or from whom they would have "borrowed" it. Borrowing is not the issue, so methodology does not have to address that. Likewise this need not concern whose ideas are derivative. There is simply common ground across the cognitive environment of the cultures of the ancient world.[11]

There is a great distance between borrowing from a particular piece of literature and resonating with the larger culture that has itself been influenced by its literatures. As a modern example, when Americans speak of the philosophy of "eat, drink, and be merry, for tomorrow we die," they are resonating with an idea that has penetrated society rather

10. For example, J. Tigay's criteria in "On Evaluating Claims of Literary Borrowing," in *The Tablet and the Scroll*, ed. M. Cohen et al. (Bethesda, MD: CDL, 1993), 250–55.

11. I use the terminology of "cognitive environment," but other terminology could serve just as well and occurs in the literature; e.g., intertextual echo (Richard Hays), shared stream of linguistic tradition or a common *Wortfeld* (Michael Fishbane), cultural codes (Daniel Boyarin), patterns of meaning (Hayden White), matrix of associations (Gershon Hepner), common conceptual milieu (J. Richard Middleton). These are conveniently presented with full bibliography by Middleton in *The Liberating Image* (Grand Rapids: Brazos, 2005), 62–64.

than borrowing from the writings of the Greek philosopher Epicurus, who is traditionally identified with promoting that approach to life. Historically the philosophy of Epicurus has seeped into the culture and can therefore be reflected in statements today. The demands of propinquity would be considerably relaxed. A cultural trail will not be as definable as a literary trail, nor will the tracking require the same criteria.

Cultural Dimensions of Literary Genre

On the whole, it is now recognized that the determination of literary dependence is not as simple as once thought, nor should it be the dominant goal of comparative studies. Rather, the careful observations of similarities and differences in pieces of literature help inform the study of both the Bible and the ancient Near East. For those who have an interest in understanding the Bible, it should be no surprise that this Israelite literature would reflect not only the specific culture of the Israelites but many aspects of the larger culture of the ancient Near East. Even when a biblical text engages in polemic or offers critiques of the larger culture, to do so its authors must be aware of and interact with current thinking and literature. When we compare the literature of the ancient Near East with the Bible, we are ultimately trying to recover aspects of the ancient cognitive environment that may help us understand the Israelite perspective a little better. By catching a glimpse of how they thought about themselves and their world, we sometimes discover ways that the Israelites would have thought that differ totally from how we think.

Beyond the words and ideas of the literature itself, another area where we must be sensitive to cultural issues is in the way we understand literary genres. It should be no surprise that Old Testament genres need to be compared to genres in the larger culture. Some genres would have operated differently in the ancient world than they do in our own culture, so we must become familiar with the mechanics of the genres represented in the ancient Near East. Whether we are looking at wisdom literature, hymnic literature, historical literature, or legal literature, we find generous doses of both similarities and differences. Understanding the genre of a piece of literature is necessary if we desire to perceive the author's intentions. Since perceiving an author's intentions is an essential ingredient to the theological and literary interpretation of a text, we recognize that understanding genre contributes to legitimate interpretation.

Where similarities can be observed between the biblical and ancient Near Eastern genres, they help us to understand the genre parameters and characteristics as they existed in the ancient mind. For instance, it is important for us to explore what defined historical writing in the ancient world. How close was it to the journalistic approach of today that relies heavily on eyewitness accounts? How did genealogies function in Old Testament times? Were they compiled for the same purpose that we compile them for?

Occasionally comparisons within genres reveal very close similarities between the biblical and ancient Near Eastern literatures on the level of content. Such similarities do not negate the individuality of either. Even if the Hebrew Bible had the very same law or the very same proverb that was found in the ancient Near East, we may find uniqueness in how that law or proverb was understood, or how it was nuanced by the literary context in which it was incorporated. At other times the Israelite version may not be noticeably different from the ancient Near Eastern example at any level.

Where there are differences it is important to understand the ancient Near Eastern genres because significant points in the biblical text may be made by means of contrast. For example, literature from Mesopotamia contains a couple of texts that recount the complaints of a righteous sufferer similar to what we find in the book of Job. The theology behind the book of Job, however, not only offers different explanations, but even uses the mentality of the ancient Near East (represented in the arguments of Job's friends) as a foil. Job maintains his integrity precisely by not adopting the appeasement mentality recommended by his friends (Job 27:1–6) that was representative of the ancient Near East. The book's message is accomplished in counterpoint. If we are unaware of the contrasts, we will miss some of the nuances. Throughout this book I will be presenting what can be understood about the cognitive environment of the ancient Near East and interspersing "Comparative Explorations" to consider specific similarities and differences found in Israel.

Cultural Dimension of Religious Practice

Another aspect of comparative study concerns comparative religion. One of the most consistent claims made within the biblical text concerns the distinctiveness of the Israelite religion. Yet at the same time the text does not hide the fact that the distinctions that were articulated in theory often did not translate into practice. Consequently, comparative study is helpful both for understanding the background religious practice to which the biblical ideal is contrasted and for understanding the syncretistic elements that were represented in common practice. Even when noticing the contrasts, however, comparative study will reveal many areas of continuity alongside the noted discontinuity. For instance, even though the biblical ideal is aniconic (no use of idols), the study of religious iconography can give understanding to objects like the ark of the covenant. As a second example, though the prophets decry the use of the high places, high places had a role even in legitimate worship in some periods.

Indeed, as much continuity as Christian theologians have developed between the religious ideas of preexilic Israel and those of Christianity, there is probably not as much common ground between them as there was between the religious ideas of Israel and the religious ideas of Babylon. When we think of Old Testament religious concepts such as ritual sacrifice, sanctuaries/sacred space, priests and their role, creation, the nature of sin, communication with deity, and many other areas, we realize that the Babylonians would have found Israelite practice much more comprehensible than we do.

In addition, though there would have been aspects of Canaanite or Babylonian religious practice (such as the ideology behind certain rituals) that were not understood clearly by the Israelites, they were well acquainted with the basic elements and ideals of their neighbors' beliefs. As H. W. F. Saggs has pointed out, for example, a man such as King Jehu of Israel must have been able to be fairly convincing as a Baal worshiper and well enough informed about the nuances of their religious practice to succeed in persuading all of the Baal worshipers to shed their weapons and come into the temple to be slaughtered (2 Kings 11:18–28). Saggs gives several other examples and makes his point persuasively.[12] We must not make a mistake in our assessment in either direction. Both similarities and differences must be observed, documented, and evaluated, not for the sake of critiquing, but for the sake of understanding. Though some use comparative studies to contradict claims made in the biblical text, the data need not be so employed.

Cultural Dimension of Theology

Including but expanding beyond religious practice is the construct termed theology. To investigate Israelite theology in relation to any other ancient theology, we must go beyond the simple identification of similarities and differences to articulate the relationships on a functional level. For example, it is one thing to say that both Israelites and Babylonians used rituals for transference of offense. It is another matter altogether to understand the function of those rituals and the role they played in the larger theology. Similarities could exist because Israel adapted something from ancient Near Eastern culture or literature, or, as previously mentioned, because they simply resonated with the culture. Differences could reflect the Israelites' rejection of an ancient Near Eastern perspective, in which a practice was either ignored or proscribed, or they might emerge in explicit Israelite polemics against the views of their neighbors, in which extended discourse drew out the distinction. In all such cases,

---

12. H. W. F. Saggs, *Encounter with the Divine in Mesopotamia and Israel* (London: Athlone, 1978), 6–8.

the theology of the text may be nuanced or clarified by an understanding of the cultural context, whether it resonates with its environment or stands in sharp relief against it.

When it comes to the formulation of our modern theology based on the biblical text, we may logically conclude that without the guidance of background studies, we are bound to misinterpret the text at some points. A text can be thought of as a web of ideas linked by threads of writing. Each phrase and each word communicates by the ideas and thoughts that it will trigger in the mind of the reader or hearer. We can then speak of the potential meanings that words point to as gaps that need to be filled with (one hopes, appropriate) meaning by the audience. The writer or speaker assumes that those gaps will be filled in particular ways based on the common language and worldview he shares with his audience. Interpreters of the Bible have the task of filling in those gaps, not with their own ideas (theological or otherwise) but with the ideas of the writer as those ideas can be understood. Often the words he uses and the ideas he is trying to convey are rooted in the culture and therefore need the assistance of background studies.[13] For example, the tower of Babel is described as being built "with its head in the heavens." Without the benefit of ancient Near Eastern backgrounds, early interpreters were inclined to provide the theological explanation that the builders were trying to build a structure that would allow them to launch an attack on the heavens. In other words, the tower was seen as a way for people to ascend to heaven. But background study has allowed modern interpreters to recognize that the tower is an expression used to describe the ziggurats of Mesopotamia that were intended to serve as a bridge or portal between heaven and earth for the gods to use. Thus comparative study offers an alternative, and arguably more accurate, interpretation of the text.[14] In Genesis the tower should be viewed as providing a way for deity to descend. In conclusion, then, as our interpretation of the text requires us to fill in the gaps, we want to be careful to consider the option of filling those gaps from the cultural context before we leap to fill them with a theological significance coming out of our own experience or understanding.

Scope of Comparative Study

As we continue to think on the level of the common cognitive environment, we will have reason to expand the focus of our comparative studies.

---

13. I am not here speaking of the sort of information that one could theoretically derive from cross-examining or even psychoanalyzing the writer. I simply refer to those elements that can be found to make sense against the backdrop of the culture.

14. See more complete discussion in "Comparative Exploration: Tower of Babel," in chap. 5.

The scholarly interest in comparative studies had formerly focused on either individual features (e.g., flood accounts from both the Bible and the ancient Near East feature birds sent out from an ark) or the literary preservation of traditions (e.g., creation accounts, vassal treaties), and many studies have been conducted with either apologetics (from confessional circles) or polemics (against confessional traditions) in mind. Those interested in the interpretation of the text have only more recently begun to recognize in addition the importance of comparative studies that focus on conceptual issues conducted with illumination of the cultural dynamics and worldview behind the text in mind.

> Comparative research in the Biblical field has often become a kind of "parallel hunting." Once it has been established that a certain biblical expression or custom has a parallel outside the Bible, the whole problem is regarded as solved. It is not asked, whether or not the extra-Biblical element has the same place in life, the same function in the context of its own culture. The first question that should be asked in comparative research is that of the *Sitz im Leben* and the meaning of the extra-Biblical parallel adduced. It is not until this has been established that the parallel can be utilized to elucidate a Biblical fact.[15]

Items for comparative research can be divided into three categories: individual elements, worldview concepts, and literary preservation. In addition, rather than simply talking about similarities and differences, we may now create a spectrum to define the varieties of differences and similarities to classify nuances of relationship more precisely. This is represented on figure 1. Each bullet point identifies a level of relationship between the Old Testament and the ancient Near East. Examples in any of the three categories listed above may be found in each of these seven levels of relationship.

Conclusions

Principles of Comparative Study

Ten important principles must be kept in mind when doing comparative studies:

1. Both similarities and differences must be considered.

15. H. Ringgren, "Israel's Place Among the Religions of the Ancient Near East," in *Studies in the Religion of Ancient Israel*, VTSup 23 (Leiden: Brill, 1972), 1; quoted in S. Talmon, "The Comparative Method in Biblical Interpretation: Principles and Problems," in *Essential Papers on Israel and the Ancient Near East*, ed. F. E. Greenspahn. (New York: New York University Press, 1991), 402.

Figure 1. Comparative/Contextual Spectrum

Differences

Similarities

- Totally ignores and presents different view
- Hazy familiarity leading to caricature and ridicule
- Accurate knowledge resulting in rejection
- Disagreement resulting in polemics, debate, or contention
- Awareness leading to adaptation or transformation
- Conscious imitation or borrowing
- Subconscious shared heritage

---

2. Similarities may suggest a common cultural heritage or cognitive environment rather than borrowing.
3. It is not uncommon to find similarities at the surface but differences at the conceptual level and vice versa.
4. All elements must be understood in their own context as accurately as possible before cross-cultural comparisons are made (i.e., careful background study must precede comparative study).
5. Proximity in time, geography, and spheres of cultural contact all increase the possibility of interaction leading to influence.
6. A case for literary borrowing requires identification of likely channels of transmission.
7. The significance of differences between two pieces of literature is minimized if the works are not the same genre.
8. Similar functions may be performed by different genres in different cultures.
9. When literary or cultural elements are borrowed they may in turn be transformed into something quite different by those who borrowed them.
10. A single culture will rarely be monolithic, either in a contemporary cross-section or in consideration of a passage of time.[16]

Goals of Background and Comparative Study

I would contend, then, that students should undertake background study with four goals in mind:

---

16. J. Walton, "Cultural Background of the Old Testament," in *Foundations for Biblical Interpretation*, ed. D. Dockery, K. Mathews, and R. Sloan (Nashville: Broadman/Holman, 1994), 256. See also Tigay, "On Evaluating Claims," 250–55.

1. Students may study the *history* of the ancient Near East as a means of recovering knowledge of the events that shaped the lives of people in the ancient world.
2. Students may study *archaeology* as a means of recovering the lifestyle reflected in the material culture of the ancient world.
3. Students may study the *literature* of the ancient Near East as a means of penetrating the heart and soul of the people who inhabited the ancient world that Israel shared.
4. Students may study the *language* of the ancient Near East as a means of gaining additional insight into the semantics, lexicography, idioms, and metaphors used in Hebrew.

These goals then each contribute to comparative studies and will help us understand the Old Testament better.

2

Comparative Studies, Scholarship, and Theology

Comparative study is used in two very different sorts of scholarly contexts and poses its own unique challenges in each one. On the one hand, it is one of the tools used by critical scholars in the scientific study of the text, particularly in historical and literary criticism. As such, it sometimes pulls in a different direction than other branches of critical scholarship. On the other hand, comparative study is a tool used in confessional contexts and likewise often pulls in a different direction than confessional scholarship has traditionally gone. We will consider the role of comparative study in each of these contexts, and consider both the resistance to comparative study that is sometimes evident in each, as well as the way it is used for polemical purposes. Finally, we will consider the integrated role of comparative study.

Comparative Study and Critical Scholarship

Critical scholarship of the nineteenth century was driven by the winds of evolution. Whatever the interconnections may have been to the scientific theories of evolution posited in Darwin's *Origin of Species*, biblical studies had its own permutations of evolutionary theory. In the literary realm, much attention was being paid to the evolution of pieces of literature—thus the compositional theories connected to literary criticism and source criticism. Likewise in the history of traditions, evolution was seen as providing the foundation for understanding that religious practice developed from lower to higher forms, and in philosophy that there was likewise a progression in the sophistication of ideas that could be traced over the millennia.

These evolutionary theories had been birthed in an environment where theorizing led to models and hypotheses—but one in which those ideas could not be tested against empirical data. As the discovery of the ancient Near East unfolded and the languages were deciphered and the texts published, the spate of primary source material allowed for the reigning theories to be placed under the microscope.

Challenges to Critical Scholarship

As is always true with theorizing, some of the conclusions that had been reached proved to be untenable. Religious or cultural ideas that were thought to be late were seen to be early. Texts that were thought to be redacted together at late dates showed signs of being unified earlier. Ideas that were thought to be too sophisticated to be found among early populations showed up.

As more and more literature became available from the Near East, scholars learned more and more about the growth of literary traditions and the composition of texts in the ancient world. Consequently, the burgeoning comparative material that was becoming available revolutionized critical theory. Apart from any gloating this might have occasioned from those who had been skeptical of the theories to begin with, such examples had the effect of demonstrating that comparative study was capable of challenging theories that had achieved a certain consensus in critical circles.

Hermann Gunkel spearheaded one of the earliest attacks on the consensus that had formed behind literary criticism. The central elements of the form criticism that he espoused were the recognition of standard forms used in communication and the importance of the *Sitz im Leben* in the interpretation of a text. Both drew heavily on ancient Near Eastern elements, as did his interests in genre (*Gattung*) and the oral traditions behind a written text. On the basis of the Babylonian texts, Gunkel had concluded that certain theories of Wellhausen, such as the late dating of Genesis 1, were simplistic. E. Gerstenberger indicates that Gunkel and his followers were looking for more.

> The new school demanded—on top of literary criticism, or better, preceding it—a comprehensive analysis of history, culture and religion. The rebels

could not content themselves with reconstructions of conceptual systems or historical social structures. They were searching for the very soul of the ancient writers, and, what is even more important, they took into account both general cultural and religious backgrounds and all those social factors which influence the growth of oral tradition.[1]

Thus comparative studies pitted critical scholars against one another.[2]

A second challenge came against literary criticism as the division of biblical texts between various sources was undermined by the suggested relationship between biblical and ancient Near Eastern texts. For example, how could J and P be considered independent, autonomous sources if in their (putatively late) combined form they proved to have a literary structure parallel to early ancient Near Eastern literature?

This challenge can be seen clearly in the book *Before Abraham Was* by I. Kikawada and A. Quinn.[3] Their contention was that Genesis 1–11 followed the same pattern as that found in the *Atrahasis Epic*. Kikawada and Quinn endorsed and developed an analysis of the coherence of the flood narrative that G. Wenham had published a few years earlier.[4] Wenham had observed: "it is strange that two accounts of the flood so different as J and P, circulating in ancient Israel, should have been combined to give our present story which has many more resemblances to the Gilgamesh version than the postulated sources."[5] D. Garrett summarized Wenham's position and drew out the centrality of comparative study in it.

> When compared form-critically to the other major ancient Near Eastern flood accounts (especially the account in Gilgamesh, but also the Atrahasis, Ras Shamra, and Sumerian versions), the Genesis narrative is found to have a remarkably high number of formal parallels to those versions. Wenham has isolated seventeen features the Genesis and Gilgamesh accounts have in common, and these usually occur in the same sequence. . . . Wenham points out that of the seventeen common formal elements, J has only twelve and P has only ten.[6]

This sort of challenge does not attempt to negate the concept of sources or the idea of long periods of composition. It merely indicates that com-

1. E. Gerstenberger, "Psalms," in *Old Testament Form Criticism*, ed. J. H. Hayes (San Antonio: Trinity University Press, 1974), 181.
2. See J. H. Hayes, *An Introduction to Old Testament Study* (Nashville: Abingdon, 1979), 123–39.
3. I. Kikawada and A. Quinn, *Before Abraham Was* (Nashville: Abingdon, 1985).
4. G. Wenham, "The Coherence of the Flood Narrative," *VT* 28 (1978): 336–48.
5. Ibid., 347.
6. Duane Garrett, *Rethinking Genesis* (Grand Rapids: Baker, 1991), 27.

parative study is capable of offering some correctives to some of the assumptions and conclusions of source theory.

A third area in which comparative study challenged the critical establishment was by providing evidence that certain cultural developments that had been supposed to be late actually came significantly earlier. In other words, the ancients had more sophistication than had been credited to them. One example of this concerned the still controversial issue of literacy. When the issue of the date of the pentateuchal materials was discussed, it was not uncommon that one of the evidences for a late date was that writing was not sufficiently developed in the circles that would have had to produce the kinds of documents involved in the Pentateuch.

Response to these challenges has resulted in some reassessment of long-standing critical theories. In other cases, critical scholars have taken up comparative studies as a tool for further advancing literary criticism. Most notable is J. Tigay's *Empirical Models for Biblical Criticism* in which he uses the long compositional history of the *Gilgamesh Epic* as a parallel for the compositional history of the Pentateuch.[7]

Resistance to the Use of Comparative Studies by Critical Scholars

Resistance to comparative studies continues in some critical circles, especially those more focused on the biblical text simply as the literary output of an ancient culture. One result of this approach to the text is the conviction that there are no real historical events behind the text to reconstruct. The current form of the text is viewed as the result of a long history of redactional activity that does not represent any specific time period or series of events. Historical criticism is therefore seen as fruitless, and literary criticism is in no need of comparative enlightenment. This trend is also fed by those who are committed to reader response hermeneutics and find it presumptuous for anyone to think that they can recover what an author meant. The task is complicated enormously when dealing with an ancient author from a totally different culture.

Related to these convictions one might find the purist insistence that comparative studies is dependent on simplistic generalizations that will always require one to compare apples to oranges. It is maintained that each culture is autonomous and unique and we dare not blur the lines of distinction by superficial correlations. Another alternative is found in those who increasingly ignore the comparative data and insist that texts be treated as self-contained interpretive units. J. J. M. Roberts assesses

---

7. J. Tigay, *Empirical Models for Biblical Criticism* (Philadelphia: University of Pennsylvania Press, 1985). This work uses the result of his more detailed treatment, *The Evolution of the Gilgamesh Epic* (Philadelphia: University of Pennsylvania Press, 1982).

this trend: "Partially it reflects a conscious theological decision about the appropriate task of the OT scholar (Childs), and partly it may reflect a loss of nerve, a decision to settle for a more controllable albeit more restricted vision."[8] Despite these pockets of resistance, critical scholarship as a whole has tended to absorb the data provided by comparative studies and adjust its theories accordingly. Comparative study poses a threat not to critical scholarship but only to occasional theories that critical scholars have espoused.

Polemical Use

The science of biblical study often does not operate under any confessional premise and therefore is most inclined to treat the Old Testament as any other piece of ancient literature, despite its literary distinctions. Since comparative studies typically draw out similarities between the Old Testament and the ancient Near East, they are at times used to contest or contradict traditional or confessional views. Occasionally this polemical use offers a necessary adjustment that does not intrinsically negate confessional positions. At other times basic convictions about the theological nature of the biblical text are undermined or challenged.

Polemical comparative studies can take many forms and in some ways can be thought of as dominating the field of study. Polemics are often encountered in the work of those who bring to the comparative task presuppositions about the biblical text that directly contradict the apparent claims of the text. When a scholar believes that Moses, Abraham, or David did not exist and that the texts are simply later legends that have grown up around fictional characters, comparative study is going to be used to substantiate that skepticism and vindicate it. Scholars who believe that no flood of cosmic proportions ever occurred will understandably be inclined to bring their comparative study to the task of demonstrating the mythological and derivative nature of the biblical text. In these cases, whether the interpreter has an ax to grind or simply presuppositions to support, the historical, literary, and eventually confessional value of the text is undermined.

Comparative Study and Confessional Scholarship

Confessional scholarship has not acclimated to comparative study with quite the ease that is evident in critical circles. Of course, confessional

---

8. J. J. M. Roberts, "The Ancient Near Eastern Environment," in *The Hebrew Bible and Its Modern Interpreters*, ed. D. A. Knight and G. M. Tucker (Chico, CA: Scholars Press, 1985), 96.

scholars who have wholeheartedly embraced the critical agenda experience no problems. But many confessional scholars still find themselves defensive concerning cherished and traditional convictions about the biblical text and therefore find certain aspects of both critical scholarship and comparative study suspect or unacceptable. Such reticence may be evident in conservative circles of Orthodox, Catholic, Protestant, or Jewish persuasions. Of these, evangelical Protestants have been perhaps the most visible in publication and will therefore be considered here.

Challenges to Confessional Scholarship

The challenges that comparative studies present to confessional and traditional scholars are manifold. Tracing the history of the conversation will show that the challenges first focused on the Old Testament texts dealing with the earliest time periods and gradually penetrated deeper into the biblical ages. The initial conversations focused on Genesis 1–11 and its parallels to the mythological literature of the ancient Near East. Earlier critical conclusions that Genesis 1–11 was the mythology of Israel were strengthened by the Babylonian account of creation and the flood found in Ashurbanipal's library.[9] Genesis 1–11 came to be explained not only as mythology, but as derivative and inferior mythology. More extensive studies brought Adam and Eve, the genealogies, the sons of God, and the tower of Babel under the same microscope with the same conclusions.

When comparative studies were applied to the patriarchal narratives, a different pattern emerged. Here the discoveries of archives such as those from Nuzi and Mari, and later even from Ebla, offered opportunities for critical scholars to defend the authenticity of the stories of Israel's ancestors. This lasted from the 1930s to the 1970s when scholars such as T. L. Thompson and J. Van Seters began to question whether the comparative evidence really lent any credibility to the narratives, or said anything about the dating of those narratives. As Genesis 1–11 had been categorized as myths, Genesis 12–50 were interpreted as founders' legends.

The exodus had been a target of critical incredulity for some time due to the miraculous elements that are so prominent. Background studies pressed the case further as evidence for the events of the exodus narrative continued to be absent on every count. It was purported that there was no evidence that the Israelites were ever in Egypt, no evidence of Moses (or Joseph) in the royal records, no evidence of the plagues, no consensus about the location of Sinai, no indications of an Israelite

---

9. Ashurbanipal was a seventh-century BC Assyrian king.

presence in the wilderness, and so on. No comparative literature comes into this discussion because that too is absent. The text does not name the pharaoh of Egypt, and the identification of the cities the Israelites built was fraught with controversy.[10]

With the discovery of the stele of Hammurabi around 1902, the law of Moses also came to be seen in a different light. Here was a Babylonian text that predated Moses by centuries and showed an already sophisticated sense of law. Again traditional views of the law proceeding from Sinai by divine communication were threatened by the similarities in content, style, and concept.

The historical narratives of the Old Testament came under fire as comparative and background studies identified problems in chronology and factual details. Literary studies found similarities between the biblical narratives and literary-historical compositions from the ancient Near East. These studies led critical scholars to question whether the biblical narratives could be used at all in the historical-critical process of reconstructing the events during the Bronze and Iron ages. A group labeled "minimalists" contended that the biblical narratives were almost entirely unusable, while "maximalists" continued to find some level of usefulness, even if it were only in some historical core.

The institutions of Israel were also evaluated in light of comparative and background information. Prophets, priests, and kings, and temple and cult were compared to, and critiqued in light of, the related institutions in the ancient Near East.

Hymnic and Wisdom literatures were challenged with regard to date, authorship, and originality. With regard to the last category, similarities between Proverbs and ancient Near Eastern wisdom pieces such as the Instruction of Amenemope, as well as similarities between certain psalms and Ugaritic literature, led once more to conclusions that Israelite compositions descended from older, venerated literary traditions.

In all of these categories, the common denominator was that the Old Testament is not unique. Some considered this a threat to their doctrine of inspiration. The sequence of logic easily moved from "not unique" to "derivative or borrowed" to "human, not divine," to "fictitious or unreliable."

10. Many of the critical conclusions from these lacunae can be seen in D. B. Redford, *Egypt, Canaan and Israel in Ancient Times* (Princeton: Princeton University Press, 1992); T. L. Thompson, "The Joseph and Moses Narratives," in *Israelite and Judaean History*, ed. J. Hayes and J. M. Miller, OTL (Philadelphia: Westminster, 1977), 149–212; C. Redmount, "Bitter Lives: Israel in and out of Egypt," in *The Oxford History of the Biblical World*, ed. M. Coogan (New York: Oxford University Press, 1998), 79–120; E. S. Frerichs and L. Lesko, *Exodus: The Egyptian Evidence* (Winona Lake, IN: Eisenbrauns, 1997).

Responses to these challenges have come from competent Assyriologists and Egyptologists such as K. A. Kitchen, D. J. Wiseman, A. R. Millard, K. L. Younger, and J. Hoffmeier,[11] who not only refute some of the charges levied by skeptics, but also provide evidence of the Bible's reliability through their cultural and comparative studies. Scholars engaged in this work use their research to challenge the conclusions of critical scholarship and in the process to authenticate the biblical text. Such studies intend to exonerate the Old Testament and defend against spurious attacks on its integrity.

Resistance to the Use of Comparative Studies by Confessional Scholars

Nonetheless, for various reasons many confessional scholars are uncomfortable with the use of comparative studies. Some still harbor the belief that similarities detract from the uniqueness of the Bible. They maintain that admittance of comparative evidence to the interpretive process is a slippery slope that will end with de-canonizing the text.

A second group claims that the text is all that we need. God has inscripturated his revelation through the use of human authors and language, but the theological meaning of the text is located in the canon, not bound up in the authors' limitations, humanity, and culture. For this group, a careful study of the text is all that is necessary to glean the truth of God's Word. In a related way, it is not uncommon for traditional interpreters to believe that the divine authorship of Scripture is mitigated if the human input into the text is used to arrive at an interpretation. Inspiration, in their view, lifts the text above its human element.

Especially in Protestant circles where the blood of the Reformers flows thick, commitment to the perspicuity of Scripture is perceived as threatened by comparative studies. Since a high level of training in specialized fields is necessary to do comparative studies, some laypeople feel that scholars are trying to take the Bible out of their hands. They feel that requiring specialized information is ultimately elitist and throws them right back into dependence on a few, as the pre-Reformation church was dependent on the clergy for interpretation. Individualism and the prospects of being able to engage in an inductive study of the text lead them to disdain any suggestion that they cannot be self-sufficient interpreters.

11. In numerous articles in addition to the following books: K. A. Kitchen, *On the Reliability of the Old Testament* (Grand Rapids: Eerdmans, 2003); A. R. Millard and D. J. Wiseman, eds., *Essays on the Patriarchal Narratives* (Winona Lake, IN: Eisenbrauns, 1983); A. R. Millard, *The Bible B.C.: What Can Archaeology Prove?* (Phillipsburg, NJ: Presbyterian & Reformed, 1977); K. L. Younger, *Ancient Conquest Accounts*, JSOTSup 98 (Sheffield: JSOT Press, 1990); J. Hoffmeier, *Israel in Egypt* (Oxford: Oxford University Press, 1997).

Finally, some object to the use of comparative study on historical grounds. Christians and Jews are intentionally dependent on the interpretations and decisions of those who have preceded them. Tradition and the creeds are nearly as foundational to doctrine as the biblical text itself. In such an environment, innovation and originality are not necessarily welcomed. How could God leave all of those generations without the wherewithal to read his Word accurately? Furthermore, if the likes of Augustine or Calvin were hampered or even crippled by the lack of cultural studies, and could perhaps even have misinterpreted passages because of their ignorance of ancient culture, the fear that Christian doctrine might be exposed as a house of cards would seem too real and threatening.

Polemical Use

Even as the use of comparative studies is suspect in some confessional quarters, others view the availability of information from the ancient Near East as an opportunity to prove that the Bible is true or to confirm a traditional date of a particular book. As was early evident in the field of biblical archaeology, many who would take upon themselves the mantle of apologist have not had the scholarly training to give them discernment for their task. Misinterpreted data, out-of-date or disproven arguments, haphazardly selected factoids, and neglect of information that would negate their point all characterize the special pleading that is too often obvious in this approach. Though lacking credibility, these polemical approaches can gain a wide following among a sometimes gullible public. This is not to label such writers as charlatans. They are zealots with a mission that in and of itself may be admirable. It is just that they are insufficiently schooled in the methods that would allow them to use properly the tools that they are exploiting.

Of course, not all apologists are lacking scholarly credentials, nor does the apologist's task necessarily involve special pleading or distortion of the data. One of the important tasks that apologists take up is the defense of the date of biblical literature. While the trends in critical study have tended to push the date of final redactions increasingly later, some use comparative studies to try to demonstrate that literary characteristics found in the biblical literature demand an earlier date. This approach is not so much an attempt to prove the Bible true as it is determination to show that the Bible's claims of chronological setting are more plausible than the critical reconstruction's alternatives.

For example, Kenneth Kitchen has provided in-depth studies of treaty forms in support of the idea that the covenant documents reflect a mid-second-millennium milieu that would have been unknown in the mid-first millennium. He has also presented evidence that the literary form in Proverbs is attested in materials that date to the beginning rather than the middle of the first millennium.

In a book like Jonah, the tug-of-war goes back and forth. Critical scholars point out that the use of the title "king of Nineveh" demonstrates that the author is writing long after the time of the Assyrian Empire. In the putative time of the prophet Jonah, Nineveh is not the capital and it is claimed that the king would be identified as the "king of Assyria." Attempts to use cultural studies to undergird the biblical text point to the anarchy in Assyria at the time and the powerful role of regional governors,[12] one of them being over the region of Nineveh.[13] Added to this is the information from the eponym lists that identify similar offices.[14] Thus the title "king of Nineveh" is presented as an authentic detail of the period that may not even have been known a generation later. A writer several centuries later would have naturally used "king of Assyria," for the knowledge of the existence of the empire was long retained. Such discussions jockey back and forth for the data that will serve the polemical desires of the interpreter.

Integrated Role

We can now speak of three different roles for comparative studies: critical analysis, defense of the biblical text, and exegesis of the biblical text (see figure 2). Each of these can be done well or done poorly.

Critical Analysis

Integrated use of comparative studies in critical analysis serves to provide a wide range of information by which we can understand in more advanced ways the history and the literature of the biblical world. Such studies are helpful in providing us the data necessary to critique and modify as necessary any given consensus. Consensus among confessional scholars is often based on tradition. These conclusions need constantly to be reevaluated with a critical eye by careful scholars who are not

12. A. K. Grayson, "The Struggle for Power in Assyria: Challenge to Absolute Monarchy in the Ninth and Eighth Centuries B.C.," in *Priests and Officials in the Ancient Near East*, ed. K. Watanabe (Heidelberg: Universitatsverlag C. Winter, 1999), 268. It should be noted, however, that Grayson is not engaging in polemics or discussing the book of Jonah.

13. P. Ferguson, "Who Was the 'King of Nineveh' in Jonah 3:6?" *TynBul* 47 (1996): 301–14.

14. A. R. Millard, *The Eponyms of the Assyrian Empire, 910–612 BC*, SAAS 2 (Helsinki: University of Helsinki Press, 1994), 7–11.

predisposed to either undermine or vindicate confessional conclusions. Consensus in critical circles has embraced theories that have created their own traditions, which need constant reevaluation. Comparative studies used for critical analysis can thereby provide a basis for us to subject our theories and traditions to accountability.

But revision is not the only possible outcome. Sometimes critical analysis can simply improve our understanding of a series of historical events as we are able to reconstruct them. The parameters of literary genres can be delineated or social institutions can be investigated and carefully nuanced. Consequently critical analysis has much to offer in its ability to illuminate the cognitive environment of the biblical world.

Defense of the Biblical Text

Though this might often be a role played by confessional scholars, nonconfessional approaches may also at times provide comparative studies that rebuff claims that have been made previously by others against the biblical text. The integrated role of comparative studies in this area recognizes the importance of a careful and balanced use rather than a haphazard and biased use of the data that emerge from cultural studies. K. A. Kitchen has done a thorough job of demonstrating the appropriate use of this approach in his book *On the Reliability of the Old Testament*, in which he seeks to validate the credibility and plausibility of the details of the biblical text by using the information from cultural studies. He especially seeks to deflect negative criticism that has made claims defaming the reliability of the text or the composition date or process of one book or another.

Exegesis of the Biblical Text

Many readers of the Bible could arguably ignore with impunity the two roles already discussed. Many people in the pew feel no need of further illumination of the background—to them it is irrelevant to God's Word. Similarly, those whose beliefs about the Bible are not under attack may feel no inclination to explore the defense of the text. They assume the text to be reliable and perhaps do not even care if others think differently. This third category, however, we ignore at our peril.

As we discussed in the previous chapter, since the biblical text is a cultural artifact (in addition to whatever theological significance and claims may be attached to it) emerging from an ancient context, we should not be surprised that there are frequent occasions in which the meaning of the text will not be immediately transparent to us. Ancient Near Eastern ideas, concepts, beliefs, or worldviews may then be necessary in order to discern the meaning of the text. The aid of comparative study might sometimes be needed to help with a minor detail. For instance, when Sennacherib sends his representatives to present terms to Hezekiah after Jerusalem has been besieged by the Assyrians, the officers are referred to as Tartan, Rab-saris, and Rabshakeh. In the American Standard Version, for one, these are treated as proper names. Comparative study has been able to clarify that these are titles of important officers, thus resulting in the NIV translation: "The king of Assyria sent his supreme commander, his chief officer and his field commander" (2 Kings 18:17). Without the comparative data, the passage was misunderstood, though admittedly at the technical level.

More important are the many occasions in which the core meaning of the text is misinterpreted for lack of assistance from the ancient Near East. This role of comparative studies is the principal focus of this book, so many examples will be offered in the following chapters. I would contend that while the committed reader of the Bible may find excuses not to care about comparative studies in the critical or defense roles, he or she cannot overlook its importance for interpretation. If we do not bring the information from the ancient cognitive environment to bear on the text, we will automatically impose the parameters of our modern worldview, thus risking serious distortion of meaning.

Figure 2. Traditional Roles for Comparative Study

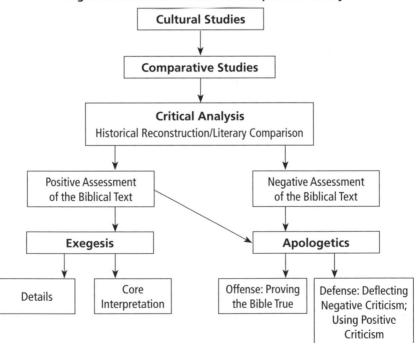

Part 2

Literature of the Ancient Near East

3

Summary of the Literature of the Ancient Near East

Myths

People define and understand "myth" in a number of different ways. It is generally understood that myths are stories in which the gods are the main characters. Since most people do not believe that "the gods" exist, they consider these stories fanciful and fictional. The Old Testament then becomes disputed territory, since, in contrast to those who believe in Marduk or Baal, a greater number of people believe that Yahweh exists and are uncomfortable with those who classify the Old Testament in the same category as the mythology of the ancient Near East.

Perhaps some resolution can be reached if we consider the basic function of mythology beyond the observation that it concerns the gods. We should ask the question of why a culture should consider stories about the gods to be important. A Babylonian would consider the myths to be important because they offered explanations of how the world functioned. The inhabitants of Mesopotamia would not have considered their myths to be fanciful or fictional, though they would not have considered a myth the same as a court chronicle. "The Sumerians seem to have perceived mythological reality as historically actual."[1] The gods were

1. D. Katz, *The Image of the Netherworld in Sumerian Sources* (Bethesda, MD: CDL, 2003), 56.

43

real to the ancients, and their stories gave account of the gods and the world in ways that were important for understanding the world and life in general. Jan Assmann's observation concerning Egypt is true across the board: "The theme of myth was not the essence of the deities, but rather . . . the essence of reality."[2] He elaborates: "Myths establish and enclose the area in which human actions and experiences can be oriented. The stories they tell about deities are supposed to bring to light the meaningful structure of reality. Myths are always set in the past, and they always refer to the present. What they relate about the past is supposed to shed light on the present."[3]

For the Israelites, the stories in the Old Testament served a similar function. Yahweh was real to them and his deeds were important. Like everyone else in the ancient world, the Israelites believed that everything that happened and everything that existed found its ultimate cause in deity. In this way of thinking, it is irrelevant whether the modern reader believes the gods of the Babylonians or the God of Israel exist. The significance and nature of the literature are not dependent on *our* assessment of their reality. These accounts serve as important sources for coming to understand the worldview of the ancients. For those who continue to accept aspects of that worldview, that is, one in which the role of deity is pivotal, there is added significance. That is why those who continue to believe in the God of Israel would not classify the Old Testament accounts and the ancient Near Eastern myths in quite the same category. But for those who have no convictions concerning the God of Israel the differences fade into insignificance, because the God of Israel is just as imaginary as the gods of Egypt or Assyria.

Sumerian

Eridu Genesis (RANE #1; COS 1.158; ANET 42–44; HTO 145–50)

This is the title given by T. Jacobsen to a collection of cosmology texts that he believes are all part of the same work.[4] Earliest copies date to about 1600 BC. As reconstructed it would contain accounts of the people becoming civilized and building cities as a prelude to the flood. The flood hero is named Ziusudra, king of Shuruppak. The texts include brief allusions to the creation of people and animals and the establishment of rituals, divination, and kingship.

2. J. Assmann, *The Search for God in Ancient Egypt* (Ithaca: Cornell University Press, 2001), 112.

3. Ibid.

4. T. Jacobsen, "The Eridu Genesis," *JBL* 100 (1981): 513–29. By "cosmology" I refer to texts that concern the origins or operations of the cosmos.

Enki and Ninmah (RANE #4; COS 1.159; HTO 151–66)

This tale recounts the circumstances that led to the creation of people. The dissatisfaction of the gods over their hard labor results in the fashioning of people from clay instigated by Enki and carried out by Nammu, his mother, with the aid of Ninmah. Enki and Ninmah subsequently engage in a contest to see if Enki can find a function for seven disabled individuals that she has created.

Enki and the Ordering of the World (RANE #3)

The copy of this text dates to about 2000 BC. In it Enki is assigning destinies in Sumer. In the process he assigns the gods their various roles that will enable the land to function.

Enki and Ninhursag (RANE #2; HTO 181–204; ANET 37–41)

The extant copies date to the Old Babylonian period (1800–1600). The subject is the island of Dilmun (modern Bahrain), which is the closest parallel in Mesopotamian thinking to the modern idea of paradise. It is described as a place where animals and people were incognizant of how they were to function. Enki begins to remedy the situation by bringing fresh water to the pristine island and establishing a city there. In the second part he couples with a series of deities to produce the various characteristics of Dilmun. The piece concludes with the production of eight exotic plants whose functions are designated when Enki eats them. The piece ends with the birthing of eight gods (corresponding to the plants), one of whom is the lord of Dilmun.

Inanna and Enki (COS 1.161)

Extant copies date to the Old Babylonian period. This piece concerns Inanna's acquisition of important functions (Sumerian ME) for the city of Uruk. The setting is a banquet in which Inanna gains possession of the functions from a drunken Enki. They are loaded on a boat and successfully transferred to Uruk. Of great significance is the list of 94 ME (functions) that provides the best source for understanding this important concept.

Inanna's Descent (ANET 52–57; HTO 205–32)

Extant texts date to the Old Babylonian period.[5] The main characters are Inanna; her shepherd lover, Dumuzi; and Ereshkigal, who rules in the

5. Compare the *Descent of Ishtar* derived from *Descent of Inanna* (*COS* 1.108; *MFM* 154–60; *FDD* 78–84).

netherworld. It is one of the most helpful sources for information about beliefs concerning the netherworld. Inanna descends to the netherworld for an undisclosed reason (perhaps to usurp the throne) and is finally brought defenseless before Ereshkigal and turned into a corpse. Having anticipated this, Inanna has arranged with her assistant, Ninshubur, to make petition for her return to the great gods should she not return in three days. Enki carries out a successful plan for her restoration, but she cannot escape without providing a substitute. Dumuzi is given over in her place but is required to stay only half of each year.

Song of the Hoe/Pickaxe (COS 1.157)

Extant copies are from the Old Babylonian period, most excavated at Nippur, like many of the above. In this piece the hoe is portrayed as the tool used by Enlil in creation. Heaven and earth are separated, and humans are caused to sprout forth from the ground. People then used hoes to build the temples. The conclusion lists various functions that make use of the hoe, including others that use the word for hoe in their name.

Sumerian Creation (BM 491–93)

The extant copies of this text date to about 1100 BC in the Middle Assyrian period.[6] It opens with reference to the separation of heaven and earth. The plan of the cosmos is laid out, and the Tigris and Euphrates are set on their course. Then the assembly of the gods meet and determine to make humans (by slaying two divine beings) to labor at irrigating the fields. Two types of human beings are then created. These were at one time thought to represent the original human pair, like Adam and Eve, but the text identifies them as deities, not humans.[7]

Akkadian

Epic of Creation/Enuma Elish (RANE #6; COS 1.111; ANET 60–72, 501–3; MFM 228–77; FDD 9–51; OTP 9–18)

One of the best-known of the ancient texts, *Enuma Elish* gets its title from the first words of the text, often translated "When on high." This text, dated to the end of the second millennium BC, is a hymn commemorating the elevation of Marduk to the head of the pantheon. It includes some of the most detailed information about divine conflict and about cosmol-

---

6. Translation can be found in R. J. Clifford, *Creation Accounts in the Ancient Near East and in the Bible* (Washington, D.C.: Catholic Biblical Association, 1994), 49–51.

7. See discussion in "Comparative Exploration: Polygenesis and Monogenesis," in chap. 9.

ogy available from ancient Mesopotamia. The first tablet opens with a cosmogony/theogony and introduces Tiamat in conflict with the gods and the slaying of Apsu, interwoven with the account of Marduk's birth.[8] The conflict escalates in tablet two as Tiamat and the rebels threaten the gods. Marduk is finally selected as the champion of the gods with the understanding that if he wins he will be elevated to the head of the pantheon. All the negotiations and preparations come to a climax in tablet four as Marduk defeats Tiamat and lays out the cosmos using Tiamat's corpse. Establishing the functions of the cosmos continues into tablet six and concludes with the creation of people from the blood of Tiamat's partner, Kingu, and the building of Babylon and a temple for Marduk. Tablet seven draws the piece to a conclusion as the fifty names of Marduk are proclaimed to name his attributes, delineate his jurisdiction, and identify his prerogatives.

Erra and Ishum (COS 1.113; MFM 282–312; FDD 132–63)

The main extant copy is on five tablets dating to the eighth century BC. Erra is another name for Nergal, the god of plague who helps rule in the netherworld. He and his general, Ishum, stand in opposition to the aged and ineffective Marduk. Ishum turns out to be the hero as he ameliorates Erra's destructive intentions. Consequently the work offers hope for the restoration of order under new leadership.

Anzu and the Tablet of Destinies (COS 3.147; ANET 111–13, 514–17; MFM 203–26; FDD 115–31)

Earliest versions date to the Old Babylonian period. Anzu is a fierce beast, a combination of eagle and lion, who has been enlisted by Enlil as a guardian but who steals the Tablet of Destinies and threatens to wreak havoc among the gods. This initiates a search for a champion who will conquer Anzu and recover the tablet. Ninurta is persuaded and proceeds to engage Anzu, though the creature's possession of the Tablet of Destinies gives him the ability to counteract any weapon used against him. Finally, Ea provides a strategy that helps Ninurta slay Anzu and the tablet is recovered. Subsequently, Ninurta is honored and declared the greatest among the gods.

Nergal and Ereshkigal (COS 1.109–10; ANET 103–4, 507–12; MFM 163–81; FDD 85–96)

The earlier version from Amarna (fourteenth century) is shorter than the Neo-Assyrian version from the seventh century BC. Both versions relate how Nergal goes to the underworld because he has insulted Eresh-

---

8. Tiamat and Apsu are both primordial deities associated with the sea.

kigal's messenger, who has come to a banquet in heaven to get a portion for his mistress, who cannot leave the netherworld. Her demand that he be punished results in Nergal's appearance before her and the resulting conflict. Nergal seizes control of the throne of the netherworld from Ereshkigal, who becomes his wife and consort.

Egyptian

Memphis Creation Account (COS 1.15; RANE #9; ANET 4–6; AEL 1:51–57; OTP 3–5)

The extant copy dates to about 700 BC, but the tradition is thought to have originated in Old Kingdom times in the last half of the third millennium. Ptah, the craftsman deity, was the patron of Memphis and is the creator god in this tradition. He speaks the Ennead, nine deities representing all of creation, into existence rather than using bodily fluids as the other traditions believe.

Heliopolis Creation Account, Pyramid Texts 246–47 (ANET 3; RANE #8)

Dating to the mid-third millennium, this tradition features Atum as the creator of the Ennead, the nine gods, from whom all the rest of creation emerges.

Hermopolis Creation Account, Leiden Papyrus I.350 (COS 1.16)

The four pairs of gods, the Ogdoad, figure prominently in this tradition in which Amun is the principal creator. Creation proceeds through an evolving process from the "first occasion" with Amun's self-generation.

Hittite/Hurrian

Kumarbi Cycle (Song of Kumarbi, ANET 120–21; Hoffner, Hittite Myths, 14; Song of Ullikummi, RANE #11; ANET 121–25; Hoffner, Hittite Myths, 18; smaller fragments in Hoffner, Hittite Myths, 15–17)

Dating to the fifteenth century, the Hurrian Kumarbi Cycle is comprised of five extant texts (songs) that concern the conflict between the sky god, Teshub, the king of the gods, and the netherworld deity, Kumarbi, who wants to displace him.[9] In the Song of Kumarbi, Anu is the king of the gods and Kumarbi, his cupbearer, revolts against him. Teshub is born from Kumarbi, and after a major battle between the gods Teshub ascends to kingship over the gods. Eventually Kumarbi fathers Ullikummi

9. Discussion in René LeBrun, "From Hittite Mythology: The Kumarbi Cycle," *CANE* 3:1971–80.

by mating with a mountain. The stone child grows up and becomes a threat to Teshub, but is eventually destroyed.

Illuyanka *(COS 1.56; ANET 125–26; Hoffner,* Hittite Myths, *1)*

Illuyanka is a serpent representing chaos who had recently defeated the storm god. The storm god's daughter, Inara, marries a mortal, Hupasiya; together they trick Illuyanka and the storm god is able to kill him. The tale functioned as part of the obscure *purulli* festival.

Wrath of Telepinu *(COS 1.57; ANET 126–28; Hoffner,* Hittite Myths, *2)*

Telepinu is son of the storm god and a deity of agriculture. He becomes angry and abandons the people, thus bringing economic disaster. Since no food was being produced, no offerings were being given and the gods too were suffering. Agents are sent far and wide to locate Telepinu. None can find him until a bee is sent and appeases the god, who then returns fertility to the land.

Ugarit

The Baal Cycle *(RANE #7; COS 1.86; ANET 129–42; Parker,* Ugaritic Narrative Poetry, *III.7–14; OTP 244–56)*

This Ugaritic text dates to the mid-second millennium.[10] The three sections of the Baal Cycle concern Baal's Conflict with Yamm, Baal's Temple, and Baal's Conflict with Mot. "Baal's Conflict with Yamm" begins with Yamm, the god of the sea and chaos, in what appears to be a kingship role with a royal residence being constructed for him. Baal's objections lead first to him being delivered over to Yamm as a captive, and second to an armed conflict between the two deities. Baal triumphs and his wife/sister, Anat, completes the destruction of Yamm's followers. In the second section Baal commissions the building of a palace for himself. In the third, Baal is challenged by Mot, the god of death, and is defeated. After a time he emerges from the netherworld and fertility returns to the earth.

Literary Texts and Epics

Literary texts begin to appear as tales of Sumerian kings from the Early Dynastic period (2900–2400), though the texts themselves are dated to the Ur III period (2100–2000) at the earliest. Ur III was a period of

---

10. N. Wyatt, *Religious Texts from Ugarit* (Sheffield: Sheffield Academic Press, 1998), 34–146.

renaissance and so the texts were collected, copied, and read. The tales concern the heroic kings of old, usually supported or opposed by the gods. They go on various quests, adventures, and exploits that exhibit their heroism and virtues or, on occasion, expose their folly.

Sumerian

Enmerkar and the Lord of Aratta (COS 1.170; HTO 275–319; Vanstiphout, Epics of Sumerian Kings, 49–96)

Enmerkar was king of Uruk, a predecessor to Gilgamesh. Aratta has not been identified but was located at the eastern boundary of their geographical knowledge. In this epic Enmerkar, using a famine sent by Inanna for leverage, is trying to frighten Aratta into submission, but the lord of Aratta will agree only if Enmerkar can meet several challenges. Enmerkar cleverly succeeds, but by the time he demands the agreed submission, the famine has been broken and Enmerkar has lost his leverage. The two cities end up striking a bartering agreement.

Lugalbanda and the Thunderbird (HTO 320–44; Vanstiphout, Epics of Sumerian Kings, 97–165)

Lugalbanda is a military officer for Enmerkar prior to succeeding him as king. On one campaign against Aratta he becomes ill and is left behind in a cave with provisions. When he recovers he attempts to find his companions, and in his journeys encounters the Thunderbird, a magical bird of prey. Lugalbanda performs services for the bird and is therefore blessed with speed and endurance (after he refuses success in battle and gifts of bounty), which allow him to find the rest of the troops. His gifts are kept secret, but they allow him to serve as a remarkably successful messenger.

Gilgamesh and Aka (COS 1.171; ANET 44–47; HTO 345–55)

In his wanderings Gilgamesh is offered hospitality by Aka, king of Kish. Aka installs him on the throne of Uruk, but Gilgamesh refuses to submit his subjects to the labor demands of Aka. The elders of the city counsel submission, but his young peers are ready to join him in revolt. When Aka lays siege to Uruk, Gilgamesh's champion, Enkidu, eventually launches a successful sortie, defeats the enemy, and captures Aka. Nevertheless, Gilgamesh is now ready to submit to Aka's suzerainty.

Curse of Akkad (ANET 646–51)

Here Naram-Sin is seen as responsible for bringing the curse of the gods on the dynasty of Akkad (2350–2100) through his desecration of the Ekur temple of Enlil at Nippur.[11] Enlil responds by bringing the barbarian Gutian hordes against the empire to destroy it.

Akkadian

Atrahasis *(RANE #5; COS 1.130; MFM 1–38; FDD 52–77; OTP 31–40)*

The *Atrahasis Epic* contains three segments also found in the Genesis account: creation, proliferation, flood.[12] Earliest surviving copies are from the Old Babylonian period. The epic opens with the gods restless and then rebellious because of the hard labor they are engaged in. People are created to lighten the load. But as the population grows, the gods are disturbed by the noise of their slave labor. After several attempts to reduce the population, the decision is made to send a flood to wipe out humanity. Atrahasis (a title rather than a name), the king of Shuruppak, learns of the planned flood, builds a boat, and thus saves himself and human civilization.

Gilgamesh *(RANE #12; COS 1.132; MFM 39–153; OTP 19–30)*

This most widely copied piece of literature in the ancient world has a long and complicated history of composition.[13] The classic form of the epic known by early in the first millennium recounts the adventures and quest of Gilgamesh, king of Uruk in the mid-third millennium BC.[14] The opening description offers a picture of a mighty but oppressive king, whose people cry out to the gods for relief from his tyranny. The gods respond by creating Enkidu, an uncivilized human living out with the animals, who eventually comes to Gilgamesh's attention. Enkidu is ensnared by a woman, civilized, and brought to Uruk, where, after a wrestling match, he and Gilgamesh become friends. Their joint exploits include a raid of the cedar forests where the guardian monster Huwawa is killed, and overcoming the Bull of Heaven sent by the gods ostensibly to punish them for the slaying of the guardian. The subsequent punishment for killing the bull is that one of them must die, and it turns out to be Enkidu. Faced with his companion's death, Gilgamesh embarks on a quest to find immortality. His journeys take him to the edge of the world, where he eventually encounters an individual who has gained

11. J. Cooper, *The Curse of Agade* (Baltimore: Johns Hopkins University Press, 1983).

12. See W. G. Lambert and A. R. Millard, *Atra-Ḫasis: The Babylonian Story of the Flood* (Oxford: Clarendon, 1969).

13. J. Tigay, *The Evolution of the Gilgamesh Epic* (Philadelphia: University of Pennsylvania Press, 1982).

14. In general see A. George, *The Babylonian Gilgamesh Epic* (New York: Oxford University Press, 2003).

immortality, Utnapishtim, the survivor of the flood. After hearing the story of the flood, and realizing that he cannot gain immortality in that way, Gilgamesh attempts several other options with Utnapishtim's well-intentioned help. When these fail he returns to Uruk to gain immortality by the only means available to him—becoming a great ruler, a great builder, and raising up the next generation.

Etana *(COS 1.131; MFM 189–202; FDD 102–14)*

The oldest extant texts date to the Old Babylonian period. Etana was king of Kish and is listed in the first dynasty after the flood in the Sumerian King List. There he is the fifteenth king in the dynasty, though this tale portrays him as the first king. The account begins with a serpent and an eagle living in a sacred tree in a symbiotic relationship. The eagle treacherously devours the serpent's young and the serpent seeks revenge. He catches the eagle unaware, plucks his feathers, and throws him into a pit to die. Etana rescues the eagle and requests that the eagle help him find a plant of birth so he can produce an heir. He ascends to heaven on the back of the eagle but he loses courage before they can accomplish their objective. The conclusion of the tale is lost due to breaks in the tablets.

Adapa *(COS 1.129; MFM 182–87; FDD 97–101)*

The earliest copy of this text was found at Amarna and dates to the mid-fourteenth century.[15] Adapa is known from the Mesopotamian traditions as the first of the *apkallu*—the sages who served as advisors to the antediluvian kings and are credited with bringing the arts of civilization to the human race. Adapa is identified as a priest of Ea in Eridu, the first city in Mesopotamian tradition. The south wind tips his boat and, by means of an incantation, he "breaks its wing." Consequently he is summoned before the high god Anu. Prior to his audience he is warned by Ea not to eat or drink anything while he is there. He follows this advice and rejects the food offered to him. Later he discovers that this was "food of life" and that he has lost a chance at immortality.

Birth Legend of Sargon *(RANE #17; COS 1.133; FDD 165–66; OTP 85)*

Though Sargon ruled in the twenty-fourth century BC, the earliest versions of this tale date only to the Neo-Assyrian period (900–600).[16]

---

15. In general see S. Izre'el, *Adapa and the South Wind* (Winona Lake, IN: Eisenbrauns, 2001).

16. J. G. Westenholz, *Legends of the Kings of Sargon* (Winona Lake, IN: Eisenbrauns, 1997), 36–49; T. Longman III, *Fictional Akkadian Autobiography* (Winona Lake, IN: Eisenbrauns, 1991), 53–60, 215–16.

In this first person account Sargon recounts how he was born to a priestess who put him in a basket boat floating down the river. He was found and raised by a gardener. Attracting the favor of Ishtar, he eventually was elevated to kingship. The remainder of the work tells of his accomplishments.

Cuthean Legend of Naram-Sin *(FDD 171–77)*

Texts of this piece date from the Old Babylonian period down into the late Neo-Babylonian period (625–539).[17] Naram-Sin was one of the kings of the dynasty of Akkad toward the end of the third millennium. Naram-Sin is compared with the ancient Sumerian king Enmerkar, who also fought the Umman-manda. Naram-Sin's enemies are considered demonic birdlike creatures, but when it is discovered that they bleed, their mortality is revealed, and Naram-Sin becomes optimistic about defeating them. Though prohibited by the gods from pressing the attack, he sends three armies and each is destroyed. He thereby becomes an example of what happens when rulers refuse to heed the advice given by the gods through diviners.

Epic of Tukulti-Ninurta *(FDD 178–96)*

This epic offers reflection on the life of an Assyrian king from the thirteenth century BC centering on his defeat of Babylon and its Kassite king Kashtiliash IV. He reports that the god Marduk abandoned his sanctuary (Tukulti-Ninurta carted the image to Assyria) due to the Babylonian king's violation of treaty agreements.

Verse Account of Nabonidus *(ANET 312–15)*

This text presents Nabonidus as an unpopular religious reformer who incited the anger of Babylon's traditional gods Marduk and Nabu by elevating the worship of the moon god Nanna/Sin. His fervor for Nanna led him to turn kingship over to his son and leave Babylon to stay in Teima. Cyrus is portrayed as coming to set all of this right and is welcomed by the inhabitants of Babylon, who have reportedly been distressed by Nabonidus's behavior.

Dream of Nabonidus/Sippar Cylinder *(COS 2.123A)*

Nabonidus is instructed by Marduk in a dream to rebuild the temple to Sin in Haran that has been sacked by the Medes. He is told that the Medes will be defeated by Cyrus and the Persians.

17. Westenholz, *Legends of the Kings*, 294–368; Longman, *Fictional Akkadian Autobiography*, 103–17, 228–31.

Egyptian

Sinuhe *(RANE #18; COS 1.38; ANET 18–22; AEL 1:222–36; OTP 129–33)*

Both the events and the earliest manuscripts date to the 12th Dynasty in the first centuries of the second millennium. In this first person narrative, Sinuhe, an official in the court of Amenemhet I, tells of his flight from Egypt fearing for his life in the instability following the death of Amenemhet. This is followed by a long period of self-imposed exile in Palestine and Syria as far as Byblos. He eventually settled down in Retenu (Canaan), where he married into a clan. The tale includes recounting of his many deeds and accomplishments and concludes with his reconciliation to the court of Egypt.

Wenamun *(RANE #83; COS 1.41; ANET 25–29; AEL 2:224–30; Nissinen, Prophets and Prophecy, 219–20; OTP 323–30)*

The reported events took place near the beginning of the eleventh century and the papyrus manuscript dates to soon after. The story's hero was an official of the temple of Amun on a trade mission to Byblos to purchase lumber. The report details difficulties encountered by Wenamun and the negotiations between the parties.

Shipwrecked Sailor *(COS 1.39; AEL 1:211–14)*

This tale dates to the Middle Kingdom (2050–1720). The setting is an attendant trying to encourage his master, who had apparently experienced failure in his mission at sea. The core of the piece is the attendant's tale of his own experience of being shipwrecked on an island, where he was aided by a serpent and eventually rescued, as the serpent had foretold.

Eloquent Peasant *(COS 1.43; ANET 407–10; AEL 1:169–83; OTP 215–22)*

From the Middle Kingdom, this is an account of a peasant who had been robbed and beaten by a steward's servant and took his case to the steward for restitution. His eloquent presentations concerning the importance of justice impressed the steward and resulted in action on his behalf.

Tale of Two Brothers *(COS 1.40; ANET 23–25; AEL 2:203–10; OTP 61–65)*

An eleventh-century papyrus records this tale of Anubis and Bata. Bata served the household of Anubis and his wife. Anubis's wife attempted to seduce Bata, who steadfastly refused. That night she accused Bata of violating her, and Anubis decided to kill Bata, who heard of the plot and took flight. Bata confronted Anubis and, declaring his innocence, emasculated himself. Bata went into self-imposed exile, while Anubis went home and executed his wife. The gods provided Bata with a wife who was so desirable that she came to the attention of the pharaoh and was taken by him and Bata was killed. Anubis searched for the heart of Bata and brought him back to life. Bata then assumed the shape of a bull and had Anubis take him to the pharaoh. When Bata confronted his wife as a bull she had him killed, and from the blood sprang two trees. When Bata confronted his wife as the tree, she had it cut down and a splinter flew into her mouth and she became pregnant. Bata was then born as the crown prince who became king, judged his treacherous wife, and elevated Anubis so that he became pharaoh after him.

Dream of Thutmose IV (ANET 449)

Thutmose IV reigned in the fifteenth century. This stele, located between the paws of the sphinx, tells of when he was yet a prince and took a nap at that spot. In a dream, the deity of the sphinx, Harmakhis tells him that he will become pharaoh and requests that he clear the sand that had built up around the sphinx.

Hittite

Proclamation of Telipinu (COS 1.76)

Documents from the thirteenth century preserve this royal decree of Hittite king Telipinu, who reigned about 1500 BC. After a history of the preceding century's conflicts, rules for succession are expounded in the context of mercy being shown to the king's opponents. Other reforms are tacked on at the end of the document.

Apology of Hattushili III (COS 1.77)

In the mid-thirteenth century this was a popular work of Hittite literature. As the youngest son of the king, Hattushili was dedicated to temple service as a child. When his older brother, Muwatalli, ascended the throne, he was given a military position. His successes in this role include participation in the Battle of Qadesh against Ramesses II. Hattushili eventually usurped the throne from his nephew Urhiteshub, who had treated him as a claimant and restricted his jurisdiction. He attributed his rise to power to the favor of Ishtar. The piece contains praise to Ishtar and the establishment of rituals honoring her. He also granted her temple a privileged tax-free status.

Deeds of Shuppiluliuma (COS 1.74)

Shuppiluliuma reigned in the first half of the fourteenth century. This literary work records his mighty deeds. It differs from chronicles and annals in that it was composed by his son and successor rather than as his own court record. Shuppiluliuma was one of the most successful Hittite kings: he was responsible for the victory over the Hurrian kingdom of Mitanni in upper Mesopotamia (1500–1350) and the subsequent expansion of the empire.

Ugarit

Kirtu *(RANE #20; COS 1.102; Parker, Ugaritic Narrative Poetry, 9–48; OTP 76–81)*

The extant copy of this work was produced in the mid-thirteenth century BC.[18] It begins with an aged king, Kirtu, who had been left with no heir. A military expedition procured a wife, who then bore him a son. Kirtu survived a mortal illness, but his disloyal son accused him of incompetence and attempted to replace his father on the throne.

Aqhat *(RANE #19; COS 1.103; Parker, Ugaritic Narrative Poetry, 49–80; OTP 66–75)*

The extant copy of this work was produced in the mid-thirteenth century BC.[19] Danel, a righteous leader of his people, had no son and requested one from the gods. Baal provided Aqhat, who was presented with a marvelous bow by the crafts deity. Anat coveted the bow, and when she could not acquire it she arranged for Aqhat's death, though his bow was broken and lost in the process. This injustice resulted in drought, which in turn led to a period of mourning and the recovery of Aqhat's remains from the eagle that had devoured them. Aqhat's sister Pagat sought revenge for his death, but it is unknown whether she found it.

Alalakh

Idrimi *(COS 1.148; ANET 557–58)*

Recorded on a statue of Idrimi, this inscription, dated to the fifteenth century, represents Idrimi's first person account of his succession to the throne of Alalakh.[20] After his family had to flee Aleppo, he settled in Emar. Subsequent travels brought him back to his home where, after some tension, he entered into a vassal treaty agreement with King Barrattarna of Mitanni. Barrattarna sets Idrimi up as king of Alalakh, where he is successful in taking territory from the Hittites. After a prosperous thirty-year reign, he is succeeded by his son.

18. Wyatt, *Religious Texts*, 176–243.
19. Ibid., 246–312.
20. Longman, *Fictional Akkadian Autobiography*, 60–66, 216–18

Ritual Texts

Information concerning the rituals of the ancient world may be found in texts that record rituals, describe rituals, or refer to rituals. Procedures had to be followed, words spoken (incantations), and careful attention paid to the time, place, and status of all participants, priestly and lay. Rituals could be related to regular occasions, unusual circumstances, or sacred activities. They served to regulate contact between humans and the divine world.

Akkadian

Akitu *(RANE #38; ANET 331)*

In Babylon the *Akitu* was a twelve-day enthronement festival that was celebrated in association with the New Year.[21] It included renewal both of kingship among the gods and of the human king. Part of it reenacted the conflict between Marduk and Tiamat that is preserved in *Enuma Elish*. It was an occasion for the destiny of the coming year to be declared. Variations of the ceremony occur as early as the third millennium and in a number of different cultures in Mesopotamia.

Substitute King *(RANE #35; ANET 355–56)*

In this practice known mostly from second-millennium Hittite texts and Neo-Assyrian (900–600) texts, the occurrence of omens that were thought to jeopardize the life of the king served as the occasion for the enthronement of a substitute king.[22] The threat was typically posed by an imminent eclipse of sun, moon, or one of the planets. The theory behind the ritual was that the negative effect of the omens would be drawn to the substitute and thus bring deliverance for the king. Chosen by the diviners, he was enthroned, dressed like the king, and given the royal insignias and a queen. He played the role of king by presenting offerings before the altar and burning incense.

Menologies/Hemerologies

These texts list particular prescriptions and proscriptions for various days of each month.[23] Activities addressed concern issues

21. J. Bidmead, *The AKITU Festival* (Piscataway, NJ: Gorgias, 2002); see also M. E. Cohen, *Cultic Calendars of the Ancient Near East* (Bethesda, MD: CDL, 1993), 400–453.

22. Most texts can be found in S. Parpola, *Letters from Assyrian and Babylonian Scholars*, SAA 10 (Helsinki: University of Helsinki Press, 1993).

23. To be published by A. Livingstone (see W. G. Lambert, *Wisdom, Gods and Literature*, ed. A. R. George and I. L. Finkel [Winona Lake, IN: Eisenbrauns, 2000], 384).

such as what one eats or drinks, whether doctor or lawyer or priest or prophet should be consulted, and rituals that should or should not be performed.

Washing of the Mouth

These Mesopotamian induction rituals helped in transition between the manufacture of the image and the installation of the image in the temple.[24] The texts are from the mid-first millennium but the ritual is referred to more than a thousand years earlier in the Ur III period. The rituals deny that the images were crafted by human hands. The craftsmen's tools are thrown into the river and the image is declared to have been born in heaven. The mouth is ritually purified and opened so that the god can speak oracles to the king and his diviners.

Zukru Festival at Emar *(RANE #37; COS 1.123)*

This Syrian New Year's festival was one of renewal focused on Dagan, the head of the pantheon at Emar.[25] Usually a one-day festival involving offerings and a procession of the deity, every seventh year it was an extended affair for which a year of preparation culminated in a seven-day celebration. The texts date to the mid-second millennium.

Namburbi Incantations

Approximately 140 texts of this type are extant.[26] They are apotropaic rites intended to undo evil or to ward off portended dangers such as ants, snakes, fungi, and monstrous births.

Bit-Rimki Rituals

Bit-Rimki means "House of Ablution."[27] These rituals were performed by the king outside the city when he had contracted ritual impurity or had violated a taboo of some sort.

---

24. The *mis pi* ("Washing of the Mouth") rituals can be found in C. Walker and M. B. Dick, *The Induction of the Cult Image in Ancient Mesopotamia: The Mesopotamian Mis Pi Ritual*, SAALT 1 (Helsinki: Neo-Assyrian Text Corpus Project, 2001); see also M. B. Dick and C. Walker, "The Induction of the Cult Image in Ancient Mesopotamia," in *Born in Heaven, Made on Earth*, ed. M. B. Dick (Winona Lake, IN: Eisenbrauns, 1999), 55–122.

25. D. E. Fleming, *Time at Emar: The Cultic Calendar and the Rituals from the Diviner's Archive*, Mesopotamian Civilizations 11 (Winona Lake, IN: Eisenbrauns, 2000).

26. R. Caplice, *The Akkadian Namburbi Texts: An Introduction* (Los Angeles: Undena, 1974).

27. J. Læssøe, *Studies on the Assyrian Ritual and Series "Bit Rimki"* (Copenhagen: Munksgaard, 1955).

Hittite

Hittite Priests *(RANE #36; COS 1.83; ANET 207)*

Dating to the mid-thirteenth century, this text instructs the priests in proper conduct with regard to the shrine and sacred things. There are regulations regarding bodily cleansings to prepare for service, and restrictions concerning the use of the food that has been brought to be offered to the gods. Instructions are given for guard duty and for sexual relations.

Mistress of the Pit

These rituals concern the procedures for consulting with the dead at a ritual pit.[28] Consultations were made with experts who knew the location of the portals where offerings could be made and the spirit of the dead summoned forth. The rituals included libations, food offering, and blood, and took place at night. Both the expert and the inquirer had roles to play.

Egyptian

Book of the Dead Negative Confession *(RANE #34; COS 2.12; ANET 34–36; AEL 2:124–32; OTP 203–7)*

First attested in the mid-second millennium, spell number 125 from the *Book of the Dead* is intended to help the person who has died to magically pass the tribunal of the gods and enter into the afterlife. He therefore protests his innocence in regard to a long series of nearly eighty potential offenses. Potential crimes range from mistreating cattle to blasphemy, from causing tears to committing adultery. In fact, the individual claims to have done no wrong at all.

Execration Texts *(COS 1.32; ANET 328–29)*

These texts occur throughout Egyptian history. By breaking items inscribed with identifications of the people or cities and their kings, curses were brought on the enemies of Egypt.[29]

Daily Ritual of Amun-Re *(COS 1.34; ANET 325–26)*

Most temples had daily rituals that were performed by the priests to honor the gods, gain their favor, and maintain the status quo. This

---

28. H. Hoffner, "Second Millennium Antecedents to the Hebrew *ʾōb*," *JBL* 86 (1967): 385–401.

29. S. Seidlmayer, "Execration Texts," *OEAE* 1:487–89.

papyrus, reflecting the practice at Thebes in the mid-first millennium, records the procedures to honor Amun-Re each morning as the temple is opened. The importance of the care and feeding of the gods is evident as the liturgy is recited and the offerings are presented.

Divination/Incantation Texts

Texts related to divination are found throughout the ancient Near East (though Egyptian material is quite limited).[30] Mesopotamian documents related to extispicy, celestial observations, chance happenings, and dreams dominate in sizable collections, but a number of other types are also extant. In all of the cultures divination is used to gain answers to oracles. The omens are used by those who must advise the king, and the incantations are used to exorcise evil or protect from it. Most of the divination literature developed over centuries before achieving the standardized form represented in the exemplars that have been preserved.

Akkadian

Shurpu *(RANE #88)*

This is a series of incantations used in rites of purification when one believes oneself to be under the influence of some sort of evil.[31] Objects were ritually identified with offenses and then burned or discarded as the incantations were recited.

Maqlu *(RANE #89)*

In contrast to *shurpu*, *maqlu* seeks to counteract magical spells and combat the practitioners of those spells.[32] Comprised of eight tablets,

30. The best summary is F. Cryer, *Divination in Ancient Israel and Its Near Eastern Environment*, JSOTSup 142 (Sheffield: JSOT Press, 1994).

31. E. Reiner, *Šurpu: A Collection of Sumerian and Akkadian Incantations*, AfO Beiheft 11 (Osnabruck: Graz, 1970).

32. Publication and treatment can be found in T. Abusch, *Babylonian Witchcraft Literature* (Atlanta: Scholars Press, 1987), and throughout many of his articles, including the following: "The Socio-Religious Framework of the Babylonian Witchcraft Ceremony *Maqlu*: Some Observations on the Introductory Section of the Text, Part 1," in *Riches Hidden in Secret Places*, ed. T. Abusch (Winona Lake, IN: Eisenbrauns, 2002), 1–34; "Ritual and Incantation: Interpretation and Textual History of *Maqlu* vii:58–105 and ix:152–59," in *Sha'arei Talmon*, ed. M. Fishbane, E. Tov, and W. W. Fields (Winona Lake, IN: Eisenbrauns, 1992), 367–81; "The Ritual Tablet and Rubrics of *Maqlu*: Toward the History of the Series," in *Ah, Assyria*, ed. M. Cogan and I. Eph'al, *Scripta Hierosolymitana* 33 (Jerusalem: Magnes, 1991), 233–53; "The Socio Religious Framework of the Babylonian Witchcraft

the ritual was performed in two stages during the night and a third stage in the morning. In the ceremony an image of the suspected witch is destroyed. Then the individual is protected from further spells, and the spirit of the witch is expelled.

Enuma Anu Enlil *(COS 1.120:16–17)*

These are celestial omens that include observations of the movements of the sun, moon, stars, and planets.[33] Issues such as the color, the juxtaposition to other bodies, and the time of appearance or disappearance were all considered important and were interpreted.

Shumma Izbu *(COS 1.120:8–15)*

These omens concern the interpretation given to various birth oddities, mostly involving the flocks and herds.[34] Observations extend to every part of the external anatomy.

Shumma Alu *(COS 1.120:18–55)*

This omen series, comprised of over a hundred tablets, concerns a wide variety of situations and events that were believed to have ominous significance.[35] Omens interpret odd behavior of animals as well as people, and situations or conditions of a city, its walls or gates, or of individual houses.

Dream Book

The Mesopotamian dream book contains dream omens as well as rituals to try to influence the dreams one has.[36]

Ceremony *Maqlu*: Some Observations on the Introductory Section of the Text, Part II," in *Solving Riddles and Untying Knots: Biblical, Epigraphic, and Semitic Studies in Honor of Jonas C. Greenfield*, ed. Z. Zevit, S. Gitin, and M. Sokoloff (Winona Lake, IN: Eisenbrauns, 1995), 467–94; and "An Early Form of the Witchcraft Ritual *Maqlu* and the Origin of a Babylonian Magical Ceremony," in *Lingering over Words: Studies in Ancient Near Eastern Literature in Honor of William L. Moran*, ed. T. Abusch, J. Huehnergard, and P. Steinkeller (Atlanta: Scholars Press, 1990), 1–58.

33. These tablets have not been fully published. Discussion, description, and bibliography can be found in D. Brown, *Mesopotamian Planetary Astronomy-Astrology* (Groningen: Styx, 2000). Reports often quoting from *Enuma Anu Enlil* have been published by H. Hunger, *Astrological Reports to Assyrian Kings*, SAA 8 (Helsinki: Neo-Assyrian Text Corpus Project, 1992).

34. E. Leichty, *The Omen Series Šumma Izbu*, TCS 4 (Locust Valley, NY: Augustin, 1970).

35. S. Freedman, *If a City Is Set on a Height* (Philadelphia: Samuel Noah Kramer Fund, 1998).

36. S. A. L. Butler, *Mesopotamian Conceptions of Dreams and Dream Rituals*, AOAT 258 (Münster: Ugarit-Verlag, 1998).

Egyptian

Egyptian Dream Oracles *(COS 1.33; ANET 495)*

The Egyptian dream book concerns mostly the interpretation of what one sees oneself doing in the dream. Incantations are included so that evil dreams can be counteracted. They are very brief and indicate a behavior, whether the behavior portends good or evil, and the nature of good or evil.

Letters

Whether letters represent domestic internal memos or international correspondence between kings, they reveal much about life and conditions of the times in which they were written.

Amarna Letters *(RANE #55; COS 3.92A–G; ANET 483–90; OTP 137–40)*

This cache of 382 tablets (349 of them letters) is from an archive at Tell el-Amarna, which was the ancient site of Akhetaten.[37] This city was newly constructed as the capital city of Pharaoh Akhenaten in the mid-fourteenth century and was occupied for only about a decade before being abandoned by his successor. Most of the letters are in a dialectal form of Babylonian Akkadian, but documents in Hittite and Hurrian are also present. The international correspondence includes letters from the Hatti, Mitanni, Assyria, Babylonia, Arzawa, and Alashiya, as well as from numerous cities-states in Syria-Palestine that were Egyptian vassals. This last group reveals the political intrigues that were occurring in the region, particularly in regard to a group known as the 'Apiru, while the former group indicates the complexities of shifting international relationships between the major powers.

Lachish Ostraca *(RANE #56; COS 3.42; ANET 321–22; OTP 188–90; Lindenberger, Ancient Aramaic and Hebrew Letters, 110–16)*

Twenty-one ostraca were found in the 1930s dating to about 600 BC, the time of the final Babylonian invasion of Judah that included the destruction of Lachish around 589.[38] The letters discussing the military situation are written to Yaush, the commander of the fortress, probably from his subordinates who were in charge of the smaller garrisons in the region.

37. W. Moran, *The Amarna Letters* (Baltimore: Johns Hopkins University Press, 1992).
38. Hebrew texts collected in G. I. Davies, *Ancient Hebrew Inscriptions* (Cambridge: Cambridge University Press, 1991), 1 10.

Arad Ostraca *(RANE #57; COS 3.43; ANET 568–69; OTP 185–87; Lindenberger, Ancient Aramaic and Hebrew Letters, 99–110)*

Over one hundred ostraca inscribed in ink with short messages, most dated to the Neo-Babylonian period, were discovered at Arad, a military center in the Negev.[39] On many of them only a few letters or words can be read. The most significant items were eighteen letters addressed to Eliashib, the commander of the fortress. They concern largely issues of rations in the years leading up to the Babylonian invasion of Judah in 597.

Royal Inscriptions

Much of the historiographical information from the ancient Near East was generated by the palace scribes. Kings kept records and commissioned inscriptions so that they could perpetuate their names and reputations to the generations yet to come.[40]

Sumerian

Gudea Temple Cylinders *(COS 2.155; ANET 268–69)*

Two cylinders dating to the late third millennium record the building of a temple for Ningirsu, patron deity of Lagash, by its ruler, Gudea.[41] The text tells of how Gudea received permission and instructions for building the temple and then records the building and dedication of the temple. It is the most complete temple building account preserved from the ancient world.

Akkadian

Shalmaneser III's Black Obelisk *(RANE #40; COS 2.113F; ANET 281; OTP 166–71)*

Combining reliefs and inscriptions, this text documents 31 years of Shalmaneser's reign. It dates to 827 BC.

Photo 2 Black Obelisk of Shalmaneser III

39. Hebrew texts collected in ibid., 11–38.
40. The royal inscriptions from Mesopotamia are being comprehensively published by the University of Toronto.
41. D. O. Edzard, *Gudea and His Dynasty*, RIME 3/1 (Toronto: University of Toronto Press, 1997).

It includes an account of the famous Battle of Qarqar and shows Shalmaneser receiving tribute from the Israelite king Jehu in 841.

Sennacherib Prism *(RANE #43; COS 2.119B; ANET 287–88; OTP 177–79)*

Sennacherib had several prisms inscribed detailing his activities.[42] The most famous includes a description of the siege of Jerusalem in 701. The Assyrian king reports that after besieging 46 fortified cities, he had Hezekiah locked up in Jerusalem like a bird in a cage. Though Sennacherib reports over two hundred thousand captives and the receipt of heavy tribute from Hezekiah later in the year, there is no indication of the outcome of the siege.

Photo 3 Sennacherib Prism

Egyptian

Ramesses II—Battle of Qadesh *(COS 2.5; AEL 2:62–71)*

Along with the relief of the battle carved on the wall of the temple of Amun-Re at Karnak (with other copies in other locations) is this literary description of the battle against the Hittites at Qadesh. It recounts his heroic deeds in battle and portrays an overwhelming victory—a claim that must be qualified in light of Hittite accounts that offer a variant perspective.

Merneptah Stele *(RANE #50; COS 2.6; ANET 376–78; AEL 2:73–78; OTP 91–93)*

This stone slab from the end of the thirteenth century records a hymn of praise to Pharaoh Merneptah. It recounts his great victories and focuses on his devastation of the Libyans. It concludes with a list of vanquished foes, including Israel. This is the earliest reference to Israel in an ancient Near Eastern document.

Hittite

Edict of Hattushili *(COS 2.15)*

This inscription, in parallel columns of Hittite and Akkadian, designates Murshili the heir to the Hittite throne. Hattushili is ill and wants to assure that the throne goes to this son instead of Labarna, whom he

---

42. L. L. Grabbe, *"Like a Bird in a Cage": The Invasion of Sennacherib in 701 BCE* (Sheffield: JSOT Press, 2003).

is disinheriting. The dying king is blunt about the faults of Labarna and effusive in his praise of Murshili, who is still a minor.

Levant (Aramaean, Phoenician, Moabite)

Zakkur Inscription *(RANE #53; COS 2.35; ANET 655–56; Nissinen, Prophets and Prophecy, 203–7)*

This Aramaic inscription is preserved on the base of a statue. It dates to about 800 BC. It is the first person report of Zakkur, king of Hamath and Luash, telling of his devotion to the god Baal-Shamayin and how the god made him king and helped him withstand a siege of a coalition of Aramaean kings led by Ben-Hadad son of Hazael. A seer delivers the favorable word of the god by means of a prophetic oracle.

Azatiwada Inscription from Karatepe *(RANE #52; COS 2.31; ANET 653–54; OTP 162–65)*

From around 700 BC, this record of accomplishments is carved in several locations in the city in both Phoenician and Luwian. Azatiwada was a local official serving the king of Danuna, known in the Bible as Que (Kue) in northern Syria (now in southern Turkey). His inscription includes military victories, domestic prosperity, grand building projects, and security and justice for the people. It closes with blessings on Azatiwada and the city, and curses on any who would erase his name or threaten the city.

Tel Dan Inscription *(RANE #54; COS 2.39; OTP 160–61)*

This Aramaic inscription from the ninth century is preserved on three fragments of what was a stone slab inscription of an Aramaean king set up in the northern Israelite city of Dan commemorating his victory over Israel and Judah.[43] Though the names of the Israelite kings are not preserved, there is a clear reference to the southern kingdom as the "house of David." This is the first reference to David in ancient Near Eastern literature.

Mesha Inscription *(RANE #51; COS 2.23; ANET 320; OTP 157–59)*

Mesha was king of Moab in the mid-ninth century, and this inscription records his military victories over Israel and his building activities.[44] The inscription names Omri of Israel and Yahweh as Israel's God. Mesha

43. G. Athas, *The Tel Dan Inscription: A Reappraisal and a New Interpretation* (New York: Continuum, 2003).
44. J. A. Dearman, *Studies in the Mesha Inscription and Moab* (Atlanta: Scholars Press, 1989).

Photo 4 Cyrus Cylinder

speaks of his god, Kemosh (Chemosh), leading him in the same ways that the Bible talks about Yahweh leading Israel's kings.

Persian

Cyrus Cylinder (RANE #44; COS 2.124; ANET 315–16; OTP 193–95)

Cyrus is known as the first king of the Medo-Persian Empire, and the one who allowed the Jews to return to their homeland and build their temple. This inscription, though not mentioning Israel, details this policy of currying favor with those who had been captive peoples and their gods by sponsoring the rebuilding of shrines all over the empire. He describes his victory over Babylon as the result of Marduk's anger at the last Babylonian rulers. He portrays himself as liberator of Babylon welcomed by the formerly oppressed people.

Behistun Inscription

In the cliff over 200 feet above the plain, this trilingual account of Darius's victories was carved in 518.[45] The Old Persian version extends to about 3,600 words. Other copies have been found including a papyrus version in Aramaic at Elephantine from over a century later. The inscription was made early in Darius's reign and records the revolts that he put down as he secured his position on the throne. While important for the history of the transition years between Cambyses and Darius, the outstanding contribution of the inscription was the opportunity that it provided for deciphering Akkadian since the unknown Akkadian could be compared with the known Old Persian.

45. See E. Yamauchi, *Persia and the Bible* (Grand Rapids: Baker, 1990), 131–34.

Annals/Chronicles

Sumerian

Sumerian King List *(RANE #45; ANET 265–66)*

In the Isin-Larsa period (around 1900), the kings produced a list of kings to legitimate their own place in this succession of worthy rulers since kingship "descended from heaven."[46] This Sumerian king list traces kingship from one city to another beginning with ten kings who are credited with enormous reigns (averaging over 24,000 years each) before the flood. One hundred thirty more names fill the gap from the flood to the kings of Isin.

Hittite

Ten Year Annals of Murshili *(COS 2.16)*

These record the major campaigns and battles of the first ten years of the reign of Murshili II toward the end of the 14th century. Key opponents include the Kashka peoples and the lands of Arzawa, Azzi, and Kinza. The annals emphasize the favor of the gods going out with his armies in battle, lest anyone think that the plague that raged during all of these years reflected the disfavor of the gods.

Akkadian

Limmu List *(ANET 274)*

Every year from about 900 until the fall of Nineveh in 612, a key administrator in Assyria was commemorated by being designated the *limmu*, the honored official, for that year, and as such the year was named after him.[47] A list covering these three centuries is preserved and is of critical importance for both relative and absolute chronology. For the latter, the year of Bur-Saggile indicates that there was a solar eclipse in that year, which we now can calculate as 763 BC.

46. In general see T. Jacobsen, *The Sumerian King List* (Chicago: University of Chicago Press, 1939). Some segments of the list are found even earlier in the Ur III period; see P. Steinkeller, "An Ur III Manuscript of the Sumerian King List," in *Literatur, Politik und Recht in Mesopotamien*, ed. W. Sallaberger, K. Volk, and A. Zgoll (Wiesbaden: Harrassowitz, 2003), 267–92.

47. A. R. Millard, *The Eponyms of the Assyrian Empire, 910–612 BC*, SAAS 2 (Helsinki: Neo-Assyrian Text Corpus Project, 1994). This practice began as early as the second millennium.

Tiglath-pileser III *(RANE #41; COS 2.117; ANET 282–84; OTP 172–73)*

A variety of annals and inscriptions recount the details of the seventeen-year reign of this founder of the Neo-Assyrian Empire in the third quarter of the eighth century.[48] He collected tribute from Menahem, king of Israel. Pekah and Hoshea are also mentioned as the campaigns of 734–732 are described.

Sargon II *(RANE #42; COS 2.118; ANET 284–87; OTP 174–76)*

Toward the end of the eighth century, Sargon had his annals carved on stone panels in his palace at Dur-Sharrukin (Khorsabad).[49] He claims to have defeated Samaria located in the land of Bit-Humri (House of Omri) and deported its population. In addition, details are given of campaigns against Ashdod, Babylon, Elam, and Urartu among others.

Weidner Chronicle *(RANE #47; COS 1.138)*

This piece, probably from the end of the second millennium (major extant copies are in Neo-Babylonian and Neo-Assyrian), focuses on the shrine of Marduk in Babylon, the temple Esagil.[50] The text offers a far-ranging assessment of Mesopotamian history premised on the idea that those who treated Esagil and Babylon with respect succeeded while those who took action against the temple and city were overthrown.

Babylonian Chronicles *(RANE #49; ANET 563–64; OTP 182–84; COS 1.137)*

This year-by-year record documents major military campaigns and other significant occurrences in summary fashion.[51] They cover the entire reign of Nabopolassar, but only part of Nebuchadrezzar's. They therefore detail the expansion of Babylon from Nabopolassar's accession to the throne in 626 to the fall of Nineveh in 612, and beyond to the Battle of Carchemish in 605. Of additional importance is the note concerning

48. H. Tadmor, *The Inscriptions of Tiglath-Pileser III* (Jerusalem: Israel Academy of Arts and Sciences, 1994).

49. H. Tadmor, "The Campaigns of Sargon II of Aššur: A Chronological-Historical Study," *JCS* 12 (1958): 22–40, 77–100.

50. A. K. Grayson, *Assyrian and Babylonian Chronicles*, TCS 5 (Locust Valley, NY: Augustin, 1975), 145–51. See B. T. Arnold, "The Weidner Chronicle and the Idea of History in Israel and Mesopotamia," in *Faith, Tradition, and History*, ed. A. R. Millard, J. K. Hoffmeier, and D. W. Baker (Winona Lake, IN: Eisenbrauns, 1994), 129–48.

51. D. J. Wiseman, *Chronicles of the Chaldaean Kings* (London: British Museum, 1956).

the campaign to Jerusalem in 597 that led to the deportation of King Jehoiachin (Chronicle 5, year 7 of Nebuchadrezzar).

Treaties

(RANE ##21–26; COS 2.17–18, 2.82, 2.127–29; ANET 199–206, 529–41, 659–61; Beckman, Hittite Diplomatic Texts; OTP 86–90)

Nearly sixty treaties from the ancient Near East are extant. More than half are Hittite treaties from the mid-second millennium, and there are a handful from Syria and another handful of Neo-Assyrian exemplars. The treaties give an indication of the historical relationship between the parties and then define the expectations that the suzerain has for the vassal (since most are vassal treaties). Curses and blessings complete the documents. The Assyrian documents tend to give many more curses, while the Hittite treaties offer more detailed blessings. Typical stipulations include loyalty, payment of tribute, reception of ambassadors, provision for garrison troops, participation in military campaigns when requested, information concerning conspiracies, and extradition of enemies.

Law Collections

The law collections known from the ancient Near East are generally comprised of laws that we would classify as either civil or criminal. The inclusion of prologue and epilogue in a few cases demonstrate that these collections were sometimes used for apologetic purposes—that is, to demonstrate to the gods that the king is carrying out his primary responsibility of maintaining justice. Most of the laws are casuistic in form (i.e., case law) and many similarities among the collections can be observed. Even the most extensive collections are not codes per se, that is, they do not provide a comprehensive view of the society's legislative corpus.

Sumerian

Shulgi/Ur-Nammu *(RANE #27; COS 2.153; ANET 523–25; Roth, Law Collections, 13–22; OTP 97–98)*

Shulgi was king of Ur during the Ur III period, the twenty-first century BC. Only 31 laws remain of this collection, and only 22 of those are legible. Categories addressed are mostly concerned with civil law, but a few paragraphs concern criminal actions.

Lipit-Ishtar *(RANE #28; COS 2.154; ANET 159–60; Roth,* Law Collections, *23–35)*

From the nineteenth century BC, this collection of 38 laws includes both a prologue and epilogue. The sponsor, Lipit-Ishtar, is the king of Isin. The laws concern civil rather than criminal matters.

Akkadian

Eshnunna *(RANE #29; COS 2.130; ANET 161–63; Roth,* Law Collections, *57–70)*

Generally associated with Dadusha from Eshnunna, these sixty paragraphs predate the Hammurabi collection by a few decades. They include criminal law paragraphs along with civil law.

Hammurabi Stele *(RANE #30; COS 2.131; ANET 163–80; Roth,* Law Collections, *71–142; OTP 101–9)*

The most famous and most extensive of the ancient collections, this stele contains a prologue, epilogue, and 282 laws. It dates to the eighteenth century and offers many insights into Old Babylonian culture and the importance and role of law in second-millennium Mesopotamia. It offers ample opportunity to compare the biblical legal material.

Middle Assyrian *(RANE #31; COS 2.132, ANET 180–88; Roth,* Law Collections, *153–94; OTP 114–23)*

Perhaps from the reign of Tiglath-pileser I in the twelfth century BC, about one hundred laws are collected on eleven tablets.

Hittite

Hittite Laws *(RANE #32; COS 2.19; ANET 188–96; Roth,* Law Collections, *213–40; OTP 110–13)*

Nearly as old as Hammurabi's collection and nearly as extensive, about two hundred laws from the seventeenth century constitute this collection.

Legal Documents

Aside from the law collections itemized above, numerous documents from the ancient Near East are legal in nature. These include contracts, family documents (dealing with adoption, marriage, inheritance, etc.), court records, and the like. While the law collections may often be considered idealistic rather than realistic, the legal documents are thought to offer more confidence about what social practices were really like.

Nuzi Adoption Text *(RANE #14; ANET 220)*

The adoption tablet of Shennima illustrates a number of important features of life at Nuzi in the mid-second millennium. It contains several clauses about marriage. Marriage variables were regulated by contract, including the use of a concubine for bearing children when the wife was barren.

Hittite Witness Deposition *(COS 3.33)*

In this document two of the queen's grooms are suspected of taking for themselves items from the queen's stables. They make statements under oath, witnesses make statements concerning their activities, and the accused respond.

Yavneh Yam Fieldworker's Plea *(RANE #58; COS 3.41; OTP 331–32; Lindenberger, Ancient Aramaic and Hebrew Letters, 96–98)*

This Hebrew ostracon from the late seventh century preserves a letter written from a fieldworker to an official concerning his supervisor, who has confiscated his cloak. It is not a formal legal document, but involves a legal plea. The worker claims innocence and requests that the cloak be returned.

Hymns and Prayers

In ancient Near Eastern traditions, not only must the gods be served and cared for, they must be praised. And since the gods were considered powerful and actively involved in the operation of the cosmos, it was natural that petitions be laid before them. Texts recording communication with the divine realm are attested very early in the literary tradition. These documents are invaluable for revealing attitudes, beliefs, and expectations concerning the gods. Most of the literature derives from official settings (palace/temple), so it does not necessarily offer the desired glimpses of personal piety or worship on the level of the common people. Scholarly discussion is ongoing regarding the extent to which the extant literatures are connected to rituals or served in standardized liturgical settings and roles.

Sumerian

Ershahunga

There are twenty-six exemplars in this category of individual laments that seek to calm the heart of the deity.[52] They are offered in the context of distress, often only generically identified, that is, attributed to the deity's anger. They include confession of sin, again in general terms. The documents date to the Kassite period and usually feature interlinear Akkadian text.

Ki-ᵈUTU-kam

Five extant pieces from the mid-second millennium show these to be incantations addressed to the rising sun (UTU) seeking purification from sin.[53]

Eršemma

The oldest of these Sumerian compositions date to the Old Babylonian period.[54] There are dozens of extant pieces. These were performed by *gala* priests and were accompanied by the *šem* drum. A number of these are connected to events of the past.

Exaltation of Inanna (COS 1.160)

Sargon's daughter, Enheduanna, high priestess of Ur, has several pieces attributed to her toward the end of the third millennium.[55] The goddess Inanna is portrayed as powerful, devastating lands by raining fire down on them. After enumerating many of the goddess's attributes, the high priestess appealed to the deity to intervene on her behalf, since she had apparently been ousted from her position of privilege.

Hymn to Enlil (ANET 573–76; HTO 101–11 [RANE #74 is another hymn to Enlil])

The praise in this composition focuses on the sacred city of Nippur, Enlil its god, and Ekur his temple. Enlil is recognized as the one who sustains all life and the orderly operation of the cosmos.

---

52. S. M. Maul, *Herberuhigungsklagen: Die sumerisch-akkadischen Eršaḫunga-Gebete* (Wiesbaden: Harrassowitz, 1988).

53. E. R. Dalglish, *Psalm Fifty-One in the Light of Ancient Near Eastern Patternism* (Leiden: Brill, 1962), 40 n. 105.

54. M. Cohen, *Sumerian Hymnology: The Eršemma* (Cincinnati: Hebrew Union College Press, 1981).

55. W. W. Hallo and J. van Dijk, *The Exaltation of Inanna* (New Haven: Yale University Press, 1968); B. D. Meador, *Inanna: Lady of the Largest Heart* (Austin: University of Texas Press, 2000), 168 91.

Akkadian

Shuilla

There are about 150 Akkadian texts in this category.[56] *Shuilla* means the "raising of the hand," which was a gesture of adoration and praise. These incantations were used in association with a number of different rituals. As with most classes of incantation, they intended to regain the favor and protection of the patron deity and to soothe the anger of any offended deity.

Dingir.ša.dib.ba

There are only a handful of examples of this specific type of incantation composition. Appeasement of an angry god is the goal.[57]

Shigu

Overlapping somewhat with several of the previous categories, this category also represents penitential prayers.[58] The word itself is an exclamation that cries out for pardon and is at times connected to rituals of release from portended or actual calamities.

Hymn to Shamash *(RANE #75; COS 1.117; FDD 254–61; BWL 121–38)*

Shamash is the sun god responsible for maintaining justice. This two-hundred-line poem praises him for many of the ways that he fulfills that responsibility in specific social contexts.

Hymn to Ishtar *(RANE #76; ANET 383–85)*

After enumerating a series of attributes characteristic of the goddess and extolling her great power, a petition follows that the deity might drive away spells and bring relief from enemies.

Hymn to Marduk *(RANE #77; ANET 389–90)*

This prayer expresses the frustration of the worshiper that his prayers have gone unanswered, and he begs the god to be appeased from his

---

56. E. Ebeling, *Die Akkadische Gebetsserie "Handerhebung"* (Berlin: Akademie-Verlag, 1953).

57. W. G. Lambert, "*Dingir.ša.dib.ba* Incantations," *JNES* 33 (1974): 267–322.

58. Discussion of the genre and translation of a couple of samples may be found in K. van der Toorn, *Sin and Sanction in Israel and Mesopotamia* (Assen: Van Gorcum, 1985), 117–33.

anger. He calls on all the great gods to intercede with Marduk on his behalf. The composition ends with pleas that the god not neglect his holy cities of Nippur, Sippar, and Babylon.

Egyptian

Hymn to Amun-Re *(RANE #72; COS 1.25; ANET 365–67)*

This great sun god of Egypt was the patron of the holy city of Thebes, but this hymn gives him preeminence over all of the cult centers. He is praised as a creator god and as king of the two lands (Upper and Lower Egypt).

Hymn to the Aten *(RANE #73; COS 1.28; ANET 369–71; AEL 2:96–99; OTP 257–61)*

Akhenaten's worship of the Aten is as close to monotheism as can be found in the ancient Near Eastern literature. Even so, it is difficult to tell how much of the theology of this hymn is simply the rhetoric of praise. Nevertheless, this is a beautiful composition that extols the sovereignty of the sun disk over all of creation.

Hittite

Plague Account of Murshili *(RANE #78; COS 1.60; ANET 394–96)*

In response to a devastating outbreak of plague that lasted for many years, prayers were composed that acknowledge royal and national sin and that ask that the gods have mercy, accept the offered restitution, and rid the land of the epidemic.

Wisdom Literature

Several subgenres make up the general category of "Wisdom literature," including short proverbs, longer "instruction" or "admonition" pieces, and philosophical treatises concerning meaning in life, theodicy, and suffering. The first and last categories are better represented in Mesopotamia, while the middle category is a popular Egyptian genre. Together they offer us a good sampling of "all of the wisdom of the east."

Sumerian

Sumerian Proverbs *(COS 1.174)*

The earliest Mesopotamian proverbs date to the Early Dynastic III period, about 2600 BC.[59] A larger collection dates to the Isin-Larsa period toward the beginning of the second millennium. Sumerian proverbs continued to be transmitted in bilingual texts in the Middle Assyrian period and even into the Neo-Assyrian period. Proverbs were frequently used for writing exercises by scribes in training. As with most proverbs of any period, they are drawn from the activities of life (such as farming and herding and housework) and from personality traits. The nature of the collection ranges from common sense to abstract ideas and in general reflects the values of society.

Man and His God *(RANE #63; COS 1.179; ANET 589–91)*

This composition dates to the early second millennium. It describes the plight of an individual who is suffering from various diseases despite his piety and faithfulness toward his god. Most of the piece is taken up by a lengthy lament and description of his suffering. It has some resemblance to lament psalms in the Old Testament, including rhetorical questions posed to the deity, vows of praise, and confessions of sin. Like individual laments, it also reports deliverance.

Akkadian

Ludlul bel Nemeqi *(RANE #64; COS 1.153; ANET 596–600; FDD 298–315; BWL 21–62)*

In this monologue of nearly five hundred lines, an individual describes how he had been abandoned by his god, Marduk. He experiences rejection from every level of humanity as he is disowned, driven out, mocked, and persecuted. Despite his sincere petitions to the gods and his pious acts, he receives no relief; instead his situation worsens and he suffers various physical ills. No one can help him identify a cause for his suffering. Finally in three dreams he is purified and promised deliverance, and, at the end, is restored to favor.

59. B. Alster, *Proverbs of Ancient Sumer*, 2 vols. (Bethesda, MD: CDL, 1997); *BWL* 222–82. Alster lists only two from this period (*Proverbs*, 1:xix, n. 15).

Babylonian Theodicy *(RANE #65; COS 1.154; ANET 601–4; OTP 223–28; FDD 316–25; BWL 63–91)*

This acrostic (the first letters in each couplet spell out the name and position of the author) is a dialogue between a man and his friend concerning injustice in the world and in his own experiences. The friend, like Job's friends, consistently defends traditional ways of thinking. The speaker laments his sad circumstances and wonders how one can find happiness. The friend expresses the remoteness of the gods and their inscrutability. No solutions result from the discussion and no change in the fortunes of the speaker is indicated. Oldest copies are from the Neo-Assyrian period.

Dialogue of Pessimism *(COS 1.155; ANET 600–601; FDD 370–72; BWL 139–49)*

This first-millennium dialogue is a satire about all of the attempts individuals make to improve their lot in life. In it a man expresses various intentions to his slave, who is able to identify the benefit to each course of action. When the master determines not to take a stated course of action, the slave proves equally able to identify reasons why the course should not be pursued. When the master despairs of taking any action and asks the slave what he should do, the slave offers the death of both of them as the most practical alternative. Proposed activities include going to the palace, eating, falling in love, sacrificing to a god, being patriotic, and so on.

Egyptian

Man and His Ba *(COS 3.146; ANET 405–7; AEL 1:163–68; OTP 203–8)*

The manuscript dates to the Middle Kingdom, but the piece may be even older. The speeches exalt the value of death over life. Egyptologists differ as to whether this is a dialogue or a monologue, but it certainly represents the situation of one who has despaired of life and, though not suicidal, welcomes death.

Instruction of Ptahhotep *(RANE #66; AEL 1:61–80; OTP 265–69)*

At least as old as the Middle Kingdom,[60] this piece features a prologue and epilogue framing 37 exhortations. Each consists of four to eighteen lines. Ptahhotep is identified as a vizier who is setting before the king advice he passed on to his son. Topics range from ethics to etiquette to the nature of human relations.

60. Lichtheim dates it to the Sixth Dynasty, *AEL* 1:62.

76

Instruction of Merikare *(RANE #67; COS 1.35; ANET 414–18; AEL 1:97–112)*

Eighteenth Dynasty (1550–1400) manuscripts attribute this instruction to an elderly king in the First Intermediate Period (2180–2000) addressing his son, Merikare. The topic of the treatise is kingship, and it is designed to outline procedures for succeeding in being a wise and just king.

Instruction of Amenemope *(RANE #69; COS 1.47; AEL 2:146–66; OTP 274–82; ANET 421–25)*

Lichtheim sees this as the zenith of the instruction genre that features a shift of emphasis "away from action and success, and toward contemplation and endurance, [which] leads to an overall regrouping of values and a redefinition of the ideal man."[61] It exalts modesty, self-control, and kindness. Consisting of thirty chapters and dating to the 20th Dynasty of the 12th century, it contains numerous parallels to Proverbs 22–23.

Instruction of Any *(RANE #68; COS 1.46; ANET 420–21; AEL 2:135–45)*

Unlike many other didactic works, this 18th Dynasty piece is addressed to the situations faced by the middle-class commoner. In it a scribe (Any) advises his son about how to get along in life. In the epilogue the son objects that all of this advice is too difficult to put into practice.

Satire on the Trades *(COS 1.48; AEL 1:184–92)*

An 18th Dynasty scribe, Dua-Khety, escorts his son to school and on the way extols the benefits of the scribal profession. In the process he describes eighteen other professions and emphasizes how difficult or unfulfilling they are—painting them in the most negative light. The list includes craftsmen such as carpenters and jewelers, as well as laborers such as reed cutters and bird catchers.

Admonitions of Ipuwer *(RANE #81; COS 1.42; AEL 1:149–62; ANET 441–44)*

Some consider this piece to have been composed about 2000 BC in the First Intermediate Period, while others date it to the late Middle Kingdom a few centuries later.[62] Sometimes categorized as a prophecy, the six poems were composed by a court sage and concern the troubled times in which he lived. Along with the social criticism and accompanying exhortations, the work anticipates the coming of an ideal king who will set things right.

---

61. *COS* 1:115.

62. The earlier date is supported by Shupak in *COS* 1:93, the later date by Lichtheim in *AEL* 1:149.

Aramaean

Words of Ahiqar (RANE #70; ANET 427–30; OTP 283–88)

Ahiqar is portrayed as an official in the Assyrian court of Sennacherib and Esarhaddon during the first half of the seventh century. The manuscript is dated a couple of centuries later. Betrayed by a treacherous adopted nephew, he was spared by an executioner whom he had rescued many years earlier. There is a gap between this narrative frame and the proverbial literature contained in the piece. Like the biblical book of Proverbs, it includes advice on child discipline and it personifies Wisdom. Piety, humility, and disciplined speech are encouraged.

Prophecy

Kings in the ancient world depended on communication from the gods to guide them in their decisions and were constantly in pursuit of the favor of the gods in projects that they undertook. Divination was the most prominent way to receive revelation from a deity, but prophets played a significant role in the ancient courts. Prophets are referred to in various sorts of literature, but two particular corpora of texts preserve the oracles given by prophets. Still there are no collections of particular prophets' oracles such as those found in the Old Testament.

Mari Prophetic Texts (RANE #79; OTP 318–22; Nissinen, Prophets and Prophecy, 13–78)

The administrative correspondence from Mari contains about fifty letters that report to King Zimri-Lim (18th century) concerning prophetic activity.[63] The oracles typically exhort Zimri-Lim to take or not to take some action and to be attentive to a deity who has been supportive of him in the past. The actions are mostly political or ritual in nature. Other oracles warn the king of danger and either urge or promise care. One oracle calls the population to repentance, but the rest pertain to the king.

---

63. The best edition of the Mari prophecies is in J. J. M. Roberts, "The Mari Prophetic Texts in Transliteration and English Translation," in *The Bible and the Ancient Near East* (Winona Lake, IN: Eisenbrauns, 2002), 157–253; see also W. Heimpel, *Letters to the King of Mari* (Winona Lake, IN: Eisenbrauns, 2003).

Neo-Assyrian Prophecies *(RANE #80; Nissinen, Prophets and Prophecy, 101–32)*

Nearly thirty prophetic texts from the reigns of Esarhaddon and Ashurbanipal are included in these reports from various officials.[64] Most derive from Ishtar of Arbela, and some have been copied secondarily into compilations. Many of the prophets were female. "Most of the prophecies can be characterized as oracles of well-being, proclaiming the reconciliation of the king with the gods. . . . The divine reconciliation is effected by the intercession of Ištar who protects the king and fights for him."[65]

Fictional Autobiography/Apocalyptic

Discussion continues regarding an appropriate label for the texts in this category. Their common features include recounting a difficult event or series of events, then projecting a time when all will be made right. The latter is usually offered in the future tense suggesting that the events were being predicted. Scholarly consensus considers them propagandistic pieces to support a monarch who has just come to the throne or is about to do so, thus characterized by *vaticinum ex eventu*—a type of pseudo-prophecy written after the events but presented as if they were written before the events.

Marduk Prophecy *(RANE #85; COS 1.149)*

Marduk speaks as one who keeps watch over the world.[66] After reciting the events surrounding the three times he left Babylon, and how on the first two occasions he returned, the prophecy section of the work then indicates his soon return from the third captivity in Elam that will happen when a new king of Babylon arises. This king will enjoy the favor of Marduk and the land will experience renewal. The work is usually connected to the time of Nebuchadnezzar I (end of the second millennium), who succeeded in subjugating Elam.

Dynastic Prophecy *(COS 1.150)*

This text is related to the events toward the end of the sixth century as the Babylonians and Nabopolassar overthrew the Assyrians.[67] As it

---

64. S. Parpola, *Assyrian Prophecies*, SAA 9 (Helsinki: University of Helsinki Press, 1998); see also M. Nissinen, *References to Prophecy in Neo-Assyrian Sources*, SAAS 7 (Helsinki: University of Helsinki Press, 1998).

65. M. Nissinen, *Prophets and Prophecy in the Ancient Near East*, SBLWAW 12 (Atlanta: SBL, 2003), 100–101.

66. Longman, *Fictional Akkadian Autobiography*, 132–42, 233–35.

67. Ibid., 149–52, 239–40.

continues, it vaguely alludes to the three successors of Nabopolassar before it speaks of one designated a "rebel prince," generally identified as Nabonidus. The "prophetic" section of the text introduces a prince of Elam (Cyrus) who will bring deliverance. Allusions continue to a few of the Persian kings and probably through Alexander into the early Seleucid kings, all of whom it sees in a negative light.

Adad-Guppi Autobiography (COS 1.147)

Adad-Guppi, the mother of Nabonidus, is the first person narrator of this account.[68] She describes her conscientious piety to the moon god Sin, whose patron city, Harran, had been overrun by the Babylonians and Medes in 610, at which time the shrine was ransacked. Her care for Sin in the subsequent years was rewarded by the succession of her son to the throne, whom she now encouraged to restore the city of Harran and the shrine of Sin. The remainder of the work contains the account of the death of the matriarch at the age of 104 and her honorable burial.

Shulgi Prophecy

Shulgi was a prominent king of the Ur III period, around 2000 BC.[69] Here he is the first person speaker who portrays himself as part of the divine assembly, able to hear the discussions as well as to contribute to them. He describes a purportedly future time of trouble that will be remedied by the appearance of an ideal king, who will restore order and prosperity to the land by reestablishing shrines and sanctuaries and resuming neglected rituals. Allusions are too vague and the text too broken to identify most of the events, though it seems that one reference is to the sack of Babylon by Tukulti-Ninurta in the thirteenth century. Like the Marduk Prophecy, this may well date to the second dynasty of Isin toward the end of the second millennium.

Uruk Prophecy (RANE #86; ANET 604)

Differences of opinion exist whether the future kings in this prophecy refer to Merodach-Baladan and his son,[70] to Nabopolassar and Nebuchadnezzar,[71] or to Nebuchadnezzar and his successor, Awel-Marduk.[72]

---

68. Ibid., 97–103, 225–28.

69. Ibid., 142–46, 236–37.

70. Toward the end of the 8th century; see J. Goldstein, "The Historical Setting of the Uruk Prophecy," *JNES* 47 (1988): 43–46.

71. W. G. Lambert, *The Background of Jewish Apocalyptic* (London: Athlone, 1978), 10–12.

72. H. Hunger and S. A. Kaufman, "A New Akkadian Prophecy Text," *JAOS* 95 (1975): 371–75.

P.-A. Beaulieu supports the last view with the distinction that rather than referring to Nebuchadnezzar's immediate son and successor, the text intends a reference to one of the Seleucid monarchs as a new Nebuchadnezzar.[73] The text considers the restoration of the *lamassu* (protective images) to Uruk by the penultimate ruler and anticipates the rise of a new ruler whose dynasty "will be established forever."[74]

Archives

Many of the textual finds from the ancient Near East occur not in isolated tablets but in major archives.[75] These archives often emerge in the excavations of public buildings (palaces or temples) in major cities. They can offer a wide perspective on history and culture through the variety of texts that they contain, but they typically represent the ruling echelon rather than the common people.

Ebla *(OTP 240–43)*

The Ebla archive is the oldest royal archive, dating to the mid-third millennium, in biblical chronology somewhere between the tower of Babel and Abraham.[76] Located in modern Syria, Ebla was a city of economic and political importance. The three- to four-thousand texts do not have any direct connection to the Bible, but they give a good idea of the historical and cultural background of the period.

Mari *(ANET 482)*

The twenty thousand texts from Mari date to the Old Babylonian period.[77] Mari was one of the major cities along the Euphrates River. The archives provided extensive historical information for the period of Hammurabi and also contain the largest collection of prophetic texts outside the Bible.

---

73. P.-A. Beaulieu, "The Historical Background of the Uruk Prophecy," in *The Tablet and the Scroll*, ed. M. E. Cohen, D. C. Snell, and D. B. Weisberg (Bethesda, MD: CDL, 1993), 41–52. He suggests Antiochus I at the beginning of the third century BC. The text was found in a Seleucid period house in Uruk.

74. Longman, *Fictional Akkadian Autobiography*, 146–49, 237–38.

75. O. Pedersén, *Archives and Libraries in the Ancient Near East* (Bethesda, MD: CDL, 1998). Many of the archives have their own series of publications for the texts. General treatment of the archives can be found in the major reference works, e.g., *OEANE, CANE,* and *ABD.*

76. G. Pettinato, *The Archives of Ebla* (Garden City, NY: Doubleday, 1981).

77. Heimpel, *Letters to the King.* Most of the texts translated in this volume are from ARM 26 (= J.-M. Durand, *Archives épistolaires de Mari*, 1/1 [Paris: Éditions recherche sur les civilizations, 1988]).

Alalakh (COS 3.99–102)

Over five hundred texts from this site in northwestern Syria date to the mid-second millennium BC. They are written in Akkadian and concern administrative matters. Many are lists of various sorts and others are legal texts (contracts, deeds, etc.). They offer a profile of everyday life in a town of this period.

Emar

The Late Bronze Age (1550–1200) town of Emar was located at the bend on the upper Euphrates. Among the most important texts found there were ritual texts from the temple library that help us to understand worship at Emar and the festivals and rituals that they observed. There are also many legal texts that continue to shed light on daily life.[78]

Nuzi

The Nuzi tablets provided family records in contrast to the national and royal archives of other city and temple archives. Some four thousand tablets dating to the fifteenth century BC offer details of many personal legal matters such as marriage, adoption, and inheritance as practiced by the Hurrians of Mitanni. Many of the practices demonstrated have also been documented in other areas of the ancient world.[79]

Ugarit

The texts from the Syrian coastal town of Ugarit date to the Late Bronze Age.[80] The population of Ugarit was probably what the Bible would refer to as Canaanite. These texts therefore give us our best picture of Canaanite culture. Most significant among the fourteen hundred tablets are the literary texts: the *Tale of Kirtu*, the *Tale of Aqhat*, and the mythological *Baal Cycle*, all mentioned earlier in this list. In addition there are a number of ritual and liturgical texts.

78. For rituals see D. Fleming, *Time at Emar* (Winona Lake, IN: Eisenbrauns, 2000); for laws see R. Westbrook, ed., *History of Ancient Near Eastern Law* (Leiden: Brill, 2003).

79. For documentation of practices see M. Selman, "Comparative Customs and the Patriarchal Age," in *Essays on Patriarchal Narratives*, ed. A. R. Millard and D. J. Wiseman (Winona Lake, IN: Eisenbrauns, 1980), 91–139.

80. Wyatt, *Religious Texts*; J. C. L. Gibson, *Canaanite Myths and Legends* (Edinburgh: T & T Clark, 1978); D. Pardee, *Ritual and Cult at Ugarit*, SBLWAW 10 (Atlanta: SBL, 2002); S. B. Parker, ed., *Ugaritic Narrative Poetry* (Atlanta: Scholars Press, 1997).

Miscellaneous

Dumuzi and Inanna *(COS 1.169; ANET 637–44; HTO 3–84; OTP 305–11)*

Dumuzi (Tammuz) is an early shepherd god whose annual death and return from the netherworld determine the change of the seasons.[81] A significant collection of poetic and liturgical Sumerian literature features love poems concerning the relationship of Dumuzi and his bride, Inanna, as well as laments for Dumuzi after his death. These texts relate to fertility and the sacred marriage rituals, and are known primarily from the Ur III period.

Lamentation over the Destruction of Sumer and Ur *(COS 1.166; ANET 611–19)*

Several city laments survive from about 2000 BC. A number of them, like this one, bemoan the fall of the city of Ur at the end of the Ur III dynasty.[82] Written a generation after the disastrous events, they offer a perspective of divine abandonment that seeks remedy in the rebuilding of ruined shrines.

Deir 'Alla Inscription *(RANE #91; COS 2.27; OTP 124–26; Nissinen, Prophets and Prophecy, 207–12)*

This Aramaic (or Canaanite) text from an Israelite provenance was written with ink on a plaster wall of a house about 800 BC.[83] In it, visions of Balaam the son of Beor, the internationally renowned prophet known from Numbers 22–25, are recorded in which El communicates coming doom. Other gods attempt to thwart El by coercing a goddess to work on their behalf. Balaam seeks to aid the goddess under duress, and in the end neither divine faction accomplishes its plans. A second part of the text appears to concern El's construction of the netherworld.

Nineteenth Dynasty Egyptian Love Poetry *(ANET 467–69; OTP 297–301)*

This collection of about fifty pieces dates from the thirteenth to the eleventh centuries BC.[84] The monologues concern the sensual (more than erotic) thoughts and emotions that accompany a courting relationship.

---

81. D. Wolkstein and S. Kramer, *Inanna, Queen of Heaven and Earth: Her Stories and Hymns from Sumer* (New York: Harper & Row, 1983). See also *Inanna's Descent* above, pp. 45–46.

82. P. Michalowski, *The Lamentation over the Destruction of Sumer and Ur* (Winona Lake, IN: Eisenbrauns, 1989).

83. J. Hackett, *The Balaam Text from Deir 'Alla*, HSM 31 (Chico, CA: Scholars Press, 1980).

84. M. Fox, *The Song of Songs and the Ancient Egyptian Love Songs* (Madison: University of Wisconsin Press, 1985).

Part 3

Religion

4

The Gods

This chapter introduces the divine world in general, including how deities functioned among themselves as cosmic overseers and how they interacted with human beings.[1]

There is no such word as "religion" in the languages of the ancient Near East. Likewise, there is no dichotomy between sacred and secular, or even between natural and supernatural. The only suitable dichotomy is between spiritual and physical, though even that would be a less meaningful distinction to them than it is to us. In the end, there is a distinction between the heavenly realm and the earthly one, but events in the two were often intertwined or parallel. It would be difficult to discuss with ancients the concept of divine intervention, because in their worldview deity was too integrated into the cosmos to intervene in it. For the most part, deity is on the inside, not the outside. All experience was religious experience, all law was spiritual in nature, all duties were duties to the gods, all events had deity as their cause. Life was religion and religion could not be compartmentalized within life.[2]

Ontology/Theogony

The mythology of both Mesopotamia and Egypt makes clear that the gods had origins. They exist in familial relationships and there are

---

1. See the appendix for an annotated list of thirty of the most significant gods.
2. For a discussion of this relative to Egypt see J. Assmann, *The Search for God in Ancient Egypt* (Ithaca: Cornell University Press, 2001), 1–3. He also provides some nuancing in the recognition that the boundaries and categories shifted over the centuries.

generations of gods.[3] When the texts speak of theogony (origins of the gods) they include a number of elements in the presentation. In Egyptian literature it is most common to think of the earliest gods coming into being through bodily fluids (the creator god spitting, sneezing, sweating, or masturbating), while the later deities are simply born to a previous generation of deity. In the *Memphite Theology* the gods are brought into being by Atum separating them from himself.[4] One way that creation was expressed was by "the mouth which pronounced the name of everything."[5] Typically the first gods created are primordial cosmic gods. Since the forces of nature are expressions and manifestations of the attributes of deities, cosmogony and theogony become intertwined as the natural world comes into being along with the gods who embody the various elements of the cosmos.

What does it mean to say that a god exists or comes into existence? The question of ontology (what it means for something to exist) is important for understanding both theogony and cosmogony because we cannot productively talk about how something came into existence until we define in some way what it means to exist.[6]

In the ancient world something came into existence when it was separated out as a distinct entity, given a function, and given a name.[7] So the *Ritual of Amun* from the second half of the second millennium identifies creation as beginning "when no god had come into being and no name had been invented for anything."[8] The first god arises on his own from the primeval waters (separates himself from them) and then separates into millions.[9] Out of this fairly restrictive sense of ontology emerges the oxymoron of nonexistent entities.[10] Prior to creation there was a unity expressed by the statement that there were "not yet two things."[11] The realm of the nonexistent remains not only at the bound-

3. See discussion in J. Bottéro, *Religion in Ancient Mesopotamia* (Chicago: University of Chicago Press, 2001), 72–77.

4. Excellent discussion in E. Hornung, *Conceptions of God in Ancient Egypt* (Ithaca: Cornell University Press, 1982), 143–51; examples in *COS* 1.8–16.

5. S. Morenz, *Egyptian Religion* (Ithaca: Cornell University Press, 1973), 164.

6. For a brief discussion on ancient Near Eastern ontology that investigates from a different angle than here, see T. Jacobsen, "The Graven Image," in *Ancient Israelite Religion: Essays in Honor of Frank Moore Cross*, ed. P. D. Miller, P. D. Hanson, and S. D. McBride (Philadelphia: Fortress, 1987), 18–20.

7. This is in distinct contrast to modern and even classical ontologies, which often see existence as defined by substance and properties—i.e., largely material in nature. In the ancient Near East, something did not necessarily exist just because it happened to be occupying space.

8. Quoted in Hornung, *Conceptions*, 148; cf. Morenz, *Egyptian Religion*, 165.

9. Hornung, *Conceptions*, 170, 176; see also Morenz, *Egyptian Religion*, 173.

10. Hornung, *Conceptions*, 172–85.

11. Ibid., 176.

aries but throughout the cosmos, and that realm can be encountered. The desert and the limitless waters are two examples.[12] The gods exist on earth only through their functions. "On earth . . . the gods live only in images, in the king as an image of god, in cult images in the temples, and in sacred animals, plants and objects."[13]

Assmann expresses this in the idea that the gods were most importantly represented through their actions.

> The cosmic dimension of the divine was not confined to the sheer materiality of cosmic elements such as earth, air, water, and so forth, or to celestial bodies such as the sun and the moon, but rather that it referred to specific complexes of actions, traits, attitudes, and qualities that were interpreted as cosmic phenomena "in action" and in which humankind also participated. Nut was not so much the sky as what the sky did.[14]

In Mesopotamia there are a number of similar issues, though the philosophy has not reached the level that we find in the extant Egyptian literature. Discussion of the origins of the gods is typically nonspecific. The procreation element is obvious in the god lists and in the many references to the familial relationships between the various gods.[15] Heaven (An) and Earth (Ki) joined in cosmic matrimony and the great gods were born. This union is the focus of the Nippur tradition of cosmogony.[16] In the Eridu traditions, Nammu is the mother of the gods: "Nammu, the primeval mother, who had given birth to all the great gods. . . ."[17] In *Ewe and Wheat* the sky god An is seen as the progenitor of the gods: "Upon the Hill of Heaven and Earth when An had spawned the divine godlings."[18] We must understand, however, that the birth of the gods does not relate to their physical or material existence. It relates to their functions and roles because their birth is connected to the origins of natural phenomena.[19]

12. Ibid., 179–80.

13. Ibid., 229. It is a confirmation of this idea of ontology that even things like temples are ritually animated in Egypt so that they took the character of dynamic entities, i.e., they were "living" and their life was sustained by virtue of the cult. See R. Gundlach, "Temples," *OEAE* 3:367.

14. Assmann, *Search for God*, 81.

15. R. J. Clifford, *Creation Accounts in the Ancient Near East and in the Bible* (Washington, D.C.: Catholic Biblical Association, 1994), 49–51. The most important and extensive of these lists is the Old Babylonian text designated by its first line "An = *Anum*."

16. Ibid., 22–32.

17. Ibid., 40, "Enki and Ninmah."

18. Ibid., 45.

19. The idea that procreation is related to role rather than to substance is evident even in the biblical statements like "You are my son, today I have begotten you" (Ps. 2:7) in which the king is born to his royal position. In Egypt the sun/sun god is born each morning

All of these references offer a procreative theogony, but no ontology. An Akkadian prayer from the Seleucid period names a list of gods that Ea creates, and with each one a function is given. This does not go as far as suggesting that the designation of a function is necessary for a god to exist, but it indicates the importance of the assigned function in the understanding of the nature of the god. The most helpful statements for discerning the Mesopotamian ideas of divine origins and ontology are found in the *Atrahasis Epic* and *Enuma Elish*. The opening line of *Atrahasis* establishes the setting as "When gods were men."[20] This is an interesting case of the nature of the gods being defined by their functions. Here their function was "humanlike."

Enuma Elish opens with the following well-known introduction:

> When skies above were not yet named
> Nor earth below pronounced by name.
> Apsu, the first one, their begetter
> And maker Tiamat, who bore them all.
> Had mixed their waters together,
> But had not formed pastures nor discovered reed-beds;
> When yet no gods were manifest,
> Nor names pronounced, nor destinies decreed,
> Then gods were born within them.
> Lahmu and Lahamu emerged, their names pronounced.[21]

Here there is no separation of the gods from one another as was seen in Egypt, but the elements of procreation (more pronounced as the text continues) and of naming are clear. In addition, the significance of destinies (which define the functions and roles) of the gods is evident. Names are related to destinies, as demonstrated in tablets six and seven of *Enuma Elish,* where the gods in assembly declare the destiny of the champion Marduk by bestowing on him fifty names, which give him all of the roles and functions necessary to exercise kingship over the gods.

Finally, mention should be made of the *Theogony of Dunnu*, dating to the early second millennium BC. It is important for the close connection that it portrays between the gods and the elements in nature with which they are associated. Clifford concludes that "the male deities appear to be

as it takes up its function anew (J. Assmann, *The Mind of Egypt* [New York: Metropolitan, 1996], 210–11).

20. This is the translation offered by B. Foster in *COS* 1.130. The earlier editions such as S. Dalley, *MFM* 9; and the critical edition by W. G. Lambert and A. R. Millard, *Atra-Hasis: The Babylonian Story of the Flood* (Oxford: Clarendon, 1969), 43, translated: "When the gods instead of man." The discussion is a complex one, but does not impact the decisions made here.

21. *MFM* 232.

Comparative Exploration: Ontology and Theogony in Israel

When we compare the ancient Near Eastern ideas of ontology and theogony to the biblical portrayal of Yahweh, we see some significant similarities and differences. The most obvious difference is seen in the absence of any theogony in Israel. The biblical text offers no indication that Israel considered Yahweh as having an origin, and there are no other gods to bring into existence either by procreation or separation. Since the cosmos is not viewed as a manifestation of divine attributes, Israel's cosmogony develops without any need of theogony. The issue of theogony is likewise foreign to contemporary Christian and Jewish theology where God is considered eternally existing.

In the area of ontology, however, there is more continuity. The name of Yahweh itself invites ontological assessments. Whether it represents a simple statement of existence or expresses a causative aspect in its verbal form, the giving of the name is surrounded by statements of identity linked with role. Though we may not go so far as to revert to G. E. Wright's "God who acts," we nevertheless cannot miss the common role-oriented descriptors when attributes are defined. More than that, the biblical depiction of Yahweh insists that he is the only God, which, given the ontology laid out above, indicates that there is no jurisdiction or role allotted to any other deity. This will be discussed at greater length in a later section on the Decalogue (p. 156).

A specific text that is informed and illuminated by this ontological understanding is Psalm 14:1 (cf. 53:1), "The fool says in his heart, 'There is no God.'" As becomes clear in the rest of the psalm, this statement implies that the "fool" has drawn the conclusion that God will not act against his corrupt ways. "Existence" can be seen to be defined in relation to the Deity's activity.

hypostases of the fertility of the flocks and the females, representatives of vegetation."[22] Though the text is fragmentary, it is clear that the gods of the city of Dunnu achieve their authority and jurisdiction through acts of parricide and incest.[23] New gods come into existence as they take over the functions of older gods.

From all of the above we can conclude that the gods came into existence through a variety of mechanisms, of which procreation is the most common. Whether any particular god was considered the product of procreation or not, the existence of the deity was defined in terms of having taken on an individual identity by being separated from the creator deity (Egypt only), by being given a name, and by being given a

22. Clifford, *Creation Accounts*, 96.
23. Ibid.

Comparative Exploration: The Name Yahweh

If ancient cultures considered something to exist when it had a name and a function, the name of a deity is more than simply a moniker by which he or she can be invoked. It is the god's identity and frames the god's "existence." The announcement to Moses at the burning bush is therefore a singular defining moment. When he asks what name he should give for the God of their fathers (Exod. 3:13), he is not expressing ignorance of the identity of their ancestral deity. It is not unusual for a single deity to have many different epithets or titles. When Marduk ascends to the head of the pantheon, *Enuma Elish* lists fifty names to delineate all of the functions and attributes that he accumulates. Amun-Re is praised as having names whose number is unknown.[1] The multiplication of names is one way to express the power and station of the deity. So Moses's question concerns which identity of the deity is pertinent to the mission on which he is being sent. A number of names had been attached to the ancestral Deity in the founding accounts, many given on the basis of an encounter in which a particular attribute was manifest. This diversity of names is also reflected in Exodus 6:2–3, where God indicates that there were some names that had been manifest to the patriarchs, but that he had not yet acted in ways that would manifest the identity bound up in the name Yahweh. His statement does not suggest that the patriarchs had never been introduced to the name Yahweh, but that he had not fulfilled that role in their experience.

What was the role attached to Yahweh? One way to answer this question

function or jurisdiction in some area (defined by the destinies decreed for them). Jurisdictions could be cosmic, terrestrial, or cultural. J. Assmann has used the designation "cosmotheism" to describe polytheistic religions that "worship the cosmos as the collective manifestation of various different deities."[24] He explains: "Gods had names, genealogies, and a mythically revealed spectrum of roles; they had a 'portfolio,' a sphere of cosmic, vegetative, or cultural competencies; and finally they had cult locations from which they exercised their earthly rule."[25]

Divine Assembly

Before addressing this topic directly, we need to make sure that we observe the obvious. All of the cultures around Israel were polytheistic.

24. Assmann, *Mind of Egypt*, 204.
25. Ibid., 205.

is through the etymology of the name. Unfortunately, the etymology is uncertain. Many, like F. Cross, analyzed the name as a causative form of the verb "to be."[2] This would identify him as one who causes to be (i.e., "creates").

As we have seen, however, to cause something to be in the ancient world means to give functions and names. We might ask if there is something specific that the name has in mind. If Cross is right in seeing a causative verbal element in the name Yahweh, there may be a parallel here to the Akkadian verb *banu*, which is used in names describing the personal god's engendering relationship to his protégé. It describes not so much a concept of actual birth as the initiating of a relationship. The name Yahweh would then designate "a God who creates" in the sense of "a God who enters a relationship."[3] This could be a rather generic epithet for a personal god, but it could also lay the foundation for the key concept of a covenant God, for this engendering becomes synonymous with choice (= election). We might recall that besides naming and giving a function, creating often involves separating—so here Israel is separated out, given a function (Exod. 19:5–6), and in that way Yahweh is causing them to exist.

In this sense, Yahweh was not presented as a name they had never heard of before, but as a name representing a function that they had not as yet experienced. The god Yahweh who had made promises of land to their forefather was now ready to function in that implied capacity—he was forming a relationship with the family of Abraham (Exod. 19:3–6; Lev. 26:12) and was electing them as a people to populate the land.

1. *COS* 1.25:40.
2. F. Cross, *Canaanite Myth and Hebrew Epic* (Cambridge: Harvard University Press, 1973), 60–71; see D. N. Freedman, *TDOT* 5:500–521.
3. Cf. Akkadian Ilum-bani, cited by F. Cross, *TDOT* 1:243.

This fact has many ramifications, some of which have already been addressed and others are still to be unveiled. Beyond the blunt fact, however, is the need to nuance that polytheism carefully. Rather than doing this by reference to the brief "monotheistic moments" (e.g., 14th-century Egypt under Akhenaten) or the inclination to aggregate divine identities to one deity in the rhetoric of praise literature, we can do so by recognizing the vestiges of a monotheistic core in the sense that the gods are traced back to one in the cosmogonies. This primordial, singular, divine entity is not represented in the head of the pantheon, and indeed is largely inactive. Jan Assmann suggests that it is the very inactivity and distance of this deity that eventuates in the need to recognize active gods that in turn become the gods who control the destinies of the human world.[26] To

26. Assmann, *Search for God*, 10–13; see also L. K. Handy, *Among the Host of Heaven* (Winona Lake, IN: Eisenbrauns, 1994), 65–130, where he divides his treatment of the gods of Ugarit into the "authoritative" gods and the "active" gods. This might also help

Comparative Exploration: Yahweh's Council

In the Old Testament, as we would expect, Yahweh is the sole authority responsible for carrying out those functions. Isaiah 40:14 insists that Yahweh has no need of consultation, yet the council has not totally disappeared. It is no longer made up of gods, and its members[1] are delegated the tasks of carrying out the decisions of the council rather than being delegated any actual authority or jurisdiction (see discussion of Decalogue on p. 156). Nevertheless, the council, under Yahweh's command, addresses the same kinds of issues as listed above.

The concerns of the assembly are like that of the divine assembly in Mesopotamian religion: upholding the moral and legal order of society, deciding about victory and defeat in war and politics,

electing and deposing kings, controlling and shaping history.[2]

Unlike the Mesopotamian council made up of the great gods, the Israelite council, similar to that of Ugarit, is made up of lesser beings. Besides the Psalms that allude to the divine council (e.g., Pss. 29, 82, 89), it appears in several other genres. In 1 Kings 22 the council appears in the vision of the prophet Micaiah. The council is deliberating about a strategy for dealing with Ahab, and the result is that a spirit[3] is sent to deceive his prophets. In Isaiah 6 the presence of the council is indicated by the use of the first person plural ("Whom shall we send and who will go for us?"), and it is possible that the seraphim are connected in some way to the council, either as attendants or as members. As in

the extent that this is true, polytheism would be a secondary construct, though it dominates the religious environment of the ancient Near East. Since their ontology was function oriented, a god who does not function or act fades into virtual nonexistence.

In the ancient world, major decisions among the gods were group decisions. Most likely a perception modeled after human government of an early period, this view understood the gods as deliberating and governing as an assembly.[27] The divine council is evidenced in many of the Ugaritic texts, as well as in a wide variety of texts from Mesopotamia. Egypt, on the other hand, understands its gods operating in much more individualistic ways. There is little to suggest assembly rule, though

---

explain why Israel would have naturally been inclined to fill in echelons of active deities even while recognizing their national deity was Yahweh.

27. Despite the common rejection these days of Jacobsen's Primitive Democracy, the core observation of the ways in which perception of the divine was modeled on human institutions remains valid. See T. Jacobsen, "Primitive Democracy in Ancient Mesopotamia," in *Toward the Image of Tammuz*, ed. W. L. Moran (Cambridge: Harvard University Press, 1970), 157–70, esp. 164.

1 Kings 22, the council is seeking a messenger to send. The book of Job opens with a council scene as the "sons of God" (an occasional label for the council members) have gathered and are being debriefed. The adversary (Heb. *satan*) comes, apparently as one of their number, and the plot begins to unfold. Finally, it is common to see the council as providing a contextual understanding of the plurals in the early chapters of Genesis (Gen. 1:26; 3:22; 11:7). It should be noted, however, that though these Genesis passages suggest deliberation, there is no distribution of power to the council members—Yahweh is the one who carries out the tasks. In contrast, the spirit in 1 Kings 22, the adversary in Job 1–2, and the prophet in Isaiah 6 are all sent from the council with a mission to accomplish.

From the Old Testament itself, it would be clear that the Israelites thought in terms of a divine council (at least 1 Kings 22 is clear). The information from the ancient Near East has provided much more information concerning how the council was believed to operate in the ancient world, and based on that information we can understand the Israelite worldview more clearly. In addition it is now possible to make sense of some passages that had previously been opaque. Without an informed understanding of the divine council it had become commonplace for interpreters to read the Trinity, or at least plurality in the godhead, into the plurals in Genesis, though most did not hesitate to admit the unlikelihood that the Isra-

elites would have understood the text in those terms.[4]

Even as we have come to understand the Old Testament better in light of the ancient worldview, we are able to see sharp contrast in the way that the concept of the council has evolved to suit the theology of Israel. This is an example of what is found many times throughout the Old Testament. Confessional scholars would not think in terms of God *revealing* the concept of a divine council to Israel. It is just there in the background, not necessarily *borrowed* from the broader culture, but simply a part of how people thought in the ancient world. Nevertheless, the thinking about it is adjusted in the Bible so that it is in line with revelation about the nature of God.

---

1. The members of the council are sometimes referred to as "the sons of God," similar to the Ugaritic designation of the council as "the sons of El."

2. P. Miller, "Cosmology and World Order in the Old Testament: The Divine Council as Cosmic-Political Symbol," in *Israelite Religion and Biblical Theology*, JSOTSup 267 (1987; repr. Sheffield: Sheffield Academic Press, 2000), 425. R. Clifford, *The Cosmic Mountain in Canaan and the Old Testament*, HSM 4 (Cambridge: Harvard University Press, 1972), 47, identifies the functions of the assembly in the OT as relating to lordship of the nations (Deut. 32:8–9), acclaiming kingship (Ps. 29), and judging (Ps. 82).

3. "Spirit" = Heb. *ruah*, the only place where this is used to designate a member of the council.

4. See fuller discussion of the hermeneutical and exegetical issues in J. Walton, *Genesis*, NIVAC (Grand Rapids: Zondervan, 2001), 128–30.

there is a concept of king of the gods as well as a hierarchical structure among the gods.[28]

The assembly in Mesopotamia was made up of the great gods, whose number, when designated, was fifty; among them were seven who determined the destinies.[29] This assembly carried the highest authority since it represented the collective community of deities. In earliest Sumerian literature, Anu is the head of the pantheon with Enlil often taking the active lead. In the second millennium Marduk takes the lead in southern Mesopotamia and Ashur in Assyria. In Ugaritic literature the head of the pantheon is El. Here the gods of the assembly appear to be lesser gods, and the role played by El is more dominant than is evidenced by the head of the pantheon in Mesopotamia.[30]

The Sumerian divine assembly gathered in Enlil's temple in Nippur. In Ugaritic literature the assembly took place at the dwelling place of El in the mountains.[31] The role of the assembly varies slightly from culture to culture, but a common profile is discernible. The following list is derived from Mesopotamian literature. Though all of the pieces are not evidenced in the extant literature of West Semitic cultures, what is found in Ugaritic and Israelite literature would not be inconsistent with these functions.

1. In the disputation *Two Insects*, the assembly creates heaven and earth and the various types of animals and assigns them their roles.[32]
2. The assembly is called together to decide either human or divine[33] court cases.[34]
3. In the *Gilgamesh Epic* the decision to send the flood is made in the council. In *Atrahasis* both that decision and the earlier attempts at limiting human population came from discussions in the assembly. Thus the fate of humankind is seen as the business of the assembly.

28. Morenz, *Egyptian Religion*, 232–33. In the *Book of the Dead* there is a group of gods who sit in judgment, though there is little sense of deliberation. The king's coronation is witnessed by deities, but this again stops short of the concepts seen elsewhere. Perhaps the clearest example is in a late-second-millennium text, *Horus and Seth*, which portrays the Ennead as a decision-making body (*AEL* 2:214–23).

29. Jacobsen, "Primitive Democracy," 404 n. 50.

30. E. T. Mullen, *The Assembly of the Gods*, HSM 24 (Chico, CA: Scholars Press, 1986), 282; Handy, *Among the Host*, 118.

31. Baal's mountain is Mt. Zaphon, and while it is the site of much activity, including banqueting of the gods, the assembly does not meet there to do business.

32. Clifford, *Creation Accounts*, 65.

33. *Enlil and Ninlil*.

34. Jacobsen, "Primitive Democracy," 166.

4. The assembly grants kingship both in the divine realm and the human realm, where cities are granted kingship[35] as well as individuals.[36]
5. In a similar way the decision to remove kingship and decree the fate of cities is the decision of the council in the city laments.

Hence the council can be seen in the role of decreeing destinies in general, both in the divine and human realm, and making ad hoc decisions that arise in the process of governing the world.

Place of the Gods in the Cosmos

Our next investigation must consider how this divine collective community relates to the cosmos and how the cosmos operates under their supervision. Every aspect of what we call the natural world was associated with some deity in the ancient Near East. The result is that the term "natural world" would be meaningless or nonsensical to them. There was nothing about the world that was natural. There was no purely natural cause and effect, no natural laws, no natural occurrences—everything was imbued with the supernatural (another artificial category).

The cosmic deities were manifest in that element of the cosmos with which they were associated, and had some jurisdiction there. Sun gods were active in and through the sun—but they did not create the sun, at least not in the material terms that we are used to thinking in. In the ontological concepts that we have already discussed above with regard to the gods, and those that we have yet to discuss with regard to the cosmos, existence is much more closely bound with function and role. Consequently, that the sun and the sun god function together and that their roles coincide suggest a modified "creative" role. The birth of the sun god is coterminous with the origin of the sun (neither functions/exists without the other), thus explaining the oft-mentioned correspondence between theogony and cosmogony. Though the god is the controlling party in the functioning partnership, the god has no existence separate from, outside, or above the sun. The sun is the manifestation of the god and the expression of the god's attributes. The god is the power behind the sun. Because of this, we might also conclude that our categories of cosmogony (origins of the cosmos) and cosmology (operations of the cosmos) are artificially distinguished with regard to the ancient world (similarly theogony and theology). In the ancient world the origins are inseparable from operations. Hence cosmogony, cosmology, theogony, and theology are all inextricably intertwined.

---

35. *Sumerian King List.*
36. Jacobsen, "Primitive Democracy," 166.

Comparative Exploration: Yahweh's Place in the Cosmos

In contrast, Yahweh is not just responsible for managing the cosmos, but is seen as the originator of its "control attributes." In Mesopotamian terms we would say that Yahweh causes the control attributes to begin functioning, as well as decreeing the destinies at every level. He is not within the system, but operates from outside the system.[1] The cosmic phenomena are not manifestations of his attributes, but instruments of his sovereignty. No control attributes have any autonomous existence. In the chapter on the cosmos where I discuss creation in more detail, I will suggest that Genesis 1 portrays Yahweh as creating the control attributes on days one through three and decreeing destinies on days four through six (pp. 194–95).

At this juncture, it is important to differentiate between how the people of the ancient Near East saw their gods operating in the cosmos and how the Bible portrays Yahweh's role. The most important difference noted in the biblical pre-sentation of what Israel's theology was supposed to look like was not the number of deities, but the place deity occupied in the cosmos. H. C. Brichto has noted: "Biblical religion not only removes the One God from the domain of mythology, but as often noted, it demythologizes creation itself, and this even while it echoes with the constructs of pagan mythology."[2] He goes on to suggest that in the Bible, nature is impersonal and the realm of ultimate power is personal, occupied by Yahweh alone. In contrast, the ancient world at large perceives nature as personal (the realm occupied by the gods) and the outside sphere of the control attributes as impersonal.[3]

1. H. C. Brichto, *The Names of God* (Oxford: Oxford University Press, 1998), 60–61.
2. Ibid., 57. I would rephrase the last clause to suggest that it is not a pagan mythology that echoes, but an ancient cognitive environment.
3. Ibid., 61.

The gods are "in" the cosmos, and so they are locked into certain parameters. How, when, and by whom were these operational parameters established? Who decides which functions and roles are filled by which entities? In Mesopotamia two important terms help us to explore these issues. The first is Sumerian ME (Akkadian *parṣu*). There is still considerable debate involved in defining (let alone translating) these terms. Translations that have been suggested include "decrees," "ordinances," "prescriptions," "rules," "attributes," "divine powers," "arts of civilization," and "cultural norms," to name just a few. For expedience I will label them here as "control attributes." Whichever translation we might choose, they are what define the parameters regarding how the world works. The second term is Sumerian NAM (Akkadian *šīmtu*), which defines the roles and functions played by individual entities within the parameters of the control attributes. These "destinies," as I will refer to them, assign entities their place in the cosmos.

As we compare these terms, we might conclude that the control attributes of something are relatively static in the sense that they are determined without being regularly revisited or addressed. Control attributes are standing orders. In contrast, the destinies are much more dynamic and are reestablished periodically. Destinies are provisional. At the same time, the control attributes need to be perfected, executed, or activated.[37] When people execute control attributes it is in the context of performance of rituals. In this sense the control attributes need to be renewed or upheld. So Rim-Sin "perfects the power and ordinances (ME GIŠ·GUR) of Eridu."[38]

The significance of these two terms that I have translated "control attributes" and "destinies" is that they help define the role of the gods in the cosmos. By the nature of the gods' interaction with them, they show that the gods are operating *within* a system that they manage. The control attributes exist independently of them while the exercise of their rule is expressed primarily through the destinies. These distinctions can be observed in the cosmogonic prologue to the bilingual *Great Astrological Treatise*. In the Sumerian version, An, Enlil, and Enki operate within the control attributes to establish the lunar cycle, days, months, and omens. The Akkadian version describes this as establishing the plans (*uṣurtu*) of heaven and earth.[39] A second prologue gives more detail using verbs such as "established, appointed, distributed, measured (the day), created (month and year)"—all summarized as making the decrees concerning heaven and earth.[40]

Attributes of Deity

What did Assyrians, Canaanites, and Egyptians believe their gods were really like? Different pictures may form depending on which genres of literature one decides to make foundational. Is the depiction in the mythical literature more reliable than the one in the hymns and prayers? Is the rhetoric found in the royal inscriptions going to give a more balanced picture than the cynicism that might be found in wisdom literature? Do the omen texts offer a more realistic and authentic portrayal of what they believed about their gods than the diplomatic treaties? The point is that it is difficult for outsiders to penetrate the rhetoric sufficiently to achieve a confident understanding of how the ancients thought about deity. The

37. Various renderings of Sumerian šu·DU, Akkadian *šuklulu*.
38. Y. Rosengarten, *Sumer et le Sacré* (Paris: Boccard, 1977), 21–22.
39. Clifford, *Creation Accounts*, 67–68.
40. Ibid., 68.

Photo 5 Sun God

rhetoric in the hymns and prayers would naturally portray worshipers as being patronizing, effusive, and flattering. The rhetoric of the royal inscriptions would be expected to represent the deities as suitably pretentious and all-encompassing. By its nature the rhetoric of wisdom will expose the raw side of uncertainty concerning the intentions of deity. Are the "real beliefs" represented in the ideals or in the praxis?

We must recognize these problems, but they need not paralyze us or force us to abandon the investigation in agnostic frustration. The setting of the literature can help adjust our assessment of the information we gain from it. For example, it would be logical to expect different perspectives when a god is approached as an individual (as in hymns and wisdom), when a god acts within the group to which he or she relates (pantheon, assembly, as in the mythology) and when the god is seen in relation to gods from other groups (often in royal inscriptions or treaties). We will approach each of these categories in search of information.

Gods as Individuals

When individual gods are addressed in prayer, attributes are often named and titles listed. It is here that we find the most optimistic portrayal of the gods. It is natural that whatever god is being praised is exalted above others without any thought of contradiction.

Anu was "the prince of the gods," but so was Sin. The "Word" of each god was "preponderant" and "was to be taken above those of the other gods," who were subjected to it, "trembling." Each god was "the ruler of Heaven and Earth," "sublime throughout the universe," supreme and "unequaled." . . . All of these superlatives were attributed not only to the gods who were traditionally recognized as being above all the others, such as An(u), Enlil, Enki/Ea, Marduk, Inanna/Ištar, Aššur, but also to Adad, Šamaš, Sin, Ninurta, Zababa, and others, who were always of lesser importance, in spite of their popularity.[41]

Photo 6 Baal Figure

Nearly any attribute that is applied to Yahweh in the Hebrew Bible can be documented with one god or another in the ancient Near East.[42] These attributes, however, have to be modified as they are informed by other genres of literature. When deities are identified as "loving" we must ask whether they love one another only, or whether they love some or all humans. Then we must peruse the other literatures to see if they act in loving ways. If they do not, then we must ask whether there is a way to justify the inconsistent behavior with a loving nature, whether a deity's behavior is inconsistent, or whether the "love" of a deity was in the hope or imagination of the one who considered the deity so. Were some gods loving and others not? This complex inquiry may be undertaken with a whole series of attributes in relation to any deity if those attributes are attested in the literature.

Gods in Community

When the gods interact with one another, their attributes emerge in their personalities and in the roles within the divine community. The deity who may be considered the hero of the narrative may be portrayed

41. Bottéro, *Religion*, 41.
42. An intriguing book that traces these similarities only within the Ugaritic literature is M. C. A. Korpel, *A Rift in the Clouds: Ugaritic and Hebrew Descriptions of the Divine*, UBL 8 (Münster: Ugarit-Verlag, 1990).

in more positive ways than other deities who may serve as opponents, foils, or supporting characters. Thus the picture of Enlil in *Atrahasis* is going to suffer in favor of Enki, and the character of Ishtar is at a disadvantage in the context of her dealings with Gilgamesh.

Gods in Conflict

Though the gods in a community clearly vie with one another for power, the conflicts of the gods emerge at yet another level when they are seen representing various polities (whether on the domestic or international level). In this context the strengths and weaknesses of deities emerge as their clients succeed or fail. In this sort of context, polemic enters the picture.

From these observations some guidelines emerge. We should not try to define the most commendable qualities of a deity from the literature that praises him or her, because in this literature we will often find expressions of what people hoped or wished the gods would be. In contrast, we can take very seriously the more offensive qualities that may be mentioned in that context. If a deity is praised for viciousness, for deception, for wanton behavior, or for treachery, we would have every reason to take those qualities as legitimate aspects of the deity's profile. Likewise, if limitations or subordination are mentioned in contexts where the deity is the hero of the tale or where the deity is the sponsor of royal or national authority, these could be included in the profile with confidence.

Beyond the attributes that may be identifiable for any particular deity, there are characteristics that apply across the board when describing the divine realm in the ancient Near East. For example, the gods are perceived in largely human terms that include, but extend well beyond the physical forms in which they are imagined. "In pagan religion, gods are born and suckled, grow to maturity, contest for satisfaction of appetites and emotions, battle for prestige and power and mastery, indulge in sex, and are subject to failure, defeat, and death."[43]

This is true not only of their personalities, but of the way in which they pursued their own individual goals.

> Mesopotamia's religion was a receptive form of polytheism, "an open system, . . . a kaleidoscopic repertoire of divinities who personify various aspects of reality." These gods, like humans, were subject to spite, lust and rage. Each one of them tried to realize his own aims, if need be to the detriment of his colleagues. Similarly to the members of an oriental court

43. H. C. Brichto, *The Names of God* (Oxford: Oxford University Press, 1998), 57.

they sought to decide upon a common course, which would be settled in their heavenly council.[44]

By this approach we can safely identify a number of features that aptly describe the polytheistic system that spanned the eras and cultures of the ancient Near East. Many of these have already been discussed above, so we can list them here in summary fashion.[45]

Divine Features

Anthropomorphic. The important aspect of anthropomorphism is not the physical shape, but the nature, character, and personality of the gods. Many of the features in the rest of the list could easily be viewed as further defining what this entails. In short, the gods were viewed as having all of the same qualities, good and bad, as humans but without as many limitations. They had more power and a longer span of existence than people. They were not *better* than people, they were simply stronger than people. Just as there was no essential qualitative difference between the commoner and the king, there was no essential qualitative difference between the king and the gods—all shared basic human traits.

Geographically and geopolitically based. A common misconception about the gods of the ancient Near East is that their power was restricted to certain geographical areas. The literature, however, does not support this view.[46] They were based in a particular area because that was where their temple was (where they dwelt) and where they were worshiped (needs were met) and recognized. The whole premise of imperialism is that the gods were capable of extending their territories from their power base. Again, their geographical and geopolitical connections can be seen as very similar to that of a king. Just as a king would think little about exercising authority over or caring about a small group of people five hundred miles away, so such concerns would not be central for the gods.

Cosmically bound. The cosmic gods were bound to particular cosmic phenomena, and therefore had little jurisdiction over other cosmic phenomena. Gods who were not cosmic gods would have no jurisdiction in the cosmic realm. Beyond this level of categorization, the gods were also bound within the cosmos. They did not transcend the cosmos, but operated only within it. We could perhaps think in terms of a company's

44. K. van der Toorn, *Sin and Sanction in Israel and Mesopotamia* (Assen: Van Gorcum, 1985), 4.

45. Many of these are discussed in Bottéro, *Religion*, 66–69.

46. H. W. F. Saggs, *Encounter with the Divine in Mesopotamia and Israel* (London: Athlone, 1978), 180–81.

board of directors and CEO. They have a great deal of power within the company (= cosmos) but they have to operate within the national and global economic situation. They run the company, but they are within the economy and subject to its status.

Procreative. Having already discussed that the gods are born and, in turn, give birth, here I simply state the implication of that, which is not merely inferred but pervades the mythology: the gods are sexually active. Logically and textually, it can also be seen that the gods have sexual needs and desires, and that they are seen as anatomically equipped both for sexual activity and for procreation. Here we can see how deeply the anthropomorphism penetrates.

Fallible. The gods make mistakes and misjudgments, and even commit crimes. They can be surprised, so it is clear that they are not considered omniscient. They experience uncertainty and confusion, and at times make ill-advised decisions.

Emotional.[47] The gods experience the whole range of human emotions, whether negative or positive. Those familiar with the Bible would find it easy to imagine the gods having joy, pride, sorrow, or anger. In the ancient Near East, however, the gods also experience emotions such as shame and fear.

Engaged in daily routines and activities.[48] The daily routines not only suggest a human-like existence (eating, sleeping, occupations), but also human-like inclinations, desires, needs, cravings, and, therefore, anatomy and psyche.

In community. It is understandable that in the ancient world, as oriented as it was to corporate identity and social integration, deity would also be seen in community. Assmann suggests that in Egyptian history the gods developed as persons in the perception of the people only in the mid-third millennium. But once that development took place, polytheism was born as a reflex to the need for community in the divine sphere.

> With the coming into being of the *persons* of deities—that is, with the personalizing and thus the anthropomorphizing of the Egyptian concept of the divine—*polytheism* came into being. As a person, a deity had need of a "sphere of belonging." He became a person only by being integrated into constellations. As a person, a deity was not conceivable without reference to other deities.[49]

47. For an excellent presentation of textual material and discussion see Korpel, *Rift*, 165–85.
48. Ibid., 364–522.
49. Assmann, *Search for God*, 101.

The gods functioned within families, within the society of the gods, and within the government structures of the gods. As with people, they drew their identity from their social relationships and roles. As in any community, they were dependent on one another in various ways. When functions and roles are defined in such a way, limitations are the inevitable result. As discussed above, the gods are assigned their roles (destinies decreed) and these assignments define their areas of jurisdiction and authority, at the same time removing them from other areas of jurisdiction and authority. In community, no god, even the head of the pantheon, can be truly omnipotent.

Divine Attributes

Given these features of the gods within the polytheism of the ancient Near East, we can now inquire concerning specific attributes that characterized the gods. Here we encounter additional problems that we must address. If it is true that the ancient world was inclined to think of deity in human terms, we must factor what we have learned about ancient ontology as well as what we can discern about ancient psychology into the discussion about the attributes of God.

We have seen that their ontology was functional, meaning that existence is defined by the functions one has. The psychology/anthropology (e.g., especially how one perceives the "self") of the ancient world will be discussed in detail in the section on family religion (p. 147–49). Here we need only note that Assyriologists have proposed that in the ancient world one's identity was found in exterior relationships, rather than in an interior sense of one's being. One's soul or essence, one's "self," was defined in exterior terms.[50] Assuming that the perceptions of self as applied to the gods, as in every other area, mimicked humanity, we may then propose the following formula:

> If ontology were defined in relation to one's function and actions, and
>
> if "self" were defined as largely exterior,
>
> then personal attributes (whether divine or human) could only be discerned at the level of one's actions—that is, they could not easily be seen as abstractions.

50. K. van der Toorn, *Family Religion in Babylonia, Syria and Israel: Continuity and Change in the Forms of Religious Life* (Leiden: Brill, 1996), 116–17; T. Abusch, "Ghost and God: Some Observations on a Babylonian Understanding of Human Nature," in *Self, Soul and Body in Religious Experience*, ed. A. Baumgarten, J. Assmann, and G. Stroumsa (Leiden: Brill, 1998), 380–81. Assmann draws similar conclusions for Egypt in "A Dialogue between Self and Soul: Papyrus Berlin 3024" in *Self, Soul and Body*, 384–403.

If the formula holds, the description of a god as good or wise would signify only that the deity was acting in what were perceived to be good or wise ways, rather than implying that the inherent essence or nature of the deity was to be good or wise. The affirmation or conviction that a deity consistently acted in good or wise ways, or the observation that goodness or wisdom persisted in all of the deity's behavior, could suggest that such an abstraction might have been accurate, but falls short of suggesting that the ancients would have been inclined to draw conclusions in the abstract realm. They were not inclined to abstractions relating to interior perceptions.

If this assessment is accurate, we should ask whether there is any concept in the ancient world of an inherent essence of the deity—or can we only say that deity is as deity does? A thorough search of the literature suggests that the latter is the case. There is little interest expressed in penetrating the inner psyche or essential nature of any deity. Bottéro notes perceptively that it is plausible that "our insistence on isolated propositions somewhat deadens, in fact deforms, the thought of those people who had neither our need for logic nor our demands for clarity."[51] The operative question in their minds, for instance, is not, "Is deity just?" but, "Does the deity administer justice?" It is not important whether the deity is inherently good—is the deity doing good for me?

When we read the hymnic and petitionary literature from the ancient Near East, we discover that the gods are praised for their majesty, glory, beauty, and splendor on the one hand, and for their power, authority, and deeds on the other. These are qualities manifested in exterior ways, rather than interior attributes. It is no surprise then that we find little evidence in the ancient Near Eastern literature that the ancients consider their gods to be just, wise, good, faithful, gracious, and so on, though they often express hope that the gods will act in those ways. The absence of such abstractions does not necessarily suggest that the gods were not characterized by those attributes, but may simply suggest that the ancients were not inclined to think in terms of abstractions. Furthermore, we cannot confidently derive abstractions from literature that has no interest in such things. Therefore, we can only consider the attributes on the level of the actions of the gods.

Justice. Deities such as Shamash in Mesopotamia are considered responsible for carrying out justice.[52] One can likewise infer that gods who rule, especially as kings and judges, are responsible for justice because that was the defining responsibility of those offices. Since they are charged with maintaining justice in the world, it is clear that they

51. Bottéro, *Religion*, 71.
52. Not yet found as connected to any of the gods of Ugarit; see Korpel, *Rift*, 286–87.

require kings to administer justice and the people to live within the framework of justice. In Egypt this is all bound up with the responsibility of establishing *maat*. The gods of Egypt are praised for doing that and are called upon to do that. But administering justice or establishing *maat* is not the same thing as being just. Are the gods bound by their character or by their duty? We might well conclude that in the ancient world it is impossible to isolate character from duty. The only way to approach it would be to ask if the gods or any particular god were capable of being unjust.

In the literature from Mesopotamia concerning the pious sufferer, one can find discussions concerning theodicy, exploring the justice of deity. But even in these, there is no suggestion that the gods are corrupt or unconcerned about justice.[53] Injustice in the world is blamed not on the gods but on demons and humans. Evil was built into the MES that controlled the cosmos, but even those had not been established by the gods.[54] It is clear that personal misfortune was considered to be the result of offending the gods, even if the offense were committed innocently. Thus it is evident that the ancients believed that rather than being unjust, the gods simply were not very forthcoming about what constituted offense. The gods were not considered unjust; they simply did not take it upon themselves to communicate their expectations. The gods, then, were believed to act justly. Shamash in particular shows no favoritism[55] and is considered "a circumspect judge."[56]

On the other hand, the gods can occasionally be seen as incompetent judges. Most notable in this regard is the implicit accusation against Enlil when Enki chastens him about sending the flood.[57] This exchange calls into question whether justice was best served by the course of action taken by Enlil. It should be noted that Enlil was attempting to act justly. Enki is suggesting that his decision was not in the best interests of justice. Like a human judge, then, the gods are doing their best to administer justice, but they do so imperfectly.

53. G. L. Mattingly, "The Pious Sufferer: Mesopotamia's Traditional Theodicy and Job's Counselors," in *Scripture in Context III: The Bible in the Light of Cuneiform Literature*, ed. W. W. Hallo, B. W. Jones, and G. L. Mattingly (Lewiston, NY: Mellen, 1990), 305–48; D. P. Bricker, "Innocent Suffering in Mesopotamia," *TynBul* (2001): 121–42.

54. A byproduct of this concept was the belief that doing justice did not necessarily eliminate all suffering. Some misfortune came about simply because of how the world was. In the *Lament over the Destruction of Ur*, the city is destroyed not as an act of justice or injustice, but because it was time for kingship to be passed on. Likewise with regard to individuals, suffering can sometimes just be one's lot in life for the present (see Mattingly, "Pious Sufferer," 320).

55. *FDD* 257.

56. *BWL* 132:101 uses *mišaru* adjectivally.

57. See the *Gilgamesh Epic*, xi:181–95.

We can now identify several ways in which one might consider whether a deity is just:

1. Deity is just (inherent quality)
2. Deity administers justice consistently (though actions are sometimes opaque)
3. Deity intends to administer justice but does so imperfectly
4. Deity is corrupt, with only a secondary interest in administering justice

In Mesopotamia the discussion hovers between options two and three. In the Hebrew Bible the discussion hovers between options one and two. Yahweh is at times declared to be just.[58] Job calls Yahweh's justice into question based on his experience (Job 40:8), but the book exonerates Deity in the end.

Another aspect of justice concerns acts of judgment. In Israel much of the prophetic literature is taken up with oracles of judgment, and both in the covenant curses and in the historical literature we see Yahweh as proactive in punishing his wayward people. In Mesopotamia it is more common for the judgment of the gods to be seen in their abandonment of subjects. Loss of the care and protection of the deity would expose the city, king, or individual to evil forces, whose activities would constitute punishment. Nevertheless, many texts speak of the gods imposing punishment on people (often in the form of illness or disease).[59]

Wisdom. The wisdom of the gods is one of the most pervasive attributes recognized in ancient Near Eastern texts, but in these texts it is not necessarily related to ethical or moral behavior. Some examples from the hymnic literature demonstrate that the wisdom of the gods often relates to their decision-making ability.

> Enlil, "knowing counselor, wise, of broad intelligence"[60]
> "Ea the wise, whose counsel is supreme"[61]
> Thoth, "wise among the Ennead"[62]
> Ninazu, "who gathers wisdom to himself"[63]
> Ishtar, "wise in understanding and perception"[64]

58. Deut. 32:4 refers to both deeds and character: "all his ways are just (*mishpat*) and he is upright (*tsaddiq*) and just (*yashar*);" Ps. 99:4 confirms his love for justice and that he has done what is right and just in Israel; Ps. 111:7 also focuses on his acts: "The works of his hands are faithful and just (*mishpat*)."

59. See *šertu* B, *CAD* Š/2: 325–26. These punishments can at times be associated with curses that are delineated on *kudurru* (boundary markers).

60. *HTO* 102. In Akkadian the term generally used is *apkallu*, "expert, knowledgeable."

61. *CAD* E: 314.

62. *AEL* 2:103.

63. *FDD* 231.

64. *FDD* 240.

The wisdom of the gods makes them a potential source of information, primarily related to divination. It marks the gods as clever and often results in power over other members of the pantheon.

It is obvious that wisdom associated with Yahweh would not be evident in any of these areas since official Yahwism does not feature divination or a pantheon in which to exercise power. In contrast, Yahweh's wisdom is related to his ability to judge. Therefore, his wisdom is sometimes linked with his power (cf. Job 9:4; Isa. 31:2; Dan. 2:20–23). Mostly, however, he acts with wisdom and gives wisdom. Yahweh is a repository of wisdom and a source of wisdom.

Goodness. It is very rare for the gods of the ancient Near East to be described as good,[65] though the hope is commonly expressed that the god will *do* good to the worshiper, that is, act favorably or for their benefit. This is an expression of favor rather than a sense of intrinsic goodness. More than any other attribute, goodness, in the abstract sense, implies correspondence to an independent standard of goodness. Such a standard does not exist in the ancient Near East.

What does an Israelite mean when he insists that Yahweh is "good" (2 Chron. 30:18; Ps. 136:1)?[66] Theologians tend to think of God's goodness as the aggregate of his moral qualities.[67] Theologians would typically understand God's goodness as affirming that God could do no evil. In the ancient Near East there would be no outside standard to measure by, so good and evil would not be categories that could easily be applied to the gods. For Yahweh the standard is Yahweh's own character, therefore making it impossible for him to do evil—good is defined by what he does. In both cases discussion and definitions quickly become either relative or circular, making the philosophical issue moot. What is important here is to see the difference between how Israel and its neighbors thought about the goodness of deity.

Faithfulness. Faithfulness is one of the most frequently affirmed attributes of Yahweh because of his covenant relationship with Israel. In contrast, it is difficult to find any such affirmation for the gods of the ancient Near East. Words that convey loyalty are never used of the gods in that way.[68] The gods have no agreements or promises to be faithful to and no obligations or commitments to fulfill.

Mercy and compassion. These are among the most commonly sought-after responses from the gods. Examples from prayers in Egypt find

65. Amun-Re, "the good god" (*COS* 1.25); Osiris, "all extol his goodness" (*COS* 1.26).
66. For more discussion see R. P. Gordon, *NIDOTTE* 2:355.
67. Millard Erickson, *Christian Theology*, 3 vols. (Grand Rapids: Baker, 1983–85), 1:283–300.
68. Cf. *kinu* and *kittu*, *CAD* K: 389–93, 468–72.

Comparative Exploration: How Is Yahweh Different from the Gods of the Ancient Near East?

Were the Israelites any different than their neighbors in the ways they thought about the nature of deity? Did they think of Yahweh as having an inherent essence or simply as a deity who acted in particular ways? How would we know? Consistency might be one way. Another might be to observe affirmations of character even when actions seemed to suggest otherwise. A third would be to observe whether they show an inclination to deduce abstractions about the deity in a way that is distinct from the others in the ancient Near East.

There is nothing to suggest that ontological thinking in Israel was any different from what is observed in the rest of the ancient Near East. While Israelite ontology seems to have focused on functions and relationships, however, it is still possible that their self-identity developed a sense of interiority to complement the more common exteriority that characterized the era. Whether an understanding of Yahweh with an interior focus led to an understanding of themselves in those terms, or vice versa, this sense of interiority on both levels is at the heart of those features that distinguish Israel from its neighbors. The belief that Yahweh had revealed himself—not only his actions, but his character—to the Israelites, and that he expected them to imitate him on both levels, was key in these developments. Consequently, in Israel people are called upon to imitate the holiness of God, and, while that holiness includes a cultic dimension, it stretches across the entire range of covenant stipulations and has a moral element to it.

What attributes did Yahweh have that other deities were not believed to have had? Prominent on the list would be those attributes relating to monotheism, interiority, moral character, and formal relationships. He was jealous of any act that acknowledged other gods and he was faithful to his covenant. Thus, though Yahweh was viewed as intensely personal, this did not lead to a polytheism that provided him with a divine community. Instead, people are created to serve as community for him, and the covenant eventually comes to give structure to that community.

Inversely, what attributes did Yahweh not have that other deities possessed? This list would include those attributes that assumed a polytheistic system or human foibles, such as craftiness, lust, deception, sexuality, and a host of others. Many more items would be included on this list than the previous one because the baser qualities came with the fact that the deities of the ancient Near East were perceived in human terms. Israelites had to be constantly reminded by the prophets that Yahweh is *not* like a human and *not* like the other gods.

Amun-Re to be "Rich in love" and "Graciously disposed when entreated."[69] He is identified as one "who loves every living soul."[70] The kindness of Osiris "overwhelms the hearts,"[71] and Amun is portrayed as one "who knows compassion, who hearkens to him who calls."[72] Similar expressions can be found throughout the Mesopotamian hymnic literature as well as in Israel's psalms.

Holiness. In Mesopotamia objects could be "holy" (precious metals, wood, garments, animals, water), meaning they were cultically pure or dedicated for cultic use.[73] Likewise people could be "pure" or "clean" (*ellu*), also referring to their cultic status.[74] In texts that list attributes, the gods are also described with the adjective *ellu*. In the absence of elaboration, it is difficult to understand what is meant by that, but in all likelihood it refers to cultic status rather than moral status.[75]

Orthodoxy

A final question to address is whether there was such a concept in the ancient world as orthodoxy. We can certainly identify an orthopraxy in the sense that rituals and incantations had to be performed with precision. But the polytheistic systems were open to gods being added ad infinitum. If a deity showed himself or herself to be influential in the affairs of a person or group, that deity would be acknowledged. The cosmos was full of spirit beings of power, and one wanted to make sure to cover all the bases. So, for instance, the Ninevites would have no skepticism about Jonah coming with a message of a God from far away who had designs against them. There was nothing improbable about that scenario, and they would not hesitate to try to appease this deity's anger. In this system there are no false gods and therefore no false beliefs. "Dogmatism and intolerance toward the beliefs of others was alien to the ancient religions, since the complete absence of the concept of false faith or of any forms of heresy were typical of them."[76]

69. *COS* 1.25.

70. From Papyrus Nakht, *Book of the Dead*, see J. L. Foster, *Hymns, Prayers, and Songs: An Anthology of Ancient Egyptian Lyric Poetry*, SBLWAW 8 (Atlanta: Scholars Press, 1995), 88.

71. *COS* 1.26.

72. *AEL* 2:112.

73. Akkadian *ebbu*, *CAD* E: 2–4.

74. Akkadian *ellu*, *CAD* E: 102–5.

75. A fairly thorough search of primary and secondary Egyptian literature produced no references to Egyptian gods being holy.

76. M. Dandamayev, "State Gods and Private Religion in the Near East in the First Millennium B.C.E.," in *Religion and Politics in the Ancient Near East*, ed. A. Berlin (Bethesda: University of Maryland Press, 1996), 35–46, quotation on 40.

What may look to us like persecution or repression of the worship of one god or another results from the political alliances that are associated with the worship of deities. This issue does not concern false faith, but which god/s has supremacy. "The images of deities of enemies were not smashed but only carried away in order to deprive the enemies of the support of their gods. For the same reasons individuals who chanced to be in a foreign land paid their respects to the local gods of that land and tried to win their favor, while at the same time retaining fidelity to their traditional gods."[77]

The gods would not be jealous of attention paid to other gods as long as their own needs were being met and their position was not in jeopardy. Again, in this way the God of Israel was very different from any other deity, and the Israelites had quite a bit of trouble adjusting their thinking to the idea that Yahweh would not tolerate the open-ended system and that there were false gods and unacceptable beliefs. This was evident especially in the Judges period during which someone like Gideon could affirm allegiance to Yahweh and wonder why he has been distant even while his father maintained a Baal altar and Asherah pole (Judg. 6:25).

77. Ibid., 40.

5

Temples and Rituals

Worship took place at temples, but temples were not designed primarily to provide a place for worship.[1] They were designed to be residences for deities and, as such, places for the performance of cultic rituals. The implications of this distinction are far-reaching and affect our understanding of deity and the role of the temple in the cosmos. Temples had names in the ancient world (since naming was an expression of function and existence), and a name such as "Bond between Heaven and Earth" certainly captures the ideology beautifully.[2]

The Temple and the God

From the standpoint of deity, the temple is his/her estate and residence. The earthly temple was a symbol, an echo, a shadow of the heavenly residence.[3] As such it served as a link, a bond, or even a

1. J.-C. Margueron, "Mesopotamian Temples," *OEANE* 5:165.
2. Several temples have similar names, but most notable is EDURANKI, the temple of Ishtar at Nippur. See A. George, *House Most High: The Temples of Ancient Mesopotamia* (Winona Lake, IN: Eisenbrauns, 1993), 80.
3. Some would suggest that this is supported by the idea that Moses was shown the heavenly prototype when given instructions for the tabernacle, e.g., in Exod. 25:9. V. Hurowitz makes a convincing case that the word NIV translates as "pattern" (Heb. *tabnit*) refers not to the heavenly prototype but to something approximating an architect's drawing or

portal to the heavenly residence. The heavenly archetypal temple can sometimes be identified as the cosmos itself.[4] In Mesopotamia the ziggurat stood beside the temple as the place where the deity descended from the heavens to reside among the people and to receive their worship. These temples were constructed to be a place of "rest" for the deity.[5] Though the concept of relaxation (or even indolence) is not lacking, rest concerns most importantly the achievement of stability, security, and order. The deity can rest in his/her temple because the threat of chaos has been dispelled. The deity then takes his/her place in the ordered, controlled cosmos with the leisure of enjoying his/her estate.

Excursus: Polytheistic Iconism

The deity's presence was marked by the image of the deity. It is therefore appropriate at this point to explore briefly the theoretical foundations of polytheistic iconism.

The existence of an idol needed to be approved by the god whose image was being made, so the gods were responsible for initiating the manufacturing process.[6] At the end of the process, rituals were performed to transfer the deity from the spiritual world to the physical world, a process that one may refer to as "actualizing the presence of the god in the temple."[7] Consequently, the production of the image was not viewed in human terms, but as a miraculous process through which the deity worked,[8] not unlike the traditional Christian concept of the inspiration of Scripture.

The most significant ritual was the mouth-washing ritual. This procedure was carried out to enable the image to eat bread, drink water, and

---

model. Even in this argument, however, he does not dispute that the heavenly temple serves as a prototype for the earthly one (*I Have Built You an Exalted House*, JSOTSup 115 [Sheffield: Sheffield Academic Press, 1992], 168–70).

4. J. D. Levenson, "The Temple and the World," *JR* 64 (1984): 275–98. Levenson uses the terminology "archetype" for the temple that is the cosmos, and "antitype" for the architectural representation; see 296.

5. Hurowitz, *I Have Built*, 330–31.

6. C. Walker and M. Dick, *The Induction of the Cult Image in Ancient Mesopotamia*, SAALT 1 (Helsinki: Neo-Assyrian Text Corpus Project, 2001), 8.

7. Ibid., 4 (quoting P. Boden's dissertation on the Mesopotamian Washing of the Mouth Ritual).

8. A. Berlejung, "Washing the Mouth: The Consecration of Divine Images in Mesopotamia," in *The Image and the Book*, ed. K. van der Toorn (Leuven: Peeters, 1997), 62. See Prayer to Ashur and Marduk, "Esarhaddon's Renewal of the Gods," in Walker and Dick, *Induction*, 25.

Photo 7 Mesopotamian Relief: Worshiper in Presence of Deity

smell incense,[9] that is, to receive worship on behalf of the deity. It purified the image from the human contamination involved in the manufacturing process, and thereby enabled the statue to function as deity.[10]

At the end of the mouth-washing ceremony, as the deity entered the inner sanctum, an incantation was pronounced indicating that hereafter the god would remain in his house, where he would receive his food day by day.[11] In this way the image mediated the worship from the people to the deity.

The image also functioned to mediate revelation from the deity. In Egypt of the early first millennium, for instance, court cases that were being tried were set before the god Amun. The various outcomes of the trial were placed oracularly before the image, which, manipulated by the priests, issued verdicts.[12]

From the above we can conclude that the material image was animated by the divine essence. Therefore it did not simply represent the deity,

9. Walker and Dick, *Induction,* 14, see incantation tablet 3, lines 70–71.

10. Walker and Dick, *Induction,* 14. For Egyptian rituals see S. Morenz, *Egyptian Religion* (Ithaca: Cornell University Press, 1973), 155–56.

11. Berlejung, "Washing," 67.

12. W. W. Hallo and W. K. Simpson, *The Ancient Near East,* rev. ed. (Fort Worth: Harcourt Brace, 1998), 285.

Comparative Exploration: Worthless Idols

Several passages in the prophets castigate the images of the foreign nations, including the ideology surrounding their manufacture and use. Most notable in this regard are Isaiah 44:9–20 and Jeremiah 10:2–16. The depiction that they offer is a polemical caricature, therefore making it difficult to assess whether the prophets are engaging in hyperbole or whether there may be true misunderstanding of the ideology.[1] Comparative study would seek to understand what the Israelite prophets believed about what their neighbors were doing when they made and worshiped idols, and whether their perception squared with how their neighbors actually thought. In addition, for the exegete, knowledge of particularly the Assyrian and Babylonian texts can clarify what the prophets are alluding to in their descriptions.

Z. Zevit considers the prophets to have presented a realistic picture of the manufacturing process, though he recognizes that they are engaged in a harangue against the stupidity of the Babylonians.[2] The description of the materials is accurate: a wooden core from special wood that is sculpted, then overlaid with precious metals. Scraps of the wood were then used for cooking a dedicatory meal, and the image was vitalized and then worshiped. Particularly lacking on the procedural level, however, is any reference by the prophets to temple, priesthood, or purifying waters.[3] On the ideological level, the prophets do not acknowledge that there is a continuing distinction between the image and the god who is transubstantiated in the image.[4] As a result, they criticize the idea that true deity could in any way be present in a humanly made

but it manifested its presence.[13] We should not conclude, however, that the image was the deity. The deity was the reality that was embodied in the image.[14]

This same concept is observable in Egyptian literature when, in the *Memphite Theology*, Ptah formed the bodies of the gods:

> He made their bodies according to their wishes.
> Thus the gods entered into their bodies,
> Of every wood, every stone, every clay,

13. Walker and Dick, *Induction*, 4 (quoting from p. 13 of I. Winter, "'Idols of the King': Royal Images as Recipients of Ritual Action in Ancient Mesopotamia," *JRitSt* 6 [1992]: 13–42).

14. Walker and Dick, *Induction*, 6. T. Jacobsen, "The Graven Image," in *Ancient Israelite Religion: Essays in Honor of Frank Moore Cross*, ed. P. D. Miller, P. D. Hanson, and S. D. McBride (Philadelphia: Fortress, 1987), 22. Walker and Dick suggest the relationship between statue and deity is somewhat like the relationship between body and soul in Aristotelian dualism.

image. They do not treat as credible the disclaimers of the craftsmen who ritually and symbolically return the image to the divine realm after its manufacture is complete. The rituals seek to accomplish just that, and the actual discussions found in Assyrian texts show that the Assyrians wrestled with these same issues.[5] While the Mesopotamians attempt to resolve the problems cultically and thus justify the continued use of the image, the prophets see the obstacles as impassable and ridicule the attempts as they flaunt the superiority of Yahweh. M. Dick concludes that the prophets are not ignorant of the ideology reflected in the use of images, but that they distort the ideology in their polemical agenda.[6] He suggests that Israelite religious practice would have been just as vulnerable to distorted polemic.

In the end, however, it is simply the prophetic position that the ritual strategies were incapable of resolving the shortcomings of the ideology. Their parodies are very well informed about the ideology and the rituals that support it, and our understanding of the biblical text is greatly enhanced from a study of the ancient Near Eastern documents and worldview.

1. M. B. Dick, "Prophetic Parodies of Making the Cult Image," in *Born in Heaven, Made on Earth*, ed. M. B. Dick (Winona Lake, IN: Eisenbrauns, 1999), 1–53.

2. Z. Zevit, *The Religions of Ancient Israel* (New York: Continuum, 2001), 524. His discussion of Jeremiah 10 is briefer, 546.

3. Zevit identifies some of the differences between Isaiah's description and Babylonian practice in ibid., 525–26.

4. Dick makes the distinction quite clear with both textual and iconographic examples, "Prophetic Parodies," 32–34.

5. Ibid., 34–44.

6. Ibid., 45.

Every thing that grows upon him
In which they came to be.[15]

In Egyptian thinking the images were animated by the deity's *ba*,[16] which united with the image thus permitting it to manifest the presence of the deity and reveal the deity—a phenomenon referred to as "habitation." In this way the image was not a physical picture of the deity, but a characterization of the divine nature.[17] The ritual performed by the king or his representative caused the *ba* of the deity to enter the image and be available for communication.[18]

We may conclude that the image functioned in the cult as a mediator of the divine presence. It was the means by which humans gained access

15. Translation from *AEL* 1:55, lines 60–61.

16. The *ba* is the soul/spirit that is able to exist apart from the body and is the representative of the essence of the person.

17. E. Hornung, *Conceptions of God in Ancient Egypt* (Ithaca: Cornell University Press, 1982), 128–35; Morenz, *Egyptian Religion*, 150–52.

18. R. Gundlach, "Temples," *OEAE* 3:373.

to the presence of deity. As such it represented the mystical unity of transcendence and immanence, a theophany transubstantiated.[19] Jacobsen therefore sees the functioning image as an act of the deity's favor: "The image represented a favor granted by the god . . . it was a sign of a benign and friendly attitude on the part of the community in which it stood."[20] Berlejung provides a useful summary of our study: "A cultic statue was never solely a religious picture, but was always an image imbued with a god, and, as such, it possessed the character of both earthly reality and divine presence."[21] From deity to people, the image mediated presence and revelation. From people to deity, the image mediated worship.

Sacred Space

The residence of the deity in the temple required the recognition of sacred space. This objective is evident in the earliest steps of temple building. The selection of the site was determined by oracle so that the god could designate a sacred site.[22] In the ancient world they believed that certain locations had gained sacred status as portals through which the gods traversed.[23] Thus sacred space was identified even before the temple was built. The construction was then carried out in such a way as to preserve the sanctity of the space. The presence of the image endorsed the sacred status of the space. All of the architecture of the temple was designed to represent and preserve the sanctity of the site, generally through the establishment of sacred zones, barriers between those zones, and limited sight lines.[24] The result of this architecture was that accessibility was limited so that nothing profane could approach. Likewise, the eyes of the curious were prevented from glimpsing the sacred image except as permitted in occasional festival processions. Israel shared in this ideology of sacred space at nearly every point.

Building accounts and dedicatory ceremonies from Mesopotamia show a striking similarity of literary form (also observable in biblical

19. Jacobsen, "Graven Image," 22–23; Berlejung, "Washing," 61.

20. Jacobsen, "Graven Image," 22.

21. Berlejung, "Washing," 46.

22. Hurowitz, *I Have Built*, 332–34, provides extensive information from the Bible and the ancient Near East to show that the deity was also considered the one who was the builder of the temple (cf., e.g., Pss. 78:69; 127:1).

23. This is evident in Gen. 28, where Jacob happens to sleep on what he later determines to be sacred space and where in his vision he sees the operation of the stairway portal. This concept is also evident in the Babylonian prayer in which a troubled individual expresses concern that he may have encroached on sacred space unwittingly.

24. For architectural and archaeological information see the entries under "Temples" in *OEANE* 5:165–79.

accounts) as they articulate some of the implications of sacred space being formalized in the temple. V. Hurowitz has done a comprehensive analysis of these and finds a common ideology concerning sacred space that stretches across all periods.[25]

The major temple complexes in Mesopotamia featured, besides the temple itself (usually including several chambers), a ziggurat and a garden. These were both considered part of sacred space. The ziggurat was simply a series of stairways and ramps that gave architectural reality to the stairway (*simmiltu*) used by the gods as they traveled between realms.

Excursus: Ziggurats

Photo 8 Arad Sanctuary

What do we know about ziggurats?[26] First we need to clarify that though they may resemble pyramids in appearance, they are nothing like them in function. There is no inside of a ziggurat. The structure was framed in mudbrick, then the core was packed with fill dirt. The façade was then completed with kiln-fired brick. Second, ziggurats were dedicated to particular deities. Any given deity might have several ziggurats dedicated to him/her in different cities. Furthermore, a given city may have several ziggurats, though the main one was associated with the patron deity of the city. Third, archaeologists have discovered nearly thirty ziggurats in the general region of Mesopotamia, and texts mention several others. The main architectural feature is the stairways or ramps that lead to the top. Texts indicate that there was a small room at the top where a bed was made and table set for the deity.[27] Ziggurats range in size at the base from sixty feet per side to almost two hundred feet per side.

25. Hurowitz, *I Have Built*.
26. Excerpted from J. Walton, "The Mesopotamian Background of the Tower of Babel and Its Implications," *BBR* 5 (1995): 155–75.
27. For a complete description see T. Jacobsen, "Notes on Ekur," *EI* 21 (1990): 40–47.

Comparative Exploration: Tower of Babel

In Genesis 11:1–9 a group settles in Shinar, which most interpreters rightly connect to the area called Sumer in southern Mesopotamia and associated in the Old Testament with Babylon. Their Mesopotamian building materials differ greatly from that which is known in Egypt and Israel, so the author explains them to us in verse 3. The ready availability of stone in Palestine meant that it could be used by even common folks for building. Still, houses in Israel would typically use stone for the foundation and mudbrick for the superstructure. Burnt brick technology was never developed because it was unnecessary. In contrast, the alluvial plains of southern Mesopotamia had no stone available. It would have to be transported many miles and was therefore expensive. As a result, as early as the Late Uruk period at the end of the fourth millennium BC we see the development of kiln-fired brick.[1] Furthermore, as the text indicates, the usual mortar used with kiln-fired brick is a bitumen-based mastic. This combination of baked brick and bitumen mastic made for waterproof buildings as sturdy as stone. The time required to fire the bricks and to procure the bitumen made this an expensive procedure. As a result, only the most important buildings were constructed with these materials.

That leads us to a consideration of what precisely was being built.

The text refers to a "city" and a "tower." If the setting is the end of the fourth millennium (to coincide with the technological developments), the events occur right at the beginning of urbanization in Mesopotamia. In the early stages of urbanization, the city was not designed to house the private sector. Common people did not live in the city. Instead it was comprised of the public buildings. The public buildings of this time (administrative buildings, granaries, etc.) were mostly congregated around the temple. Consequently, the city is, in effect, a temple complex.[2] A number of these buildings would have used at least some kiln-fired brick. Such structures were known throughout the biblical period and were still visible in Nebuchadnezzar's Babylon.

This brings us to the "tower." The word used in the Hebrew text is generic and can be used for any sort of tower. In the Old Testament the towers most frequently referred to are defense towers or watchtowers. But the text is not describing an Israelite city; it is describing a Mesopotamian city.[3] The most prominent building in the temple complex from earliest times was the ziggurat. Most interpreters have identified the tower of Babel as a ziggurat, and with good cause. Not only is it

Most important is the function of the ziggurat. The first puzzle to note in this regard is that the ziggurat does not play a part in any of the rituals that are known to us from Mesopotamia. If known literature were our only guide we would have to conclude that common people did not use the ziggurat for anything. The ziggurat was sacred space, and would have been strictly off limits to profane use. Though the structure at the

sociologically right for the context, even the terminology supports it. Throughout Mesopotamian literature, almost every occurrence of the expression describing a building "with its head in the heavens" refers to a temple with a ziggurat.[4] For example, here is the description by Warad-Sin, king of Larsa, who built the temple É-eš-ki-te: "He made it as high as a mountain and made its head touch heaven. On account of this deed the gods Nanna and Ningal rejoiced. May they grant to him a destiny of life, a long reign, and a firm foundation."[5]

The ziggurat was the most dominant building of the temple complex, so it is no surprise that it draws the attention of the author of Genesis. In summary, the project is a temple complex featuring a ziggurat, which was designed to make it convenient for the god to come down to his temple, bless his people, and receive their worship. This understanding of ziggurats makes an important point drawn from the ancient Near Eastern context to clarify the biblical text: the tower of Babel was not built for people to go up,

but for the god to come down. So with Dostoevsky we can affirm that the tower was not to mount from heaven to earth, but to set up heaven on earth.[6]

1. Much more detail of all of the issues of the tower of Babel narrative can be found in my article, "The Mesopotamian Background of the Tower of Babel Account and Its Implications," *BBR* 5 (1995): 155–75, from which this sidebar has been excerpted.

2. For a thorough discussion of the origins and early stages of urbanization, see M. van de Mieroop, *The Ancient Mesopotamian City* (Oxford: Oxford University Press, 1999), 24–38.

3. It is the context that tells us that this is not just any tower, but the ziggurat tower. One could claim that nothing in the phrase "Berlin Wall" suggests it could not be any old wall in Berlin, and in a wooden sense that is true, but the context tells us differently.

4. NIV's "tower that reaches to the heavens" can be misleading. The Hebrew expression "with its head in the heavens" is idiomatic, just like our English "skyscraper." This is not a siege tower, as the early rabbis had suggested.

5. D. Frayne, *Royal Inscriptions of Mesopotamia: Old Babylonian Period* (Toronto: University of Toronto Press, 1990), 208.

6. F. Dostoevsky, *Brothers Karamazov* (New York: Knopf, 1992), chapter one.

top was designed to accommodate the god, it was not a temple where people would go to worship. There was no image or any other representation of the deity there. The ziggurat was typically accompanied by an adjoining temple near its base where the image was housed and where worship took place.

The best indication of the function of the ziggurats comes from the names that are given to them. For instance, the name of the ziggurat at Babylon, Etemenanki, means "temple of the foundation of heaven and earth."[28] One at Larsa means "temple that links heaven and earth." Most significant is the name of the ziggurat at Sippar, "temple of the stairway to pure heaven." The word translated "stairway" in this last example is used in the mythology as the means by which the messenger of the

28. "Temple" in these names is simply a designation of sacred space.

gods moved between heaven, earth, and the netherworld.[29] As a result of these data, we would conclude that the ziggurat was a structure that was built to support the stairway. This stairway was a visual representation of that which was believed to be used by the gods to travel from one realm to another. It was solely for the convenience of the gods and was maintained in order to provide the deity with the amenities that would refresh him/her along the way. At the top of the ziggurat was the gate of the gods, the entrance into their heavenly abode. At the bottom was the temple, where the people hoped the god would descend to receive the gifts and worship of his/her people.

Temple complexes also sometimes featured gardens that symbolized the fertility provided by the deity.[30] The produce of these temple gardens was used in offerings to the deity, just as the temple flocks and herds were used for sacrificial purposes. The gardens were watered from the fertile waters that flowed from temples.[31] The idea of four streams flowing from the temple or palace to water the four corners of the earth is represented graphically in a couple of places. In the eighteenth-century BC palace of Zimri-Lim at Mari, there is an investiture scene fresco on the walls. In one of the panels two goddesses hold jars and out of each flows four streams of water going off in different directions. Similarly, an ivory inlay from thirteenth-century Ashur (Assur) features a god in the middle from whom four streams of water flow. He is flanked by two sacred trees, which in turn are flanked by winged bulls.[32] The artifactual and archaeological evidence offer more information about palace gardens than about temple gardens.[33] Archaeologists have discovered a temple near Ashur with many rows of tree pits in the courtyard.[34] In Egypt a divine grove at times was associated with a temple. Artificial pools, exotic trees and plants, fish and water fowl, and produce grown for the provi-

29. The *Myth of Nergal and Ereshkigal*. The Hebrew cognate of this word is also used in the story of Jacob's "ladder," which serves the very same purpose as the stairways of the ziggurat.

30. K. Gleason, "Gardens," *OEANE* 2:383. All of these elements are also discussed by I. Cornelius, *NIDOTTE* 1:875–78.

31. J. Lundquist, "What Is a Temple?" in *The Quest for the Kingdom of God: Studies in Honor of G. E. Mendenhall*, ed. H. B. Huffmon, F. A. Spina, and A. R. W. Green (Winona Lake, IN: Eisenbrauns, 1983), 208–9.

32. For photographs see L. Stager, "Jerusalem as Eden," *Biblical Archaeology Review* 26/3 (2000): 38, 41.

33. See K. Gleason, "Gardens," *OEANE* 2:383. It should be noted that temples and palaces often shared adjoining space (E. Bloch-Smith, "'Who Is the King of Glory?' Solomon's Temple and Symbolism," in *Scripture and Other Artifacts: Essays on the Bible and Archaeology in Honor of Philip J. King*, ed. M. Coogan, J. C. Exum, and L. Stager [Louisville: Westminster John Knox, 1994], 26).

34. L. Stager, "Jerusalem as Eden," *BAR* 26 (2000): 43.

sion of the gods were all features of these temple gardens. Their fertility and ordered arrangement symbolized order in the cosmos.[35]

> The temple is often associated with the waters of life which flow forth from a spring within the building itself—or rather the temple is viewed as incorporating within itself or as having been built upon such a spring. The reason such springs exist in temples is that they are perceived as the primeval waters of creation, Nun in Egypt, Abzu in Mesopotamia. The temple is thus founded on and stands in contact with the primeval waters.[36]

In the Bible, Ezekiel's vision of a temple also features fertile waters flowing out from the threshold of the sanctuary (Ezek. 47:1–12). Eden is also portrayed as having a garden accompanying sacred space watered by fertile streams and featuring animals and exotic plants.[37]

The Temple and the Cosmos

Since the temple on earth was considered only a type of the larger, archetypal cosmic temple, many images and symbols evoke the relationship between temple and cosmos.[38] The temple is considered the center of the cosmos,[39] and in itself a microcosmos.[40]

In Egypt the temple contained within its sacred precincts a representation of the original primeval hillock that emerges from the cosmic

---

35. R. Germer, "Gardens," *OEAE* 2:5.

36. Lundquist, "What Is a Temple?" 208.

37. M. Dietrich, "Das biblische Paradies und der babylonische Tempelgarten. Überlegungen zur Lage des Gartens Eden," in *Das biblische Weltbild und seine altorientalischen Kontexte*, ed. B. Janowski and B. Ego, FAT 32 (Tübingen: Mohr Siebeck, 2001), 281–323; Stager, "Jerusalem," 36–47; G. J. Wenham, "Sanctuary Symbolism in the Garden of Eden Story," in *Proceedings of the Ninth World Congress of Jewish Studies, Division A: The Period of the Bible* (Jerusalem: World Union of Jewish Studies, 1986), 19–25; repr. in *I Studied Inscriptions from Before the Flood*, ed. R. S. Hess and D. Tsumura, SBTS 4 (Winona Lake, IN: Eisenbrauns, 1994), 399–404.

38. B. Janowski, "Der Himmel auf Erden: Zur kosmologischen Bedeutung des Tempels in der Umwelt Israels," in *Biblische Weltbild*, ed. Janowski and Ego, 229–60.

39. Levenson, "Temple," 283–84, drawing from M. Eliade, *The Sacred and the Profane* (New York: Harper & Row, 1961), 36–47.

40. Levenson, "Temple," 284–88. See also his citation of G. Ahlström's statement that Syro-Palestinian temples were meant to be heaven on earth, 295; G. Ahlström, *The History of Ancient Palestine* (Minneapolis: Fortress, 1993), 256–57; cf. Hornung, *Conceptions*, 229. As an example from Mesopotamia, part of the temple of Nippur was called *ki-ùr* and bore the epithet "the great land" (R. J. Clifford, *Creation Accounts in the Ancient Near East and in the Bible* (Washington, D.C.: Catholic Biblical Association, 1994), 26; cf. L. R. Fisher, "Creation at Ugarit and in the Old Testament," *VT* 15 (1965): 318–19.

Comparative Exploration: Garden of Eden

The text of Genesis describes a situation that was very well known in the ancient world: a sacred spot featuring a spring with an adjoining, well-watered park, stocked with specimens of trees and animals.[1]

At the same time, we should realize that the geography used here is not a topographical geography, but a cosmic geography. (Concepts like the tropic of Capricorn are parts of our cosmic geography. It is real, but not in the same topographical category as the Thames.) Though the four rivers were real bodies of water, their description here concerns their cosmic role. The river of Eden was the place of God's abode and was the source of life-giving water that flowed through the rivers, benefiting all the earth.[2]

We must first recognize that the garden of Eden was not, strictly speaking, a garden for man, but was the garden of *God* (Isa. 51:3; Ezek. 28:13). "The garden of Eden is not viewed by the author of Genesis simply as a piece of Mesopotamian farmland, but as an archetypal sanctuary, that is, a place where God dwells and where man should worship him. Many of the features of the garden may also be found in later sanctuaries, particularly the tabernacle or Jerusalem temple. These parallels suggest that the garden itself is understood as a sort of sanctuary."[3] The presence of God was the key to the garden and was understood by author and audience as a given from the ancient worldview. His presence is seen as the fertile source of all life-giving waters. "It is not only the dwelling place of God. It is also the source of all the creative forces that flow forth from the Divine Presence, that energize and give life to the creation in a constant, unceasing outflow of vivifying power."[4] This concept is well known in the Bible. Ezekiel 47:1–12 shows the life-giving waters flowing from the temple. Briefer references can be found in Zechariah 14:8 and Psalm 46:4. Perhaps the most familiar picture, however, comes in Revelation 22:1–2, where the river of the water of life flows from the throne of God.

This association between ancient Near Eastern temples and spring waters is well attested. In fact, some temples in Mesopotamia, Egypt, and in the Ugaritic myth of Baal were considered to have been founded upon springs (likened to the primeval waters), which sometimes flowed from the buildings themselves. Thus the symbolic cosmic mountain (temple) stood upon the symbolic primeval waters (spring).[5]

On this point, then, the ancient world and the biblical picture agree. When we

waters.[41] In short, the temple was considered deity's cosmic domain. This concept is represented even in the design of the temples.

> The [Egyptian] temple is a depiction of the world: the wave-shaped structure of the enclosure wall is a representation of the opposition between dry

41. Lundquist, "What Is a Temple?" 208.

see that creation as a whole was understood in terms of a cosmic temple complex, it would be logical to understand the garden as the antechamber to the holy of holies. Eden proper would be the holy of holies, and the garden adjoins it as the antechamber. In this regard it is of importance to note that the objects that were kept in the antechamber of the sanctuary are images intended to evoke the garden.[6] The menorah is a symbol of the tree of life[7] and the table for the bread of the Presence provided food for the priests. In conclusion, then, the garden is understood to be comparable to the antechamber of the holy of holies (Eden) in the cosmic temple complex. It is presented as a real place, but the significance of it is to be found in what it represents theologically and literarily. With this understanding, one can appreciate that in the aftermath of the fall, the greatest loss was not paradise but God's presence. The temple provided for a partial return of that presence, and the antechamber of the temple was reminiscent of the proximity to God's presence that had once been enjoyed.

Genesis 2 is not trying to develop the idea that Eden is the place of God's presence, or the holy of holies of the cosmic temple. Those are givens that are simply assumed by author and audience. The text is most interested in the garden as the means by which God provided food for people (v. 9). Trees of the garden provided food, not for the Deity (as in the parks that sometimes adjoined temples) but for the people who served the Deity. By providing food, the garden actualized the benefits that had been granted in the blessing in Genesis 1:29–30.

1. For extensive discussion in a biblical theology context, see G. Beale, *The Temple and the Church's Mission* (Downers Grove, IL: InterVarsity Press, 2004), 66–80.
2. For in-depth discussion see Stager, "Jerusalem," 36–47.
3. Wenham, "Sanctuary," 19.
4. D. Neiman, "Gihon and Pishon: Mythological Antecedents of the Two Enigmatic Rivers of Eden," *Proceedings of the Sixth World Congress of Jewish Studies* (1973), 324.
5. Lundquist, "What Is a Temple?" 208.
6. Bloch-Smith, "'Who Is the King?'" 27.
7. Meyers, *ABD* 4:142.

land and the primeval ocean, while the pylon, with its two pylon towers and the recess between them within the gateway, represents the horizon. The temple building itself is the cosmos: the temple ceiling with its depictions of birds, for instance, is the sky; the bark shrine and the cultic image chamber are identified as the vault of the heavens.[42]

In Mesopotamia the primary imagery of the temple was that it was the center of the cosmos. From the early second millennium this perspective is articulated in Gudea's temple building text, which enumerates the temple's cosmic qualities.

42. R. Gundlach, "Temples," *OEAE* 3:372; see also, J. Assmann, *The Search for God in Ancient Egypt* (Ithaca: Cornell University Press, 2001), 35–40.

Photo 9 Canaanite High Place

> The temple, mooring pole of the land
> which grows [high] between heaven and earth
> the Eninnu, the true brickwork, [for] which Enlil decreed a good
>   destiny
> the beautiful mountain range, which stands out as a marvel
> [and] which towers above the mountains
> the temple, being a big mountain, reached up to heaven
> being Utu, it filled heaven's midst.[43]

The concepts are present with little change in the mid-first millennium in Neo-Assyrian texts.

> When the second year came
> I raised to heaven the head of Esarra, my lord Assur's dwelling.
> Above, heavenward, I raised high its head
> Below, in the underworld, I made firm its foundations
> Ehursaggula (meaning) House of the Great Mountain
> I made beautiful as the heavenly writing . . .
> Its lofty high head scraped the sky
> below, its roots spread in the subterranean water.[44]

43. Gudea Cylinder B: i. 1–7, *COS* 2.155.
44. Esarhaddon's description of Esarra is quoted from Hurowitz, *I Have Built*, 245.

Comparative Exploration: Cosmos and Temple in Israel

In Isaiah 66:1 the Lord indicates: "Heaven is my throne and the earth is my footstool, where is the house you will build for me, where will my resting place be?" This is not like the claim in Jeremiah 10, where the human craftsmanship of the idols invalidates their role. God is not suggesting that a human temple is somehow sacrilegious and incompatible with his transcendence. But he is referring to the inadequacy of a human-made temple as being considered the true temple (cf. 1 Kings 8:27). It is only a micro-scale representation of the cosmic temple. Psalm 78:69 communicates a similar idea when it indicates that the temple was built on the model of the cosmos. Ideas like these are also found in literature from Mesopotamia that compares temples to the heavens and the earth and gives them a cosmic location and function.[1] It is evident, then, that Israel and their neighbors shared an ideology that understood the cosmos in temple terms and viewed the temple as a model of the cosmos or as the cosmic temple.

1. Hurowitz, *I Have Built*, 335–37.

In Syro-Palestine the temple was the architectural embodiment of the cosmic mountain.[45] This concept is represented in Ugaritic literature[46] as well as in the Bible, where Mount Zion is understood as the mountain of the Lord (e.g., Ps. 48) and the place where his temple, a representation of Eden, was built. "For ancient Israel, the Temple of Solomon—indeed, the Temple Mount and all Jerusalem—was a symbol as well as a reality, a mythopoeic realization of heaven on earth, Paradise, the Garden of Eden."[47]

The Temple and the Human World

Because of the significance that the temple had in the divine and cosmic realms, it took on unparalleled significance in the human world as well. It was considered the center of power, control, and order from which deity brings order to the human world. Fertility, prosperity, peace, and justice emanate from his presence there. Note this example from the Gudea Cylinders in the speech of the god Ningirsu:

45. Lundquist, "What Is a Temple?" 207.
46. R. J. Clifford, *The Cosmic Mountain in Canaan and the Old Testament*, HSM 4 (Cambridge: Harvard University Press), 34–97.
47. Stager, "Jerusalem," 37.

O faithful shepherd Gudea,
When you bring your hand to bear for me
I will cry out to heaven for rain.
From heaven let abundance come to you,
Let the people receive abundance with you,
With the founding of my temple
Let abundance come!
The great fields will lift up their hands to you,
The canal will stretch out its neck to you . . .
Sumer will pour out abundant oil because of you,
Will weigh out abundant wool because of you.[48]

Therefore the temple is not only the cosmic center, it is the economic and moral center of the cosmos, which Lundquist refers to as "the central, organizing, unifying institution in ancient Near Eastern society."[49] J. N. Postgate refers to it as "a bond holding the community together, a source of wealth and goods, a center of law and a focal point for all communal activities."[50]

Yet the temple was not only the center of gravity for society, it was the ultimate focus of much of human activity. "To the members of any ancient Mesopotamian urban community, the vast economic resources and complex administrative apparatus of its temple existed in order to minister to the needs and comfort of the city's patron god or goddess, for his or her numinous presence therein was believed to be the fundamental prerequisite for success in all human endeavors."[51]

Thus the temple existed as a fulcrum of mutual dependence. The gods had their needs met through the temple and their image was resident in its midst, and the people had their needs met by the beneficence of the contented deity. An inscription of Arik-din-ili from just before 1300 BC distills the essence of the ideology when it indicates that the king built the temple of Shamash "in order that the harvest of my land might prosper."[52] The prosperous harvest then becomes the resource for bountiful offerings to be made to the temple—the cycle of cosmic life in the ancient Near East.

48. *COS* 2.155, Gudea Cylinder A: xi. 5–13, 16–17.
49. Lundquist, "What Is a Temple?" 213; see also Levenson, "Temple and World," 298.
50. J. N. Postgate, "The Role of the Temple in the Mesopotamian Secular Community," in *Man, Settlement, and Urbanism*, ed. P. Ucko, R. Tringham, and G. W. Dimbleby (Cambridge, MA: Schenkman, 1972), 811–25, esp. 813–14.
51. J. Robertson, "The Social and Economic Organization of Ancient Mesopotamian Temples," *CANE* 1:444.
52. Cited in Hurowitz, *I Have Built*, in the appendix on "Temple Building and Fertility," 322–23, where he also discusses Hag. 2:15–19.

Comparative Exploration: Temple Functions in Israel

In Solomon's temple dedication prayer in 1 Kings 8:27–53 he expresses his hopes for what the temple will accomplish in the midst of the city of Jerusalem and how God's presence there will affect the kingdom. Functions are introduced by the request that God would hear from his temple the supplications that are made by his people in a variety of situations that are enumerated, including:

- Judging the innocent and the guilty in response to oaths (vv. 31–32)
- Delivering from invading enemies in response to confession (vv. 33–34)
- Ending drought, famine, or plague in response to confession (vv. 35–40)
- Responding to the foreigner (vv. 41–43)
- Bringing victory or deliverance in warfare (vv. 44–45)
- Deliverance from captivity and exile in response to confession (vv. 46–53)

These are the benefits made available by the presence of a deity among people. We would find the same expectations among the people of any ancient Near Eastern city. The civil, political, and cosmic jurisdiction of the deity is recognized in these expectations. In these particulars we can see that the ideology of the temple is not noticeably different in Israel than it is in the ancient Near East. The difference is in the God, not in the way the temple functions in relation to the God. The cycle of cosmic life is construed differently in Israel since God's provision of food does not ultimately serve his own purposes by meeting his own needs. Yet the idea that all of human experience is centered on the deity's presence in the temple is common to all of these cultures.

Zechariah's visions offer additional indication of the expected function of the temple. Each of the seven visions has some connection to temple building.[1] Most notable in the functions that are indicated are the following:

- Deliverance from enemies and political order established (Zech. 1:7–17 and 4:1–14)
- Protection of the people even without city walls (Zech. 2:1–5)
- Calling oath breakers to account (Zech. 5:1–4)
- Base of divine operations throughout the world (Zech. 6:1–8)

In this way the rebuilding of the temple is promoted on the premise that when God again takes up his residence among his people, he will be able to establish justice in their land, protect them from enemies, and resume the fulfillment of the long-term plan for his people that had been temporarily interrupted by the exile.

1. B. Halpern, "The Ritual Background of Zechariah's Temple Song," *CBQ* 40 (1978): 167–90.

The Temple and the Rituals

The gods' needs were not cared for just so that the people would be graced with good harvests. The temple was the control center for order in the cosmos and that order had to be maintained. The deity needed to be cared for so that he/she could focus his/her energies on the important work of holding forces of chaos at bay. The rituals, therefore, served not simply as gifts to the deity or mechanical liturgical words and actions. The rituals provided a means by which humans could play a role in maintaining order in the cosmos.[53]

Priests were the specialists who possessed the knowledge and the responsibility for ensuring that access to sacred space was protected and that rituals were properly performed. The god's privacy needed to be guarded and his needs met so that he could be about his cosmic business. Creation was renewed and maintained through the various rituals and ceremonies.[54]

Egyptian thinking attached this function not only to the role of priests but also to the role of the king. In Egypt priests operated only by authority delegated from the king, who had the sole right to perform the rituals of the cult.[55] It was his task "to complete what was unfinished, and to preserve the existent, not as a status quo but in a continuing, dynamic, even revolutionary process of remodeling and improvement."[56] Thus in the ritual observances the order of the cosmos not only was maintained but was transferred to society, resulting in political and social order.[57] "The royal performance of the cult, generally speaking, invoked the sacred power for the preservation of *maat*, the order of the world."[58]

Assmann summarizes the system well: "The world thus maintained is a world of meaning, of language, of knowledge, of relations and reflections, an anthropomorphic reading of the universe with a correspondingly cosmomorphic image of human order. The hourly ritual bans cosmic chaos, and with it the chaos in man himself."[59]

Sacrifices played an important role in this system. As the food of the gods, it is arguably the most important provision to sustain their presence, favor, and the smooth operation of the cosmos. Conventions for the trans-

53. J. Assmann, *The Mind of Egypt* (New York: Metropolitan, 1996), 205; Hornung, *Conceptions*, 229.

54. Stager, "Jerusalem," 37.

55. Gundlach, "Temples," *OEAE* 3:373.

56. Hornung, *Conceptions*, 183.

57. Assmann, *Mind of Egypt*, 205, refers to the sociologist Talcott Parsons, who labels these polytheistic communities with the blanket term "cosmological societies." A cosmological society lives by a model of cosmic forms of order, which it transforms into political and social order by means of meticulous observation and performance of rituals.

58. Gundlach, "Temples," *OEAE* 3:365.

59. Assmann, *Mind of Egypt*, 211.

Comparative Exploration: Role of Ritual

Once we understand the underlying ideology of ritual in the ancient world and the role that it plays we can explore the Israelite ideology and use of ritual. Here we can begin with the way that sacrifice was understood, but we also want to move beyond that to the larger ritual ideology.

Though the language associated with the understanding that sacrifice provided nourishment for deity is still observable in the biblical text,[1] there are scattered disclaimers that lead us to infer that such terms became lexical vestiges. Certainly the strongest such disclaimer is found in Psalm 50, where Yahweh denies that he grows hungry or needs Israelite sacrifices for food. The distinction is reinforced in the fact that the presentation of offerings to Yahweh takes place at the altar in the outer courtyard in full view, thus resisting the idea of a god partaking of food in mystical ways in secret chambers.[2] Despite the fact that this element is denied a place in the ideal Israelite ideology of sacrifice, the idea of offering gifts to deity in gratitude and petition is common to all systems. Likewise, despite differences from one culture to another in their confidence in being able to identify offense, the response to having offended deity included the offering of sacrifice.

The blood rites familiar in the Bible are not replicated in other cultures,[3] but the idea that sacred space needs to be symbolically cleansed from impurity is commonplace. The differences in the ritual details and procedures notwithstanding, the ritual world of Israel shared a common foundation with what is known in the ancient world.

Leviticus 16 offers a comparative window into this world as an annual rite where the sanctity of the sanctuary is ritually returned to equilibrium to preserve the presence of deity and order in the cosmos.[4] In the Babylonian New Year ritual the priest slaughters a ram to be used in purging the sanctuary. This is accomplished by incantations to exorcise demons. The king declares himself free of a number of crimes concerning his office, and the body of the ram is thrown into the river.[5] The difference in Israel is that the sins of all the people are addressed by the ritual rather than the offenses of the king or the threat of demonic presence. Still, the idea is that whatever constitutes the most significant threat to the sanctity of the temple is purged. It is done ritually with the same ultimate goal in mind—that the deity would be pleased to remain in his temple and that cosmic stability would thereby be retained.

Babylonians threw a slaughtered ram into the river and Israelites chased a goat into the wilderness. Along this same line of thought, a number of Hittite rituals feature the transfer of evil to an animal that is then sent away.[6] In some cases the animal is considered a gift to appease the gods or a type of sacrifice to the gods, but in others it is simply a means of disposing of the evil. Mesopotamian rituals that transfer impurity often see the animal as a substitute for an individual—a substitute who will now become the object of demonic attack rather than the person. In the *Asakki Marsuti* ritual for fever, the goat that is the substitute for the sick man is sent out into the wilderness.[7] All of these differ significantly from Israelite practice in that they are enacted by means of incantations—a concept totally absent from Israelite ritual. Additionally the Israelite practice shows no intention to appease the anger of deity or demon, whereas this is the most common motivation of the ancient Near Eastern rituals. Milgrom summarizes the similarities and differences as follows:

> Mesopotamian elimination rites resemble the biblical scapegoat rite in that an object that is selected to draw the evil from the affected person is consequently disposed of. The differences between them are more significant: (1) In Mesopotamia, the evil removed by such rites is demonic and very real; in the Bible, while the impurity is real, it does not possess the vitality and independence of demonic evil. (2) There are no group transfer rites in Mesopotamia: the biblical scapegoat, in contrast, removes the sins of the entire nation. (3) The Mesopotamian rites seek the aid of the deities of the wilderness to accept the evils; in the Bible, the entire rite is done under the aegis of its one God. (4) The Bible rejects the idea of substitution, which presupposes demonic attack and the appeasement of threatening demons.[8]

One more point needs to be stressed concerning the role of ritual within the spectrum of religious responses. In the ancient Near East at large, the performance of the cult was central and foundational to their religion. It was their principal responsibility and superseded the element of belief (the mental affirmation of doctrinal convictions). In today's view of religion, belief is more foundational, with some even viewing performance as rote and thus empty or hypocritical. We dare not impose that perception on the ancient world.

The world of the deities of Egypt was not an object of belief, but rather of knowledge: knowledge of names, processes, actions, and events that were superimposed, in a manner that explained and made sense of, saved, transfigured, on the realm of manifestations in the cult and in nature.[9]

The shape of one's belief was less significant in the ancient world. It was not belief that counted, but performance of the cult. In Israel it was not performance of the cult that was the essential expression of belief, but adherence to the covenant, which included cultic performance but was not dominated by it.

1. Pleasing aroma, the altar as a table, and the idea of communal meals as sharing a meal with deity. In addition, one interpretation of the dietary laws is that a model for what people could eat was provided by understanding what deity could "eat"; see E. Firmage, "The Biblical Dietary Laws and the Concept of Holiness," in *Studies in the Pentateuch*, ed. J. A. Emerton, VTSup 41 (Leiden: Brill, 1990), 177–208.

2. J. Milgrom, *Leviticus*, CC (Minneapolis: Fortress, 2004), 21.

3. See T. Abusch, "Blood in Israel and Mesopotamia," in *Emanuel: Studies in Hebrew Bible, Septuagint, and Dead Sea Scrolls in Honor of Emanuel Tov*, ed. S. M. Paul et al., VTSup 94 (Leiden: Brill, 2003), 675–84. Beckman indicates that among the Hittites the throat of the animal was slit with the blood being squirted toward the statue, and blood was used in purification ceremonies ("How Religion Was Done," 349–50).

4. See R. Gane, *Cult and Character* (Winona Lake, IN: Eisenbrauns, 2005).

5. This occurs on day five of the twelve-day ritual. Cf. J. Bidmead, *The Akitu Festival* (Piscataway, NJ: Gorgias, 2002), 70–74.

6. D. Wright, *The Disposal of Impurity*, SBLDS 101 (Atlanta: Scholars Press, 1987), 15–74. Cf. J. Milgrom, *Leviticus 1–16*, AB (New York: Doubleday, 1991), 1071–79.

7. Milgrom, *Leviticus 1–16*, 1078.

8. Ibid., 1079.

9. Assmann, *Search for God*, 94–95.

Photo 10 Offering Scene

ference of the food to the divine realm varied from culture to culture—from formal presentation of the offering on a stand of some sort to a ritual of destruction. Beckman places Hittite practice in the latter category: "The general principle underlying Hittite offering technique was that the material presented had to be destroyed, in whole or in part, in order to pass over to the intended recipient in the para-human world. Thus liquids were poured out (on the ground, offering table, or altar), breads were broken or crumbled, vessels were smashed, and animals were killed."[60]

It would be a mistake to think that sacrifices primarily involved the ritual slaughter of animals. Other typical foodstuffs included grain products, dairy products, baked goods, fruit, eggs, and a variety of liquids, from beer or wine to milk to honey or oil. When animals were offered, they tended to be the domesticated animals that had a role in the economy.[61] In Mesopotamia bulls and sheep were most common, but offerings also included birds, fish, or bandicoot rats.[62] Pigs and dogs would typically

60. G. Beckman, "How Religion Was Done," in *The Companion to the Ancient Near East*, ed. D. Snell (Oxford: Blackwell, 2005), 349.

61. Occasional sacrifices of wild animals, especially gazelles, can be found. See ibid., 348.

62. J. Scurlock, "Animal Sacrifice in Ancient Mesopotamia," in *History of the Animal World in the Ancient Near East*, ed. B. J. Collins (Leiden: Brill, 2002), 392.

be offered only to chthonic deities or in offerings to the dead.[63] In Egypt meat was not a common element in the sacrificial ritual, but it was present in most other cultures.[64] In most cases the meat then became the basis for a feast shared by the deity, the offering priest, and the worshiper. The parts given to deity varied. Hittite practice shows some similarity to Israelite rituals: "The gods preferred the fat and those organs thought to be the seat of life and emotions—liver and heart above all, but also the gall bladder and the kidneys. These entrails were roasted over the flame, chopped and served to the recipient on bread. The remainder of the carcass was dismembered, cooked as a stew, and shared by the humans present."[65]

In all of these areas we can see that the actual ritual practices show some degree of commonality across the ancient world, including Israel. Likewise the role of ritual as undergirding the smooth operation of the cosmos and securing the favor and presence of the deity is everywhere evident. The main difference seen in the cognitive worldview of Israel concerned the extent to which Yahweh had needs that were met by rituals, or the way in which the giving of gifts influenced deity.

63. Ibid., 392–93.
64. Ibid., 389–404, for Mesopotamia.
65. Beckman, "How Religion Was Done," 350.

6

State and Family Religion

J. Bottéro has summarized Mesopotamian religiosity in the following terms:

> [Mesopotamian religiosity] was made up above all of a "centrifugal" feeling of fear, respect, and servility with regard to the divine; that the divine was portrayed in the human model (*anthropomorphism*) and was spread out over a whole society of supernatural beings, gods (*polytheism*), whose needs people were expected to fulfill and whose orders were to be carried out with all the devotion, submission, but also generosity and ostentation that were thought to be expected by such lofty figures. Furthermore, it was resolutely and exclusively a prehistoric religion without holy scriptures, religious authorities, dogmas, orthodoxy, orthopraxy, or fanaticism.[1]

Much of what we know about the religious practice of the ancient Near East concerns what would be called the state religion. This is because most written documents (the primary sources available to us) derive from the palaces and temples. The ordinary commoner in the ancient world had little relationship with religion at that level (aside from the festivals and other spectacle events). The religion practiced at the popular level can be called "family religion" because it had its base in the family unit

---

1. J. Bottéro, *Religion in Ancient Mesopotamia* (Chicago: University of Chicago Press, 2001), 6.

(rather than in the individual).[2] Our understanding of family religion is informed by some texts, but is also dependent on archaeological finds (particularly cultic objects) found in private homes. In this section we will first address state religion, then family religion.

Though the gods often had their own individual purposes, as a group they were unanimous in their general expectations of people: "Their servants were expected to be quiet, to keep the land in good order and to attend to the needs of their creators."[3] The gods had needs, the gods had jobs, and the gods had whims—these were all addressed in the practice of religion at the state level.

State Religion: What the Gods Want

Needs of the Gods

The literature from throughout the ancient Near East clearly addresses the fact that the gods have needs that are met by human beings. As mentioned in the last chapter, rituals and other cultic activities were designed to address those needs.[4] The king and the priests each had duties in the process.

All public worship revolved around the image. It marked the deity's presence and was the center of any ceremony involving the divine.[5] It was awakened in the morning, washed, clothed, fed two sumptuous meals each day (while music was played in its presence), and put to bed at night.[6] Thus worship took place by caring for the needs of the god through his image. This care was intended to ensure the continued presence of the deity in the image.

What confidence did the people have that the needs of the gods were being met adequately and appropriately? The traditions that dictated the terms of this care had been developed over centuries through information gleaned from common sense and experimentation. In terms of common sense, they simply treated the god with the same deference, bounty, and

2. K. van der Toorn, *Family Religion in Babylonia, Syria and Israel: Continuity and Change in the Forms of Religious Life* (Leiden: Brill, 1996).

3. K. van der Toorn, *Sin and Sanction in Israel and Mesopotamia* (Assen: Van Gorcum, 1985), 4.

4. Bottéro, *Religion*, 125–33.

5. C. Walker and M. B. Dick, *The Induction of the Cult Image in Ancient Mesopotamia: The Mesopotamian Mis Pi Ritual*, SAALT 1 (Helsinki: Neo-Assyrian Text Corpus Project, 2001), 5.

6. A. L. Oppenheim, *Ancient Mesopotamia* (1964, repr. Chicago: University of Chicago Press, 1977), 188–90. For Egypt see S. Morenz, *Egyptian Religion* (Ithaca: Cornell University Press, 1973), 88.

luxury that would be appropriate for a king. This made sense based on the premise that what the god wanted was to be cared for. In addition to the intuitive nature of such a response, commands from the gods to care for them are known from the literature.[7] On the experimentation level, when circumstances, omens, or prophetic oracles suggested that the deity was displeased, divinatory procedures would be initiated to attempt to identify an appropriate course of action. Once this course of action was followed and deemed successful, additions might be made to the ritual traditions.

The point to be made is that ritual procedures were not the result of revelation in anything like the sense that is found in the Pentateuch (instructions from Sinai). While it is true that divinatory procedures were considered to result in divine revelation (see the fuller treatment in chap. 11 on divination and omens), high levels of insecurity and anxiety plagued the system.

Situations were bound to develop in which the divine will might not be so clear. Did the god want a new high priest or high priestess and, if so, whom? Did the god wish that his old temple be rebuilt now or later? Or not at all? Did he think one should go to war against an encroaching neighbor, or was he inclined to use diplomatic means? And, of course, the god might harbor a wish that one could not guess, but which nevertheless had to be divined and carried out.

> For such cases—one might call them the "specific orders"—the ruler had to rely on messages from the gods in dreams or visions, on signs and portents, or on one of the traditional ways in which one would approach the gods and obtain—if one was lucky—an answer.[8]

Thus in the ancient Near East there was much uncertainty about what was to be done to please the gods. Nevertheless, the accumulated tradition gave them the sense of doing something, which they could only hope would be sufficient. They believed themselves to be following the commands of deity, though those commands were often tailored to specific circumstances rather than addressing lifestyle or ethical behavior.

Jobs of the Gods

The gods have destinies decreed for them through the divine hierarchy, and at least some of those jobs were enabled through the ritual process, as already mentioned. The gods also expected that the officials

---

7. Morenz, *Egyptian Religion*, 60.

8. T. Jacobsen, *Treasures of Darkness* (New Haven: Yale University Press, 1976), 84. For the similar situation in Egypt see Morenz, *Egyptian Religion*, 31–33.

of the land would help the gods to do their jobs. Maintaining justice, the job of the gods, was delegated to the king so that appropriate verdicts and decrees could be made and enforced. The gods expected this to be done. On the stele of Hammurabi, the picture shows Shamash extending authority to Hammurabi, and in the prologue Hammurabi reports that he has fulfilled his duty to be a just king. More of this will be explored in chapter 13 on law.

Whims of the Gods

The gods are easily offended, and neither avoiding their anger nor appeasing it was intuitive. The anger of the gods was perceived from either circumstances or omens. When such anger seemed evident, one would attempt to appease the anger of the gods. On the state level, divination might suggest a solution: increase the offerings, remodel the temple, cease hostilities with a neighboring country, and so on.

An example of this whole procedure on the state level can be seen in the "substitute king ritual." In this case omens, usually an eclipse, would indicate that the deity was displeased with the king.[9] If the divination priests concluded through their arts that the omens suggested that the king's life was in jeopardy, he would step down from his throne and a substitute would be enthroned for a period of time to be determined, usually a maximum of one hundred days. Chosen by the diviners, he was enthroned, dressed like the king, and given the royal insignias (crown, mantle, weapon, scepter).[10] He was given a queen, who eventually shared his fate. He played the role of king by presenting offerings before the altar and burning incense. At the same time, he was made to recite omen litanies and thereby take the evil omens on himself.[11] The final act by which the transference of the evil omens was accomplished came at the end of the period when the substitute was put to death. In so doing, the omens were cancelled. He was put to death for the sake of the king and his prince, and accomplished their redemption. The substitution was seen as a way of allowing the gods to do what they wanted to do. The omens had indicated that the gods desired to act against someone. The ritual was not intended to fool the gods, but to give them a ready victim on whom to carry out their intentions.[12] It

---

9. S. Parpola, *Letters from Assyrian and Babylonian Scholars*, SAA 10 (Helsinki: University of Helsinki Press, 1993); cf. discussion in J. Bottéro, "The Substitute King and His Fate," *Akkadica* 9 (1978): 2–24, repr. in *Mesopotamia: Writing, Reasoning, and the Gods* (Chicago: University of Chicago Press, 1992), 138–55.

10. *LABS* #189.

11. *LABS* #351.

12. Bottéro, *Religion*, 142.

Photo 11 Beersheba Horned Altar

would never be known in this case what the gods had been angry about. It only gave them a target to inflict their anger on, which would result in their appeasement.[13]

At another level, political sins could be committed for which evidence existed not from omens, but in the ill fortune that a country or city faced. One of the best-known examples is contained in the Hittite *Plague Account of Murshili*.[14] In Egypt the royal instruction genre at times alludes to this phenomenon (e.g., *Instructions of Merikare*),[15] and in Mesopotamia the *Curse of Akkad*[16] suggests the displeasure of the gods over Naram-Sin's desecrations in the third millennium, while the accusations against Nabonidus stand as testimony to this mentality in the first millennium.[17] Corporate identity meant that many offenses would be considered corporate offenses and solutions would be corporate solutions. Common folks counted on the king and the priests to maintain the favor of the god at this corporate level. They expected that this would result in fertility and

13. Summary adapted from J. Walton, "The Imagery of the Substitute King Ritual in Isaiah's Fourth Servant Song," *JBL* 122 (2003): 734–43.

14. See chap. 3, p. 74.

15. Morenz, *Egyptian Religion*, 58–59.

16. See chap. 3, p. 50.

17. *Verse Account of Nabonidus* (*ANET* 312–15); see chap. 3, p. 53.

Comparative Exploration: State Religion in Israel

Though the Old Testament posits a role for Yahweh since the very beginning, the Yahwism associated with Israel began with Abraham as a family religion and emerged over time as a state religion.[1] To some extent this transition began in the exodus narratives as Yahweh took his place as a national God. It took on a new dimension in the development of the monarchy when the associated institutions of kingship and temple (in a fixed cult center) came into existence and the profile of a state God was established. Yahwism is the only recognized example of this sort of development. The intermediate phase between the family religion of Abraham and the state religion of the monarchy is what might be called the clan or tribal religion that is most evident in the judges period.

The state religion of the monarchy shared many common features with the state religions known in the ancient Near East, such that to an outside observer much would have looked the same. The public role of the king, the functions of the temple and the priests, and the maintenance rituals on behalf of the kingdom all would have had a familiar feel.

Nonetheless, the literature of the Old Testament insists that Yahweh is not like any other god. Those elements that often served as the underlying foundations of state religion in the ancient Near East were unacceptable in the ideals and values that the prophets presented for Yahwism. These differences can be explored by using the same three categories addressed under the previous heading "State Religion: What the Gods Want": needs, jobs, and whims.

Needs of Yahweh

In the Old Testament this is, of course, an oxymoron. Yahweh has no needs and therefore the state religion has no underlying rationale that is based on the premise of meeting those needs. There is no image to mediate the care of Yahweh. The rituals respond to requirements rather than to needs. The splendor of the temple honors Yahweh just as the splendor of Marduk's temple honors Marduk. Sacrifices and the maintenance of sacred space are designed to attract and preserve the deity's vital presence. Gifts are an expression of gratitude. So much is the same in the rhetoric, yet in the ancient Near East the gods willingly own their neediness and admittedly rely on human support. In Israel every aspect, however traditional, has an alternative rationale. The state religion highlights the needs of the people more than the needs of Yahweh. Reciprocity and mutual dependence have no place in the rhetoric. Whatever obligations Yahweh has to Israel come not because they serve his needs, but because of the covenant agreement. The people serve Yahweh by faithfulness to the covenant expectations.

Jobs of Yahweh

The jobs that Yahweh does in Israel are not perceived that differently from those that were undertaken by other deities in the ancient Near East, and religious practice also was seen as a means of coming alongside Yahweh and participating along with him (though again, it is clear that he is not in need of help). The responsibility to maintain justice and order was imposed on the king, priests, and people by the covenant. Yahweh has no destinies decreed for him, and he is not subject to control attributes (such as the MEs) that operate independently of him. Though arguable, it is worth considering whether one could draw the following contrast: ancient Near Eastern gods have jobs while Yahweh has a plan. Both concepts ("jobs" and "plan") offer ways to discuss the outworking of the deity's attributes in the world. The difference is that justice emanates from the nature of Yahweh, while justice is simply the responsibility of a deity such as Shamash. This may be a distinction without a difference, depending on how closely we associate function (jurisdiction) with identity (nature).[2] It is important to resist simplistic contrasts, yet it is difficult to escape the conclusion that the Israelites maintained unique categories in which to understand God.

Whims of Yahweh

Unlike the view of the gods in the ancient Near Eastern literature, the Old Testament does not recognize that Yahweh has whims. Nevertheless, sometimes Yahweh's actions are considered troublesome, seem incomprehensible, or seem inconsistent. The complaint of the Israelites of the Babylonian period that "the fathers eat sour grapes and the children's teeth are set on edge" is only one example. At other times drought or famine occurs without ready explanation. The prophets and biblical authors, however, are never content to let stand the conclusion that the events in question simply represent divine whim. The prophets identify causes for the treatment of the nation. The Chronicler builds his whole theology on the consistency of retribution. The psalmist, though often confused about Yahweh's apparent unresponsiveness, has no room for the idea that Yahweh is anything less than consistent. The wrath of Yahweh against Nadab and Abihu, Korah, Achan, Hophni and Phinehas, Uzzah, and others like them always comes with justification. It is true that Babylonians likewise sought reasons, but only so that appeasement

could proceed rather than being driven by any need to reconcile the divine behavior with the divine nature. The point is that there is no indication that the Israelite state religion viewed appeasement as related to divine whims.

Many of the religious problems targeted in the Deuteronomistic History, Chronicles, and the prophets concerned issues connected to state religion. In the division of the monarchy into north and south, there was no dispute about which god was worshiped. Instead, the differences arose over state sanctuaries, the integrated role of the Davidic kings with the capital city, Jerusalem, and the temple there, and the priesthood and festivals. These are all related to the practice of religion at the state level.

The conflict between Elijah and Ahab and Jezebel concerned a challenge to Yahweh's role as state god. Previous unfaithfulness going back into the period of the judges and continuing at the high places merely showed the adoption of fertility and nature gods at the clan or family level. Ahab and Jezebel championed Baal as a replacement for Yahweh at the national level.

State-sponsored innovations under kings such as Manasseh and Ahaz featured other deities brought in alongside Yahweh and perhaps being prioritized over him because of state associations.[3] The Old Testament also speaks of state-sponsored reforms, notably those of Hezekiah and Josiah. These sought to cleanse the state religion of syncretistic elements—the very ones that had been part of the politically motivated innovations of their predecessors.

None of these divisions, challenges, innovations, or reforms necessarily had much impact on the religious practice of the families of Israel. In the polytheistic religions of the ancient world it was not considered obligatory for individuals to worship the state gods. It might be to their advantage and coincide with their self-interests to do so, but the state god would hardly be offended by their worship of their local or ancestral deities. This observation brings considerable clarity to the centuries-long struggle of the Israelites to understand that Yahweh's status as state God excluded the worship of local gods, nature gods, or ancestral gods. Their native mentality would have seen no conflict. They could willingly acknowledge Yahweh as the national God and as the supreme God, but such conclusions would not require sole worship of Yahweh. State religion was an entirely different issue than family religion. The uniqueness of Israel is that here we can see an attempt to merge those two horizons. Every indication is that they were consistently syncretistic throughout the monarchy period,[4] though the prophets had high hopes that they would recant of their syncretism and adopt covenant faithfulness to Yahweh wholeheartedly.

The key to the state religion of Israel and to an understanding of its uniqueness in the ancient world is found in that the corporate identity of Israel was based on their covenant relationship with Yahweh. The covenant is at the foundation of Yahweh's role as their national deity and is the primary element in their understanding of the king, the temple, and the purpose behind their rituals. It is the covenant that dictates their behavior and that explains Yahweh's behavior.

Although the covenant offered information from and about God that other nations did not enjoy, Israel had the same difficulty with receiving "special orders" from deity as anyone else did. Answers were sought through quasi-divinatory methods that were legitimized for Israel such as consulting the Urim and Thummim or consulting the prophets. Both of these have significant phenomenological continuity with the ancient Near East. However, since they were not based on the premise that deity needed to be taken care of, the standing orders were a different matter entirely. This is where the revelation from Sinai came in.

1. In general see P. Miller, *The Religion of Ancient Israel* (Louisville: Westminster John Knox, 2000), 87–94.
2. This takes us back to the discussion of ontology of the gods; see chap. 4.
3. S. Holloway argues the limited nature of religious impositions by the Assyrians on subject states, *Aššur Is King! Aššur Is King! Religion in the Exercise of Power in the Neo-Assyrian Empire* (Leiden: Brill, 2002).
4. The details of this are traceable in part through the iconography of the various periods; see O. Keel and C. Uehlinger, *Gods, Goddesses, and Images of God in Ancient Israel* (Minneapolis: Fortress, 1998).

prosperity for their land and nation, success in international relations, and a sense of peace and security.

Family Religion: What the Gods Want

The nature of polytheism significantly affects the distinction between state and family religion. Since the gods were viewed as operating within a hierarchical system, there was a bureaucracy and a division of labor.

While the state religion would be focused primarily on the gods connected to the major temples in the city (and particularly the patron god of the city), most families would feel that they had little access to those great gods.[18] Likewise, those gods would not likely be concerned about them or hear their requests.[19] It was not considered obligatory for individuals to worship the state gods.[20] Consequently, the common people tended to turn to their family and ancestral gods, who would more likely take an interest in them. In turn, one might on occasion ask those deities to try to influence the great gods.[21]

> The god Babylonian citizens elected to be theirs had to be near. In theory, this nearness meant physical proximity. Few gods being omnipresent, it was of little avail to have a mighty god as one's helper if he had his temple miles away. People wanted to worship a god within reach. When the god they worshipped belonged to the lower echelons of the divine hierarchy, there is a fair degree of probability that the god in question had a temple or a shrine in the neighbourhood.[22]

In Mesopotamia the ancestors who had died were often mixed in with the family gods, in which case the family religion at least included a cult of the ancestors.[23] Babylonians referred to their family gods in relational terms, thus paralleling the biblical expression "God of your fathers."[24]

Worshipers throughout the ancient Near East looked to their gods to bring them a sound reputation, social success, material prosperity, and, of course, the ability to have children.[25] They expected their gods to show them favor in their various endeavors. They were therefore very

18. Van der Toorn, *Family Religion*, 81.

19. G. del Olmo Lete, *Canaanite Religion According to the Liturgical Texts of Ugarit* (Winona Lake, IN: Eisenbrauns, 2004), 44–45.

20. M. Dandamayev, "State Gods and Private Religion in the Near East in the First Millennium B.C.E.," in *Religion and Politics in the Ancient Near East*, ed. A. Berlin (Bethesda: University of Maryland Press, 1996), 42.

21. Van der Toorn, *Family Religion*, 136–37. On occasion it could be the other way around and a higher god may be asked to exert pressure on the personal god; cf. P. D. Miller, *They Cried to the Lord* (Minneapolis: Fortress, 1994), 22–23.

22. Van der Toorn, *Family Religion*, 82.

23. Ibid., 55–58.

24. Ibid., 75. Ancestral deities are not as recognizable in Egyptian religion. Here the family religion is even more difficult to penetrate; see J. Baines, "Society, Morality and Religious Practice," in *Religion in Ancient Egypt*, ed. B. Shafer (Ithaca: Cornell University Press, 1991), 128. In Israel, by the time the Patriarchal Narratives were written, the ancestral "God of the Fathers" had transitioned to the status of national God.

25. T. Abusch, "Ghost and God: Some Observations on a Babylonian Understanding of Human Nature," in *Self, Soul and Body in Religious Experience*, ed. A. Baumgarten, J. Assmann, and G. Stroumsa (Leiden: Brill, 1998), 381.

interested in how to attain the favor of the gods. "The many facets of the care of the personal god can be summarized in the phrase that the god wishes to give his human servant life in abundance," sometimes referred to as fullness of life.[26]

But the relationship with the gods was a fragile symbiosis. Inadvertent actions by the individual could suddenly draw the wrath of the deity. Since a relationship with a personal god offered protection and prosperity, if the god withdrew in anger, sudden vulnerability resulted.[27] Sicknesses, failure of crops, and for that matter personal disasters of every sort were attributed to desertion by the deity and the concomitant exposure to demons and evil from a variety of sources. The utmost priority in such circumstances became the appeasement of the deity, but here the procedures were uncertain. In human relationships, if there is a falling out such that reconciliation is needed and desired, two paths are possible. If the offense is known, one can ask forgiveness and stop the offensive behavior. If there is no easily identified offense, one can seek reconciliation by acts of kindness or generosity toward the offended party.

In the ancient Near East it was the rare exception that anyone thought that they could identify with confidence the cause of the deity's anger. Since there was no revealed code of conduct, only obvious offenses (stealing from the temple? neglecting the required sacrifices?) would be recognizable. That generally not being the case, the other path would be followed. The individual would seek to soothe the anger by acts of kindness and generosity. The theory in Mesopotamia was laid out clearly enough:

> Every day worship your god.
> Sacrifice and Benediction are the proper accompaniment of
>   incense.
> Present your free-will offering to your god,
> For this is proper toward the gods.
> Prayer, supplication and prostration
> Offer him daily, and you will get your reward.
> Then you will have full communion with your god.
> In your wisdom study the tablet.
> Reverence begets favor,
> Sacrifice prolongs life,
> Prayer atones for guilt.[28]

26. Van der Toorn, *Family Religion*, 105.
27. Miller, *They Cried*, 17.
28. *BWL* 105:135–45, *Counsels of Wisdom*.

But theory is for the realm of the hypothetical. Reality often found less optimism. One well-known sufferer, after pursuing many ritual courses of action, sadly confesses his confusion and frustration:

> I wish I knew that these things were pleasing to one's god!
> What is proper to oneself is an offence to one's god;
> What in one's own heart seems despicable is proper to one's god.
> Who knows the will of the gods in heaven?
> Who understands the plans of the underworld gods?
> Where have mortals learnt the way of a god?[29]

With no revelation, however, there was no way to know what pleased and what angered. In a well-known Assyrian prayer entitled *A Prayer to Every God*, the worshiper is seeking to appease a deity from anger over an offense that the worshiper has presumably committed. There are only two problems: he does not know which god is angry, and he does not know of anything he has done wrong. He therefore addresses each confession he makes to "the god I know or do not know, the goddess I know or do not know." He is ready to confess ignorantly eating forbidden food or invading sacred space . . . anything to appease.[30] His frustration overwhelms us with sympathy as he expresses his hopelessness:

> Although I am constantly looking for help, no one takes me by the
>   hand;
> When I weep, they do not come to my side.
> I utter laments, but no one hears me;
> I am troubled; I am overwhelmed; I cannot see.
>
> Man is dumb; he knows nothing;
> Mankind, everyone that exists—what does he know?
> Whether he is committing sin or doing good, he does not even
>   know.[31]

This is the plight of those who live in a world without revelation. In the end, for all of their conscientious ritual, they did not know what deity wanted—they could only adhere to traditions and ride out the storm. The ritual actions were typically combined with prayer, so we now turn our attention to that area.

29. *BWL* 41:33–38, *Ludlul bel nemeqi*.
30. Lists of offenses were compiled in appeasement rituals that would be recited in the confessions of those who felt that they had become objects of the wrath of the gods. Most notable in this regard is the list in the second tablet of *šurpu*. See van der Toorn, *Sin and Sanction*, 97.
31. *ANET* 391–92, lines 35–38, 51–53.

The Role of Prayer and Piety

People's prayers reveal their priorities and their values.[32] Prayers of praise demonstrate the importance placed on exalting deity. It is not always easy to discern whether that exercise simply reflects true adoration or whether it is part of a more complex scheme driven by self-interests—as Bottéro quips, stemming not from piety, but from prudence. Most of us would have trouble making such distinctions in the roots of our own prayers and should be reluctant to draw conclusions from the literary prayers that are preserved from the ancient world.

When we enter the realm of supplication and petition, however, self-interest is intrinsic to the setting, so motivations, values, and priorities are more discernible.[33] Since the culture of ancient times tended to value a person in light of the role performance, personal values also follow that path. Van der Toorn finds a "priority of shame over guilt, of honour over self-esteem, and of success over integrity."[34] Since misfortune of any sort was inferred to derive from having offended deity, the "offender" inevitably experienced social rejection. No one wanted to suffer from guilt by association and likewise attract the ire of some god. Therefore, though the sufferer felt no guilt (the sufferer had no idea what he might have done wrong,[35] though he was ready to acknowledge any offense if only he were informed what to acknowledge), he was overwhelmed with shame from society's response to his difficult circumstance. He felt the humiliation of public disgrace and suffered consequences in disintegrating relationships in his town and in his family. Prayers therefore seek restoration of the god's favor, which is expected to result in the renewal of one's social well-being rather than in the renewal of one's personal or spiritual well-being. Shame would be resolved and honor restored. Such restoration and renewal stand as the religious objectives and the anticipated outcome of prayer.

Israelites may have shared the same anthropological focus in prioritizing social role over personal consciousness and conscience. The concept of shame is ubiquitous in the book of Psalms. But, of course, the knowledge of the Torah created a far different situation concerning their awareness of offense and their ability to confess offense. The ability

32. For an excellent presentation of prayer in the ancient Near East see Miller, *They Cried*, 5–31.

33. Examples can be found in W. W. Hallo, "Individual Prayer in Sumerian: The Continuity of a Tradition," *JAOS* 88 (1968): 71–89.

34. Van der Toorn, *Family Religion*, 118. He is quick to caution, however, that this does not suggest that the Babylonians were incapable of feelings of guilt and self-esteem or that they lacked a concern for personal integrity.

35. This, of course, adds poignancy to Paul's observations about the law and its effects in Rom. 7:7–13.

to identify offense and the sense of having done wrong provides a fertile environment for guilt to emerge at a different level. As a result, in Israel guilt does not replace shame on the list of values, but it is promoted to somewhat more equal status.

Is there piety outside of the ritual/prayer matrix that contributes to a healthy relationship between a person and his or her god? Early analysis suggested that there was little evidence of piety in the Mesopotamian religious system.[36] More recent analysis of ancient anthropology has opened up the possibility that it may not be that piety is absent, but that it would be expressed in different ways at different levels. K. van der Toorn concludes: "The Babylonians did not have an introspective tradition, and had little sense of interiority. Subjectivity had not been invented yet. . . . Individual identity, in this view, is not what you are deep down, but what you manifest to be: it is public and social."[37] T. Abusch adds: "Human beings attain their identity in no small measure from their social contexts."[38]

The most relevant anthropological term to describe one's self-identity in Akkadian, *ṭemu*, is defined as "plan, inspiration, or intelligence as well as the verbal formulation that conveys or expresses these."[39] This is not "self" in the sense of "interiority." Abusch concludes: "The Mesopotamian did not formulate his own personal psychology primarily in the form of internal categories; rather he objectified and externalized major aspects of self."[40] In that sense, soul and self are external identity constructs rather than internal ones.

In Egyptian thinking, anthropology had some aspects that differed from Mesopotamia. One could speak of the *ba*-soul and the *ka*-soul.[41] Assmann labels this anthropology as "constellative":

> A person comes into being, lives, grows, and exists by building up such a sphere of social and bodily "constellations." A constellative anthropology stresses the ties, roles, and functions that bind the constituent parts

36. A. L. Oppenheim, *Letters from Mesopotamia* (Chicago: University of Chicago Press, 1967), 29.

37. Van der Toorn, *Family Religion*, 116–17. See also D. C. Snell, "The Invention of the Individual," in *Companion to the Ancient Near East*, ed. D. Snell (Oxford: Blackwell, 2005), 357–69.

38. Abusch, "Ghost and God," 381.

39. Ibid., 378. He suggests that through a series of wordplays the human *ṭemu* had been granted by the blood of the slain deity that was used in the creation of human beings (371).

40. Ibid., 380.

41. See definitions in Baines, "Society," 145; Morenz, *Egyptian Religion*, 157 (*ba*), and 170 (*ka*); and entries in *OEAE*. Basically the *ba* is the person's essence, while the *ka* is the vital force.

together. It abhors the ideas of isolation, solitude, self-sufficiency, and independence, and considers them symptoms of death, dissolution, and destruction. Life is interdependence, interconnection, and communication within those webs of interaction and interlocution that constitute reality.[42]

He draws a tight relationship between the individual's sense of self and the conditions of society in which he lives. "The Egyptian individual is dependent on social coherence in order to be able to maintain his personal coherence. The Egyptian ideal is constellative integratedness, which depends on both the person's connective virtues and the social conditions."[43] Assmann concludes with the statement that Egyptian culture "constructs the person in terms of plurality."[44]

Though the differences between Egyptian and Mesopotamian anthropology are readily observable in the details, the broader similarity exists in the outward, social, communal orientation of self-perception. If this is indeed the way that ancient Near Eastern peoples thought, we should consider whether Israelites shared this same foundation in their anthropology. Cultural foundations found in cosmology, ontology, and anthropology are not matters of revelation in the biblical literature. The basic defaults from the common cognitive environment are in place and generally represent the way Israelites thought. Certain modifications may have come about as a result of their theology, but the foundations show little evidence of innovation.

In biblical texts piety is more related to the *nephesh* ("soul, self") than to the *leb* ("heart"). The Hebrew usage of *nephesh* is paralleled by the semantic range of the cognates found in Akkadian (*napištu*) and Ugaritic (*npš*). In neither of those literatures, however, is it well established as an anthropological term such as can be found in Hebrew.[45] The LXX often translates *nephesh* with *psychē*, but studies have indicated that it is likely following pre-Platonic use of the noun, which is remarkably close to the Hebrew usage of *nephesh*.[46]

Perhaps among the most familiar expressions of piety in the Old Testament are the Psalms that speak of the *nephesh* thirsting or longing for God (Pss. 42:2; 63:2; 119:20, 81; 143:6; cf. Isa. 26:8). H. Seebass concludes that these are expressions of "life" longing for Yahweh, who

42. J. Assmann, "Dialogue Between Self and Soul: Papyrus Berlin 3024," in *Self, Soul and Body*, ed. Baumgarten, Assmann, and Stroumsa, 386.
43. Ibid., 401.
44. Ibid., 403.
45. Seebass, *TDOT* 9:499–503.
46. *TDOT* 9:503.

is the source of life.[47] Just as we spoke previously of the need of connectiveness to society, in Israel there is a need of vibrant connectiveness to
God.[48] "A person does not *have* a vital self but *is* a vital self."[49] Human
vitality finds its source in God.[50] This vitality remains something that
is exterior rather than interior, but at the same time offers a dimension
not observable in the ancient Near East.

In the ancient world, Israel included, piety was expressed by outward
acts more than by inner feelings of devotion, awe, or adoration. It was
not so much an inner attitude of spirituality, but an exterior expression of oneself in acts that reflected the religious values of the culture.
For the ancient Near East these were typically social, public acts.
Additionally in Israel we find evidence of their need to be connected
to the vitality of life from God. This understanding of religious duty
may offer alternative interpretations of some biblical passages. Just
as we should avoid imposing our ontology and cosmology on Israel,
we should also avoid imposing our anthropology on them and their
texts. This is not a matter of Israel "borrowing" from their neighbors,
but a reflection of concepts that Israel held in common with the world
around them.

The Role of Ethics and Morality

Definitions of ethics and morality are variable depending on the source,
and at times the terms are viewed as synonymous.[51] I will use "morality"
to refer to the behavior that results from inner convictions about right
and wrong, and "ethics" to refer to those actions that represent attempts
to conform to the best expectations of society.[52] Obviously, there is significant overlap and it is not always easy to determine what motivates
behavior. Given the anthropological assessment offered above, it would
be logical to question whether, within such an exteriorized perception
of self as is evidenced in the ancient Near East, there could be such a
thing as morality as I have defined it. Information is available in primary
sources such as exhortations that occur throughout the literature and

47. *TDOT* 9:508.
48. Assmann, "Dialogue," 400–401.
49. *TDOT* 9:512. Of course, this is also true of God, who is described in numerous
passages as having a *nephesh* (516–17).
50. *TDOT* 9:508.
51. See Baines, "Society," 130–31, for some discussion of the terminology.
52. In that sense we are not speaking of ethics as the modern discipline. Instead, ethics
will speak of the exterior element of connectivity while morality will be used to refer to
the interior elements. I grant that these definitions are arguable and perhaps prejudicial,
but I beg the reader's indulgence as I use them to address the issues.

Comparative Exploration: Religion of Abraham

The information that has been presented here concerning family religion in the ancient Near East now offers us a new perspective for exploring the religious experience of Abraham.

T. Jacobsen has identified the primary development within Mesopotamian religion during the second millennium as the idea of a "personal god," which van der Toorn has shown is to be understood as the equivalent to the family god.[1] Typically the role of personal god was played by minor deities,[2] though it is not impossible that the great cosmic deities could so function. In return for obedience and worship, these deities provided for the well-being of their worshipers.

> Close and personal relations—relations such as he had to the authorities in his family: father, mother, older brother and sister—the individual had only to one deity, to his personal god. The personal god was usually some minor deity in the pantheon who took a special interest in a man's family or had taken a fancy to the man himself. In a sense, and probably this is the original aspect, the personal god appears as the personification of a man's luck and success.[3]

It is clear from the Mesopotamian texts that this deity was not worshiped exclusively, but he did dominate the personal aspect of the individual's religious practice. "To his personal god, then, before any other a man owed worship and obedience."[4]

While this bears little resemblance to philosophical monotheism, it may have often taken the appearance of a practical monotheism. It is this trend more than any other that characterizes the period during which the patriarchs emerged from Mesopotamia.

The Hebrew Bible makes clear that Abraham's monotheism was not part of his religious heritage. Abraham was of general Semitic stock described in the Pentateuch as "Aramaean" (Gen. 25:20; 28:5; Deut. 26:5). Joshua 24:2 and 14 assert that the relatives of Abraham, including his father, served other gods, and the text of Genesis gives us no reason to question that assessment. Jacob has to urge his company to put away their other gods (Gen. 35:2–4), and *teraphim*, the images of the ancestral family gods,[5] are important in Laban's religious practices (Gen. 31). It is clear, then, that the biblical record does not attribute monotheism of any sort to the family of Abraham. In addition, we would search in vain for any passage in which Abraham or any of the patriarchs deny the existence of other gods. Nevertheless, the perspective of the biblical text is that all of the worship of Abraham that is recorded is focused on a single deity, though that deity is called by different names. The Bible, however, nowhere explicitly insists that this is the only God that Abraham ever worshiped. It can be safely inferred from the biblical data that Abraham showed a distinct preferential loyalty for a single god.

Is it possible that Abraham's perception of Yahweh/El Shaddai would have been similar to the typical Mesopotamian's perception of his personal deity? The way in which Abraham and his God interact would certainly suit the paradigm of relationship with a personal god in Mesopotamia. Yahweh provides for Abraham and protects him, while obedience and loyalty are given in return. One major difference, however, is that our clearest picture of the personal god in Mesopotamia comes from the many laments that are offered as individuals seek favors from deity or complain about his neglect of them. There is no hint of this in Abraham's approach to Yahweh. In the depiction in the text, Abraham maintains an elevated view of deity that is much more characteristic of the overall biblical view of deity than it is of the Mesopotamian perspective. On the whole, however, it is not impossible, and may even be likely, that Abraham's understanding of his relationship to Yahweh, in the beginning at least, was similar to the Mesopotamian idea of the personal god. In Mesopotamian language, Abraham would have been described as having "acquired a god."[6] That he was led to a new land and separated from his father's household would have effectively cut any ties with previous deities (located in city and family), and opened the way for Yahweh to be understood as the only deity to which Abraham had any obligation. By making a break with his land, his family, and his inheritance, Abraham was also breaking all of his religious ties. In his new land Abraham would have no territorial gods; as a new people he would have brought no family gods; having left his country he would have no national or city gods; and it was Yahweh who filled this void, becoming the "God of Abraham, Isaac, and Jacob," the "God of the Fathers."[7] But it is only in Israel, Jacobsen observes, that the idea of the personal god made the transition from the personal realm to the national realm.[8] Van der Toorn adds, "Family religion was the ground from which national religion eventually sprang."[9]

1. Van der Toorn, *Family Religion*, 3–4.
2. Ibid., 78.
3. T. Jacobsen, "Mesopotamia," in H. Frankfort, H. A. Frankfort, J. A. Wilson, and T. Jacobsen, *The Intellectual Adventure of Ancient Man* (Chicago: University of Chicago Press, 1946), 203; cf. Abusch, "Ghost and God," 382.
4. Jacobsen, "Mesopotamia," 204.
5. T. Lewis, "Teraphim," *DDD*, 844–50; K. van der Toorn, "The Nature of the Biblical Teraphim in the Light of the Cuneiform Evidence," *CBQ* 52 (1990): 203–22.
6. Van der Toorn, *Family Religion*, 113; Jacobsen, *Treasures of Darkness*, 155–56.
7. Van der Toorn, *Family Religion*, 72–73.
8. Jacobsen, *Treasures of Darkness*, 164.
9. Van der Toorn, *Family Religion*, 265.

the hymns that address behavior.[53] The line connecting social (ethical) responsibility and customs on the one hand and moral integrity on the other is not ostensibly crossed in their minds. For example, strict rules may dictate that prostitutes be unveiled, or observations may even be made about the social disintegration that could result from prostitution, but no consideration is given concerning the immorality of prostitution.[54] M. Dandamayev sums this up with the observation: "In ancient polytheistic societies, there existed no dogmatic religions with firmly fixed norms, and as a result of this there emerged various modifications of the same religious conceptions."[55]

53. W. G. Lambert, "Morals in Ancient Mesopotamia," *JEOL* 15 (1958): 184–96. Many of these are published in Lambert's *BWL*.
54. See discussion in Lambert, "Morals," 195.
55. Dandamayev, "State Gods," 40.

Van der Toorn does indeed follow the anthropological evidence to the conclusion that behavior was linked to the maintenance of the social order.[56] By my definitions, this suggests that there was no moral system, but a tightly regulated ethical system that had an exteriorized focus concerned with maintaining order. Lambert draws a similar distinction between the value of morality and of order: "Everything in the universe, material or immaterial, human or divine, was laid down by decrees. Man's duty was to conform to these regulations. The contrast was not, as among the Hebrews, between morally right and wrong, but between order and disorder. Civilization was the ideal: the well-ordered society."[57]

Bottéro echoes this same direction of thought as he sees the Isra-elites as the ones who replaced the obligation to care for the gods with moral obligation.

> Did *morality*, honest and righteous behavior, have an authentic religious and cultural value, a place in the practice of religion, a direct influence on the gods? We have never found any response, in all of our documentation, to such a question, a question that we ask ourselves from our own religious and "biblical" point of view. The ancient Mesopotamians never overtly concerned themselves with or imagined such preoccupations, which are so familiar to us. This must have been one of Moses's great revolutions in Israel: to replace the purely material maintenance of the gods with the single and sole "liturgical" obligation in life to obey a moral law, thereby truly rendering to God the only homage worthy of him.[58]

Similar observations can be made concerning Egypt, where the focus is on the concept of *maat*. *Maat* is the goal of existence for both human-ity and the gods. It is the ideal that all beings try to achieve. J. Assmann translates it "connective justice" and defines it as "the principle that forms individuals into communities and that gives their actions meaning and direction by ensuring that good is rewarded and evil punished."[59] He elaborates that it is "the spirit of mutual understanding, solidarity, and community that is the indispensable foundation of civil society."[60] It is the foundation of their sense of ethics.

In the ancient Near East, then, we could say that the people are in-formed by a socially attuned conscience. As a result, we could conclude

56. Van der Toorn, *Family Religion*, 94–95.
57. W. G. Lambert, "Destiny and Divine Intervention in Babylon and Israel," *OtSt* 17 (1972): 65–72, quotation on 67; see also G. Buccellati, "Ethics and Piety in the Ancient Near East," *CANE* 3:1685–96.
58. Bottéro, *Religion*, 169.
59. J. Assmann, *The Mind of Egypt* (New York: Metropolitan, 1996), 126–27, with discus-sion through many following pages as he traces the concept through various stages.
60. Assmann, "Dialogue," 395–402.

that ethical responsibility, not morality, is the basis of conscience in the ancient Near East.[61]

In general, norms included in each of the ethical systems in the ancient Near East, including Israel, can be seen as having some level of universal continuity,[62] though they may be supported by varying senses of self and may result in various mores or legal formulations within society. At issue for our purposes is the extent to which the norms of behavior are configured in ancient societies in religious terms or are motivated by religious obligation. In studies done in the twentieth century, it was not unusual to see a reductionism that suggested that the Mesopotamians knew only a ritual obligation with no sense of moral and ethical responsibility before the gods.[63] This perspective has been modified as a more nuanced understanding has emerged from more recent studies.[64] Van der Toorn identifies religious obligation in Mesopotamia not, ultimately, in terms of propositional norms, but in terms of "fear of the god."

> Religion, in Babylonian parlance, is "fear of the god" (*palaḥ ilim*). This term is not concerned with the acceptance of a set of propositions relating to metaphysical realities, but with proper religious and social behaviour. "Fear of the god" is tangible in acts of human kindness and in dutiful observance of the cultic worship of the gods. It is the safeguard of social decency: as soon as people forget their gods they start using uncivilized language. "Fear of the god" is not belief (belief being tacitly taken for granted) but the manifestation of an attitude of reverence for the gods and love of one's fellow human beings.[65]

In general in the ancient Near East, people gain the favor of the god by serving the god, which people were created to do. In this regard, one can find pertinent illustrations in either Egyptian or Mesopotamian literature. The Egyptian *Instruction of Merikare* advises that one should "Make ample the daily offerings" because "It profits him who does it."[66] Yet toward the end of the piece the exhortation shifts from ritual to ethics:

61. Van der Toorn, *Sin and Sanction*, 92.
62. Note the development by C. S. Lewis in *Mere Christianity* (London: G. Bles, 1952) and the expression of the inverse in Rom. 1.
63. Oppenheim, *Ancient Mesopotamia*, 29, 176.
64. Van der Toorn, *Sin and Sanction*, 39.
65. Van der Toorn, *Family Religion*, 106–7. It is interesting that Akkadian has no word translated "faith," and the word translated "believe, trust" (*qâpu*) does not take deity as its object.
66. *AEL* 1:102.

Make firm your station in the graveyard,
By being upright, by doing justice,
Upon which men's hearts rely.
The loaf of the upright is preferred to the ox of the evildoer.[67]

Despite the importance of ethics in Egyptian life, S. Morenz can still conclude: "piety and ritual are the flesh and blood of Egyptian religion."[68] Yet ethical behavior is connected to the gods through the central concept of *maat*. Judgment in the afterlife was in accordance with *maat*.[69] The ways of *maat* are not revealed by the gods but can be taught and learned through experience. It is more comparable to wisdom than to righteousness, though the latter is not excluded.

The relationship between ethics and service to the gods is forged in the context of the role of humanity in cosmos and society. Order was the highest value among gods and humans. Ritual supported order in the cosmos; ethical behavior supported order in society, which in turn contributed to order in the cosmos. Preservation of cosmic and social order gained the favor of the gods. Thus an ethical system that preserved order was expected by the gods and violations were punishable by the gods.

In contrast, any sense of moral rectitude in the abstract can only be achieved from reaching outside of the experiential parameters of cosmos and civilization.[70] In other words, an abstraction of moral right and wrong can only take root in the character of God. There was a strong sense of ethical obligation in the ancient world as one of the principal elements of order, which was in turn the goal of religious behavior.[71] But the abstractions of right and wrong had not been invented yet. Therefore it was left to Israel to develop the theology of morality (in the restricted ways that I have defined it). This development came through a combination of (1) the instigation of guilt through the Torah, thus opening up an interiorized anthropology; and (2) the mandate to imitate God, thus relocating the foundation of ethical responsibility (in the character of God) and thereby fostering a sense of abstract right and wrong.[72] Israel

67. *AEL* 1:106.

68. Morenz, *Egyptian Religion*, 110.

69. Ibid., 113–30.

70. The Egyptian word often translated as "wrong," *izfet*, means "disorder." Cf. Baines, "Society," 163.

71. Van der Toorn has provided an extensive investigation of the concerns about ethical conduct available in the literature from Mesopotamia in *Sin and Sanction*.

72. J. J. Finkelstein, "Bible and Babel: A Comparative Study of the Hebrew and Babylonian Religious Spirit," in *Essential Papers on Israel and the Ancient Near East*, ed. F. Greenspahn (New York: New York University Press, 1991), 371. The concept of conscience and interior feelings of guilt continue to be subjects of controversy. J. Milgrom seeks to

saw this not as their philosophical innovation, but as the result of reve-lation from God concerning what he was like and the implications of his character in their lives. This revelation provided knowledge, which then translated into a new level of awareness of sin that was unknown in the rest of the ancient world. Babylonians would sense sin based on how their consciences had been tuned by society. Israelites had additional elements informing their consciences.

H. W. F. Saggs has attempted to build a case that the life of an Israelite was more dominated by religion than that of a Mesopotamian counter-part.[73] That is probably not sustainable. The key difference occurs in what was construed as serving the god. In the ancient Near East at large this service was accomplished in terms of caring for the god through ritual and preserving order in society and the cosmos. In Israel it was accomplished by obeying the Torah, which showed them how to love the Lord their God with all their hearts and minds and strength and be holy as Yahweh was holy. The high ideal of imitating the deity did not exist in any other ancient Near Eastern culture.[74] Ethical behavior had its foundations in the nature of society, not in the nature of the gods.

Comparative Exploration: Commandments 1–4

No contrasts between the religious beliefs of Israel concerning Yahweh and those of the ancient Near East can be clearer than those that emerge from the first four commandments of the Deca-logue.[1] Yet at the same time, our study of the religious ideas and practices of the ancient Near East has put us in a position to understand these commandments in a different light as the texts of the ancient Near East have given us windows into the cognitive environment that dominated the cultures of the time.

Commandment 1

As we have seen, the gods in the ancient Near East operated in a pantheon and de-cisions were made in the divine assembly. In addition, the principal deities typically had consorts. The lifestyle and operations system for deity, then, was a community experience. The destinies of the gods were decreed in assembly as were the destinies of kings, cities, temples, and people. The business of the gods was carried out in the presence of other gods.

---

establish a sense of conscience and guilt among the Israelites in his lexical study of *'asham* in *Cult and Conscience* (Leiden: Brill, 1976). Van der Toorn contests his findings in *Sin and Sanction*, 92–93.

73. H. W. F. Saggs, *The Encounter with the Divine in Mesopotamia and Israel* (London: Athlone, 1978), 153–88.

74. Finkelstein, "Bible and Babel," 368–69.

Such information suggests a straightforward comparative understanding of the first commandment. The Israelites were being commanded not to construe Yahweh as operating within a community of gods. There was to be no thought of pantheon or consort. He does not function as the head of a pantheon with a divine assembly. In short, he works alone. The significance of this is that the pantheon/divine assembly concept carried with it the idea of distribution of power among many divine beings. The first commandment becomes a simple statement that Yahweh's power is absolute, not being distributed among other deities or limited by the will of the assembly.

Israel's thinking was to be distinct from the nations around them. That is the very point of the prohibition. But the text can be misunderstood if the interpreter is not aware of what exactly is being rejected. The first commandment is not just promoting monolatry; it is getting at monotheism another way. Although it does not say explicitly that no other gods exist, it does remove them from the presence of Yahweh. If Yahweh does not share power, authority, or jurisdiction with them, they are not gods in any meaningful sense of the word.[2] The first commandment does not insist that the other gods are nonexistent, but that they are powerless; it disenfranchises them. It does not simply say that they should not be worshiped; it leaves them with no status worthy of worship.[3]

Commandment 2

In Israel the temple housed the presence of Yahweh, but did not mediate that presence. The ark mediated the presence of Deity in a limited fashion, but not in the same way that an image did. It did not contain the divine essence. Furthermore, it did not mediate revelation or worship.

The priests served a mediatorial role, but their role was to present the offerings on behalf of the people rather than to receive the offerings on behalf of the Deity.

We can now interpret the second commandment in light of the ancient Near Eastern data. No image is to be used as the mediator of revelation or presence from Deity to people, or as the mediator of worship from the people to Deity. The prohibition particularly excludes that sort of worship that is understood as meeting the needs of the Deity through the image. This differs from the traditional interpretations of the commandment in that rather than insisting that God is transcendent or not to be replaced by material things, it specifically targets mediation.[4]

Commandment 3

The name is equivalent to the identity of the Deity and expresses the Deity's essence,[5] and the divine identity can be commandeered for illicit use. We are familiar with identity theft today, when a symbol such as a credit card number or social security number can be used to abuse or

Photo 12 Ashkelon Calf

exploit the economic power or authority of an individual. Commandment three works on the same premise and prohibits divine identity theft.

In light of this information, the third commandment when read as ancient Near Eastern literature concerns how Yahweh's power/authority was not to be perceived—people were to recognize it by refraining from attempts to control or misuse it. It was not to be thought of as an efficacious symbol that could be used to pursue one's self-interests.

Commandment 4

For several decades it was popular to posit ancient Near Eastern precursors to Sabbath observance.[6] But it is now widely acknowledged that no such observance has yet been found. The key to understanding the Sabbath rest for people is found in the Sabbath rest for Yahweh on the seventh day of creation, as the command in Exodus tells us. The concept of divine rest can, in turn, be elucidated by ancient Near Eastern literature, which demonstrates that deity's rest is achieved in a temple, generally as a result of chaos having been dispelled. The rest, while it represents *disengagement* from any process of establishing order (whether through conflict with other deities or not), is more importantly an expression of *engagement* as the deity takes his place at the helm to maintain an ordered, secure, and stable cosmos. Six aspects of divine rest in the ancient Near East culled from primary and secondary sources will illustrate the nature of the concept.

1. The divine rest is disturbed by rebellion

In *Enuma Elish*:

> Apsu made ready to speak
> Saying to her, Tiamat, in a loud voice,

Their [the gods'] behavior is noisome to me
By day I have no rest, at night I do not sleep
I wish to put an end to their behavior, to do away with it!
Let silence reign that we may sleep.[7]
He [Marduk] caused a wave and it roiled Tiamat
Tiamat was roiled, churning day and night
The gods, finding no rest, bore the brunt of each wind.[8]

2. The divine rest is achieved after conflict

In *Enuma Elish* after Ea kills Apsu and captures Mummu:

> He founded his dwelling upon Apsu,
> He secured Mummu, held (him) firm by a lead rope,
> After Ea had captured and vanquished his foes,
> Had won the victory over his opponents,
> In his chamber, in profound quiet, he rested.[9]

3. The divine rest is achieved after order-bringing acts of creation[10]

In the *Memphite Theology*:

> So has Ptah come to rest after his making everything and every divine speech as well, having given birth to the gods, having made their towns, having founded their nomes, having set the gods in their cult places, having made sure their bread offerings, having founded their shrines, having modeled their bodies to what contents them.[11]

4. The divine rest is achieved in the temple[12]

Marduk's temple in *Enuma Elish* is described to the gods:

> When you go up from Apsu to
> assembly,
> Let your stopping places be there to
> receive you.
> When you come down from heaven
> to [assembly],
> Let your stopping places be there to
> receive you.[13]

This concept of rest can also be illustrated by evaluating the names of temples. Those built at Ur by Warad-Sin and Rim-Sin are called '*ki-tuš ni-dub-bu-da-ni*' ("his dwelling place which will provide rest").[14]

5. The divine rest is characterized by ongoing control and stability (rather than simply sleeping peacefully, which is another concept in the ancient Near East)

Marduk's intentions in *Enuma Elish*:
> A house I shall build, let it be the
> abode of my pleasure.
> Within it I shall establish its holy
> place,
> I shall appoint my (holy) chambers,
> I shall establish my kingship.[15]

Marduk's thirteenth name in *Enuma Elish* indicates his control by his sustaining of rest:

> Tutu is he who effected their
> restoration,
> He shall purify their shrines that
> they may be at rest,
> He shall devise the spell that the
> gods may be calm.
> Should they rise in anger, they
> shall turn back.
> He shall be supreme in the assembly
> of the gods his fathers.
> No one among the gods shall make
> himself equal to him.[16]

N.-E. Andreasen concludes, "We can say then that the gods seek rest, and that their rest implies stability for the world order. The gods rest because they want to see the world ordered."[17] He sees a reflection of this same concept in Psalm 132:13–14:

> For the Lord has chosen Zion,
> He has desired it for his dwelling:
> "This is my resting place for ever
> and ever;
> Here I will sit enthroned, for I have
> desired it."

Verses 15–18 conclude the psalm by enumerating all that God will provide from his throne as he assures the stability of the king and the people. The order in the cosmos is sustained not by God's being inactive, but precisely by his continued activity.[18]

6. In the ancient Near East the divine rest is achieved in part by the gods' creation of people to work in their place and on their behalf. A. Millard recognized that the biblical viewpoint represented a stark contrast to this picture in that in the Old Testament the people work for their own benefit and provision, rather than to meet the needs of God or to do his work for him.[19] They are commanded to share the rest of God on the Sabbath, not to participate in it per se, but in order to recognize his work of bringing and maintaining order. His control is represented in his rest and is recognized by yielding for the day their own attempts to provide for themselves.[20]

Having now conducted a summary study of the first four commandments, I can propose that the understanding provided by cultural and comparative studies aligns them in two sets of juxtaposed commandments. The first set juxtaposed commandments 1 and 2 as dealing with Yahweh's mode of operating in the two realms.

Photo 13 Taanach Cult Stand

- Commandment 1 concerned how Yahweh was not to be perceived as operating in the divine realm—no distribution of authority to other divinities.
- Commandment 2 concerned how Yahweh was not to be perceived as operating in the human realm—no iconographic mediator of his presence, revelation, or of worship offered to him.

The second set juxtaposed commandments 3 and 4 as dealing with the recognition of Yahweh's power.

- Commandment 3 concerned how Yahweh's power/authority was not to be perceived—people were to recognize it by refraining from attempts to control it.
- Commandment 4 concerned how Yahweh's power/authority was to be perceived—people were to recog-

nize it by refraining from attempts to control their own lives on the Sabbath.

In commandments 1–3 the Israelites are being warned not to perceive Yahweh in the manner in which the gods were perceived in the cultures around them. For example, Assmann identifies three major dimensions of contact with the divine in Egyptian religion: cosmic (the sphere of divine action), cultic (deities' representation in cult statues), and mythic (how the names of the gods are elaborated into stories about the gods as they fulfill their names).[21] These transparently relate to the first three commandments as Yahweh is seen as existing within a different sphere of action, is not represented in cult statue, and whose name is not to be elaborated into myth. Commandment 4 is positive rather than negative because there is nothing like a Sabbath observance in the ancient Near East. Nevertheless, our comprehension in this case remains dependent on the concept of divine rest as understood in the ancient Near East.

1. Commandments 5–9 are explored in Mesopotamian contexts in van der Toorn, *Sin and Sanction*, 13–20, though the study is descriptive rather than comparative.

2. This coincides with the ontology of the ancient Near East that we have discussed—something was not considered to exist if it had not been assigned a name, a place, and a function. If this concept holds, other gods, given no place or function, would not be considered to exist.

3. Wright approaches this: "The fundamental thrust of the verse is not Yahweh's sole deity, but Yahweh's sole sovereignty over Israel" (D. Wright, *The Disposal of Impurity*, SBLDS 101 [Atlanta: Scholars Press, 1987], 15–74, quotation on 68).

4. This was precisely an issue that Israel struggled with as early as Mt. Sinai. There Moses had been the human mediator of God's presence and revelation. When he appeared to have left them, they substituted the gold calf as a replacement mediator of God's presence.

5. J. Assmann, *The Search for God in Ancient Egypt* (Ithaca: Cornell University Press, 2001), 83–84.

6. See a helpful summary in J. J. Stamm and M. E. Andrew, *The Ten Commandments in Recent Research*, Studies in Biblical Theology 2/2 (London: SCM, 1967), 90–95.

7. *COS* 1.111, tablet 1:35–40.

8. *COS* 1.111, tablet 1:108–10.

9. *COS* 1.111, tablet 1:71–75.

10. B. Batto, "The Sleeping God: An Ancient Near Eastern Motif of Divine Sovereignty," *Bib* 68 (1987): 153–77, esp. 156.

11. *COS* 1.15, cols. 60–61.

12. The material in support of this is conveniently gathered together by Victor Hurowitz, *I Have Built You an Exalted House*, JSOTSup 115 (repr. Sheffield: JSOT Press, 1992), 330–31. Other key articles are M. Weinfeld, "Sabbath, Temple, and the Enthronement of the Lord—The Problem of the Sitz im Leben of Genesis 1.1–2.3," in *Mélanges bibliques et orientaux en l'honneur de M. Henri Cazelles*, ed. A. Caquot and M. Delcor, AOAT 212 (Neukirchen-Vluyn: Neukirchener Verlag, 1981), 501–12; S. Loewenstamm, "Biblical Studies in the Light of Akkadian Texts," in *From Babylon to Canaan* (Jerusalem: Magnes, 1992),

256–64; P. Machinist, "Rest and Violence in the Poem of Erra," *JAOS* 103 (1983): 221–26; Batto, "Sleeping God"; John Lundquist, "What Is a Temple? A Preliminary Typology," in *The Quest for the Kingdom of God: Studies in Honor of G. E. Mendenhall*, ed. H. B. Huffmon, F. A. Spina, and A. R. W. Green (Winona Lake, IN: Eisenbrauns, 1983), 205–19.

13. *COS* 1.111, tablet V: 125–28.

14. Hurowitz, *I Have Built*, 330.

15. *COS* 1.111, tablet V: 122–24.

16. *COS* 1.111, tablet VII: 9–14; *FDD* 45.

17. N.-E. Andreasen, *The Old Testament Sabbath: A Tradition-Historical Investigation*, SBLDS (Missoula, MT: Society of Biblical Literature, 1972), 182.

18. Ibid., 183.

19. A. R. Millard, "A New Babylonian 'Genesis' Story," *TynBul* 18 (1967): 3–18.

20. J. Durham, *Exodus*, WBC (Waco: Word, 1987), 290; and P. Craigie, *Book of Deuteronomy*, NICOT (Grand Rapids: Eerdmans, 1976), 157, come to a similar conclusion in general, but do not show any use of the ancient Near Eastern literature to get there and therefore can do little more than make a general statement.

21. Assmann, *Search for God*, 8.

One final consideration in this category that highlights a difference between Israel and the rest of the ancient Near East concerns the issue of disinterested righteousness. If ethical behavior has an exterior foundation, a person behaves ethically because of the consequences—rewards or punishments—that are built into the system, whether by society or the gods. Disinterested righteousness can only be a viable option if a more abstract sense of righteousness exists. The adversary's question in Job asked whether Job served God for nothing. Though Job's friends encourage him to take the Mesopotamian path of appeasement (confess anything to restore favor with deity), Job maintains his integrity (see his conclusion in Job 27:1–5) demonstrating that he did possess an abstract interiorized standard of righteousness apart from a system of consequences.

None of the Mesopotamian literature that deals with the pious sufferer shows this dimension of thinking. These individuals can only claim that they have done everything they know to do in terms of ritual and ethical responsibility. They have no basis to proclaim their innocence, only their ignorance and confusion. They make no attempt to call deity into legal disputation—they only plead for mercy. The book of Job therefore stands as stark testimony to the differences in perception between Israel and the ancient Near East as it seeks to demonstrate that there *is* such a thing as disinterested righteousness.

Joyful Pursuit of Deity

What characterized the religiosity of ancient peoples? Did they delight in their gods? Did they find their religious experience to be psychologically rewarding? Bottéro describes Mesopotamian sentiment as reflecting fear rather than exaltation. "The divine, in its multiple, personalized presentations, was above all considered to be something grandiose, inaccessible, dominating, and to be feared."[75] He observes that the gods were not the object of enthusiastic pursuit. The people sought the gods for protection and assistance, not for relationship. "One submitted to them, one feared them, one bowed down and trembled before them: one did not 'love' or 'like' them."[76] Yet this must be qualified somewhat by the recognition of a certain level of relational rhetoric in the ways that people interacted with the gods. This element is perhaps more evident in Egypt than in Mesopotamia, and perhaps more in the Amarna period in Egypt than in other periods.

75. Bottéro, *Religion*, 37.
76. Ibid.

Part 4

Cosmos

7

Cosmic Geography

Cosmic geography concerns how people envision the shape and structure of the world around them. According to our modern cosmic geography, we live on a sphere of continents surrounded by oceans. We believe that this sphere is part of a solar system of planets that revolve around the sun, which is a star. Our planet rotates as well, and the moon revolves around our planet. Our solar system is part of a galaxy, which along with many other galaxies make up the universe. What we perceive as stars are far away, and some are other galaxies while many others are suns. That this seems so elementary and basic shows how deeply rooted it is in our understanding of ourselves. Everyone has a cosmic geography and knows what it is—it is second nature.

The point is that a culture's cosmic geography plays a significant role in shaping its worldview and offers explanations for the things we observe and experience. For example, notice a few of the implications of the cosmic geography just described:

- It suggests our relative insignificance in the vastness of the universe.
- It is the basis for understanding weather and time.
- It works on the premise that cosmic geography is physical and material.
- It operates with consistency and predictability based on physical properties and laws of motion.

This cosmic geography has been deduced over centuries through a process of observation, experimentation, and deduction. We are fully convinced that it is "true," though minor adjustments take place all the time. It is the result of what we call "science."

In the ancient world they also had a cosmic geography that was just as intrinsic to their thinking, just as fundamental to their worldview, just as influential in every aspect of their lives, and just as true in their minds. And it differs from ours at every point. If we aspire to understand the culture and literature of the ancient world, whether Canaanite, Babylonian, Egyptian, or Israelite, it is therefore essential that we understand their cosmic geography.[1] Despite variations from one ancient Near Eastern culture to another, there are certain elements that characterize all of them.

What kept the sky suspended above the earth and held back the heavenly waters? What kept the sea from overwhelming the land? What prevented the earth from sinking into the cosmic waters? These were the questions people asked in the ancient world, and the answers they arrived at are embodied in the cosmic geography. Egyptians, Mesopotamians, Canaanites, Hittites, and Israelites all thought of the cosmos in terms of tiers: the earth was in the middle with the heavens above and the netherworld beneath. In general people believed that there was a single continent that was disk-shaped. This continent had high mountains at the edges that held up the sky, which they thought was somewhat solid (whether it was envisioned as a tent or as a more substantial dome). The heavens where deity dwelt were above the sky, and the netherworld was beneath the earth. In some of the Mesopotamian literature the heavens were understood to be made up of three superimposed disks with pavements of various materials.[2] What they observed led them to conclude that the sun and the moon moved in roughly the same spheres and in similar ways. The sun moved through the sky during the day and then moved during the night into the netherworld, where it traversed under the earth to its place of rising for the next day. The stars were engraved on the sky and moved in tracks through their ordained stations. Flowing all around this cosmos were the cosmic waters, which were held back by the sky, and on which the earth floated,

---

1. The most significant reference sources include W. Horowitz, *Mesopotamian Cosmic Geography* (Winona Lake, IN: Eisenbrauns, 1998); B. Janowski and B. Ego, *Das biblische Weltbild und seine altorientalischen Kontexte* (Tübingen: Mohr Siebeck, 2001); O. Keel, *The Symbolism of the Biblical World* (New York: Seabury, 1978); L. Stadelmann, *The Hebrew Conception of the World*, AnBib 39 (Rome: Biblical Institute Press, 1970); P. Seely, "The Firmament and the Water Above," *WTJ* 54 (1992): 31–46; idem, "The Geographical Meaning of 'Earth' and 'Seas' in Genesis 1:10," *WTJ* 59 (1997): 231–55; I. Cornelius, "The Visual Representation of the World in the Ancient Near East and the Hebrew Bible," *JNSL* 20/2 (1994): 193–218; J. E. Wright, "Biblical Versus Israelite Images of the Heavenly Realm," *JSOT* 93 (2001): 59–75; C. Blacker and M. Loewe, eds., *Ancient Cosmologies* (London: Allen & Unwin, 1975); D. Tsumura, *The Earth and the Waters in Genesis 1 and 2*, JSOTSup 83 (Sheffield: JSOT Press, 1989).

2. Details in Horowitz, *Mesopotamian Cosmic Geography*; brief treatment in Cornelius, "Visual Representation," 198, with citations.

though they conceived of the earth as supported on pillars. Precipitation originated from waters held back by the sky and fell to the earth through openings in the sky. Similar views of the structure of the cosmos were common throughout the ancient world and persisted in popular perception until the Copernican revolution and the Enlightenment.[3] These were not mathematically deduced realities, but the reality of how things looked to them. The language of the Old Testament reflects this view, and no texts in the Bible seek to correct or refute it.[4]

Beyond this physical description, it is important to realize that their cosmic geography was predominantly metaphysical and only secondarily physical/material. The role and manifestation of the gods in the cosmic geography was primary. For example, in Mesopotamian thinking, cables held by the gods connected the heavens and earth and held the sun in the sky.[5] In Egypt the sun god sailed in his barque across the heavens during the day and through the netherworld at night. The stars of the Egyptian sky were portrayed as emblazoned across the arched body of the sky goddess, who was held up by the god of the air. Egyptian art is more explicit than Mesopotamian art at portraying the divine powers behind the natural phenomena.[6]

Structure versus Function

In chapter 4 I presented the concept that ontology in the ancient world was more connected to function than to substance. In other words, something exists when it has a function, not when it takes up space or is a substance characterized by material properties. This applies to everything in the cosmos, where various elements come into being when they are given a role and function within the cosmos. The neglect of curiosity about the physical structure of the cosmos is therefore not simply a consequence of their inability to investigate their physical world. The physical aspects of the cosmos did not define its existence or its importance; they were merely the tools the gods used for carrying out their purposes. The purposes of the gods were of prime interest to them.

The Egyptian materials are most obvious in their depiction of this concept as the gods are portrayed as standing in for the physical ele-

---

3. Seely, "Geographical Meaning."

4. See a similar description based on biblical terminology drawing heavily on Prov. 8:24–29 in M. Fox, *Proverbs 1–9*, AB (New York: Doubleday, 2000), 281–82.

5. Horowitz, *Mesopotamian Cosmic Geography*, 120, 265; W. G. Lambert, "The Cosmology of Sumer and Babylon" in *Ancient Cosmologies*, ed. Blacker and Loewe, 62; see *Enuma Elish* V:59–68.

6. Cornelius, "Visual Representation," 196–97.

ments of the cosmos. Mesopotamian iconography is less consistent on this, though both the *kudurru*s (boundary markers) and the Shamash plaque (see cover illlustration) clearly portray this interrelationship. Even when the Mesopotamian texts discuss issues such as the structure of the heavens and speak of the three levels having three pavements of different sorts of stone (an obviously material statement), the real issue is which gods occupy each level.

Structure of the Heavens

The heavens were primarily the place where the gods dwelt. In Mesopotamian literature Adapa ascends there to meet with Anu. The heavenly temples of the great gods were located there. Variations permit one, three, or seven levels of heaven,[7] usually with the purpose of portraying distinct levels for the habitation of different deities relative to their hierarchical position within the pantheon.[8] In Mesopotamia they had theories regarding distances within the heavens[9] and the shape of the heavens. In Canaan they believed the gods lived at the tops of mountains, but this is not a contradiction because the heavens are at the tops of the mountains.

The Shamash plaque is particularly informative as it shows worshipers who, though physically in the earthly temple, view themselves before Shamash's heavenly throne. The heavenly waters arc bcneath his feet and the stars are shown in the sky across the bottom of the picture.[10] On a Babylonian *kudurru* (boundary marker) the symbols of the main celestial gods are portrayed in the top register, which represents the heavenly sphere.

In the Old Testament little is said about the geographical aspects of the heavens, mainly expressing that God dwells there and that he created them.[11]

Sky

The boundary between the heavens and the earth I will call the sky. Its main function is to hold back the waters above. Some mountains are identified as intersecting the sky and perhaps holding it up. In other

7. Current also in rabbinic literature (Midrash Rabbah, Deuteronomy); cf. Stadelmann, *Hebrew Conception*, 41.
8. Horowitz, *Mesopotamian Cosmic Geography*, 244–52.
9. Ibid., 177–88.
10. C. Woods, "The Sun-God Tablet of Nabu-apla-iddina Revisited," *JCS* 56 (2004): 23–103.
11. For discussion of a few scattered vague comments in the text, see Stadelmann, *Hebrew Conception*, 45–46.

contexts (e.g., *Enuma Elish*) there is no mention of what holds up the sky. Besides the sky being portrayed as a pavement of blue (Mesopotamian *saggilmud*-stone = blue/lapis/sapphire),[12] Mesopotamian literature at times suggests that it is some sort of skin.[13] It is represented by Nut in Egyptian iconography. In *Pyramid Text* 1040c the mountains hold up the sky, which can only happen if it is considered solid.[14] The Hebrew term used for "sky" (*raqiʻa*) is of unspecified material, but in at least one text the reference is to something solid (Ezek. 1:25–26).[15] We have no reason to suppose that the Israelites thought about the composition of the sky any differently than those around them. We know from Exodus 24:10 that they shared the idea of a pavement in God's abode—and it is even of sapphire, as in the Mesopotamian texts.

P. Seely has traced the developments of beliefs about the sky. He demonstrates that intertestamental and rabbinic speculation sometimes focused on the material that the *raqiʻa* was made of and how thick it was.[16] The church fathers likewise were united in their belief that the *raqiʻa* was solid.[17] Seely concludes: "Astonishing as it may seem to the modern mind, with very rare exceptions the idea that the sky is not solid is a distinctly modern one. Historical evidence shows that virtually everyone in the ancient world believed in a solid firmament."[18]

Weather and the Waters Above

The waters above (held back by the sky) are represented iconographically in the Mesopotamian Shamash plaque (see cover illustration) and a number of Egyptian paintings, particularly on sarcophagi.[19] In Mesopotamia Marduk assigns guards to keep the heavenly waters from flooding the earth.[20] These waters are the remnants of Tiamat's body, which was split

12. Horowitz, *Mesopotamian Cosmic Geography*, 263; cf. Exod. 24:10.

13. *Enuma Elish* IV:139–40; cf. Horowitz, *Mesopotamian Cosmic Geography*, 262, with support of *CAD* Š/1:22a but against *CAD* M/1:342a.

14. Seely, "Geographical Meaning," 233; see also *Pyramid Text* 299a. If wordplays are to be taken seriously, the Egyptians may have believed that the heavens were made of meteoric iron, since pieces of it occasionally fell to earth; see L. Lesko, "Ancient Egyptian Cosmogonies and Cosmology," in *Religion in Ancient Egypt*, ed. B. Shafer (Ithaca: Cornell University Press, 1991), 117.

15. See also Job 37:18 and Prov. 8:28, where rather than *raqiʻa*, the Hebrew word *shehaqim* is used. Stadelmann translated the term as referring to the high cirrus clouds (*Hebrew Conception*, 98), and by metonymy it can refer to the overcast sky.

16. P. Seely, "The Firmament and the Water Above, Part I: The Meaning of *raqiʻa* in Gen 1:6–8," *WTJ* 53 (1991): 236.

17. Ibid.

18. Ibid.

19. Keel, *Symbolism*, 35–47.

20. *Enuma Elish* IV:139–40; see Horowitz, *Mesopotamian Cosmic Geography*, 262.

to form the waters above and the waters below after she was defeated by Marduk. Egyptian texts refer to the heavenly ocean as *ḳbḥw-Ḥr*, the cool or upper waters of Horus.[21] The sun god's barque travels from horizon to horizon across this heavenly ocean. In the Old Testament the heavenly waters are sometimes called the *mabbul* above which Yahweh is enthroned (Ps. 29:10) and which were released in the time of Noah (Gen. 7:10).[22]

The concept of heavenly waters is the natural deduction to draw from the experience of precipitation.[23] Since moisture comes from the sky, there must be moisture up there. Thus the sky becomes the pivotal phenomenon associated with weather. The Mesopotamian imagery refers to "breasts of heaven" through which rain comes.[24] Ugaritic texts use the symbolism of the clouds serving as buckets to deliver the rain.[25] In both Egyptian and Mesopotamian thinking, entrance through the vault of the sky to become visible was made through gates. Sun, moon, stars, constellations, planets, and clouds all enter through such gates.[26] The Old Testament refers to these gates as "windows" (*'arabot*)[27] when they are only for rain, not for the celestial bodies. Job 38:22 also poetically speaks of storehouses for snow and hail. All precipitation (including dew; see Prov. 3:19–20) comes from above, and thus weather is regulated by the sky.

Celestial Bodies

Sun, moon, stars, and planets[28] were all considered in the same category and were believed to occupy the same region, the air, since they could be seen beneath the sky. Mesopotamians viewed the stars as engraved on the underside of the sky and assigned them paths of movement (three tracks, the paths of Anu, Enlil, and Ea) with the heavens divided into thirty-six zones.[29] Constellations were recognized and named, including the zodiacal constellations, though the concept of the zodiac was a later development.[30]

21. Keel, *Symbolism*, 37.
22. Both Pss. 104:13 and 148:4 refer to waters above but do not use *mabbul*.
23. Horowitz, *Mesopotamian Cosmic Geography*, 262.
24. Ibid., 262–63.
25. Stadelmann, *Hebrew Conception*, 132.
26. Horowitz, *Mesopotamian Cosmic Geography*, 266, summarizes and provides bibliography in n. 33.
27. Gen. 7:11; 8:2; 2 Kings 7:2, 19; Isa. 24:18; Mal. 3:10. See extensive discussion in Stadelmann, *Hebrew Conception*, 120–26. For similar terminology in Ugaritic, see M. Weinfeld, "Gen. 7:11, 8:1,2 Against the Background of Ancient Near Eastern Tradition," *Die Welt des Orients* 9 (1978): 242–48.
28. Mercury, Mars, Venus, Jupiter, and Saturn were the planets they recognized.
29. Horowitz, *Mesopotamian Cosmic Geography*, 256.
30. Stadelmann, *Hebrew Conception*, 87.

In Egypt, Mesopotamia, and Canaan, when the sun set in the west it entered the netherworld, where it passed from west to east to rise again in the morning. In Babylonian thought Shamash traveled through the netherworld dispensing food and light to its denizens. Egyptian thinking involved more trauma. As Re travels on his night barque with stars serving as his oarsmen, he is threatened by various demons. The Old Testament does not indicate where the Israelites believed the sun went during the night, though the term used for the setting of the sun is "to enter."[31] The sun is more often recognized as a source of heat than as a source of light,[32] though one of its functions in Genesis 1:17 is to give light.

Photo 14 Babylonian Map of the World

The main significance of the moon was found in its cycle, which regulated the calendar. All of the ancient cultures operated on a lunar-based calendar, often periodically adjusted by calculations of the solar or sidereal year. The planets and stars have less significance in the cosmic geography, though their movements were tracked and they were the source of omens.[33]

Structure of the Earth

Diagrams and texts that convey how the ancients thought about the world around them exist both in Mesopotamia (Babylonian world map) and Egypt (Egyptian sarcophagus).[34] These confirm the unanimity with

31. Ibid., 66.

32. Ibid., 68; see also Horowitz, *Mesopotamian Cosmic Geography*, 138–39, where he presents a Sumerian bilingual text that refers to heaven shining rather than the sun.

33. H. Hunger, *Astrological Reports to Assyrian Kings*, SAA 8 (Helsinki: University of Helsinki Press, 1992). See further discussion below in chap. 11 on divination.

34. Keel, *Symbolism*, 37–39; Cornelius, "Visual Representation," 196–98, fig. 2.

which all parties considered the earth to be a flat disk.[35] The sarcophagus stylizes political, theological, and cosmic concepts. The Babylonian world map, in contrast, stylizes political, cosmic, and topographical concepts.[36] Concepts expressed by both can be summarized as follows.

Political

Both see their own area as the center of the earth. On the sarcophagus, the Duat (world of the dead) is in the center, surrounded by the standards of the forty-one nomes of Egypt. The next circle out has identifications of foreign lands. On the world map Babylon is in the center with a few other geographical locations placed around (Susa, Assyria, Urartu, Habban, Bit-Yakin). Five triangular areas are identified as *nagu*, referring to islands of the sea.[37]

Cosmic

Both see the cosmic waters as disk shaped, surrounding a single disk-shaped land mass. The sarcophagus has the other realms (heavens and netherworld) represented, while the world map only shows the terrestrial features.

Topographical

There are no topographical indications on the sarcophagus, but the world map shows mountains at the top, the Euphrates, a canal, and a swamp. The locations given to these are generally correct, though not at all precise.[38]

Theological

The sarcophagus includes a number of features: represented deities include Anubis, Nun, Nut, and Re, but these are all connected to cosmic features rather than to specifically terrestrial features. No theological indications appear on the world map.

Some of the most helpful speculative information about the middle

35. Egypt: Keel, *Symbolism*, 37; Mesopotamia: Horowitz, *Mesopotamian Cosmic Geography*, 334; Israel: Seely, "Geographical Meaning," 238; see Isa. 40:22.

36. Horowitz, *Mesopotamian Cosmic Geography*, 20–42.

37. These are areas traveled to by sea, though they could still be what we call continents. See discussion in Horowitz, *Mesopotamian Cosmic Geography*, 30–33.

38. See Horowitz, *Mesopotamian Cosmic Geography*, 29, for adjustments.

level of the cosmos comes from the *Epic of Etana*, where the hero is carried up to heaven on the back of an eagle. This literary piece tries to portray the land and sea as they would look at different heights.[39] Horowitz summarizes the description represented in two images.

> First, the sea is described as encircling the land just as the cosmic ocean *marratu* encircles the central continent on the World Map. Second, the author describes the land and sea in terms of agricultural features (gardener's ditch, garden, animal pen, irrigation ditch, trough) as the earth's surface appears to decrease in size when viewed from the heights of three, four, and five leagues.[40]

These images suggest that the sea was not understood to be as extensive as the land, since it is compared to a boundary ditch that surrounds a plot of land or a fence that surrounds an animal pen. Akkadian texts estimate the land surface of the earth to be equivalent to a diameter of about 3,000 miles stretching from the mountains of southern Turkey in the north where the sources of the Tigris and Euphrates are, to southeast Iran in the south (just beyond Susa). To the east it extended to the Zagros Mountains and the Iranian plateau, but the sources are less clear about the western boundaries. They were certainly aware of the Mediterranean and considered that the main western boundary.[41]

Mountains at the edges of the known world were viewed as intersecting the sky, perhaps supporting it, and having roots in the netherworld. Sometimes they were viewed as a boundary to the cosmic waters.[42] As an example of some of these perspectives, Mount Simirria is described in one of Sargon's inscriptions as follows: "Mount Simirria, a mighty mountain-peak, which spikes upward like the cutting-edge of a spear, on top of the mountain-range, the dwelling of Belet-ili, rears its head. Above, its peak leans on the heavens, below, its roots reach into the netherworld."[43]

The Egyptians also sometimes thought of mountains as holding up the sky, though other models can be found. "Above the earth was the expanse of the sky, separated from the earth by the air, and held aloft like a great flat plate by four supports at the corners of the earth. In some representations these supports are shown as poles or forked branches,

39. Ibid., 43–66.
40. Ibid., 60–61.
41. Much of this is derived from the *Sargon Geography*; see ibid., 67–95.
42. For discussion see ibid., 331–32. Cf. F. Wiggermann, "Mythological Foundations of Nature," in *Natural Phenomena: Their Meaning, Depiction and Description in the Ancient Near East*, ed. D. J. W. Meijer (Amsterdam: Royal Netherlands Academy of Arts and Sciences, 1992), 286.
43. Translation from Horowitz, *Mesopotamian Cosmic Geography*, 98; cf. also the description in *Gilgamesh IX* of Mt. Mashu.

Comparative Exploration: Biblical Terminology Related to Cosmic Geography

A careful reading of the biblical text demonstrates that many of the concepts of cosmic geography summarized in this chapter are also present in Israelite thinking.

Job 22:14—circle (vault) of heaven

Ezekiel 1:22—"expanse" (*raqi'a*) of crystal

Exodus 24:10—sapphire pavement at the top of the mountain when meeting God

Job 38:19—the abode of the light

Job 38:22—storehouses of snow and hail

Psalm 8:3—heavens as the work of God's fingers

Psalm 104:3—beams of upper chambers laid in the waters (above the earth?)

Proverbs 3:19–20—*tehom* broken up (*bq'* = split), the skies drip with dew

Psalm 24:2—earth founded on the seas

Deuteronomy 32:22—Sheol and the foundations of the mountains

Job 9:6–7—pillars of the earth; stars sealed/engraved

Job 26:7—north hung on "nothing" (= *tohu*, the trackless waste of primordial waters)

Job 26:10—horizon as boundary

Job 38:4–6—Earth's foundations, footings, cornerstone

Proverbs 8:27—inscribed the horizon on the seas

Isaiah 40:22—circle of the earth

Job 36:27—water cycle: raindrops drawn out of the waters above the heavens

such as might be used for holding up the corners of an awning. In other instances they were spoken of as being four great mountains."[44]

When we turn our attention from the edges of the known world to the center, we also find several different images. As previously mentioned, from a political standpoint it was commonplace for peoples of any area to see themselves and their land or their capital city as at the center of the earth.[45] In cosmic terms the center of the earth was often conceived of either in terms of a world tree or a cosmic mountain.[46]

44. J. M. Plumley, "The Cosmology of Ancient Egypt," in *Ancient Cosmologies*, ed. Blacker and Loewe, 20–21; see also J. Hoffmeier, "Some Thoughts on Genesis 1 and 2 and Egyptian Cosmology," *JANES* 15 (1983): 39–49.

45. For Jerusalem so viewed see Ezek. 5:5; 38:12. Cf. D. Bodi, *The Book of Ezekiel and the Poem of Erra*, Orbis biblicus et orientalis 104 (Freiburg, Switzerland: Universitätsverlag, 1991), 219–30; Stadelmann, *Hebrew Conception*, 147; R. J. Clifford, *The Cosmic Mountain in Canaan and the Old Testament*, HSM 4 (Cambridge: Harvard University Press), 135, 183.

46. In the Sumerian myth *Lugalbanda and Anzu* these two images are combined; see H. Vanstiphout, *Epics of Sumerian Kings*, SBLWAW 20 (Atlanta: SBL, 2003), 136–39; R. S.

Job 38:10—doors and bars of the sea
Psalm 104:9—boundaries for the waters

Yahweh did not reveal an alternative cosmic geography to Israel in the Old Testament. But there can be no discussion of creation or many other important issues without presupposing some sort of cosmic geography. With no alternative presented, and no refutation of the traditional ancient Near Eastern elements, it is no surprise that much of Israel's cosmic geography is at home in the ancient world rather than in the modern world. Nevertheless, as I. Cornelius indicates, theological distinctions did arise in the way that deity was seen as operating within the familiar system.

The Hebrew Bible uses central concepts and ideas typical of the cosmology of ancient Near Eastern times. . . . However, the biblical writers seem to have given their own interpretation to many of these concepts. Heaven and primeval ocean are no longer divine powers, but only the creation of YHWH. YHWH is the one who upholds the pillars of the earth; he alone created the heaven and stars and can decide who goes to the underworld and leaves it. The biggest difference lies in the fact that according to ancient Hebrew thought, YHWH established the earth through wisdom.[1]

Cornelius's observation can be extended throughout the range of cosmic geography. Israel shared the cosmic geography that was common throughout the ancient world. The difference was that the natural phenomena were emptied of deity. Rather than manifestations of the attributes of deity, they were instruments for his purposes.

1. I. Cornelius, "The Visual Representation of the World in the Ancient Near East and the Hebrew Bible," *JNSL* 20/2 (1994): 202–3.

The idea of a mountain at the center is found in the Old Testament with regard to Zion (Mic. 4:1–2) and Gerizim (Judg. 9:37). It is more prominent in Ugaritic literature since the area of Syria was mountainous. The central mountain concept is less prominent in Egypt and Mesopotamia since civilization there was centered on the plains and in the river basins.[47] In these the cosmic center was located in the temple,[48] which in Egypt at times contained in it the primeval hillock that first emerged from the cosmic waters.[49]

Another common perception in the ancient world is that a great tree stood in the center, sometimes referred to as a "world tree" or a "tree of life."[50] Its roots are fed by the great subterranean ocean and its top

Falkowitz, "Notes on 'Lugalbanda and Enmerkar,'" in *Studies in Literature from the Ancient Near East*, ed. J. M. Sasson (New Haven: AOS, 1984), 105.

47. Clifford, *Cosmic Mountain*, 9–10.

48. Ibid., 25.

49. Ibid., 27–29.

50. Several scholarly treatments are more interested in the tree as a symbol of divine order and representing the king; see S. Parpola, "The Assyrian Tree of Life," *JNES* 52

merges with the clouds, and thus binds together the heavens, the earth, and the netherworld. In the *Story of Erra and Ishum*, Marduk speaks of the *mesu* tree, whose roots reach down through the oceans to the netherworld and whose top is above the heavens.

> Where is the *mesu*-wood, flesh of the gods,
> The proper insignia of the King of the World,
> The pure timber, tall youth, who is made into a lord,
> Whose roots reach down into the vast ocean
> Through a hundred miles of water, to the base of Arallu,
> Whose topknot above rests on the heaven of Anu?[51]

In the Sumerian epic *Lugalbanda and Enmerkar*, the "eagle-tree" has a similar role. In Assyrian contexts the motif of a sacred tree is also well known. Some have called it a tree of life, and some also associate it with this world tree. It is often flanked by animals or by human or divine figures. A winged disk is typically centrally located over the top of the tree. The king is represented as the human personification of this tree. The tree is thought to represent the divine world order, but textual discussion of it is lacking.[52]

Finally, the earth was believed to be undergirded by pillars, but also supported by the roots of the mountains that reached down into the netherworld. These images must be combined with the idea that the earth floated on the underground waters.

The Sea

The cosmic sea (which encircles the land),[53] the waters beneath the earth, and waters above were not considered separate and distinct bodies of water.[54] That there was fresh water and salt water was recognized, but did not suggest separation (after all, the fresh water rivers flowed into the salt water seas). Metaphors such as locks, bolts, bars, nets, and so on

(1993): 161–208; P. Lapinkivi, *The Sumerian Sacred Marriage in Light of Comparative Evidence*, SAAS 15 (Helsinki: Neo-Assyrian Text Corpus Project, 2004), 111–18; M. Henze, *The Madness of Nebuchadnezzar: The Ancient Near Eastern Origins and Early History of Interpretation of Daniel 4* (Leiden: Brill, 1999), 75–90. Biblical references of interest occur in Dan. 4 and Ezek. 31.

51. *Erra and Ishum*, MFM 291.
52. Parpola, "Assyrian Tree."
53. Seely, "Geographical Meaning," 243; Egyptians at times referred to the Mediterranean as *shenwer*, the "great encircler"; see Lesko, "Ancient Egyptian Cosmogonies," 117.
54. Seely, "Geographical Meaning," 253; Horowitz, *Mesopotamian Cosmic Geography*, 325ff.; Tsumura, *Earth*, 61. In Mesopotamian literature Adad was considered the god associated with the flow of water from both above and below. See Weinfeld, "Gen. 7:11," 244–45.

were used to express how the sea was kept in its place. These were all established and maintained by deity, who ultimately set the boundaries.[55]

In flood traditions in the ancient Near East, the waters that flood the earth come from a variety of sources.

Atrahasis:

Anzu tore the sky with his talons and the flood (*abubu*)[56] came out.[57]
Torrent (*radu*),[58] storm (*mehu*)[59] and flood (*abubu*) came on.[60]

Gilgamesh:

Erakal pulled out the mooring poles; Ninurta marched on and made the weirs overflow.[61]
Flood (*abubu*) and tempest (*mehu*) overwhelmed the land.[62]

Genesis:

I am going to bring floodwaters (*mabbul*) on the earth (Gen. 6:17).
Seven days from now I will send rain (*mamtir*) on the earth (Gen. 7:4).[63]
On that day all the springs of the great deep (*ma'yenot tehom*) burst forth, and the floodgates (*'arubbot*) of the heavens were opened, and rain (*geshem*) fell on the earth (Gen. 7:11–12).

In all of these texts it is the cosmic waters of every sort that are involved in the flood. The act of creation had involved setting boundaries for the cosmic waters. In the flood the restraints were removed, thus bringing destruction.

Structure of the Netherworld

In this category we find the most notable distinctions between Egypt and the rest of the ancient world, so we will have to deal with them

---

55. Horowitz, *Mesopotamian Cosmic Geography*, 326–27.
56. Here *abubu* comes from the skies whereas in other texts it rises from the bowels of the earth; see *CAD* A/1: 80.
57. *MFM* 31, III.iii.7–11.
58. Akkadian *radu* is the word for rainstorm or cloudburst; cf. *CAD* R: 60–61.
59. Akkadian *mehu* is generally associated with wind, dust, and fire more than water; cf. *CAD* M/2: 4–6.
60. *MFM* 33, III.iv.25.
61. XI.102–3; see *MFM* 112.
62. XI.129; see *MFM* 113.
63. After seven days the floodwaters come (7:10), thus equating the two terms.

separately. In Egypt the place of the dead, Duat, was subterranean and was entered from the western horizon. The Duat was inhabited by numerous gods, most importantly Anubis and Osiris. The *Book of Nut* says that "Every place void of sky and void of land, that is the entire Duat."[64] This netherworld needed to be crossed, and the eventual goal was to travel with the sun god to the Field of Reeds or the Field of Offerings. These issues will be dealt with more fully in our discussion of afterlife in chapter 14. Here it is the shape of the netherworld and its place in the cosmic geography that concern us.

The journey of the dead began in the west as one entered the netherworld with the sun god as he set. In the New Kingdom book called Amduat, the netherworld is referred to as the "Great City," and the gate into it is called the "Swallower of all."[65] It is a watery place at first, hence one crosses it in the barque of the sun god. Then one encounters a desert area where there are obstacles including various gates to pass through, darkness, a lake of flames, and serpents. In the middle of the journey one encounters a waterhole filled with the primeval waters. Moving on, the barque is threatened by the great chaos serpent Apophis.

The rest of the ancient world shared a different view than Egypt and one that, in its broad outlines, was fairly homogeneous. In Mesopotamia the terminology used is KUR when people are involved, and ARALI when evil spirits are discussed.[66] A Babylonian *kudurru* (boundary marker) from the Kassite period portrays the netherworld as a city. In the city were the palaces of the netherworld deities. Like any city, it had a sociopolitical hierarchy.[67] Myths such as the *Descent of Ishtar* and the *Gilgamesh Epic* provide information concerning the seven gates that must be passed through and the treatment of the inhabitants. Entry into the netherworld was through the grave, thus explaining why proper burial was so important.

64. *COS* 1.1.

65. E. Hornung, *The Ancient Egyptian Books of the Afterlife* (Ithaca: Cornell University Press, 1999), 34.

66. D. Katz, *The Image of the Netherworld in the Sumerian Sources* (Bethesda, MD: CDL, 2003), 58–59.

67. Katz, *Image*, 113–96.

8

Cosmology and Cosmogony

Ontology: Substance versus Function

As is immediately evident upon even a cursory reading of the texts, very little in these cosmologies relates strictly to manufacture of the material cosmos. The creator gods at times bring forth other gods (and in the process the cosmic phenomena they are associated with), while at other times they are engaged in organization and ordering of the elements of the cosmos. These observations are fundamental to an understanding of the underlying cognitive environment.[1] If we are to

1. The most important secondary resources include: J. Allen, *Genesis in Egypt* (New Haven: Yale University Press, 1988); C. Blacker and M. Loewe, eds., *Ancient Cosmologies* (London: Allen & Unwin, 1975); E. Hornung, *Conceptions of God in Ancient Egypt* (Ithaca: Cornell University Press, 1982); R. J. Clifford, *Creation Accounts in the Ancient Near East and in the Bible*, CBQMS 26 (Washington, D.C.: Catholic Biblical Association of America, 1994); G. F. Hasel, "The Significance of the Cosmology in Genesis 1 in Relation to Ancient Near Eastern Parallels," *Andrews University Seminary Studies* 10 (1972): 1–20; J. D. Levenson, "The Temple and the World," *JR* 64 (1984): 275–98; S. Morenz, *Egyptian Religion* (Ithaca: Cornell University Press, 1973), 168–71; B. Batto, *Slaying the Dragon* (Louisville: Westminster John Knox, 1992); O. Keel, *The Symbolism of the Biblical World* (New York: Seabury, 1978); J. Day, *God's Conflict with the Dragon and the Sea* (Cambridge: Cambridge University Press, 1985); C. Kloos, *Yhwh's Combat with the Sea: A Canaanite Tradition in the Religion of Ancient Israel* (Leiden: Brill, 1986).

Comparative Exploration: Functional Emphasis in Day One

In Genesis 1:3–5, in the discussion of the first day's light, it becomes clear that also for the Israelites function, not substance, was the focus of creation. In Genesis 1:5a the NIV translates, "God called the light (*'or*) 'day' (*yom*) and the darkness he called 'night.'" If God called the light *yom*, why do the authors continue throughout the Old Testament to call light *'or*? It is a question anyone could answer with a little thought: it was not the element of light itself (as physicists would discuss it) that God called *yom*, but the *period* of light. There is a term for the semantic phenomenon that is observed here, namely, metonymy. In metonymy the meaning of a word is extended to include things closely related to it. When the White House makes a statement, it is understood that the building is not talking. Consequently, it is not the physicist's light that is being named *yom*, it is the period of light—obvious enough because that is what *yom* is often used to refer to in the rest of Scripture. But if the word *'or* refers to a period of light in verse 5, what about in verse 4? There God separates the light from the darkness. Again we find "period of light" much more plausible here. The physicist's light cannot be separated from darkness, but alternating periods of light and darkness can be set up. Still we cannot stop there. If the text means for us to understand "period of light" in both verses 4 and 5, what about verse 3? Hermeneutical consistency, I think, would lead us to believe that when God said "Let there be *'or*," we must then understand it as "Let there be a period of light." We could only conclude, then, that day one does not concern itself with the creation of the physicist's light, that is, "light" as a physical element with physical properties. Day one concerns something much more significant, something much more elemental to the functioning of the cosmos and to our experience of the cosmos. On day one, God created *time*.

understand ancient views about bringing the cosmos *into existence* (creation cosmology), it is essential that we understand ancient views about what constitutes *existence* (creation ontology). As I noted when discussing the origins of the gods, in the ancient world something came into existence when it was separated out as a distinct entity, given a function, and given a name. For purposes of discussion I will label this approach to ontology as "function-oriented." This is in stark contrast to modern ontology, which is much more interested in what might be called the structure or substance of something along with its properties. In modern popular thinking (as opposed to technical philosophical discussion), the existence of the world is perceived in physical, material terms. For discussion I will designate this approach to ontology as "substance-oriented." In the ancient Near East, something did not necessarily exist just because it happened to occupy space. Tobin captures this distinction between a material definition of the cosmos and a functional one based on order.

> When the Egyptians contemplated the created universe through their myths and rituals, they would have been aware that the world around them was not simply a collection of material things. The universe was for them an awesome system of living divine beings. . . . Egyptian creation myth emphasized the fact that there was order and continuity in all things and thus gave the optimistic assurance that the natural, social, and political order would remain stable and secure.[2]

Like everyone else in the ancient world, Egyptians were less interested in that which was physical than in that which was metaphysical—what lies beyond physical reality.[3] Nut, as the sky goddess, is portrayed arching her body over the disk-shaped earth. She is often supported by the hands of the god of the air while the earth god, Geb, lies prone at her feet. This is not a physical representation. The Egyptians did not believe that one could go step on Nut's toes, or throw a rock and hit her knees. Instead the portrayal communicates important truths concerning what the Egyptians believed about authority and jurisdiction in the cosmos. These truths concern function, not substance. Though they may not deal with the material world per se, they represent reality—a greater reality than the material world offered. The cosmos functioned by means of the gods playing out their roles. Whatever the physical structure of the heavens, it was not a priority to them. To describe creation is to describe the establishment of the functioning cosmos, not the origins of the material structure or substance of the cosmos. Material substance had relatively little importance or relevance to their understanding of the world.

What Does It Mean to "Create?"

If ontology in the ancient world is function-oriented, then to create something (i.e., bring it into existence) would mean to give it a function or a role within an ordered cosmos. In Egyptian texts the most prevalent element in this function orientation is the process of separation. So J. Allen summarizes by saying: "Creation is the process through which the One became the Many."[4] The naming and giving of roles (decreeing destinies) are more prominent in Mesopotamia. Each of these elements

2. V. Tobin, "Myths: Creation Myths," *OEAE* 2:471.
3. Allen, *Genesis*, 56.
4. Ibid., 57.

will be discussed in more detail below, but first we must take a brief look at the terminology that is used for creating.

The main Akkadian verbs for "create" are *banû*[5] and *bašāmu*.[6] The former is used generally with a whole range of meanings, including "build, construct, form, make, manufacture," and is sometimes translated as "create." When deity is the subject in a cosmic context, objects are the following:

- humankind or individual humans
- heavens (see, "When Anu had created the heaven, the heaven had created the earth, the earth had created the rivers, etc."[7])
- offices (high priestess, kingship)
- mountains
- various abstract features (e.g., womb that produces features, warfare, conjuration, justice)
- cosmic features (e.g., evil wind, barley and flax)
- functions (created stars to destroy evil ones)
- a plan or a situation

The term *bašāmu* is used more reservedly. Its objects include:

- buildings or plans for them (usually sanctuaries)
- pictures (e.g., reliefs on steles)
- arable land (e.g., by building dikes)
- people in the womb
- strategies
- weapons (magical ones for the gods)
- divine images
- cosmic components (constellations, firmament [*burumu*])

Fewer resources are available for doing lexical and concordance investigations in Egyptian. A number of Egyptian words are occasionally translated "create." The main ones are *ḫpr/sḫpr*, "to evolve"; *írí*, "to make"; *msì*, "to beget"; and *km3*, "to form, fashion."[8] My own survey of the literature readily available showed that in cosmic contexts where deity is the subject, the objects of these verbs indicate a larger functional sense rather than anything strictly material, much in line with what emerged in the other languages.

5. *CAD* B: 88–89. See some discussion in Clifford, *Creation Accounts*, 71–72.
6. *CAD* B: 137–38.
7. Clifford, *Worm and the Toothache* in *Creation Accounts*, 55.
8. J. Bergman, *TDOT* 2.242–44.

Comparative Exploration: Hebrew *bara'*

One can argue that the Hebrew verb *bara'* ("create") carries the same functional meaning as other ancient Near Eastern verbs for "create," though it has not generally been recognized.[1] The verb occurs about fifty times in the Old Testament and has some curious features worth noting. First, it takes only God as its subject, and therefore must be identified as a characteristically divine activity. Second, its objects are widely varied. Objects of the verb include people groups (Ps. 102:19; Ezek. 21:35); Jerusalem (Isa. 65:18); nonmaterial phenomena such as wind, fire, cloud, destruction, calamity, or darkness (Exod. 34:10; Num. 16:30; Isa. 45:7; Amos 4:13); and abstractions such as righteousness, purity, or praise (Ps. 51:21; Isa. 57:19). Even when the object is something more tangible (sea creatures in Gen. 1:21), the point is not necessarily physical manufacturing as much as assigning roles. This direction is picked up nicely in Genesis 5:2, where God creates people male and female, that is, with gender roles. In all of these cases something is brought into existence functionally, not necessarily materially; rarely would the statement concern the issue of matter. Indeed, the text never uses *bara'* in a context in which materials are mentioned. Thus instead of suggesting manufacture of matter out of nothing (as many have inferred in the past), that materials are not mentioned suggests that manufacture is not the issue. Rather, the lexical analysis suggests that the essence of the word that the text has chosen, *bara'*, concerns bringing heaven and earth into existence by focusing on operation through organization and assignment of roles and functions. Even in English we use the verb "create" within a broad range of contexts, but rarely apply it to material things (i.e., parallel in concept to "manufacture"). One can create a piece of art, but that expression does not suggest manufacture of the canvas or paint. Even more abstractly, one can create a situation (e.g., havoc) or a condition (an atmosphere). In these cases the verb indicates a role or function. When someone creates a department, a committee, a curriculum, or an advertising campaign, it is an organizational task. One puts it together and makes it work. In this category Hebrew use of *bara'* is very similar. Perhaps an English verb that captures this idea less ambiguously is "to design" (though *bara'* would include both planning and implementing the design).

The interpretation the above analysis suggests is that the text asserts that in the seven-day initial period God brought the cosmos into operation (a condition that defines existence in the ancient worldview) by assigning roles and functions. Though theological belief based on all of Scripture may affirm that God made all the matter of which the cosmos is composed (and that he made it out of nothing), lexical analysis does not lead to the conclusion that Genesis 1 is making such a statement by the use of *bara'*. The origin of matter is what our society has taught us is important (indeed, that matter is all there is), but we cannot afford to be distracted by our cultural ideas. Matter was not the concern of the author of Genesis. The author's concerns were much like those in the ancient Near East. There the greatest exercise of the power of the gods was not demonstrated in the manufacture of matter, but in the fixing of destinies.

1. Much of this discussion is drawn from my commentary on *Genesis*, NIVAC (Grand Rapids: Zondervan, 2001), 70–72.

These data demonstrate that there is no language for creation in the literatures of Egypt or Mesopotamia that focuses attention solely or even primarily on "things." Even on those occasions where the object of the verb is a thing, the context often indicates a functional orientation.[9]

A function-oriented ontology/cosmology bypasses the questions that modern scholars often ask of the ancient world: Did they have a concept of "creation out of nothing?" Did they believe in the eternal existence of matter? These questions have significance only in a material ontology. Those who posit creation out of nothing want to know whether "things" were created without using preexistent materials. If creation is not viewed as concerned with the physical making of things, these questions cannot be approached through the texts.

The result of this study is the suggestion that in the ancient Near East "to create" meant to assign roles and functions, rather than to give substance to the material objects that make up the universe. Something could conceivably exist materially by my definitions, yet in their view of cosmology not be created yet. An obvious case in point is that in Egypt creation took place all over again every morning.

Chaos and Order: The Precosmic Condition

It is important to be careful with terminology here. Words like "chaos" and even the word I have been using freely, "cosmos," came from Greek and in that language carried certain nuances, which may or may not carry over into English usage. In early classical literature such as Hesiod's *Theogony* and Virgil's *Aeneid*, Chaos is personified as the primal state in which earth, sky, and seas were all merged.[10] More generically, *chaos* is the opposite of *cosmos*, which refers to the ordered whole.[11] It is this latter juxtaposition that is more evident in the ancient Near East. Egyptian philosophers conceived of the precreation state as opposite of the created state. "What lies outside the biosphere of earth, sky, and Duat is not 'nothingness' but a universe that is the antithesis of all that defines the world. It is infinite, where the world is bounded; formless and chaotic, where the world is shaped and ordered; inert, where the world is active; and wholly uniform in substance (water), where the world is materially diverse."[12]

---

9. Clifford, *Creation Accounts*, 8–9.

10. *Aeneid* 4.707; *Theogony* 2:116–53. This was adopted and further refined by the Gnostics; see Hornung, *Conceptions*, 177 n. 127.

11. G. E. R. Lloyd, "Greek Cosmologies," in *Ancient Cosmologies*, ed. C. Blacker and M. Loewe (London: Allen & Unwin, 1975), 200.

12. Allen, *Genesis*, 57.

Photo 15 Seven-headed Chaos Beast

In the ancient Near East the precreation condition is therefore neither an abstraction nor personified, though the primordial sea, which is the principal element of the precreation condition, is personified by Nammu in Sumer and by Nun in Egypt. In Mesopotamia chaos is personified only secondarily in the conflict myths that recount jeopardy to the created order. In this cosmological literature the threatening creatures must be overthrown and order reestablished.[13]

It would perhaps be best to use terminology such as "precosmic" condition (with the earlier Greek understanding that "cosmos" implies order). The precosmic condition was not lacking in that which was material, it was lacking in order and differentiation. Thus the accounts regularly begin with a precosmic, unordered, nonfunctional world.[14] Creation then takes place by giving things order, function, and purpose, which is synonymous with giving them existence. Once established, the order that exists in the cosmos is constantly threatened with being undone. As a result creation is not restricted to a one-time event. Whether the jeopardy derives from the cosmic waters, from what we would term "natural" occurrences, from supernatural beings, from human behavior,

13. Here I refer to creatures such as Tiamat and her cohorts in *Enuma Elish* and Anzu in the *Tale of Anzu*. Cf. R. Simkins, *Creator and Creation* (Peabody, MA: Hendrickson, 1994), 78.

14. In Egypt this includes undifferentiated singularity. This focus does not mean that they believed matter to be eternal—they simply did not consider matter to be a category worth discussing.

Photo 16 *Enuma Elish*

or simply from the darkness of each night, the gods are responsible for reestablishing order day by day and moment by moment.

In Egypt, on the "First Occasion"[15] the god Amun is by himself, the first of the gods.[16] Despite the fact that Amun was said to exist before everything, he emerged from the waters. Egyptian cosmology started with the "nonexistent," which included the absence of space and forms (i.e., some material aspects), but which was also made up of water and darkness, in which nothing was named or distinct.[17] In their thinking this nonexistent realm continued to be present in the sea, in the dark night sky, and even in the desert—places without role or function. Creation began with the first hillock emerging from the unbounded waters,[18] which had been portrayed in the form of Nun, representing primeval waters in every direction. Ancient sources are unanimous that the precosmic condition included water and darkness. Sumerian texts describe lack of functions, undifferentiated heaven and earth, darkness, and water.[19] In early Mesopotamian sources the condition prior to the separation of heaven and earth finds those two elements together represented in the "Holy Mound" (du_6-$k\dot{u}$), which had its foundation on the *apsu* with the ancient city of the gods on top of it.[20] In *Enuma Elish*

15. This phrase in many ways is similar to the phrase in Gen. 1:1, "In the beginning"; see Morenz, *Egyptian Religion*, 166–68.

16. Hermopolis, Papyrus Leiden I 350, chap. 80 line 13; 100 line 2.

17. Hornung, *Conceptions*, 175–77.

18. Allen, *Genesis*, 10, 14.

19. Clifford, *Creation Accounts*, 28.

20. F. Wiggermann, "Mythological Foundations of Nature," in *Natural Phenomena: Their Meaning, Depiction and Description in the Ancient Near East*, ed. D. J. W. Meijer (Amsterdam: Royal Netherlands Academy of Arts and Sciences, 1992), 279–306, quotation on 285.

Comparative Exploration: Precosmic Condition and Order

The precosmic condition in the Genesis account is described in Genesis 1:2 with the Hebrew expression *tohu wabohu* ("formless and empty").[1] No one suggests that this verse indicates that matter had not been shaped or that the cosmos described in verse 2 is empty of matter. By logic alone the words could be seen to concern functionality, and analysis of the Hebrew confirms the conclusion that these terms indicate that the cosmos was empty of purpose, meaning, and function—a place that had no order or intelligibility. D. Tsumura concludes that "the term *tohu* seems to refer to a situation which lacks something abstract that should be there, such as worth, purpose, truth, profit and integrity."[2]

The ordered cosmos in the ancient Near East was focused on the world of the gods. Organization had been brought to the divine realm through birth of deities and assignment of roles in the ordered world. As previously discussed, the gods lived in society with hierarchical structures by which they related and operated. The equivalent of civilization existed at this level, and the features of that civilization were an important part of the ordered cosmos. When people were created by the gods, they shared in this established order and benefited by it. In some texts the preordered condition is described by the absence of civilized behavior.[3]

In the view offered in Genesis, God does not operate within a society of gods, and people function in a different role. The role of people will be explored in chapter 9, but here what is important is that the order imposed through the creation narrative in Genesis 1 sees people, rather than the gods, as the keystone in the definition of order. The biblical text repeatedly offers the formula "it was good" to describe the successful setting of each piece in its ordered place. The functions described are designed for the benefit of humans. For example, the sun and moon are given for measuring time and for establishing festivals (signs and seasons).[4] This functional nuance of "good" in the biblical text is confirmed by a comparison of what is not good—that is, it is not good for man to be alone (2:18). In other words, in the perspective of Genesis the cosmos cannot be functional without the presence of people, because the functions are aimed at people.[5]

1. Note also that a separate sort of precosmic lack of order serves as the introduction to the second creation account in Gen. 2:5–6.

2. D. Tsumura, *The Earth and the Waters in Genesis 1 and 2*, JSOTSup 83 (Sheffield: JSOT Press, 1989), 31.

3. Cf. *Enki and Ninhursag*; see Clifford, *Creation Accounts*, 36–37.

4. W. Vogels, "The Cultic and Civil Calendars of the Fourth Day of Creation (Gen 1,14b)," *SJOT* 11 (1997): 163–80.

5. This is rather like the question about whether a tree that falls in the forest makes any noise if no one is there to hear it. At the same time, Job 38 recognizes that people continue to be substantially ignorant of the role that every created thing has.

the emphasis is on the absence of names and gods, and the lack of differentiation, but it begins with Apsu and Tiamat, together representing the primeval waters.[21] In Israel the precreation condition also is characterized by darkness on the face of the deep (Gen. 1:2).

Functional Aspects: Name, Separation, Role

Naming

Generally in the ancient world, the assignment of role and function is connected to the giving of names. Egyptian literature identified the creator god as the one who pronounced the name of everything.[22] In this way of thinking, things did not exist unless they were named. "It was believed that the name of a living being or an object was not just a simple or practical designation to facilitate the exchange of ideas between persons but that it was the very essence of what was defined, and that the actual pronouncing of a name was to create what was spoken."[23] Likewise, *Enuma Elish* begins with the heavens and the earth not yet named, and when the gods had not yet been given names. Then Lahmu and Lahamu emerge and their names are pronounced.

Separation

Egyptians thought of the universe as a limitless ocean (Nun) above the sky paralleled by waters under the earth.[24] These had been separated when the god of the air, Shu, came into being as the space between them. But beyond the separation of heaven and earth, all existence was associated with something having been differentiated. The god Atum is conceptualized as the primordial monad—the singularity embodying all the potential of the cosmos, from whom all things were separated and thereby were created.[25]

Turning to Mesopotamia, in one of the most familiar scenes of *Enuma Elish*, the victorious Marduk splits the corpse of the vanquished Tiamat

21. "Primeval Apsu was their progenitor, and matrix-Tiamat was she who bore them all, They were mingling their waters together" (*COS* 1.111, tablet 1:3–5). Cf. the bilingual "Foundation of Eridu": "All the lands were sea" (Clifford, *Creation Accounts*, 63).

22. *Memphite Theology*, line 55.

23. J. M. Plumley, "The Cosmology of Ancient Egypt," in *Ancient Cosmologies*, ed. Blacker and Loewe, 38.

24. Allen, *Genesis*, 4.

25. Ibid., 57–58: "Creation is the process through which the One became the Many."

dividing her waters in half (above and below).[26] In an earlier Sumerian account, *Praise of the Pickax*, the first few lines read

> The lord brought into being the beginnings splendidly,
> The lord, whose decisions cannot be changed,
> Enlil, to make the seed of the Kalam sprout from the earth/the
>   netherworld,
> To separate heaven from earth he hastened,
> To separate earth from heaven he hastened,
> To make the light shine in Uzumua.[27]

Israel had no need to divide a god as in *Enuma Elish*, or to interject a god as in Egyptian literature, but saw the waters as simply divided by an act of God. Nonetheless, it should be noticed that even as Genesis distances itself from the ancient theology, it communicates within the ancient perspective of the cosmology by retaining the view of waters above and below being separated from each other. Likewise in the Genesis account day and night are separated as well as the sea and dry land.

Role

Texts easily blend together functions in various categories, as can be seen in the opening lines of the Sumerian piece entitled *The* Huluppu *Tree*, a section in *Gilgamesh, Enkidu, and the Netherworld*:

> In the first nights, in the very first nights,
> In the first years, in the very first years,
> In the first days when everything needed was brought into being,
> In the first days when everything needed was properly nourished,
> When bread was baked in the shrines of the land,
> And bread was tasted in the homes of the land,
> When heaven had moved away from earth,
> And earth had separated from heaven,
> And the name of man was fixed;
> When the Sky God, An, had carried off the heavens,
> And the Air God, Enlil, had carried off the earth,
> When the Queen of the Great Below, Ereshkigal, was given the
>   underworld.[28]

26. *Enuma Elish* IV:135–38; also note the concept in Hittite, *The Song of Ullikummi*, in H. Hoffner, *Hittite Myths*, SBLWAW 2 (Atlanta: SBL, 1990), 59 §§61, 63.

27. Lines 1–5 (Clifford, *Creation Accounts*, 31); *Enki and Ninmah* has fates decreed after heavens and earth were split (Clifford, *Creation Accounts*, 40).

28. D. Wolkstein and S. Kramer, *Inanna: Queen of Heaven and Earth* (New York: Harper & Row, 1983), 4.

Comparative Exploration:
Created Functions—Naming, Separating, Giving Roles

In Genesis God initiates the creative act with a spoken word and finalizes the act with the giving of a name. Separation is a common element and delineation of roles and functions pervade the description. The acts of creation in Genesis consist of bringing order to the cosmos in the same terms that are observed in the ancient Near East, despite the fact that God's role and relationship to the cosmos differ from those of deity elsewhere in the ancient Near East. The underlying cosmological concepts remain similar to the rest of the ancient world. Instead of understanding creation as making things, the Hebrew authors saw God establishing a reality continuum. The reality of how we experience the cosmos does not need to be informed by a description of the shape or structure of the cosmos, or its formational history. The text communicates a universal reality—how all peoples throughout time have *experienced* the cosmos.

I have already suggested that day one concerns not the creation of the substance physicists call light, but involves the setting up of the cycle of day and night—the creation of the basis for time. As the functional approach continues, day two in Genesis demonstrates God's setting up the basis for weather. In the ancient understanding of the cosmos as discussed in chapter 7 on cosmic geography, the *raqiʻa* ("sky, firmament") is closely tied to the weather. Here the biblical text is using the cosmic geography of the day to indicate that the function of weather is being created. The third day, in its two parts, sets up the basis for fecundity. This is accomplished by providing for water sources, soil, and the biological principle that seeds will continue to propagate each species. It is, in effect, the provision of food.

That these three primary functions, time, weather, and fecundity, or vegetation, are in view can be confirmed from Genesis 8:22, when the primary functions are restored after the flood. The flood had represented the return of precosmic disorder (the waters of the cosmos) being brought as a response to the disorder/chaos created by the violence of the human race. When order was again restored (in terms strikingly parallel with the creation account throughout), God says:

A later Egyptian text[29] lists eighteen "creations," only one or two of which refer to structural components (e.g., sweet water). The remainder of the list contains things such as summer/winter, birth, sleep, remedies, dreams, wealth/poverty, and succession of generations.[30] In Mesopotamia the roles are usually found in the control attributes and the destinies that are decreed.

29. Papyrus Insinger, a copy of a composition judged by Lichtheim to date to the Ptolemaic period; *AEL* 3:184.
30. *AEL* 3:210–11, lines 32:1–17.

As long as the earth endures,
Seedtime and harvest,
Cold and heat,
Summer and winter,
Day and night
Will never cease.

This is a reaffirmation of the three functions established in Genesis 1 on days one through three, and demonstrates that functions are at issue throughout.

In a fragmentary section of tablet 5, *Enuma Elish* contains a similar sequence of functions. Lines 39–40 refer to the day and the year, and are followed up in line 46 by a reference to the watches of the night. In lines 47–52 Marduk creates precipitation accompanied by clouds, winds, and fog. Then in lines 53–58 water sources on earth are set up and dirt is piled up.[1] Thus we could see time, weather, and vegetation addressed in order and in functional terms. Compare the familiarity of this summary description by a modern Assyriologist of Mesopotamian creation after the separation of heaven and earth:

> With Enlil, the modern universe is founded; he establishes just rule, and with the other Anunna decides the fates on the Holy Mound. Darkness turns into

light, the moon and the sun, Nanna and Utu are born, Summer and Winter brought forth by Enlil and Ḫursag; undefined time turns into days, months, seasons and years.[2]

All of this demonstrates the radical contrast between the terms in which the Israelites thought about cosmic origins and the terms in which we think about them. When *we* ask "How does the cosmos work?" we seek an answer that discusses physical laws and structures. In our cognitive environment, function is a consequence of physical properties and natural laws, and a discussion of creation therefore must, *of course*, direct itself to the making of things. In contrast, when Israelites asked "How does the cosmos work?" they sought a totally different answer, because in the ancient worldview *function is a consequence of purpose*. Thus the Israelites can be seen to have the same functional approach to creation as is evident in the ancient Near East.

1. W. Horowitz, *Mesopotamian Cosmic Geography* (Winona Lake, IN: Eisenbrauns, 1998), 117–18.
2. Wiggermann, "Mythological Foundations," 279–306, quotation on 286.

Control Attributes and Destinies

In chapter 4, I introduced Akkadian *parṣu* ("control attributes") and *šimati* ("destinies") as terms that described the ways that the gods interacted with the cosmos as well as with one another.[31] There I noted that the cosmic control attributes were entrusted to the three main

31. These concepts have been clarified by the following studies: W. G. Lambert, "Destiny and Divine Intervention in Babylon and Israel," *OtSt* 17 (1972): 65–72; J. Lawson, *The Concept of Fate in Ancient Mesopotamia of the First Millennium* (Wiesbaden: Harrassowitz,

gods, Anu, Enlil, and Enki, who were not the originators of them, and were bound by them. They were stewards of the control attributes and were administrators of them as their control extended down through the various levels of the cosmos.

In Mesopotamia both the role of the control attributes and the assigning of functions (fixing of destinies) are of central importance in the original creation as well as in the continual renewal of creation. The operation of the cosmos is based on the control attributes. The following segment of the bilingual *Great Astrological Treatise* will illustrate the range and contexts of the terms.

Sumerian

> When Anu, Enlil, and Enki, the great gods
> In their infallible counsel
> Among the great laws (ME) of heaven and earth,
> Had established the crescent of the moon,
> Which brought forth day,
> Established the months
> And furnished omens
> Drawn from heaven and earth,
> This crescent shone in the heaven,
> And one saw the stars shining in highest heaven.

Akkadian

> When Anu, Enlil, and Enki, the great gods
> Had in their counsel
> Established the plans of heaven and earth
> And when they had charged the great astral gods
> To produce (*banû*) day
> And to assure the regular sequence of months
> For the (astrological) observation of humans
> One saw the sun rising
> And the stars shone forever in highest heaven.[32]

A second prologue talks about these gods creating (*banû*) the heavens and earth, installing the stars, measuring the length of day and night, creating (*banû*) month and year, and ordering the paths for Sin (moon) and Shamash (sun). So they "made the decrees for heaven and earth."[33]

1994); Y. Rosengarten, *Sumer et le Sacré* (Paris: Boccard, 1977); A. R. George, "Sennacherib and the Tablet of Destinies," *Iraq* 48 (1986): 133–46.

32. Clifford, *Creation Accounts*, 67–68.

33. Ibid., 68.

Ninety-four control attributes associated with Uruk and its patron deity, Inanna, are listed in *Inanna and Enki*.

> Governorship, priesthood, godship, mighty legitimate crown, throne of kingship, noble scepter, noble dress, shepherdship, truth, descending to netherworld, rebellious lands, kindness, kingship, sword and club, temple servant, colorful dress, black dress, quiver, love-making, kissing, prostitution, running speech, slander, cajoling, security at home, crafts, pure tavern, resounding lute, singing, wise old age, heroism, power, dishonesty, righteousness, plundering lamentations, rejoicing, deceit, understanding, knowledge, sheepfold, traveling, washing rites, kindling fire, hard work, assembled family, descendants, dispute, triumph, counseling, deliberation, jurisdiction, decision-making, holy shrine, and fear/awe.[34]

The list is instructive for showing what belongs in the category of control attributes. Surveying the list, one can see various aspects of culture, social institutions, abstractions, behaviors, ideals, and values. It is also evident that the list is not intended to choose only the best and most desirable elements. The functional orientation is clear. These control attributes concern roles in the ordered cosmos. There are, however, no cosmic elements here. The list consists of the control attributes that are being granted to Inanna's city of Uruk, so cosmic elements would have been inappropriate.

In the discussion of cosmology, it is important to observe that the control attributes are not set up, established, or invented by the gods. Rather creation is the process of operating within the parameters of these control attributes, or even manipulating or assigning them. In *Enuma Elish* Marduk is said to "make his control attributes" (*ubašimu parṣišu*).[35] This is the only occurrence of *parṣu* as the object of one of the verbs of creation. The parallel in the previous phrase ("rites") suggests, however, that it should be understood as referring to the control attributes of ritual procedures rather than of the cosmos.[36] The control attributes are carried, gathered, exercised, held in the hand, granted, and organized by the gods, but not initiated.

The second term, *šimtu*, is represented prominently in a tablet held by the gods, usually referred to as the Tablet of Destinies. The Tablet of Des-

---

34. G. Farber-Flugge, *Der Mythos "Inanna und Enki" unter besonderer Berücksichtigung der Liste der me*, Studia Pohl, Dissertationes scientificae de rebus orientis antiqui 10 (Rome: Biblical Institute Press, 1973).

35. *Enuma Elish* V:67.

36. *CAD* B: 138: "fixed the ceremonial, established the order of rank." *MFM* 257: "designed its cult, created its rites." *COS* 1.111 (Foster): "designed his prerogatives and devised his responsibilities." Horowitz, *Mesopotamian Cosmic Geography*, 119: "He designed his rites, made his rules."

Comparative Exploration: Control Attributes and Destinies

Each year at the all-important *Akitu*, Babylon's New Year's enthronement festival, the gods fixed the destinies for the coming year, thus reasserting their power. Authority was then transferred to the king as he took the hand of Marduk. Then the deity took up his rest in the temple. Here in Genesis one might suggest that Israel's God also demonstrates his power by the assigning of roles and functions. Genesis distances itself from the ancient Near East by portraying God's power as so much greater than the gods of Mesopotamia. But it conforms to the ancient Near East by evaluating his power in the categories typically addressed in that cognitive environment.

Though there are no recognized Hebrew terms coinciding to the Akkadian ones for control attributes and destinies, some have already recognized the *concept* at least tangentially in the biblical material.[1] It is possible to understand Genesis 1 in light of the concepts represented in the Sumerian/Akkadian terms. God's creative activities would be seen both as establishing and as maintaining order, just as the control attributes do in Mesopotamia.

In distinct contrast to Mesopotamian beliefs, however, Genesis 1, if dealing with the control attributes, positions them differently. Rather than positing deity as guardian of the cosmic control attributes, Genesis portrays God as the one who initiates them. This is similar to the idea that in Israel Yahweh is considered the source and embodiment of justice, whereas in Mesopotamia Shamash is the guardian of justice (see chap. 13).[2] Moving from the control attributes to the destinies, Yahweh does not need his destiny to be decreed, nor does he decree the destiny of other deities.[3] Predictably, the Israelite God does not delegate powers out to other gods, but brings order to the cosmos by determining the destinies of the inhabitants of the cosmos. Along the same line of logic, there is no tablet of destinies. Yahweh needs no emblem because he does not have to protect his power from usurpation by those such as Anzu or Kingu.

When we look at Genesis 1 in light of control attributes and destinies, we find

tinies has been described both as the bond that holds the cosmos together and as the reins by which deity exercises control over the cosmos.[37] This tablet is used to assign the semipermanent roles and functions of gods, temples, and cities. Kings and people have their destinies proclaimed annually at the *Akitu* festival.[38] In *Enuma Elish* Marduk retrieves the Tablet of Destinies from Kingu and then, by the authority of the tablet, restructures the cosmos under his own control. The destinies determine what roles are assigned to gods, temples, and people. Mother deities such as Nintu or Mamitu are referred to as the "creatrix of destinies" (using

37. Lawson, *Concept of Fate*, 24; see George, "Sennacherib."
38. J. Bidmead, *The Akitu Festival* (Piscataway, NJ: Gorgias, 2002), 92.

that the role of the spoken word would take on a new level of comparison, since the control attributes were also established by the spoken word.[4] We find, in addition, that the control attributes were considered "good"—the best possible expression of world order.[5] Days one–three, which concern the three core functions of the cosmos (time, weather, fecundity), would consequently be viewed as not just activating but establishing the control attributes of the cosmos, while days four–six could be seen as determining the destinies of the functionaries within the cosmos. When the destinies of the gods were determined in the ancient Near East, powers and responsibilities could be delegated. As a result, other gods became "working Enlils" as control attributes were granted to them.[6] This would bear some resemblance to people being created in the image of God and becoming Elohim operatives—a concept to be discussed when we talk about the creation and role of people (see chap. 9).[7]

The significance of the control attributes and destinies for Genesis 1 will be more evident as we explore the relationship between cosmology and temple building.

1. Gen. 8:21 is connected with ME/NAM by H. W. F. Saggs, *Encounter with the Divine in Mesopotamia and Israel* (London: Athlone, 1978), 74.

2. Law would be counted among the control attributes. Yahweh would be the source of all control attributes, whereas the Mesopotamian gods are typically simply guardians. This goes back to the concept discussed in chap. 4, that Yahweh is outside the cosmos, while the ancient Near Eastern gods are within the cosmos.

3. The closest hint to anything like this in the OT would be in Deut. 32:8 if the variant reading is correct and "sons of God" should be read instead of "sons of Israel." See M. S. Heiser, "Deuteronomy 32:8 and the Sons of God," *BSac* 158 (2001): 52–74.

4. Y. Rosengarten, *Sumer et le Sacré* (Paris: Boccard, 1977), 219–20.

5. Ibid., 12, 74.

6. Ibid., 120, *Enliluti* ("l'Enlillité").

7. Elohim operatives were designated to carry out the work of Elohim, in whose image they are made.

a feminine noun related to *banû*). There is no evidence that the cosmos as a whole has a destiny decreed for it, though it is clearly characterized by control attributes. Of course, there is no need to decree destinies for the cosmic elements themselves when the destinies of the gods are being decreed. The gods maintain the operation of the cosmos, so decreeing their destinies maintains operations.

Creation cosmology in Mesopotamia involves the wielding or activating of the control attributes and the decreeing of destinies. J. Lawson concludes: "The gods and their individual offices may give form and direction to this power [the control attributes] but they are not the final masters over the cosmos or even their own fates."[39] The gods are engaged in devising a cosmic plan, but that is independent of the control attributes and is carried out through the decreeing of the destinies of deities.

39. Lawson, *Concept of Fate*, 39.

Temple, Cosmos, and Rest

In previous chapters we have already explored the concept that the temple is viewed as a microcosmos while the cosmos is viewed in temple terms.[40] We have also seen the significance of the concept of rest as it relates to the function, indeed the purpose, of the temple.[41] Establishing control over an ordered cosmos is followed by building a temple (which represents that ordered cosmos) for the deity in which he can take up his rest.

Portraying the cosmos as a temple can be seen as a common element throughout the ancient Near East. In Ugaritic mythology the house Baal seeks for himself is a cosmic temple.[42] In Sumerian literature Gudea's account of building the Eninnu (the temple to Ningirsu), of the completion and confirmation of the architectural plan, is described in cosmological terms.

> Gudea lay down as an oracular dreamer;
> A command went forth to him.
> The building of the temple of his king,
> The separation of the Eninnu from heaven and earth,
> Was displayed there for him before his eyes.[43]

A prayer to dedicate the foundation brick of a temple shows the close connection between cosmos and temple in Akkadian thinking:

> When Anu, Enlil and Ea had a (first) idea of heaven and earth, they found a wise means of providing for the support of the gods: They prepared, in the land, a pleasant dwelling, and the gods were installed in this dwelling: their principal temple. Then they entrusted to the king the responsibility of assuring them regular choice offerings. And for the feast of the gods, they established the required food offering! The gods loved this dwelling! Thus did they institute their hold over what became the principal land of humans.[44]

40. See "Temple and Cosmos" in chap. 5.
41. See the discussion of the Fourth Commandment in the comparative sidebar at the end of chap. 6.
42. L. R. Fisher ("Creation at Ugarit and in the Old Testament," *VT* 15 [1965]: 313–24) seeks to demonstrate that in the *Baal Epic* "conflict, kingship, ordering of chaos, and temple building are all related to an overarching theme" that he labels "creation" (316). He not only sees the temple as a microcosmos, but sees the ordering of the temple as resembling the creation of the cosmos (318–19).
43. *COS* 2.155, Gudea Cylinder A: xx. 7–11.
44. Clifford, *Creation Accounts*, 61–62.

Besides the cosmological texts such as *Enuma Elish*, where Marduk organizes the universe, then has a shrine constructed, Mesopotamian temple building texts contribute to this association.[45] If it is accurate to consider the temple and cosmos to be closely related, indeed, to be reflections of one another, then it would naturally follow that cosmology texts should have a lot in common with temple construction texts. "We should not be surprised to find that the texts describing the creation of the world and those describing the construction of a shrine are parallel. The Temple and the world stand in an intimate and intrinsic connection. The two projects cannot ultimately be distinguished or disengaged. Each recounts how God brought about an environment in which he can find 'rest.'"[46]

We find, then, that cosmology and temple converge in the issue of divine rest. Cosmological texts provide accounts of order and security

---

Comparative Exploration: Genesis 1 and Temple Building

If the cosmos is to be viewed as a temple, then it is possible that a cosmological text could adopt the metaphor of temple building and dedication.[1] This course of analogy and logic results in the understanding that Genesis 1 is framed in terms of the creation of the cosmos as a temple in which Yahweh takes up his repose.[2] A fresh look at the Gudea temple building and dedication text offers some intriguing comparisons that might commend seeing Genesis 1 in these terms.

First, we encounter the common idea that the sanctuary is being constructed in order to provide a resting place, in Gudea's case for Ningirsu and his consort, Bau. Genesis 1 likewise finds its conclusion in Yahweh's taking up his rest.[3] As developed earlier, "rest" does not imply relaxation, but more like achieving equilibrium and stability. He is making a place of rest for himself, a rest provided for by the completed cosmos. Inhabiting his resting place is the equivalent to being enthroned—it is connected to taking up his role as sovereign ruler of the cosmos. The temple simply provides a symbolic reality for this concept as demonstrated by its role in the *Akitu* enthronement festival in Babylon. Psalm 104:2–4 captures this as the elements of the cosmos serve as functionaries for Yahweh's rule. Further confirmation exists in the presence of the ark in the most sacred area of the temple representing the footstool of God's throne (Ps. 132:7–8).[4]

---

45. V. Hurowitz, *I Have Built You an Exalted House*, JSOTSup 115 (Sheffield: Sheffield Academic Press, 1992): 335–37. Hurowitz further identifies the temples of the gods in *Enuma Elish* as being "simultaneously earthly temples and cosmic regions associated with various gods" (*I Have Built*, 333).

46. Levenson, "Temple," 288.

Second, we find that the dedication ceremonies sometimes last seven days.[5] This element in Gudea can also be seen in various biblical accounts that have to do with sanctuary building and dedication.[6]

In Genesis 1 we have the provision of rest for the deity occurring after a six-day period during which functions are established and functionaries installed through a procedure that has striking similarities to the decreeing of destinies, itself deeply embedded in temple dedications.

The focus on decrees for functions and functionaries constitutes the third item of significance. The dedication ceremony in Gudea Cylinder B: vi-xii touches on many of the pertinent elements that we recognize from Genesis 1. The Sabbath element in Genesis not only helps us to recognize the temple-cosmos equation in Genesis, but also to realize the contextual significance of the functions (days 1–3) and functionaries (days 4–6) in the creation narrative. Just as Gudea's account established functions for the temple and then supplied functionaries that operate in it, the Genesis account set up functions (days 1–3) and functionaries (days 4–6) for the cosmic temple. Genesis 2:1 indicates this as it refers to the creation of heaven and earth (the cosmos with its functions) and *all their hosts* (the functionaries in the various realms of the cosmos). In a temple construction project, the structure would be built, and the furniture and trappings would be made in preparation for the moment when all was ready for the dedication of the temple. On this occasion, often a seven-day celebration, the functions of the temple would be declared, the furniture and hangings would be put in place, the priests would be installed, and the appropriate sacrifices would be made to initiate the temple's operation. Somewhere in the process, the image of the deity would be brought into the temple to take up his repose in his new residence. On the basis of all of this, Genesis 1 can be viewed as using the metaphor of temple dedication as it portrays God's creation (= making functional/operational) his cosmos (which is his temple, Isa. 66:1).

Fourth, V. Hurowitz has noticed that the description of the temple construction is not architectural in nature. Despite the detail, the accounts "do not enable the reader to visualize the shape of the temple, even partially or schematically."[7] This is in accord with what has been discussed above about the creation account of Genesis being functional rather than structural.

The connections that underline the temple-cosmos relationship in Genesis 1–2 are numerous. The celestial bodies are referred to using the unusual term "lights" that through the rest of the Pentateuch refers to the lights of the lampstand that functions to give light in the tabernacle.[8] It should also be noted that the idea of rivers flowing from the holy place is found both in Genesis 2 (which portrays Eden as the holy of holies)[9] and in Ezekiel's temple (Ezek. 47:1). A third element is that when people are assigned their function in 2:15, priestly terms (*'abad* and *shmr*) are used.[10] The main connection, however, is the rest motif, for rest is the principal function of a temple, and a temple is always where deity finds rest.[11]

In summary, the cognitive environment from the ancient Near East as it is reflected in Genesis 1 includes:

- Ontology—Israel thinks of existence in terms of role and function in an orderly cosmos, and that is the level of existence that creation initiates.
- Cosmic geography—Israel continues to imagine a three-tiered

cosmos and creation is described against that backdrop.

- Centrality of control attributes and destinies—Israel considers God's creative activity in terms of establishing significant control attributes and decreeing destinies for the inhabitants of the cosmos.
- Rest and its temple implications—Israel sees the cosmos in temple terms and God's rest as a result of having established order in the cosmos.

At the same time, some significant theological departures from the ancient Near Eastern cognitive environment must be recognized:

- Theomachy (warfare among the gods)—contrary to what we often find in the ancient Near East, Genesis 1 does not portray the ordering of the cosmos and the rest of deity as the result of resolved conflict in the divine realm.[12]
- Theogony—as discussed in chapter 4, there is no origin of Yahweh nor does cosmogony depend on theogony.
- God's relationship to the control attributes—since Yahweh is perceived as being outside of the cosmos, the control attributes cannot exist

independent of him. So creation involves not only the decreeing of destinies, but the actual initiation of the control attributes.

1. Much of this can be seen worked out in detail and placed within the context of biblical theology in G. Beale, *The Temple and the Church's Mission* (Downers Grove, IL: InterVarsity Press, 2004). See especially his extensive treatment of the cosmic symbolism of temples, 29–80.

2. See further discussion in J. Walton, *Genesis*, NIVAC (Grand Rapids: Zondervan, 2001), 146–57.

3. A comprehensive treatment of rest as a theme in biblical theology can be found in J. Laansma, *I Will Give You Rest* (Tubingen: Mohr, 1997). See especially his thorough treatment of OT and ancient Near Eastern texts, 17–76.

4. See also 1 Sam. 4:4; 2 Sam. 6:2; Isa. 6:1.

5. Gudea Cylinder B: xvii. 18–19; see Hurowitz, *I Have Built*, 271.

6. Levenson, "Temple," 288–89; see Hurowitz, *I Have Built*, 275–76.

7. Hurowitz, *I Have Built*, 40 n. 5.

8. Vogels, "Cultic and Civil Calendars," 175.

9. Beale, *Temple*, 66–80.

10. Walton, *Genesis*, 172–74.

11. Ps. 132:13–14.

12. Notice that the construction of the tabernacle comes on the heels of the defeat of Yahweh's and Israel's enemies, the Egyptians, so that now they might enjoy rest; see Beale, *Temple*, 63–64. It also should be noted that there are vestigial references to theomachy in Psalms such as 74 and 89. For a thorough study of the Chaoskampf Motif see R. Watson, *Chaos Uncreated*, BZAW 341 (Berlin: Walter de Gruyter, 2005).

being established, and the temple is where that order and security are maintained and enjoyed. In Mesopotamia this rest is often achieved through conflict (theomachy) and is enabled by the organization of the cosmos through the means of the control attributes and the decree of destinies.

Part 5

People

9

Understanding the Past

Human Origins and Role

Without a sense of the past there is no memory, no conscience, no responsibility.[1]

If we seek to understand the cognitive environment of the ancient world, we must try to comprehend how people thought about the past. How people understand the past provides a key for action in the present. This topic is divided into two chapters: the first deals with the origins and role of the human race; the second deals with the ancients' understanding and writing of history.

Accounts of Human Origins

Accounts of or allusions to human origins are found in Sumerian, Akkadian, and Egyptian texts. Most of the accounts are brief (a couple of lines), with the longest ones (*Enki and Ninmah* and *Atrahasis*) extending for several dozen lines.

1. J. Assmann, "A Dialogue Between Self and Soul: Papyrus Berlin 3024," in *Self, Soul and Body in Religious Experience*, ed. A. I. Baumgarten, J. Assmann, and G. G. Stroumsa (Leiden: Brill, 1998), 396.

Sumerian

- *Song of the Hoe*[2]
- *Hymn to E-engura*[3]
- *Enki and Ninmah*[4]
- *KAR 4*[5]

Akkadian

- *Atrahasis*[6]
- *Enuma Elish*[7]

Egyptian[8]

- *Pyramid Texts* 445, 522 (Khnum on potter's wheel)
- *Coffin Texts* (II:43, spell 80)[9]
- *Coffin Text* spell 1130[10]
- *Instruction of Merikare*[11]

Neither Egyptian nor Sumerian accounts put human origins in the context of conflict among the gods as the Akkadian accounts do, though two of the Sumerian accounts (*Enlil and Ninmah*, *KAR* 4) indicate that people are taking over the work of the gods.[12] The accounts typically focus on the process and materials of creation, and the roles or functions of humankind.

2. *COS* 1.157. Also called "Praise of the Pickax"; see R. J. Clifford, *Creation Accounts in the Ancient Near East and the Bible*, CBQMS 26 (Washington, D.C.: Catholic Biblical Association), 31.

3. Clifford, *Creation Accounts*, 29–30.

4. *COS* 1.159.

5. Clifford, *Creation Accounts*, 50–51.

6. *COS* 1.130.

7. *COS* 1.111.

8. J. Allen, *Genesis in Egypt* (New Haven: Yale University Press, 1988); E. Wasilewska, *Creation Stories of the Middle East* (London: Jessica Kingsley, 2000); J. Hoffmeier, "Some Thoughts on Genesis 1 & 2 and Egyptian Cosmology," *JANES* 15 (1983): 39–49.

9. *COS* 1.8.

10. *COS* 1.17; see also 1.9.

11. *COS* 1.35.

12. A broken line in *Enki and Ninmah* suggests that the gods are smashing their tools, but it is difficult to interpret with certainty.

Comparative Exploration: Polygenesis and Monogenesis

The ancient Near Eastern texts typically speak of human origins in collective terms (polygenesis). There is no indication of an original human pair that became the progenitors of the entire human race (monogenesis). This is one of the distinctives of the Genesis account. The only extant text that has been suspected of depicting an original human pair is *KAR* 4. This idiosyncratic text has both Akkadian and Sumerian versions, with the main exemplar from Ashur dated to about 1100 BC.[1] The most important lines (19–49) describe all the intended functions of the human beings that the gods are planning to create (the text never reports their actual creation, only the plan to do so). Line 39 says, "They will be named Ullegarra and Annegarra." The problem is that these names, which seem like they could be the names of the first humans in the context, are preceded by the divine determinative, which suggests that they belong to the divine realm.[2] This text still has many uncertainties connected to its reading and interpretation. The text then sees people multiplying (line 40) and anticipates that "learned person after learned person, unlearned after unlearned will spring up like the grain" (line 44; notice "springing up," not "being born"). This is still far from the Israelite view of Adam (or Noah for that matter) as the progenitor of the race.

1. E. Ebeling, *KAR: Erster Band* (28 Wissenschaftliche Veröffentlichung der deutschen Orientgesellschaft) 1919; (Leipzig: J. C. Hinrichs'sche, 1919, 1923). Translation of the text and a limited commentary (no discussion of monogenism/polygenism) in Clifford, *Creation Accounts*, 49–51. For translation, transliteration, and commentary see G. Pettinato, *Das altorientalisch Menschenbild und die sumerischen und akkadischen Schöpfungomythen* (Heidelberg: Carl Winter Universitätsverlag, 1971), 74–81.

2. Earlier lines speak of slaying two gods whose blood will be used to create humans. Since the two beings named here are gods, there may be some connection to those who were slain.

What Are Humans Made Of?

Though there are numerous common motifs, there is no consensus in the ancient Near East concerning what humans are made of. Two Sumerian accounts portray people breaking out from the ground (*Song of the Hoe, Hymn to E-engura*). Clay alone is used in the Egyptian Pyramid Texts (using a potter's wheel) and in one Sumerian account (*Enki and Ninmah*[13]). Some Egyptian accounts use a product from the liv-

13. This may refer to special clay since it is gotten from the "heart" of clay on the top of the Abzu—perhaps suggesting clay that has regenerative qualities. Jacobsen translates it a "fathering clay" in *HTO* 156. Lambert ("The Relationship of Sumerian and Babylonian Myth as Seen in Accounts of Creation," in *La Circulation des biens, des personnes et des idées dans le Proche-Orient ancient*, ed. D. Charpin and F. Joannès [Paris: Recherche sur la

ing creator deity (tears[14] in the *Coffin Texts*, his body in *Instruction of Merikare*), whereas Akkadian accounts use products from a slain rebel deity. In *Atrahasis* both flesh and blood are used, whereas in *Enuma Elish* and *KAR* 4[15] only the blood is mentioned. Only in *Atrahasis* is there a combination of common and divine materials.[16] Divine infusion may be represented by means of the mother goddess giving birth to humans (*Enki and Ninmah*) or by the divine breath (*Coffin Texts*, *Instruction of Merikare*). Thus in the *Coffin Texts* deity states: "I will lead them and enliven them, through my mouth, which is life in their nostrils. I will lead my breath into their throats" (refers to all creatures, not just humans).

In the Israelite account the elements are dust and the breath of Deity. These have a ring of familiarity about them, but with some important distinctions. Like a number of the ancient Near Eastern accounts, there is no physical element provided by Deity (tears, blood, or flesh). The breath, as in the Egyptian accounts, is not a part of Deity, though it indicates that Deity is the source of life. In both Egypt and Israel, the breath of the deity characterizes all sentient life, not just humans. Furthermore, one should notice that with regard to the nondivine ingredients from which living beings are made, there is a difference between clay and dust. In the ancient Near East, clay is a means to impose form for the body. Dust cannot be used the same way, since it is not able to be molded. Clay has significance for the artistic process.[17] Though clay is not explicitly connected to death in these works as dust is in Genesis, *Erra and Ishum* indicates that clay is what is left behind after the blood (life/intellect) is gone.[18] A. Kilmer suggested that the appearance of the placenta, since it bore some resemblance to clay, led the ancients to infer that clay was the stuff of creation. The placenta may have been viewed as the leftover stuff from the formation of the fetus in the uterus.[19] Dust

---

Civilisations, 1992], 134) believes that blood may well be mentioned in the previous line, but not the blood of a slain deity—perhaps Enki's own blood. The text is very difficult. Note also that in the *Atrahasis Epic* the Igigi and Anunna gods all spit on the clay before it is put to use (lines 233–34).

14. In Egyptian the word for "tears" (*rmwt*) is very similar to the word for "people" (*rmtn*); see J. van Dijk, "Myth and Mythmaking in Ancient Egypt," *CANE* 3:1707. See *Coffin Text* spell 1130 in *COS* 1.17, p. 27.

15. There is no indication in *KAR* 4 that the two slain deities are rebels.

16. The bilingual version of *Enki and Ninmah* suggests that mixture may also occur there. See Lambert, "Relationship," 129–35.

17. T. Abusch, "Ghost and God: Some Observations on a Babylonian Understanding of Human Nature," in *Self, Soul and Body*, ed. Baumgarten, Assmann, and Stroumsa, 371: "represents the material form of man and serves as a base."

18. Cattle turn to clay upon death in *Erra and Ishum* I.74 (*COS* 1.113).

19. A. D. Kilmer, "The Brick of Birth," *JNES* 46 (1987): 211–13.

is not fertile, nor is it able to be shaped; it represents a connection to the earth only in death.

The ingredients used in human creation offer an archetypal analysis of what was believed about the nature of humanity by those who preserved these accounts. The difference between polygenism and monogenism points, among other things, to a basic difference in the role the archetype plays and how humanity is subsequently viewed. It is therefore beneficial to investigate how archetypal humanity is represented textually.[20] Archetypal humanity is represented in Mesopotamian texts in at least two identifiable ways. The first and most common is in its corporate and collective representation. This corporate identity makes clear that the accounts of human origins, featuring discussions of role and ingredients, extend broadly to all of humanity. A second representation is in *Enki and Ninmah*, in which the mother goddess, *Ninmah*, undertakes the challenge of creating archetypes of certain handicapped or defective classes of humans for which Enki, the god of wisdom, has to find a role.[21] Though these are individuals, they function as archetypes and are textually significant only as archetypes. The focus on roles and functions is obvious, and is the basis of the contest.

Archetypal discussions by definition focus on connectedness and relationship because archetypes offer a paradigm or an exemplar. The archetypes establish a pattern and stand as a representative of a specified class. Connectivity and relationship are vital in trying to understand an ancient sense of personal and corporate identity. One aspect of this can be seen in an Akkadian wordplay that connects the term for "man" (*awilu*) with the term for "god" (*ilu*).[22] Hebrew also offers wordplay connections of an archetypal nature by indicating the term *'adam* is appropriate since he is drawn from *'adamah* ("ground") and *'iššah* ("woman") is taken from *'iš* ("man"). By offering an understanding of how things fit together these wordplays reflect a sense of order. They naturally also address roles in the cosmos and in society. Several associations of archetypal relationship are addressed in the ancient world:

- humans to deity
- male to female
- humans to created world
- humans to previous and future generations

20. Consider R. Hess's discussion of the use of Hebrew *'adam* in Gen. 1–5. R. Hess, "Splitting the Adam: The Usage of 'Adam in Genesis i–iv," in *Studies in the Pentateuch*, ed. J. A. Emerton, VTSup 41 (Leiden: Brill, 1990), 1–16.
21. These include the crippled, blind, barren, and those lacking genitalia.
22. For further discussion of wordplays see Abusch, "Ghost and God," 368.

Comparative Exploration: Archetypal Humanity in Israel and the Ancient Near East

Would Israelites believe that all men were created out of dust? Certainly, because "dust you are and to dust you shall return" is not applicable only to Adam. Are women made of dust as well? On two counts, yes. First because Eve is made from the "side" of Adam—from Adam-parts; and second because the return to dust applies to her as well. Are all women built from the side of man? Given the narrator's comment in Genesis 2:24, the indication is that this connectedness through the "rib" is characteristic of the race. It should be noted in this regard that in Genesis the woman is technically built from the "side" (Heb. *tsela'*) of man. The word is usually architectural,[1] and is used anatomically only here in the Old Testament. In Akkadian the cognate term, *ṣelu*, is also both architectural and anatomical. Its anatomical uses generally refer not just to bone but to bones and flesh.[2] One could then ask whether it is also true that all men and women are to be viewed as two sides of an original whole.[3] All of this suggests that the dust/rib element is significant not primarily for the individuals but for the archetypes.[4] Every man is made from dust and every woman from the side of man. Male and female are also archetypal descriptions. What are the implications of these observations for interpreting the biblical account?

Ancient Near Eastern anthropology suggests that Adam and Eve should be understood in archetypal terms stressing the elements of connectivity that are inherent in their labels. All people are connected to the ground and are mortal (made of dust). All men and women are connected to one another (rib) with stronger connectivity links than to mother and father. They become functional not only as images of God, but as beings interconnected to the cosmos, to God, and to one another. Though their importance as archetypes does not rule out understanding them as individuals, it is worth noticing that the Old Testament never mentions them after Genesis 5[5] and the New Testament often treats them archetypally.

Summary

Differences in archetypal presentation:

Ancient Near East: Collective archetype
Connection to deity through ingredients
Doing corvée labor of the gods
Israel: Human couple archetypes
Connection to ground in death
Male and female connection
Connection to deity in role only, not in ingredients

Similarities in archetypal presentation:

Task of growing food is a principal role (Israel outside garden/ancient Near East providing for deity)
Mortality is an important concern (Israel as a result of disobedience/ancient Near East *Atrahasis* after the flood[6])
Image of god (see discussion under the following heading "What Is a Human?" for additional nuances)

1. See Exod. 25:14; 36:31–32; 1 Kings 6:5; Ezek. 41:5–9. For full discussion see H.-J. Fabry, *TDOT* 12:401.

2. *CAD Ṣ*: 125. Compare a "side" of beef or a rack of ribs.

3. B. Batto, *Slaying the Dragon* (Louisville: Westminster John Knox, 1992), 54, suggests that Gen. 2 be interpreted this way: that as Adam slept God virtually divided him in half to create Eve.

4. The recognition of an archetypal focus for the biblical account of human origins does not affect the debate in confessional (particularly evangelical) circles concerning the historicity of Adam and Eve. Archetypal identity neither affirms nor denies the existence of the individual. For instance, Abraham has his greatest significance as an archetype—within the covenant and in relation to the people of Israel—but that does not imply that he is not to be viewed as a historical individual. In this way of thinking, the distinction should be made that the sin of the archetypes Adam and Eve has significance for all humanity because they are archetypes, not because they are genetic parents. The faithfulness of the archetype Abraham has significance for all the Israelites, not because he is the genetic parent, but because

he is an archetype. Indeed, he is the father of all who believe. Paul certainly treats Adam as an archetype, but it is the nuancing and implications of that term that would be controversial in the study of Rom. 5.

5. Except for 1 Chron. 1:1, the reference to Adam at the beginning of the Chronicler's genealogy.

6. W. G. Lambert, "The Theology of Death," in *Death in Mesopotamia*, ed. Bendt Alster, Mesopotamia 8/RAI 26 (Copenhagen: Akademisk, 1980), 53–66, specifically 58, where he offers the reconstruction of tablet III, col. VI, lines 47–50: "[You] birth goddess, creatress of destinies; [assign death] to the peoples." Accepted by B. Foster, see *COS* 1.131:452; Abusch, "Ghost and God," 367; and B. Batto, "Creation Theology in Genesis," in *Creation in the Biblical Traditions*, ed. R. J. Clifford and J. J. Collins (Washington, D.C.: Catholic Biblical Association, 1992), 24. This destiny of natural death is in contrast to the former situation in which humans could have died through violent means. In *Atrahasis* this step would represent a concession to resolve the original "noise" problem and the overpopulation.

Every account of human origins seeks to address similar archetypal issues. They mirror what we already found in our discussion of cosmology—they focus on functional issues rather than material ones. This may sound like an unusual statement to make since all of these accounts make specific references to the materials used for the creation of humans. But the materials mentioned serve to address archetypal issues (connectivity, relationships, roles) rather than to penetrate material ontology (let alone chemical composition). This is not to say that the ancients were speaking metaphorically rather than literally, for this goes far beyond a literary or rhetorical device. The accounts address the topic by using archetypes, which express the most important realities in this cognitive environment. Materials are mentioned for their archetypal significance, not for their physical significance. Blood and flesh of the deity signify connection to deity. Clay or dust signifies connection to the land. The connections described by these archetypes offer information concerning the ancient corporate self-understanding.

In the ancient Near East, one might claim that, given the collective nature of their self-understanding, even self-awareness had a fundamentally archetypal value.

An appraisal of the Babylonian conception of the person should begin with the reminder that the notion of personhood is not a universal and innate category. The modern concept of person is in fact a long way removed from the view of the ancients. . . . In ancient cultures, such as Mesopotamia, the human person is understood as a character or a role, rather than as a personality; the individual is not a *personne* (person) but a *personage* (character).[23]

In this regard it would be inherently contradictory for the Akkadian literature to begin with individual persons. It is to some degree anachronistic for us to raise such issues.[24]

What Is a Human? (Body, Soul, Spirit)

Even modern theologians argue whether the human person is best understood by trichotomy (body/soul/spirit), dichotomy (body/soul-spirit), or unity. The ancient world shared some of our concern for understanding the human person, but it viewed the person quite differently than we do.

In Mesopotamia the clearest information comes in the *Epic of Atrahasis*,[25] where the various ingredients used to create humankind appear to correspond to the various aspects of human nature. According to the interpretation of T. Abusch, the human ghost (*etemmu*) derives from the flesh of the god, while the blood (*damu*) of the god provides the human intellect (*temu*), self, or soul.[26] "The blood is the dynamic quality of intelligence, and the flesh is the form of the body that is imposed on the clay."[27]

Egyptian and Israelite literatures portray the deity giving the breath of life to mundane materials, invigorating them to serve in the role of divine images. In Egyptian thinking human nature was composed of the body (*djet*-body as well as the *ha'u*-body), the *akh*, the *ka*, and the *ba*, and designations such as heart, belly, shadow, and name.[28] The terms *ka* and *ba* are impossible to translate adequately into English (or to Greek or Latin) because they do not have equivalent ideas in Western culture.

---

23. K. van der Toorn, *Family Religion in Babylonia, Syria and Israel: Continuity and Change in the Forms of Religious Life* (Leiden: Brill, 1996), 115. See D. Snell, "The Invention of the Individual," in *Companion to the Ancient Near East*, ed. D. Snell (Oxford: Blackwell, 2005), 357–69.

24. The issue of interiority and individualism was discussed in more detail in chap. 6 in the section on family religion.

25. *COS* 1.130:210–30.

26. Abusch, "Ghost and God," 363–83.

27. Ibid., 371–72.

28. Assmann, "Dialogue," 384.

Ka

A distinction must be drawn between an internal *ka* and an external one. The internal *ka* reflected that aspect of human nature that had ties to the supernatural and, at least in some vague way, ties to future generations.

Ka could designate human individuality as a whole, and in different contexts it could be translated as "character," "nature," "temperament," or "disposition." Since character to a great extent preordains the life of an individual, *ka* also means "destiny" or "providence." This use of the word engendered a tradition of interpreting the *ka* as a kind of universal vital force, but this idea is too abstract since it loses its association with personality.[29]

The external *ka* was like an invisible twin born with the person and associated with the placenta. The *ka* continued to live into the afterlife and received offerings on the individual's behalf.

Ba

The *ba* is connected to cognition and other mental capacities. It is often translated "soul" despite the inaccuracies of the identification. The *ba* is the aspect of a person reflected to the world around him or her. One's reputation and public persona project one's *ba*.[30] One's *ba* exists independently of one's body in what one accomplishes and how one is thought about and spoken of. The *ba* leaves the body at death and continues to exist after death. The *ba* of a deity is what enters the image to make it usable and living in the cult. This might approximate the Akkadian *ṭemu*. Perhaps it overlaps most with the modern concept of personality.

Akh

The *akh* is often translated "spirit," and also survives after death, somewhat like a ghost.[31] The *akh* of a person, in either life or death, was capable of effecting either good or ill. If "ghost" goes in the right direction, there would be some overlap between *akh* and the Akkadian *eṭemmu*.

29. A. Bolshakov, "Ka," *OEAE* 2:215. The reader might get the best idea of this by comparing to what we understand of DNA, which represents our unique individuality, has a large role in determining what kind of person we are, and extends into future generations.

30. J. Allen, "Ba," *OEAE* 1:161–62.

31. But a distinction should be made with the word *šuy,t* which refers to a person's "shade"; see L. Lesko, "Death and the Afterlife in Ancient Egyptian Thought," *CANE* 3:1763–74.

Comparative Exploration: Image of God

Throughout the ancient Near East, it is usually the king who is seen as representing the image of God.[1] One exception is in the early-second-millennium Egyptian *Instruction of Merikare*, which applies the idea to all people. The image was seen as possessing the essence of the deity that empowered it to carry out divine functions.[2] In her study of royal images I. Winter concludes that the representations of the king were not intended to capture his physical features. In an image it was not physical likeness that was important, but a more abstract, idealized representation of identity relating to the office/role and the value connected to the image.[3] In this context, Akkadian *ṣalmu* does not refer to the physical relief but to the abstract imagery, the conceptual idea, that represents the attributes of the deity. When the Assyrian king Esarhaddon is referred to as "the perfect likeness of the god," it is his qualities and his attributes that are meant.[4] That the king has been imbued with the image of the deity is the source of his power and prerogative.

An understanding of what it means for people to be in the image of god in the ancient world can be enhanced by exploring other uses of "image" as well. For instance, in both Egypt and Mesopotamia an idol contained the image of the deity.[5] This allowed the image to possess the attributes of the deity, function as mediator of worship to the deity, and serve as indicator of the presence of the deity. In another reflection, the image of a king was considered to be present in monuments set up in territories he had conquered.[6]

Across the ancient world, the image of God did the work of God on the earth. In the Israelite context as portrayed in the Hebrew Bible, people are in the image of God in that they embody his qualities and do his work. They are symbols of his presence and act on his behalf as his representatives.

In the most significant parallel to the image of God in Genesis 1 from the ancient world, the Aramaic portion of the bilingual inscription from Tell Fekheriye uses cognates of both of the Hebrew terms appearing in Genesis 1:26–27 to indicate that the statue both contains the essence and represents the substance of Hadad-Yith'i, king of Guzan.[7]

Hebrew terminology does not correspond with Egyptian or Mesopotamian terminology any better than it corresponds with modern English. The Egyptian *akh* may bring to mind the way the *ruah-yhwh* came upon individuals to make them effective either for good (in most cases, e.g., the judges) or for ill (e.g., Saul). Yet some have made a case for Hebrew *nephesh* as being equivalent to Akkadian *eṭemmu*.[32] The Israelite concepts of *basar* ("flesh"), *nephesh* (often translated

---

32. J. C. Greenfield, "Un rite religieux araméen et ses parallèles," *RB* 80 (1973): 46–50. It should be noted that Hebrew *nephesh* has cognates in Akkadian and Ugaritic that partially overlap semantically.

1. E. M. Curtis, *Man as the Image of God in Genesis in Light of Ancient Near Eastern Parallels* (Ann Arbor: University Microfilms, 1984), 80–90; the earliest such use is in Egypt in the 18th Dynasty, second half of the second millennium BC. In Mesopotamia most examples are Neo-Assyrian, with the earliest being Middle Assyrian (13th century), by Tukulti-Ninurta I. Another thorough and helpful treatment of the image of God in ancient Near Eastern texts can be found in J. R. Middleton, *The Liberating Image* (Grand Rapids: Brazos, 2005), 93–231.

2. W. W. Hallo, "Cult Statue and Divine Image: A Preliminary Study," in *Scripture in Context II*, ed. W. W. Hallo, J. C. Moyer, and L. G. Perdue (Winona Lake, IN: Eisenbrauns, 1983), 1–18; I. J. Winter, "Art in Empire: The Royal Image and the Visual Dimensions of Assyrian Ideology," in *Assyria 1995*, ed. S. Parpola and R. M. Whiting (Helsinki: Neo-Assyrian Text Corpus Project, 1997), 359–81;

B. F. Batto, "The Divine Sovereign: The Image of God in the Priestly Creation Account," in *David and Zion*, ed. B. Batto and K. L. Roberts (Winona Lake, IN: Eisenbrauns, 2004), 143–86. Curtis, *Man as the Image*, and Middleton, *Liberating Image*, offer the most thorough defense of the functional understanding of the image.

3. Winter, "Art," 373–76.

4. S. Parpola, *Letters from Assyrian and Babylonian Scholars*, SAA 10 (Helsinki: University of Helsinki Press, 1993), #207. This same text refers to a "well-known proverb" that "Man is the shadow of god." See *BWL*, 282.

5. Curtis, *Man as the Image*, 97–113.

6. Ibid., 119–20; M. Cogan, *Imperialism and Religion: Assyria, Judah and Israel in the Eighth and Seventh Centuries B.C.E.*, SBLMS 19 (Missoula, MT: Scholars Press, 1974), 58–61.

7. *COS* 2.34.

"soul" or "self"), and *ruah* (usually translated "spirit") do not overlay transparently on either Mesopotamian or Egyptian models. At the most basic level, this could be explained by the facts that the Egyptian concepts are largely developed in relationship to what they believed about death and afterlife (i.e., in light of teleology), while the Mesopotamian concepts are elaborated in relationship to what they believed about human beginnings (i.e., in light of protology). Concepts conveyed in the Hebrew Bible, in contrast to the ancient Near East, are consciously linked not to protology or teleology, but to theology—the relationship to God.

Nephesh

Hebrew *nephesh*, despite its traditional translation "soul," never refers to that which continues to exist after death,[33] though the *nephesh* departs when one dies (Gen. 35:18). In this connection, H. W. Wolff observes, "man does not *have* [*nephesh*], he *is* [*nephesh*], he lives as [*nephesh*]."[34] God also is characterized by *nephesh* (e.g., Isa. 1:14).[35] Though it was granted to Adam when God breathed into him (Gen. 2:7), it is not a "piece" of the divine, but only finds its source there. As the part of the

33. H. Seebass, *TDOT* 9:515–16; Ps. 16:10 is the most ambiguous, but is not clear enough to make the case.

34. H. W. Wolff, *Anthropology of the Old Testament* (Philadelphia: Fortress, 1974), 10.

35. See full discussion in Seebass, *TDOT* 9:516–17.

body that receives food and breathes, the *nephesh* is connected to the throat. In the metaphysical realm, the *nephesh* is that which experiences life and represents living (notice that the life, *nephesh,* is in the blood, Lev. 17:11, and the blood is the *nephesh*, Deut. 12:23). In the plural it can refer to persons, and is often related to the "self."[36]

Ruah

Where the *nephesh* feels and senses, the *ruah* acts.[37] Where the *nephesh* is related to awareness and perception, the *ruah* is related to consciousness and vitality. Like *nephesh,* the *ruah* is not understood as continuing to exist once the person dies. Indeed, it is difficult to demonstrate that a person has his/her own *ruah*. Rather each person has God's *ruah*.[38] God also has a *ruah* and his *ruah* sustains human life (Job 34:14; Ps. 104:29). The *ruah* of all creatures returns to God because it is his.[39] Israel's ideas of human composition express most centrally the individual's relationship to God in life and dependence on God for life. What continues to exist in Sheol after death is neither *nephesh* nor *ruah*.

What then is the impact of comparative studies on the understanding of the metaphysics of anthropology? On the basis of this brief study, we have seen that there are some overlapping categories, but that it is difficult to establish any one-to-one correspondences. The comparative data may, as always, urge restraint on our inclination to impose modern categories on the ancient texts, but they do not give us any greater understanding of Israelite metaphysical anthropology. Concerning the cognitive environment, we can see that the ancient views tended to focus more on theological and functional categories than on psychological (e.g., Freudian) or philosophical (e.g., Platonic) ones.

What Is the Human Role in the Cosmos? (Why Were Humans Created and What Is the Decreed Destiny of Humanity?)

The roles assigned to humans bind them together in their common plight and bind them to the gods in servitude. Egyptian sources offer no explanation for the creation of humans. Sumerian and Akkadian sources

36. In this semantic range Hebrew *nephesh* overlaps considerably with Akkadian *napištu* (*CAD* N/1: 296–304).

37. In general see H.-J. Fabry, *TDOT* 13:365–402. Akkadian and Sumerian have no cognates. The Ugaritic cognate is not as clearly or as essentially an anthropological term.

38. Ibid., 386–87; note esp. Job 27:3–4. Most ambiguous on this point is Zech. 12:1.

39. Ibid., 387–88.

consistently portray people as having been created to do the work of the gods—work that is essential for the continuing existence of the gods, and work that they have tired of doing for themselves.

Enki and Ninmah: servants for the gods: "The corvée of the gods has been forced on it."

KAR 4: "The corvée of the gods will be their corvée: They will fix the boundaries of the fields once and for all, and take in their hands hoes and baskets, to benefit the House of the great gods."[40]

Atrahasis: "Let him bear the yoke, the task of Enlil, Let man assume the drudgery of god."[41]

Enuma Elish: To bear the gods' burden that those may rest.[42]

In Israel people also believed that they had been created to serve God. The difference was that they saw humanity as having been given a priestly role in sacred space[43] rather than as slave labor to meet the needs of deity. God planted the garden to provide food for people rather than people providing food for the gods.[44] The explanation offered in *KAR* 4 shows that the priestly role of people was included in the profile, but still in terms of providing sustenance for the gods. The shared cognitive environment is evident in that all across the ancient world there was interest in exploring the divine component of humankind and the ontological relationship between the human and divine. In Mesopotamia the cosmos functions for the gods and in relation to them. People are an afterthought, seen as just another part of the cosmos that helps the gods function. In Israel the cosmos functions for people and in relationship to them. God does not need the cosmos, but it is his temple. It functions for people.

With this understanding of human origins, history has begun and the stage is set for it to unfold. We will now explore how this unfolding drama was understood and transmitted.

---

40. Clifford, *Creation Accounts*, 50 (lines 21–23).
41. *COS* 1.130:196–97.
42. *Enuma Elish*, VI:8, 34, 36.
43. J. Walton, *Genesis*, NIVAC (Grand Rapids: Zondervan, 2001), 172–74.
44. Note the combination of digging ditches and caring for sacred space in *KAR* 4, where people are doing manual labor in the care of sacred space (lines 27–51). See D. Callender, *Adam in Myth and History*, HSS 48 (Winona Lake, IN: Eisenbrauns, 2000), 57.

10

Understanding the Past

Historiography

At some point, if a record of events is to be preserved, it must be incorporated into a written form.[1] Such an undertaking requires the compiler

1. After the survey by J. van Seters, "The Historiography of the Ancient Near East," *CANE* 4:2433–44, key resources include: B. Albrektson, *History and the Gods*, ConBOT 1 (Lund: Gleerup, 1967); B. T. Arnold, "The Weidner Chronicle and the Idea of History in Israel and Mesopotamia," in *Faith, Tradition, and History*, ed. A. R. Millard, J. K. Hoffmeier, and D. W. Baker (Winona Lake, IN: Eisenbrauns, 1994), 129–48; R. E. Averbeck, "Sumer, the Bible, and Comparative Method: Historiography and Temple Building," in *Mesopotamia and the Bible*, ed. M. W. Chavalas and K. L. Younger Jr. (Grand Rapids: Baker, 2002), 88–125; idem, "Ancient Near Eastern Mythography as It Relates to Historiography in the Hebrew Bible: Genesis 3 and the Cosmic Battle," in *The Future of Biblical Archaeology: Reassessing Methods and Assumptions*, ed. J. K. Hoffmeier and A. R. Millard (Grand Rapids: Eerdmans, 2004), 328–57; T. M. Bolin, "History, Historiography, and the Use of the Past in the Hebrew Bible," in *Limits of Historiography*, ed. C. S. Kraus (Leiden: Brill, 1999), 113–40; A. K. Grayson, "Assyria and Babylonia," *Or* 49 (1980): 140–94; W. W. Hallo, "Sumerian Historiography," in *History, Historiography and Interpretation*, ed. H. Tadmor and M. Weinfeld (Jerusalem: Magnes, 1983), 9–20; idem, "Biblical History in Its Near Eastern Setting," in *Scripture in Context: Essays on the Comparative Method*, ed. C. Evans, W. Hallo, and J. White (Pittsburgh: Pickwick, 1980), 1–26; B. Halpern, *The First Historians: The Hebrew Bible and History* (San Francisco: Harper & Row, 1988), 1–13; W. G. Lambert, "Destiny and Divine Intervention in Babylon and Israel," *OtSt* 17 (1972): 65–72; J. Licht, "Biblical Historicism," in *History, Historiography and Interpretation*, ed. Tadmor and Weinfeld, 107–20; M. Liverani, *Myth and Politics in Ancient Near Eastern His-*

to work under a set of guiding principles, conscious and subconscious. It is this set of guiding principles that constitutes one's historiography. Opinions about the appropriate form, content, and structure of a preserved record of events constitute part of this historiography, but they are only the surface issues. What is important about the events of the past? Why is the account being compiled? How do events come to pass? What causes or forces drive history? Are there patterns in history? Is there design in history? The answers to these questions will play a significant role in determining how history will be written. It goes without saying that different individuals, and different cultures, will answer the questions in different ways. Thus any given historical record is going to represent a particular perspective about the events of the past. The shape of one's historiography is going to be determined by the questions the compiler is seeking to answer. In this light *any* historiography should, by rights, be referred to as "perspectives on history." Any historiography must, in some sense, be viewed as an editorial column.

The study of historiography is not necessarily the study of a genre of literature. Rather, the cultures of the ancient world express their historiography in a variety of genres. The genres that dominate are useful in

toriography (Ithaca: Cornell University Press, 2004); V. P. Long, *The Art of Biblical History* (Grand Rapids: Zondervan, 1994); V. P. Long, D. Baker, and G. Wenham, *Windows into Old Testament History* (Grand Rapids: Eerdmans, 2002); P. Machinist, "The Voice of the Historian in the Ancient Near Eastern and Mediterranean World," *Interpretation* 57 (2003): 117–37; P. Michalowski, "Commemoration, Writing, and Genre in Ancient Mesopotamia," in *Limits of Historiography*, ed. Kraus, 69–90; A. R. Millard, "History and Legend in Early Babylonia," in *Windows into Old Testament History*, ed. Long, Baker, and Wenham, 103–10; I. Provan, V. P. Long, and T. Longman, *A Biblical History of Israel* (Louisville: Westminster John Knox, 2003); I. Provan, "Ideologies, Literary and Critical: Reflections on Recent Writing on the History of Israel," *JBL* 114 (1995): 585–606; idem, "In the Stable with the Dwarves: Testimony, Interpretation, Faith and the History of Israel," in *Congress Volume: Oslo 1998*, ed. A. Lemaire and M. Sæbø, VTSup 80 (Leiden: Brill, 2000), 281–319; repr. in *Windows into Old Testament History*, ed. Long, Baker, and Wenham, 161–97; J. J. M. Roberts, "Myth versus History: Relaying the Comparative Foundations," in *The Bible and the Ancient Near East* (Winona Lake, IN: Eisenbrauns, 2002), 59–71; H. W. F. Saggs, *The Encounter with the Divine in Mesopotamia and Israel* (London: Athlone, 1978), 64–92; E. A. Speiser, "The Biblical Idea of History in Its Common Near Eastern Setting" (1957); repr. in *Oriental and Biblical Studies*, ed. J. J. Finkelstein and M. Greenberg (Philadelphia: University of Pennsylvania Press, 1967), 187–212; H. Tadmor, "Propaganda, Literature, Historiography: Cracking the Code of the Assyrian Royal Inscriptions," in *Assyria 1995*, ed. S. Parpola and R. M. Whiting (Helsinki: Neo-Assyrian Text Corpus Project, 1997), 325–38; M. Van de Mieroop, *Cuneiform Texts and the Writing of History* (London: Routledge, 1999); J. Van Seters, *In Search of History* (New Haven: Yale University Press, 1983); N. Winther-Nielsen, "Fact, Fiction, and Language Use: Can Modern Pragmatics Improve on Halpern's Case for History in Judges?" in *Windows into Old Testament History*, ed. Long, Baker, and Wenham, 44–81; K. L. Younger, *Ancient Conquest Accounts*, JSOTSup 98 (Sheffield: JSOT Press, 1990); Z. Zevit, *Religions of Ancient Israel* (New York: Continuum, 2001), 27–80.

providing insight into the values of historiography and the view of history in that culture. Even when the genres differ from culture to culture, they can be compared with regard to their historiography. Legitimate comparison can be made in a variety of ways, because the literatures serve similar sociological functions.[2]

Genres

Numerous genres are used in Mesopotamian historiography. M. van de Mieroop classifies historiographic texts into two larger categories: commemorative records and chronographic texts.[3] The former includes annals, building accounts, and royal inscriptions of various sorts that were inscribed on stone and set up in public places. They narrowly focus on a particular king and his accomplishments. In contrast, the chronographic texts include treatment of kings of the past presented in a variety of forms from lists to narratives.[4] Narrative works such as the *Dynastic Prophecy* and the *Weidner Chronicle* are more literary in nature. Historical epics such as the Sumerian tales of Lugalbanda or Enmerkar,[5] and Akkadian legends of Sargon or Naram-Sin (kings of Akkad) to the *Epic of Tukulti-Ninurta* (Middle Assyrian), are also important exemplars of historiography. Egyptian, Hittite, and Syro-Palestinian sources can be represented in similar categories, though not evidencing as broad a range.[6]

---

2. Averbeck, "Sumer," 112–13.

3. Van de Mieroop, *Cuneiform*, 25. Note also the classification of categories offered by J. Glassner, *Mesopotamian Chronicles*, SBLWAW 19 (Atlanta: SBL, 2004), 15–21.

4. Many translated in Glassner, *Mesopotamian Chronicles*.

5. H. Vanstiphout, *Epics of Sumerian Kings*, SBLWAW 20 (Atlanta: SBL, 2003).

6. None of these has been studied as broadly as Mesopotamian historiography. My treatment in this chapter will occasionally refer to Egyptian or Hittite ideas, but deals primarily with Mesopotamia for a number of defensible or heuristic reasons. Hittite historiography is sometimes touted as the earliest historiography, while Egyptologists wonder whether, despite the Egyptian interest in the past, any of their literature could be termed historiographic. Among a number of important studies of Hittite historiography are: H. A. Hoffner, "Histories and Historians of the Ancient Near East: The Hittites," *Or* 49 (1980): 283–332; idem, "Propaganda and Political Justification in Hittite Historiography," in *Unity and Diversity*, ed. H. Goedicke and J. J. M. Roberts (Baltimore: Johns Hopkins University Press, 1975), 49–64; A. Malamat, "Doctrines of Causality in Hittite and Biblical Historiography: A Parallel," *VT* 5 (1955): 1–12; Y. Cohen, "The Image of the 'Other' and Hittite Historiography," in *Historiography in the Cuneiform World*, ed. T. Abusch et al., RAI 45, Part 1 (Bethesda, MD: CDL, 2001), 113–30; G. McMahon, "History and Legend in Early Hittite Historiography," in *Faith, Tradition, and History*, ed. Millard, Hoffmeier, and Baker, 149–58; A. Uchitel, "Local versus General History in Old Hittite Historiography," in *Limits of Historiography*, ed. Kraus, 55–68; H. Güterbock, "Hittite Historiography: A Survey," in *History, Historiography and Interpretation*, ed. Tadmor and Weinfeld, 21–35.

In this section we will attempt to understand the cognitive environment of the ancient world with regard to history and historiography. Our discussion will address (1) the role of deity (theology), (2) the view of time and history (epistemology), (3) how historiography signifies (semiotics/hermeneutics), and (4) what values motivated the historiographical enterprise.

The Role of Deity in Historiography

The worldview of the historian will have far-reaching effects on one's view of history and on one's writing of history. Until the Enlightenment it was common for a person's worldview to be thoroughly supernaturalistic (transcendent). The role of deity was admitted and the belief in occurrences that defied easy explanation was commonplace. With the Enlightenment and the philosophies of Descartes, Spinoza, Hume, Voltaire, and Hegel, a significant shift occurred. The resulting historical-critical method "presupposes that all historical phenomena are subject to analogous experience, in terms of other similar phenomena."[7] It suggests that one can accept as true only that which can be empirically proven. It is concerned only with natural cause and effect in history.[8] This is largely the view adopted by our contemporary Western culture. "The positivist thrust . . . which claimed adequacy and authority on the grounds of reasoned analysis led eventually to the weakening of metaphysical explanations for historical events characteristic of pre-academic history and theology."[9]

The result is that the worldview of our contemporary society differs dramatically from the worldview of the ancient historians. While the ancients would not deny the existence of natural cause and effect in history, they were much more interested in the divine role in history. A modern empiricist historian's response to ancient (especially Israelite) transcendent historiography might be: "it has not provided information that is reliable, since it is so full of deity." The ancient historian's response to modern empiricist historiography might be: "it has not provided information that is worthwhile, since it is so empty of deity." The denial of supernatural

---

Egypt has far less, but see G. Kadish, "Historiography," *OEAE* 2:108–11; D. B. Redford, "Historiography of Ancient Egypt," in *Egyptology and the Social Sciences*, ed. K. Weeks (Cairo: American University in Cairo, 1979), 3–19.

7. M. Chavalas, "The Historian, the Believer, and the Old Testament: A Study in the Supposed Conflict of Faith and Reason," *JETS* 36 (1993): 145–62.

8. B. Spinoza, *Theologico-Political Treatise: Tractatus VI* (New York: Dover, 1990).

9. Zevit, *Religions*, 31. He goes on to talk about further developments in structuralism and eventually into postmodernism to arrive at contemporary views of historiography.

causation by many of today's historians means that any ancient document used in reconstructing a history that conforms to present-day standards needs to be "adjusted" by the modern historian to delete its nonempirical data and eliminate its supernaturalistic bias. Such may be considered necessary in order to present ancient history to a modern reader, who will want to read history expressed in the context of his or her own cognitive environment, but it represents cultural imperialism.

When we study the historiography of a pre-Enlightenment culture, it is important to recognize the cognitive environment that drives that historiography and to respect the integrity of it. The cognitive environment in the ancient world is one in which the directive activity of deity is of primary importance. This view extends far beyond the recognition of occasional supernatural interventions. In fact, even the word "intervention" is inappropriate because it implies that there are some historical events that are not supernaturally driven. In the view of the ancient Near East, even "natural" occurrences are the result of divine activity.[10]

Historical records in the ancient Near East do not claim to be revelation from deity, but they do show great interest in discerning the activities of the gods. The polytheistic nature of ancient Near Eastern religion impedes the development of any concept of a singular divine plan encompassing all of history. At best the reigning dynasty may identify a divine plan in establishing and sustaining that dynasty. Some documents look back into the distant past to see a pattern that led to the present (e.g., *Weidner Chronicle, Akitu Chronicle*). These typically concern not what the deity has done, but what has been done to the deity. In Mesopotamia it is assumed that deity plays an active part in the cause-and-effect process that comprises history. The causation of the gods is understood to be impromptu rather than in accordance with any overarching plan or grand design. As P. D. Hanson observes,

> An historical sequence spanning centuries in an unbroken development could not be recognized, for in reflecting cosmic events, history was reflecting timeless episodes. The rise and fall of empires reflected decisions in a divine assembly which was not bound by any historical sequence. One decision leads to the rise of Akkad to hegemony over the city states, another to its fall; again to the rise of Babylon, and its fall. No common line connects these separate phases in an unbroken development. They are but separate episodes reflecting isolated decisions in the divine assembly.[11]

10. S. Parker, *Stories in Scripture and Inscriptions* (Oxford: Oxford University Press, 1997), 75. For more detailed analysis expanded to all ancient conquest accounts see Younger, *Ancient Conquest Accounts*.

11. Paul Hanson, "Jewish Apocalyptic Against Its Near Eastern Environment," *RB* 78 (1971): 38–39.

Whether deity is understood to be working according to a long-term plan or not, the involvement of deity in history is clear. Without deity there is no history. Historiography provides little coherence if it leaves deity out of the picture. This is not to say that every piece of historiographic literature contains blatant and explicit theology.[12] But even though it is true that some types of accounts (e.g., building project reports) do not offer the explicit theological orientation, the cognitive environment is clear. Even when one genre or another deviates from the norm by its silence, throughout the ancient world history was considered the doings of the deity revealing the will of deity.[13]

Time and History

Thinking about Time

In contemporary Western societies we tend to imagine ourselves on the linear path of time (the pervasive timeline) with the past behind us, striding into the future, which is shrouded in mist. In the ancient Near East, in contrast, terminology indicates that the people viewed themselves positioned at the convergence of fields representing the past and the future. At this convergence they were oriented toward the past with its ancestors and traditions, while the future was obscured behind them.[14]

Important elements to the ancient understanding of time and history were recurrence and endurance.[15] This perspective is not without linear aspects, but the linear element is not the default mode. The passage of time was significant, but precision about the passage of time, particularly when the period transcended the life of the particular king and perhaps his predecessor, is not important. Continuity from the past in a succession of days and months, seasons and years, extended under the auspices of the present reign of the king, and eventually in the light of his memory and legacy in the future was of ultimate value.[16] Whereas continuity is embodied in the idea of endurance, a level of discontinuity is reflected in the cyclic concept of recurrence.[17] Whether it is the

12. Parker, *Stories*, 139.

13. Albrektson, *History*, 14, 100, and *passim*.

14. Glassner, *Mesopotamian Chronicles*, 7.

15. Ibid. For Egyptian reflections J. Assmann uses the categories of "change" and "completion" (*The Search for God in Ancient Egypt* [Ithaca: Cornell University Press, 2001], 74–77).

16. See the comparison of long periods in Mesopotamian chronicles offered by Glassner (*Mesopotamian Chronicles*, 7–8).

17. Based not on repetition but on similarity; see ibid., 10; G. W. Trompf, "Notions of Historical Recurrence in Classical Hebrew Historiography," in *Studies in the Historical*

Photo 17 Thutmose III—List of Defeated Kings

seasons, the generations of families, the prominence of cities, the reigns of kings and dynasties, or the rule of empires that come and go, the arrival of one means the end of another, and thus discontinuity prevails even as patterns continue.[18]

Thinking about History

Most peoples of the ancient world found the past interesting and significant and found in it a key to social coherence lending meaning to life in the present.[19] It is this quest for meaning that makes history

---

Books of the Old Testament, ed. J. A. Emerton, VTSup 30 (Leiden: Brill, 1979), 213–29. Retaining this idea should not be mistaken for agreement with J. J. Finkelstein's theories on the role of historical omens as the earliest and primary form of historiography. See J. J. Finkelstein, "Mesopotamian Historiography," *Proceedings of the American Philosophical Society* 107:6 (1963): 461–72, and the early refutation by W. G. Lambert, "Berossus and Babylonian Eschatology," *Iraq* 38 (1976): 171–73 and a more recent assessment in Michalowski, "Commemoration."

18. Glassner, *Mesopotamian Chronicles*, 8.

19. J. Assmann, "A Dialogue Between Self and Soul: Papyrus Berlin 3024," in *Self, Soul and Body in Religious Experience*, ed. A. I. Baumgarten, J. Assmann, and G. G. Stroumsa (Leiden: Brill, 1998), 396.

important. History should not be seen naïvely as an attempt to recount what really happened. The epistemological question concerns the extent to which we could ever know what *really* happened. When we ask that question about events that unfold day by day, we gain our answers through reports that offer glimpses from participants or eyewitnesses, and perspectives and opinions from those who might have some insight into the events. Though we are well aware of its deficiencies, this gathering of information takes place in individual circumstances all the time, and on the professional level is performed by journalists, whose findings eventually serve as resources for historians.

We have become so intrigued with what journalism provides for us that we have tried to extend its work into the writing of history (historiography). Modern-day historians probe into the past seeking similar reports (e.g., letters, diaries, journals) and perspectives that can help us portray history through the eyes of witnesses to the events. In this approach to history, we reflect a certain set of values that privileges the eyewitness and places the reconstruction of an event or sequence of events as the highest objective. It reflects the cultural values of our contemporary Western cognitive environment, which shows a strong inclination to atomization and individualization. This tendency is manifested in modern Western culture when we individualize events rather than seeking coherence in a collection or sequence.

Not all cultures think about history the same way. In the ancient world it is difficult to find anyone who could legitimately be identified as a historian or journalist. Their cognitive environment had no need of such professions. In the ancient Near East visible events on earth were reflections of the activity of the gods.[20] Consequently, rather than providing journalists who could seek out eyewitnesses, they needed experts who could interpret what deity was communicating through events (priests and palace officials), and those who could be part of building the documentation that would serve to elevate and legitimize the king (public relations departments for the palace). In Israel it was the prophets who most commonly provided the interpretation of history.[21]

In this sense one could perhaps go so far as to claim that there is no such thing as history, only the recounted interpretation of the past. B. Halpern refers to history as a "more or less useful coherence imposed by reason on reality."[22] It is an understanding about how this coherence was

---

20. This statement of connectedness should not be mistaken as expressing agreement with the merger of myth and history.

21. Hanson, "Jewish Apocalyptic," 31–58. Hanson sees the merging of the past and the future in Jewish eschatology. Both are interpreted by the prophets based on their access to the divine council (p. 35).

22. Halpern, *First Historians*, 7.

perceived and achieved that will lead us to the epistemology underlying the ancient view of history.

Coherence

We might then define historiography using the words of Egyptologist J. Assmann as the production of texts that "lend cohesion to the world of appearances in a way that gives meaning to it."[23] When knowledge of the past is based on its coherence, history is defined by its outcomes more than by its events.[24] Assmann captures this contrast in the Egyptian understanding of reality as based on the pursuit of *maat* rather than on an understanding of events, whether ordinary or extraordinary, which he elsewhere labels "resultativity."[25] The consequence of this focus on outcomes and resultativity is that historiography is teleological. "A chain of episodes is connected into a story in such a way that it is directed toward a goal. It is not the fact that the episodes stand in a cause-and-effect relationship, but that they lead teleologically to a good or bad ending, that determines the coherence of a story."[26]

Both history and the writing of it are "going somewhere" driven by divine purpose. In Egypt the attainment of *maat* is no divine plan, only a divine goal. In Mesopotamia the goal is legitimation of the king, which creates harmony between the divine and human realms. In Israel the goal is the reestablishment of divine presence and the achievement of right relationship in a community of people with their God. This goal is pursued through a divine plan embodied in the covenant.

This teleology is a result of divine purpose and therefore is absent from modern perceptions just as teleology is absent from modern perceptions of creation.[27] In the ancient world, creation and history flow together seamlessly, bound together by divine purpose and activity (see table 1). It is this teleological perspective that is the common ground of the ancient cognitive environment, even though it is reflected in vastly different ways from culture to culture.

23. Assmann, *Search for God*, 95.
24. It may be of interest to note that this epistemology can also be noted in the NT in examples like the man born blind in John 9 and in Pauline theology as expressed in Romans 8:28—both oriented toward outcomes.
25. Assmann, *Search for God*, 4, 77.
26. Ibid., 111.
27. Since modern Western thinking allows for no personal divine purposes in creation or history, it is by default dysteleological. Modern historiography is still interested in coherence but achieves it through an attempt to identify rational cause-and-effect sequences that uncover the role of human choices.

**Table 1. Similar Perspectives on Creation
and History in the Ancient World**

	Creation	History
Divine role	Both focus on divine cause and effect	
Perspective	Both driven by purpose (teleological)	
Foundation	Order	Pattern
Focus	Function	Outcome/Legacy
De-emphasized	Structures/physical laws	Eyewitnessed events

In the ancient pursuit of coherence, hindsight was not only important, it was essential. Likewise, a transcendent view of history was essential.[28] A sense of what "really happened" was gained in light of the outcome, not in light of what any given eyewitness thinks he might have seen, since eyewitnesses were also limited by their perspective and compromised by their opinions. What one saw could barely begin to offer insight into what *really* happened. Indeed, it was particularly what could not be seen that was often critical. It was only as events blended together into a continuum that significance could be identified. Individual events find their value in the continuity and relationship they share with other events. Time and hindsight therefore allow for increasing coherence, the hallmark of narrative historiography.

The particular cognitive environment of the ancient world led to a focus on certain anticipated outcomes. The outcomes that were most important were of an ideological nature, and therefore the historiographers typically offered theological and/or political interpretation of events (with the understanding that what was political was still ultimately theological). Their interest in the past was concerned primarily with actions of the deity and the legitimation of the king. These had priority over any mere recitation or reconstruction of the events.[29] Consider E. A. Speiser's remark: "The Bible is not so much a chronicle of events worth recording, or thought to be worth recording, as an interpretation of significant happenings."[30]

---

28. This is not to suggest that they had no empiricist interests or were incapable of empiricism (being hopelessly mythopoeic), only that their societal values pointed away from a dependency on empiricism. For a helpful discussion of the presence of empiricism see P. Machinist, "On Self-Consciousness in Mesopotamia," in *The Origins and Diversity of Axial Age Civilizations*, ed. S. N. Eisenstadt (New York: SUNY Press, 1986), 183–202.

29. Zevit suggests that the compilation of events is similar to the testimony by witnesses called to the stand in a trial, while the interpretation of those testimonies is offered by the respective attorneys and those interpretations are assessed by the judge or jury (Zevit, *Religions*, 27). This type of contrast may be seen as similar to disease being understood symptomatically rather than ontologically, and perhaps even similar to the function/structure contrast suggested in the discussion in chap. 8.

30. Speiser, "Biblical Idea," 2.

The events had to be seen in light of the outcome, and the outcome had to be understood in light of the royal and the divine. The events were shaped to give fullest articulation of outcome and the patterns that can be identified in a series of outcomes. The events were reported not as an eyewitness would have seen them, but as part of the interpretation of the outcome. They knew what they knew about the past because it had been interpreted for them. This interpretive testimony is what they gathered and preserved. Since all testimony has come through an interpreter to take the form of a record (oral, written, or artifactual), we must now delve into the poetics of historiography.

Poetics of Historiography in the Ancient World

Narrative and the Poetics of Historiography

All historiography is a literary construct artistically rendered. It therefore must be understood to operate by means of literary conventions common to the author and his audience—a key to communication that represents its poetics.[31] As a result, the reader must understand the literature before trying to understand the history.

Z. Zevit has noted that we have yet to develop a poetics of history writing for the ancient world. He considers historiography in the context of "truth-telling literature" and is concerned about how skepticism has been wielded as a historical hermeneutic. He uses the concept of "possible worlds"[32] to suggest that the major test to be applied to self-consciously truth-telling literature is not whether it can be considered plausible from the reader's perspective, but whether it can be effectively disproved or denied; that is, the criterion should be deniability.[33] K. L. Younger likewise stresses that intentionality is the principal criterion. "History writing is not a record of fact—of what 'really happened'—but a discourse that claims to be a record of fact. Nor is fiction writing a tissue of free inventions but a discourse that claims freedom of invention. The antithesis lies not in the presence or absence of truth value, but of the commitment to truth value."[34]

---

31. Liverani, *Myth and Politics*, 94–96, provides a good example of this in his analysis of the inscription of Idrimi.

32. A "possible world" as used by Zevit refers to the view of one whose "natural world is identical to what is known in the real world of the here and now, but differs from it with regard to what goes on" (*Religions*, 76). Those who lived in this possible world considered their view of reality just as certain as we consider our own current view of reality. That is, they are not dream worlds or made-up worlds.

33. Zevit, *Religions*, 78–79. See also Provan, Long, and Longman, *Biblical History of Israel*, 55.

34. Younger, *Ancient Conquest Accounts*, 43.

Photo 18 Relief: Siege of Lachish

B. Halpern applies this same sort of thinking as he considers the alternative: intentional disinformation. "If the author . . . attempts knowingly to perpetrate on the reader a fraudulent reconstruction contradicted or unsupported by evidence, then the author is not engaged in writing history. Quite the opposite: the author is attempting to fob off as history a text known to be something else. Whether a text is a history, then, depends on what its author meant to do."[35]

Narrative historiography intends to be persuasive and operates in the ideological world of the writer. Far from engaging in fabrication, the author seeks to reinforce ideas that he believes to be true.[36] Though the author does not intend to mislead, the slant is sometimes so transparent as to lead to incredulity on the part of the modern reader. This has long been the response of modern scholars to the Assyrian royal inscriptions.[37]

Historiography is not intrinsically bound to the narrative form—that is only one of its possible expressions, and arguably not the best (depending on what one is seeking).[38] It is important to distinguish between historical documents, such as king lists, which may have only a passive, sublimated historiography, and narrative in which historiography is more overt. When historiography is rendered in narrative form, one still has to ask what purpose the narrator has in doing so. Incorporation of historical information into a narrative does not demand or imply that the narrator's intention is to recite history. Indeed, narrative proves to be a disruptive force in historical recitation since it inevitably imposes a contrived literary form on the events to arrive at an outcome. In other words, narrative does not concern itself primarily with the event—it is much more interested in the outcome.

35. Halpern, *First Historians*, 8.
36. Provan, Long, and Longman, *Biblical History of Israel*, 49.
37. Ibid., 67.
38. Van de Mieroop, *Cuneiform Texts*, 84.

When history is reduced to narrative its outcomes can be identified, because in narrative, history is provided with a beginning, a middle, and an end, as well as with transitions, connectedness, and causation. These all can be somewhat artificial and represent the interpretation of the narrator.

> The narrative form of historical discourse also presents a fundamental paradox to the historian: its order, coherence, and completeness are appealing and intelligible, but are imaginary. Reality does not present itself in the form of ready-made stories that come to a logical conclusion. Events occur in a sequence that often has no beginning or end, that lacks coherence, and surely does not exclude extraneous facts. The realism of narrative historical representation is a dream.[39]

Participants in, witnesses to, and interpreters of history all give testimony that serves as the quintessential source for historiography. "We know about the past, to the extent that we know about it at all, *primarily* through the testimony of others. Testimony lies at the very heart of our access to the past."[40] Consequently, interpretation is unavoidable. "We cannot avoid testimony, and we cannot avoid interpretation. We also cannot avoid faith. . . . What we call knowledge of the past is more accurately described as faith in the testimony, in the interpretation of the past offered by others."[41]

Historiography is therefore driven by the values held by those whose testimony provides the framework.[42] Different values will result in different histories. Therefore we must next turn our attention to the values that served as the foundation for ancient historiography.

Values

Historiography "always has a subject: it can be about one thing, and ignore other things; but it must always be *about something.*"[43] Different values and different objectives are evident depending on what segment(s) of society sponsors the writing of history (e.g., academics, clans, temple, ruling elites, professional guild), but since in the ancient Near East most record keeping was done under the aegis of the ruling elites, reports of events offer that perspective and serve the ends of that group. The

39. Ibid., 79.
40. Provan, Long, and Longman, *Biblical History of Israel*, 37.
41. Provan, "In the Stable," 168.
42. See Liverani's treatment of the introductions to Hittite treaties in *Myth and Politics*, 78–79.
43. Halpern, *First Historians*, 6–7.

record of the past served the purposes of the present by legitimating the king.[44]

Legitimation in the present also extends into the future in the form of legacy. In the ancient world, legacy is more important than history, and history is seen primarily through the eyes of legacy. Both legitimation and legacy concern the image of the king. "Assyrian scribes were, in fact, more concerned about the *image* of the king and his activity as a warrior than about merely recording the facts of his reign."[45]

The historiography of the ancient Near East, whether represented in royal inscriptions or chronicles, king lists or annals, has by all accounts a polemical agenda that is intended to reinforce the royal political ideology. As in the campaign speeches of our day, facts can be useful, but they are not central or essential. The intention of the preserved records is not to serve the reader, but to serve the king. The recorder is trying to provide answers to the question: "Why should you consider this king to be a good and successful king?" In most cases it cannot be determined whether concealment and/or disinformation are part of the strategy, but negative information is uniformly lacking. We do receive negative assessments of some kings, but, as we might expect, they come from later dynasties seeking to enhance their own reputations.

Royal inscriptions are therefore working from a predetermined outcome: that the gods favor the king. Therefore all events are presented in a way that will support that predetermined outcome. It is the predetermined outcome that causes it to be labeled as propaganda, or, more accurately, political polemic.[46] The outcome is not open to an alternative interpretation, at least not until the next dynasty or next empire comes along.[47]

The values of historiographical literature can therefore be identified in terms of (1) the sponsor, (2) what or whom the literature promotes, and (3) the intended audience. Beyond these literary basics, the existential position of the authors and their matrix for interpreting reality would be significant in how they chose to write their history.[48] The literature would have to be read differently depending on these literary and philosophical

44. F. Cryer, *Divination in Ancient Israel and Its Near Eastern Environment*, JSOTSup 142 (Sheffield: Sheffield Academic Press, 1994), 189–90; reinforced by van de Mieroop, *Cuneiform Texts*, 47.

45. Provan, Long, and Longman, *Biblical History of Israel*, 67.

46. Because of the many different ways that the term "propaganda" has been used (derogatorily and neutrally), "political polemic" is the preferred descriptor. See H. Tadmor, "Propaganda, Literature, Historiography: Cracking the Code of the Assyrian Royal Inscriptions," in *Assyria 1995*, ed. S. Parpola and R. M. Whiting (Helsinki: Neo-Assyrian Text Corpus Project, 1997), 332–33.

47. Provan, Long, and Longman, *Biblical History of Israel*, 66.

48. Liverani, *Myth and Politics*, 98.

issues. By attending to them, we will find that the values emerge. The following list offers some of the possible ideas or people that may be promoted by historiographical literature.

- *epic history*: promotes artistic recounting of events of the past
- *didactic history*: promotes a lesson to be learned derived from an interpretation of a sequence of events in juxtaposition
- *legitimation history*: promotes an elite sponsor and interprets events and outcomes to offer support to claims being made
- *theological history*: promotes the role of deity as events are presented as God's expression of his attributes
- *foundation history*: promotes information concerning origins of people groups, practices, institutions, and political situations
- *polemical history*: promotes discussion to challenge people to re-examine beliefs or knowledge
- *journalistic history*: promotes eyewitness accounts of observation focusing on events rather than outcomes
- *academic history*: promotes analytical or critical evaluation of the past in line with rules of the academy

These categories do not constitute mechanisms of distortion; they represent how the authors got at what they considered the most important values and truths. In modern terms, for instance, Tennyson's *Charge of the Light Brigade* or Longfellow's *Midnight Ride of Paul Revere* do not use their epic style in order to have the freedom to fabricate or distort. Rather, these modern poets believe that there is a value and truth to be communicated that cannot be captured by pedestrian prose reports of eyewitnesses. What they communicate in their epics is arguably a more important truth about those events, as only epics can do.

In the ancient world many of these categories are attested, though the last two, which are arguably the most common today, are not. In Mesopotamia, legitimation history is the most common, represented particularly in the Assyrian royal inscriptions. A much smaller number of texts would be classified as epic, didactic, or theological history. Foundation narratives tend to be mythographical rather than historiographical.[49]

Finally, the intentions of the royal inscriptions can be judged not only in terms of the values associated with their goals and what they promote, but also in terms of their intended audience. Given that most of the population was not able to read Akkadian, and that the royal inscrip-

---

49. Exceptions might be found in epics like *Enmerkar and the Lord of Aratta*, where a historiographical piece of literature provides an explanation for the beginning of writing.

Comparative Exploration: Israelite Historiography

Genres

The Israelite historiography preserved in the Hebrew Bible offers very little to compare on the genre level. Though it includes genealogies and lists of various sorts, it retains only vestiges of anything like the annals, chronicles, and royal inscriptions that make up the bulk of the historiography in the other cultures. Instead, nearly all of its historiography is offered in narrative form, and that material is still distinct at many points from the literary epics scattered throughout the ancient Near Eastern corpora.[1]

Role of Deity

As in the rest of the ancient world, Israel considered God the cause of every effect and as actively shaping events. Their historiography was not intended to be simply a record of events or an assemblage of facts, but a record of the ways in which God had acted in history. There is no Israelite historiography that is secular. Yahweh is the driving force of history and the raison d'être of historiography. This transcendent view of history characterizes both Israelite and ancient Near Eastern historiography.

In many areas of comparative work, we have seen a difference in Israelite thinking that is due to the ideals of monotheism. Here that aspect does not figure prominently because the inscriptional material tends to focus singular attention on the national deity. For instance, S. Parker demonstrates that in Northwest Semitic inscriptions there is a focus on the national deity that causes those accounts to look as monotheistic as Israelite accounts.[2] Rather than monotheism, it is the covenant that stands at the center of Israel's unique historiography. The covenant was the foundation of God's activities in the past as well as for the future and therefore offered the defining paradigm for action in the present.[3]

Another area in which Israelite historiography begins to evidence distinctiveness is in their belief that Yahweh is not only the primary subject of the historiographical material, but also the source of the interpretation offered in the literature. In the supernaturalistic view of the ancient world, events were revelation, the result of divine activity. Those events, however, required interpretation to discern why the gods were doing what they did. In Israel's view not only were events revelation, but historiography was revelation. That is, God took it upon himself not only to act, but to provide an interpretation of his acts through the prophets or Levites,[4] communicating why they were done and what purposes they served. In theological terms we would say that the general revelation of history was supplemented by the special revelation of historiography.

In summary, then, in contrast to our modern historiography, Israel shared with the ancient world the idea that events are revelation. In contrast to both modern and other ancient historiography, Israel distinctively believed that their historiography was also revelation. Above all, Israelites understood their history and wrote their history in light of the covenant.

Coherence

As indicated in the last section, the centrality of the covenant is what gave coherence to Israelite historiography. Like their ancient Near Eastern counterparts, the Israelites were more interested in outcomes than in events. Continuity was found in their identity as God's covenant people, and hindsight provided the perspective that became the foundation of the great historiographic works of the Hebrew Bible, the Deuteronomistic History and Chronicles. As in the ancient Near East, events are reported not as eyewitness accounts, but as an interpretation of events in light of the covenant.

The ancient Near Eastern confidence that deity had chosen the king can be seen in the Davidic covenant, but that is subordinate to the larger confidence that God had chosen Israel. Thus the status of the king becomes only a corollary to the status of the people as a guiding concept.

Poetics

Like all truly historiographic literature, Israel's historiography is self-consciously truth-telling literature. This quality is not compromised by the facts that it is transcendent in perspective and covenant focused. These represent the central truths of their understanding of the world. Their historiography is intended to make sense of the past and the present, and they achieve this through a combination of the views of history and historiography current in the ancient world with their own distinctive theology of covenant.[5]

These were serious historians assessing the past with an eye toward synthesizing their values for the reader in a literary fashion following standard literary and cultural conventions.[6] "Our historian, and some of the authors whose work he used, believed that the evidence sustained their historical theses. Metahistory is the point of the history: it demands persuasive research."[7] And research it was, for "No historical narrator evinces an aesthetic predilection for self-contradiction."[8]

Values, Sponsors, and What Is Promoted

The obvious sponsorship by ruling elites in the ancient Near East is not matched in Israel, where it is much more debatable under whose sponsorship the great historiographical works were written and edited over time. The preponderance of negative press for the monarchy, even the Davidides, rules out the palace as a likely sponsor.[9] This continues to be one of the great debates about Israelite historiography, but no matter what the final conclusion is, here the Israelite historiography departs from the standard ancient Near Eastern pattern.

The values inherent in the literature can be assessed first of all by identifying the questions it seeks to answer. In the larger ancient Near East the principal question we identified was, "Why should you believe that this king is a good and successful king who enjoys the support and favor of the gods and should continue to receive that support and favor?" Israelite historians, in contrast, appear to be asking, "Why should you believe that Israel has been chosen by Yahweh as his covenant people and that he is sovereign over all history and nations?" Subordinate questions would include, "Why should you believe that the Davidic dynasty was chosen by Yahweh? Why did Jerusalem fall? Why should Israel continue to have hope in God's favor and support?"

We could thus suggest that whereas the highest value in the ancient Near East was the legitimation of the king, in Israel the highest value was the legitimation of the covenant. Ancient Near Eastern historiography desired to reveal the king to the people and to the deity. Israelite historiography desired to reveal the Deity to the king and the people. Here we have an important reversal similar to that which has been noted in other chapters. In Israel the historiography purports to be communication *from* the Deity, whereas in the ancient Near East the royal inscriptions serve as communication *to* the deity.[10] Consequently, the audience is neither future kings nor the gods—it is the people of the covenant: "Then you will know that I, Yahweh, am God—there is no other."

It is common to find the suggestion that Israelite historiography is legitimation history not very different from that found in the rest of the ancient world. This is especially identified in the books of Samuel, as they clearly offer legitimation for the Davidic dynasty and justify the replacement of Saul.

But of course the books of Samuel are only one part of a much larger historiographical enterprise. In the historiography of the Hebrew Bible, revelation given about individuals invariably contains favorable as well as unfavorable information—and this is true even of the portrayal of David in the books of Samuel. The same is true for the corporate people of Israel. As a result this material would be very ineffective political polemic, though undoubtedly some parts could serve that purpose for some individuals. The Bible also makes clear throughout that its purpose is not to offer revelation of any particular person or group, but to serve as Yahweh's revelation of himself. In a canonical perspective, that is its historiographical purpose. Since the revelation of Yahweh is consistently positive, one might claim that this is polemic devised by Israel on behalf of their God. This polemic would indirectly work to their advantage, for it would substantiate their claims of election. The objection to this is that it stretches our credulity to suppose that such a long-lasting practice of self-effacement could be sustained to support the effort. Such altruism runs counter to the nature of political polemic. Further-

more, while it is not inaccurate to say that the revelation of Yahweh is consistently positive, it must be admitted that the portrayal of him is not always pleasant from a human perspective. Characters who felt the harsh sting of discipline (e.g., Adam and Eve, Moses, Nadab and Abihu, Saul, Uzzah) may have had less than positive impressions. Individuals who had to endure difficult trials at the behest of their God (e.g., Abraham, Job, Hosea, Jeremiah, Ezekiel) would have been less than convinced that he was involved in promoting his reputation. In these ways the OT does not hesitate to present a "negative" picture of God.

When we revisit the categories of what might possibly be promoted in historiographical literature presented above, we find a different profile in Israelite historiography than what we found in the ancient Near East. Instead of legitimation history being prominent, we find that theological history is by far the dominant form. Second would be foundation history as found in Genesis and Exodus. Epic (e.g., Deborah's Song in Judg. 5) and legitimation history (e.g., Succession Narrative in 2 Sam. 9–1 Kings 2) would be other forms represented, though not in any major way.

How Does All of This Change How We Read the Old Testament?

We cannot read the Hebrew Bible as if it were journalistic or academic history such as might be written today. Such reading would compromise the intentions, presuppositions, values, and poetics of the literature and its authors. When we critique the literature, we should critique it in terms of its own guiding criteria rather than expecting it to reflect our own and dismissing it when it does not. When we critique the literature in terms of its emphasis on outcomes rather than

Table 2. Modern, Ancient, and Israelite Perspectives on History and Historiography

	Modern	Ancient	Israelite
History	Outcomes are a consequence of events shaped by human choices	Outcomes are a consequence of purpose crafted by divine choices	Outcomes are a consequence of purpose carried out through a divine plan (articulated in the covenant and its elaboration by the prophets)
Historiography	Designed to reconstruct the events as fully as possible and interpret the outcomes with the intention of legitimating ideas (e.g., democracy, tolerance, diversity, power, ideology)	Designed to interpret outcomes with the intention of legitimating the king	Designed to interpret outcomes with the intention of legitimating the covenant

events and precise details, it may help us to understand some of what may be considered the foibles of an author like the Chronicler, who, for instance, may have neither the means nor the inclination to investigate the factual accuracy of some of his sources' details. The precision of the numbers, for instance, is insignificant—though the general nature of the quantification is not without importance. The integrity of the text is linked to its interpretation of the outcome.

Consider Halpern's assessment of the Deuteronomistic Historian:

> H(Dtr) takes a partisan view, in the company of Gibbon, Macaulay, Mommsen, Syme, and any outstanding historian. He uses paradigmatic, or ideological, sources, and substantive sources; and, of the latter, some are physical, some antiquarian, and some, such as votives, not antiquarian but celebratory. His work is sometimes inaccurate—what historical work is not? He selects his data, taps only some of his resources (the chronicles), and his choices are, in part, ideologically conditioned. He sits squarely in the mainstream of narrative history, from Herodotus to the present.[11]

This sort of assessment is likely to rankle both critical and confessional scholars; the former for the degree of vindication that it pronounces for the biblical historian and the latter for the assessment of inaccuracy.

It is clear, then, that sensitivity to the poetics of ancient historiography complicates both the critical scholars' dismissal of the validity of biblical historiography as well as confessional scholars' apologetic approaches and doctrinal convictions. Critical scholarship needs to rethink its imperialistic and anachronistic imposition of modern standards and values on ancient texts. Confessional scholars need to rethink precisely what constitutes the truth of the text that they seek to defend in light of the text's own poetics and perspectives.[12] In this light N. Winther-Nielsen sounds the death knell for the popular activities of proving and disproving the Bible that have prevailed in academia since the Enlightenment. "All current and past history writing will call on our hermeneutical trust, and the days of confessionalist, positivist, or minimalist absolute 'proof' are gone forever."[13]

No amount of empirical information is able to accomplish that end. The extent to which deity is involved in events or outcomes can never be either verified or falsified empirically. Our dogged empiricism betrays us. The texts offer a different sort of testimony that we must respect.

1. See the introductory discussion in Parker, *Stories*, 6–8.

2. Here he refers to the role of Chemosh in the *Mesha Inscription* and the role of Hadad in the *Tel Dan Inscription*. Similar examples could be found relating to Ashur in Assyrian inscriptions or to Marduk in Babylonian inscriptions.

3. This goes beyond the question of divine plan, which was the focus of Albrektson's *History*; he called it only a difference of degree and concluded that there was not a major distinction in this category (96). This idea was rebutted in the years that followed by W. G. Lambert and H. W. F. Saggs among others (Lambert, "Destiny"; Saggs, *Encounter*, 64–92).

4. In the prophetic books an interpretation of history is offered, but what of the great historiographical pieces of the Deuteronomist and Chronicler? I accept that these are essentially prophetic if only in their extensive use of prophetic sources. P. K. McCarter sees even the pre-Deuteronomist material as a prophetic history (*1 Samuel*, AB [Garden City, NY: Doubleday, 1980], 18–23). Regarding the Deuteronomist, whether a school, a

series of redactors, or a single author, most would connect the resulting history to prophetic schools. See a summary treatment by S. McKenzie, "Deuteronomistic History," *ABD* 2:160–68. Concerning the prophetic nature of the Chronicler see M. Fishbane, *Biblical Interpretation in Ancient Israel* (Oxford: Oxford University Press, 1985), 385–92; W. Schniedewind, "Prophets and Prophecy in the Books of Chronicles," in *The Chronicler as Historian*, ed. M. P. Graham et al., JSOTSup 238 (Sheffield: Sheffield Academic Press, 1997), 204–24. H. G. M. Williamson seems willing still to accept that the Chronicler, in addition, was a Levite or an ardent supporter closely associated with the Levites (*1 and 2 Chronicles*, New Century Bible Commentary [Grand Rapids: Eerdmans, 1982], 17).

5. J. Licht, *History, Historiography and Interpretation*, ed. H. Tadmor and M. Weinfeld (Jerusalem: Magnes, 1983), 115. Cf. Averbeck, "Sumer," 113.

6. R. Chisholm, "History or Story? The Literary Dimension in Narrative Texts," in *Giving the Sense: Understanding and Using Old Testament Historical Texts*, ed. D. Howard and M. Grisanti (Grand Rapids: Kregel, 2003), 54–73.

7. Halpern, *First Historians*, 242.

8. Ibid.

9. Of course kings who come out reasonably well (Solomon, Hezekiah, Josiah) have often been suggested as potential sponsors of one or the other levels of redaction, but these fail to account for the whole.

10. Similar reversals are addressed in chap. 13 on law, and in chap. 8 on cosmology, where the ancient Near Eastern view is that humans provide for the gods whereas the garden of Eden shows God planting food for people.

11. Halpern, *First Historians*, 234.

12. Consider the extensive and insightful work of K. L. Younger on reading Joshua in light of ancient Near Eastern conquest accounts in *Ancient Conquest*.

13. Winther-Nielsen, "Fact, Fiction," 76. Compare Halpern's statement that "history, ultimately, is susceptible to evidence, but not to proof" (*First Historians*, 13).

tions were often set up where there would be little access to them, the textual information would not have had wide currency. Yet by their very presence they could convey the greatness of the king iconographically if not literarily.[50] The inscriptions are ostensibly addressed to a future king

50. The iconographic power could be achieved even if there were only text on the monument, for the inscription itself was an icon attesting to the power and prestige of the king.

who might read them and be impressed by the achievements recounted in them. H. Tadmor suggests that, more importantly, the intended audience was the gods.[51] Characteristic of reports, the focus is going to be on what the king wants the gods to know. The expectation is that through such reports the gods will be convinced that the king is doing the job well for which he was chosen and that they should continue to give him their support and favor. Their role should be adequately recognized and they should believe that their reputations and stature are growing as a result of the king's activities. Thus as Mesopotamian historiography legitimates the king it also serves to enhance the reputation of the deity.

51. Tadmor, "Propaganda," 331; see also Albrektson, *History*, 43.

11

Encountering the Present

Guidance for Life—Divination and Omens

We now turn our attention from the focus of the last two chapters, on how people thought about the past, to how they encountered the present. The next three chapters will help us understand what ideas governed the ways they lived their lives. One major factor in this equation has already been discussed: that of religion and the religious ideas that dominated their lives. In modern terms we might be inclined to say that we are now turning attention to the secular side of their lives, but that would create a distinction that did not exist in the ancient world. The cognitive environment of the ancient Near East was thoroughly transcendent, and this was reflected in how their lives were shaped day by day. There was no divide between secular and sacred. The supernatural blended seamlessly into what our contemporary culture might be inclined to label the natural world or the everyday aspects of life. We will therefore see repeatedly that the divine pervades every component of culture.

In previous chapters we have tried to penetrate the ancients' ways of thinking: their ontology, cosmology, theology, anthropology, and historiosophy. As we engage the area of divination, we are ultimately inquiring into their epistemology, for divination is driven by theories of knowledge.[1]

---

1. A. K. Guinan, "A Severed Head Laughed: Stories of Divinatory Interpretation," in *Magic and Divination in the Ancient World*, ed. L. Ciraolo and J. Seidel, Ancient Magic and Divination 2 (Leiden: Brill/Styx, 2002), 4–40, quotation on 10.

This will also lead us into a discussion of magic (the exploitation of specialized knowledge to exert power over others) and its practitioners.[2]

Categories of Divination

Divination has been divided into two major categories ("Inspired" and "Deductive"), and several forms of divination operate in each category.

Inspired

Inspired divination is initiated in the divine realm and uses a human intermediary.[3] The message may come by means of a human messenger (i.e., prophet) to the target audience or in the form of a dream directly to the targeted individual.

Official Prophecy

In the ancient world people could train to be prophets, could play an active role in cultivating prophetic messages, and could serve under the sponsorship of the king as professional advisors who were paid for their services. The most obvious examples of this are found in the Neo-Assyrian period in the reigns of Esarhaddon and Ashurbanipal,[4] and about a century earlier in Israel when Ahab and Jezebel sponsored hundreds of prophets of Baal and Asherah (1 Kings 18:19).

Informal Prophecy

The hallmark of informal prophecy is that it is more spontaneous and occasional. The recipient could be either a layperson or a priest. These

2. I do not address the history of divination, which has its roots in the second half of the third millennium BC. Sumerian sources do not provide any divination texts, but it is clear that they were already practicing extispicy. Celestial divination developed largely in the Old Babylonian period. There is no question that there is development from one period to another in terms of the practice of divination and of the worldview behind it. Discussion of this history can be found conveniently in a number of the sources listed in the footnotes that follow.

3. The categories "Inspired" and "Deductive" are introduced by J. Bottéro, *Religion in Ancient Mesopotamia* (Chicago: University of Chicago Press, 2001), 170–71. Nissinen uses "noninductive" rather than "inspired" (*Prophets and Prophecy in the Ancient Near East*, SBLWAW 12 [Atlanta: SBL, 2003], 1).

4. Sources for the Neo-Assyrian prophetic corpus are the following: M. Nissinen, *References to Prophecy in Neo-Assyrian Sources*, SAAS 7 (Helsinki: University of Helsinki Press, 1998); idem, *Prophecy in Its Near Eastern Context* (Atlanta: SBL, 2000); idem, *Prophets and Prophecy*; S. Parpola, *Assyrian Prophecies*, SAA 9 (Helsinki: University of Helsinki Press, 1998).

prophetic messages often came in dreams or during ecstatic experiences. About fifty reports of such prophecies are included among the letters found at Mari from the eighteenth century BC.[5] Numerous examples of informal prophecy are also known in Israel, including writing prophets such as Amos, as well as from incidents in the historical literature such as the account of Saul and his men (1 Sam. 19:19–24).

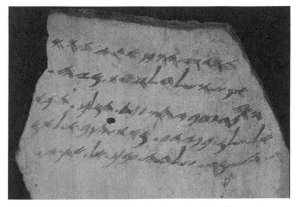

Photo 19 Lachish Letter Referring to a Prophet

Prophecies in the ancient Near East generally focused on the king's activities and responsibilities. They usually concerned politics, military campaigns, and cultic activities.[6] Most prophets were associated with particular deities and identified themselves as servants of that deity.[7] The prophecies were not intended to reveal the nature of deity; they simply functioned to advise the king in a course of action. At times the prophets served as ritual enforcers.

Dreams

Dreams were usually received spontaneously, but on occasion people desiring communication from the divine realm could actively seek to experience a dream. Such attempts are labeled incubation. Incubation dreams were often sought by royalty and involved sleeping in a sacred space. The resulting dreams, as with prophetic dreams, involved deity speaking to the dreamer. The most prominent example is Gudea, the governor of Lagash in the early second millennium, as he engaged in

5. Sources for the Mari archive include: W. Heimpel, *Letters to the King of Mari* (Winona Lake, IN: Eisenbrauns, 2003); J. J. M. Roberts, "The Mari Prophetic Texts in Transliteration and English Translation," in *The Bible and the Ancient Near East* (Winona Lake, IN: Eisenbrauns, 2002), 157–253; Nissinen, *Prophets and Prophecy*. See also the two prophecies from Eshnunna published by M. deJong Ellis, "The Goddess Kititum Speaks to King Ibalpiel: Oracle Texts from Ischali," *MARI* 5 (1987): 235–66.

6. In addition to the sources already mentioned, helpful treatments of ancient Near Eastern prophecy include: M. deJong Ellis, "Observations on Mesopotamian Orac Prophetic Texts," *JCS* 41:2 (1989): 127–86; A. Malamat, "A Forerunner of Biblical Pr The Mari Documents," in *Ancient Israelite Religion: Essays in Honor of Frank Moore* ed. P. D. Miller, P. D. Hanson, and S. D. McBride (Philadelphia: Fortress, 1987), 33–

7. Nissinen, *Prophets and Prophecy*, 16.

incubation seeking guidance for building a temple. The list of others could perhaps include Solomon of Israel in the early first millennium (1 Kings 3).[8]

The majority of dreams, however, simply came to people in the normal course of their lives. They did not involve a speaking deity, but the recipients nevertheless believed that the gods were communicating through the symbols of the dream, so they desired interpretation of these symbols. This demand resulted in the accumulation of an extensive literature in both Mesopotamia and Egypt to provide resources for the dream interpreters, often formulated in catalogs of conditional statements.[9] The protases ("If . . .") identify the content of the dream and involve activities, travels (including distinct omens for various cities), what one eats, what one wears, what someone gives to the dreamer, animals, deities, or realms (e.g., the netherworld) encountered, or doing various sorts of labor. The apodoses ("Then . . .") offering the interpretation are largely binary (good or bad results), even when directed to a specific category. They pertain to the aspects of life that are of concern to most people of any culture or era: life, property, family, health, and success.

Many interpretations are counterintuitive. For example:[10]

- If the feet of a man are lame, downfall of his ill-wisher (258a)
- If a man in his dream ascends to heaven and the gods bless him, this man will die (259a)
- If he eats human meat, he will have great riches (271a)

Others may be of the sort that at some level would be logical or expected:

- If he pours his urine into a well, he will lose his property (265b)
- If he goes to plant a field, he will be free of hardship (269a)

Most feature what seem to us to be random connections:

- If a man flies repeatedly, whatever he owns will be lost (258b)

8. S. A. L. Butler, *Mesopotamian Conceptions of Dreams and Dream Rituals*, AOAT 258 (Münster: Ugarit-Verlag, 1998), 217–40; J.-M. Husser, *Dreams and Dream Narratives in the Biblical World* (Sheffield: JSOT Press, 1999).

9. See Butler, *Mesopotamian Conceptions*, for an extensive treatment. The Assyrian dream book was published by A. L. Oppenheim, *The Interpretation of Dreams in the Ancient Near East*, Transactions of the American Philosophical Society 46/3 (Philadelphia: American Philosophical Society, 1956).

10. All examples are from Oppenheim, *Interpretation*, with page number and column indicated in parentheses.

Comparative Exploration: Dreams and Dream Interpreters in Israel

In Israel, as in the ancient Near East, dreams were considered to be important, whether they came to private individuals (Jacob, Gen. 28; Joseph, Gen. 37) or to leaders (e.g., Gideon, Judg. 7; Solomon, 1 Kings 3). Most prominent are the dreams of foreign rulers (local ones such as Abimelech, Gen. 20; or world leaders such as Pharaoh, Gen. 41, or Nebuchadnezzar, Dan. 2, 4).

In the realm of prophecy, it was recognized that God could choose to communicate through dreams, but the spoken word of God was privileged over dreams (Jer. 23:28). Dreaming prophets are referred to disparagingly, classified as lying prophets speaking the delusions of their minds (Jer. 23:26). Furthermore, dream interpreters are classified along with sorcerers and mediums (Jer. 27:9; 29:8). The classical prophets never offer a word of the Lord received in a dream, though they do occasionally have visions.

In Israel two famous dream interpreters served foreign rulers, Joseph and Daniel. Both offered their interpretations as having been given by God (Gen. 41:16; Dan. 2:27–28; 4:18). The difference between them is that Joseph's ability is informal, whereas Daniel's is most likely associated with his training (Dan. 1:4). His education in the "language and literature of the Babylonians" prepared him to be an advisor to the king, so it is likely that the curriculum includes the omen literature with the expectation that he will serve as a *baru* (expert in divination). It is difficult to know whether trainees were exposed to all the reference literature

(dream books, celestial omen collections, extispicy manuals, etc.) or would have specialized in one area. Daniel is most involved with dream interpretation, but also shows some awareness of celestial omens in the interpretation of the handwriting on the wall.[1] It is also possible that he shows awareness of the anomalies collection (*šumma izbu*) in the vision of the beasts that emerge from the sea (Dan. 7).[2]

In Israel dream interpretation is given acceptable status only when God's direct involvement in the interpretation can be affirmed. Israelites preserved no standard, formalized understanding of how dreams signify, nor is there a hermeneutic for scholarly interpretation. Israel agreed with the rest of the ancient Near East that deity could and did communicate through dreams. But they had no semiotic system by which to decipher dreams and no hermeneutic of interpretation that was considered reliable.

1. A. Wolters, "An Allusion to Libra in Daniel 5," in *Die Rolle der Astronomie in den Kulturen Mesopotamiens*, Beitrage zum 3 (Graz: Grazer Morgenlandischen Symposion, 1991), 291–306; idem, "The Riddle of the Scales in Daniel 5," *HUCA* 62 (1991): 155–77.

2. The *šumma izbu* series concerns either odd appearances or birth defects in animals and humans, thus "birth anomalies." P. Porter, *Metaphors and Monsters: A Literary-Critical Study of Daniel 7 and 8*, ConBOT 20 (Lund: Gleerup, 1983), 17–22; J. Walton, "The Anzu Myth as Relevant Background for Daniel 7?" in *The Book of Daniel: Composition and Reception*, ed. J. Collins and P. W. Flint, 2 vols., VTSup 83 (Leiden: Brill, 2001), 1:69–89.

Comparative Exploration: Terminology Related to Pronouncements regarding the Future

Plan: What someone intends to do in the future; may be circumstantial or conditional.[1]

Prediction: A foretelling of what the future holds that is specific and immutable.

Forecast: Like weather forecasting or economic forecasting, this identifies expectations derived from observed indicators that are considered reliable and thus can be interpreted with a high level of probability. Requires knowledge of signs.

Prognosis: Anticipation of likely outcomes based on knowledge or insight into the parties involved and factors to be considered (e.g., political, economic). Requires knowledge of activities and disposition of deity or king.

Vision cast: Identifies an ideal picture of what the future could or should look like and provides a target to aim for.

1. These are not strict dictionary definitions, where these terms are sometimes considered synonymous, but are provisional definitions used in this chapter for the purposes of careful nuancing.

- If he does the work of a leather-worker, the god Shamash has a claim for a vow which was neglected against him (263b)
- If he eats the head of an animal, he will have barley (270b)
- If he meets a pig he will have sons, his mind will be at peace (275a)

Inspired Divination and Its Cognitive Environment

The primary intention of inspired divination was neither to make the god known nor to make the future known, though either of those exigencies could result incidentally. Dreams led people to consult experts, mostly out of either the anxiety or the curiosity that they occasioned. Since deity had seen fit to communicate, it behooved the dreamer to discover what was being communicated, for one ignored divine communication at one's peril. From their dreams they could get a sense of direction in some area that they had concerns about or should pay attention to. Such information had the potential for affecting their lives and should figure in their decision-making process. In contrast, prophecy served to express the support of the gods for the king, and in the process often gave awareness of mitigating factors and relevant issues. Five categories (for a detailed account see table 4 on p. 250) can help us to identify the focus of prophetic oracles. They may be illustrated by the following examples:[11]

11. None of the oracles has all of these elements, and most only have one or two. An example of an oracle that has most of them is Nur-Sin's letter to Zimri Lim (#1) in Nissinen, *Prophets and Prophecy*, 17–21.

Indictment: has not responded to repeated demands for a particular sacrifice

History: I raised him and restored him to his ancestral throne

Judgment: threat of taking away estate and patrimony

Instruction: make the sacrifice

Support: "If he fulfills my desire I shall give him throne upon throne, city upon city. I shall give him the land from the rising of the sun to its setting."

Table 3. Ancient Near Eastern Prophetic Oracles

Numbering system of Nissinen, *Prophets and Prophecy*

Period		Indictment	Judgment (deity action)	Instruction (king action)	Support (future promise)	Warning (foe action)	Support (deity support)
Old Babylonian	1a	Ritual neglect	Take away land	Make sacrifice	Conquest		Gave throne
	1b			Do justice	Conquest		Gave throne
	2	Abandoned cause	Took away land	Do justice	Conquest		Gave land
	3			Temple repair			
	4			Gifts to temple	Conquest		Gave victory
	5				Punish enemies	Treachery	
	6		On Eshnunna		Victory		
	7		On Eshnunna		Victory	Treachery	
	8	Cultic neglect					
	9			Consult deity	Victory	Treachery	
	10					Uprising	
	12			Consult deity		Treachery	
	14			Consult deity			
	15			Perform ritual	Victory		
	16		Plague will come	Return taboo			
	17				Victory		
	18				Protection		
	21				Victory		
	23				Protection	Revolt	
	24	(Neglect)			Victory		

Period		Indictment	Judgment (deity action)	Instruction (king action)	Support (future promise)	Warning (foe action)	Support (deity support)
Old Babylonian	25	Cultic neglect		Cultic provision			
	26					Be careful	
	27	Cultic neglect		Cultic provision	Victory		Cared for you
	28	Cultic neglect			Name established		
	29	Cultic neglect		Cultic provision?			
	30			Perform ritual			
	31			Perform ritual			
	32		Disaster will come	Build city gate			
	38	Cultic neglect		Consult deity	Victory		
	39			Cease building			
	40					Invasion	
	43					Be careful	
	66				Conquest		
Neo-Assyrian	68				Victory		Gave victory
	69				Victory		
	71				Protection		Protected you
	73				Endless days		Protected you
	74				Victory		
	77				Safety/ dynasty		
	78				Throne established		
	79				Protection/ victory		
	80			Cultic provision	Safety/ dynasty/ victory		
	81				Protection		
	82				Defeat of enemies		Protected you

Period		Indictment	Judgment (deity action)	Instruction (king action)	Support (future promise)	Warning (foe action)	Support (deity support)
Neo-Assyrian	83				Protection		
	85				Victory		
	86				Defeat of enemies		
	88	Cultic neglect			Defeat of traitors		Gave victory
	89				Defeat of traitors		
	90				Protection/ victory		
	92				Care/ dominion		
	93				Victory		
	94				Divine sponsorship		
	95				Victory		

Indictment typically identifies neglectful or offensive behavior. These clauses occur in nine oracles, all Old Babylonian except one.[12] All of these indictments refer to general cultic neglect or the neglect or omission of a particular ritual, with one exception. In #2, Abiya the prophet of Adad indicates that Yahdun-Lim had "abandoned my cause" and therefore lost the land.

Judgment oracles proclaim what deity either has done (current trouble) or what he intends to do (future action). Judgment clauses against the recipient occur in only four oracles (##1, 2, 16, 32). Of these four, one refers to judgment in the past (just referred to, when the land was taken from Yahdun-Lim). The other three indicate impending judgment: that the deity will take away the land, that a plague will come, and that disaster will occur. There are also four oracles that pronounce judgment on an enemy land, city, or king.[13] Like the Israelite prophecies against foreign nations, these are intended to serve as statements of support and hope for the recipient.

Instruction conveys what the deity expects to be done to remedy the situation, to avoid judgment, or to bring about benefits. Instructions offered to the king occur in eighteen of the oracles, all Old Babylonian

12. Mari texts (Old Babylonian) ##1, 2, 8, 25, 27, 28, 29, 38 and Neo-Assyrian #88. Numbers used here and in the following footnotes are from Nissinen, *Prophets and Prophecy*.
13. #6, Eshnunna; ##19, 22 Babylon/Hammurabi; #47 Ishme-Dagan.

except one.[14] All but three of these involve cult or ritual. Variations include performance of a ritual (##1, 15, 30, 31), consulting the deity (##9, 12, 14, 38), repairing a temple (#3), returning taboo items (#16), or making some kind of cultic provision (##4, 25, 27, 29, 80). The three that focus on something other than ritual advise: doing justice (##1, 2), building the city gate (#32), and stopping a building project (#39).

Warning clauses inform of threatening actions by enemies domestic or foreign. Warnings occur only in the Old Babylonian corpus and concern treachery or uprisings, or simply encourage the king to be careful and not to leave the city.

Support clauses express intended future actions by deity in support of the king. These are the dominant feature of ancient Near Eastern prophecy. The support of the deity is usually expressed in terms of victory in a specific context (Old Babylonian ##6, 7, 9, 15, 17, 21, 24, 27, 38; Neo-Assyrian ##68, 69, 74, 79, 80, 85, 90, 93, 95), future conquests in general (Old Babylonian ##1, 2, 4, 66), punishment or defeat of enemies (Old Babylonian #5; Neo-Assyrian ##82, 86, 88, 89), protection, safety or care (Old Babylonian ##18, 23; Neo-Assyrian ##71, 77, 79, 80, 81, 83, 90), or establishment of name or successors (Old Babylonian #28; Neo-Assyrian ##73, 77, 78, 80). There are single examples that express extensive dominion (Neo-Assyrian #92) and continuing divine sponsorship (Neo-Assyrian #94). One other element that should be mentioned is that some oracles include statements of past support by the deity. These include that the deity put the king on the throne (##1, 2), gave victory in the past (##4, 66, 88), or provided care and protection (##27, 71, 73, 82).

As can be deduced from table 4, the main objective of the Old Babylonian oracles is generally found in either the instruction or the expression of support, though occasionally the purpose is only to give warning. Nearly every example bears this out. The main objective of the Neo-Assyrian oracles is to give expressions of support. Every oracle features this, and almost no other elements are present. Consequently, it can be inferred that the king, upon receiving prophetic messages, could feel confidence in taking a number of different courses of action of a ritual and/or political or military nature. There is little here that the king would mistake as offering prediction of the future or guarantees, except that the deity supports him. There would be no concern about false predictions, though it is clear that the king would want assurance that the prophet was reliable and at times would take the trouble of verifying the prophecy by means of extispicy (divination by means of examining the entrails, the *exta* of sacrificed animals).

14. ##1, 2, 3, 4, 8, 12, 14, 15, 16, 25, 27, 29, 30, 31, 32, 38, 39, and the Neo-Assyrian one, #80.

No plan of deity is offered in these oracles, only the current posture of deity. The support oracles focus mostly on the near term with only a couple of general statements (future land expansion, succeeded by sons) that offer a view into the distance. The king's hope would be buoyed in these expressions of support as he found in them affirmations of his endeavors.

While dreams offer a sort of forecasting of what direction the future is going, prophecy offers prognostication in terms of indication of what support the king can expect from the deity. Both can potentially result in the recipient feeling either affirmation in what he or she is doing, or warning concerning threats or particular courses of action.

Deductive

Deductive divination is no less initiated from the divine realm, but its revelation is communicated through events and phenomena that can be observed.[15] Note that in Israelite thinking that which is in the category of inspired divination is allowed—God speaks; but that which is in the category of deductive divination is forbidden—God does not write that way (e.g., on the entrails). This type of divination is found in Mesopotamia as early as the third millennium. Though many of the cultures of the ancient Near East practiced deductive divination, only in Mesopotamia are the written sources available.

Deductive Divination and Its Cognitive Environment

Connectedness. J. Bottéro uses the analogy of writing to clarify the phenomenon of deductive divination, which he suggests works along the same semiotic pattern.[16] In writing, meaning is signified by symbols. He suggests that the gods "wrote" in a similar way. Reading omens required knowing the signs, just like we need to know the alphabet and vocabulary in order to read a document. The connectedness that thus inheres in the cosmos may be expressed simply as: "All divine action causes material reaction."[17]

Not only was there a connectedness between signs and events, there was also a connectedness between the signs that could be observed in various spheres. Interpretation often required the specialist to weave together a variety of signs. The uncertainty associated with the interpretation process is reflected in a number of different ways. First of all, messages from inspired divination were often checked by seeking

15. Bottéro, *Religion*, 171.
16. Ibid., 178.
17. A. M. Kitz, "Prophecy as Divination," *CBQ* 65 (2003): 22–42, quotation on 24.

Comparative Exploration: Prophecy in Israel and the Ancient Near East

One fitting way to compare biblical and ancient Near Eastern prophecy is through the types of oracles that are used to relay the message. Israelite prophecy tended to come in four oracular catego- ries that diverge in part from those found in ancient Near Eastern prophecy: indict- ment, judgment, instruction, and after- math (see table 4).

Table 4. Israelite Prophetic Oracles

Period	Prophet	Indictment	Judgment	Instruction	Aftermath
Assyrian	Jonah	None	Destruction of Nineveh	None	None
	Amos	Social injustice, empty ritual (5:21–23)	Overrun by enemy, destruction (3:11; 5:2; 7:9; 9:8)	Do justice (5:14–15, 24)	Restoration (9:11–15)
	Hosea	Unfaithfulness, syncretism	Covenant blessings and protection retracted	Acknowledge guilt, seek the Lord (5:15); return (14:1)	God's faithfulness can be restored (chs. 2, 6, 14)
	Micah	Injustice (against upper classes); idolatry	Destruction, exile	Justice (6:8)	Return of remnant (chs. 4–5); restoration, dominion, peace, prosperity, theocratic and messianic kingship (4:7; 5:2)
	Isaiah	Trusting others rather than the Lord; worship practices	Delivered into hands of enemy	Trust, purification, repentance, return to the Lord	Political and spiritual restoration; coming messianic king, peace, dominion for Jerusalem, proper worship, God's reign
Babylonian	Nahum	None	Fall of Nineveh	None	Hope for restoration for Judah (2:2)
	Habakkuk	Judah— Injustice Babylon— violence, bloodshed, oppression	Against Judah: Babylonian invasion Against Babylon: victimized, shamed	Living faithfully (2:4)	None

Period	Prophet	Indictment	Judgment	Instruction	Aftermath
Babylonian	Zephaniah	Pagan worship	Destruction (no mention of exile)	Seek the Lord (1:3); judgment can be avoided (2:1–3)	Remnant left, gathering of oppressed (3:12–20) God's kingship (3:15)
	Jeremiah	Treachery in forsaking the Lord and departing from the covenant	An enemy from the north	Repent	New covenant; return from exile
	Ezekiel	False worship (chs. 8–11); unfaithfulness and rebellion against God; injustice among rulers	God will leave temple; Jerusalem and temple destroyed; exile	Repent (14:6; 18:30–31; 33:11); do justice (45:9–10)	Regather, restore people; return of God's presence, new covenant; David's line restored
	Daniel	None	Fall of Babylon; future troubles for Jerusalem	None	Four kingdoms, then the kingdom of God; Jerusalem rebuilt; Anointed One
Persian	Haggai	Self-centered, proud	Bad harvests already experienced	Adjust priorities and perspectives; build temple	Bumper crops; Zerubbabel as signet
	Zechariah	Covenant violations	Enemies will come against Jerusalem in judgment but God will deliver the city in the end	Repent, return; establish justice	Restoration of people, city, and temple; prosperity; deliverance from enemies; kingship
	Joel	None specified	Locust plague (current); Day of the Lord	Repentance; spiritual renewal	Renewed prosperity; Spirit, signs, and deliverance
	Obadiah	Edom's mistreatment of Judah	Destruction of Edom	None	Deliverance for Israel
	Malachi	Improper sacrifices; intermarriage; robbing God;	Purifying judgment	Offer appropriate sacrifice; honor marriage; bring tithe	Coming of Elijah

Indictment in Israel focused on covenant violations. It is much more prominent in classical prophecy than in ancient Near Eastern oracles. Most frequent violations included social injustice and unfaithfulness to Yahweh. Israelite oracles offer no hint of cultic neglect, and ancient Near Eastern oracles show little to compare to the Israelite offenses. Here the two are quite different, not only in content, but in the role of indictment. In Israelite prophecy indictment often appears to be what motivates the prophetic speech.[1] Indictment in Israel comes out of the prophets' role as covenant enforcers. Indictment in the ancient Near East comes out of the prophetic role as ritual enforcers.

Judgment in the ancient Near Eastern oracles is nearly nonexistent, while in Israel about half of all prophetic oracles contain an element of judgment. In preexilic classical prophecy, the oracles of judgment tend to focus on prognostication of the future and are paired with indictment. In postexilic prophecy, the judgment has often already come (e.g., Joel's locusts). This Israelite style of prophecy is the opposite of the ancient Near Eastern style, where divine support is the focus. In Israel divine disfavor is the focus, standing in opposition to the status quo.[2] In Israel support of the deity is withdrawn more often than assured, and victory is projected for enemies rather than for Israel. The capital is to be destroyed rather than secure, and the dynasty is in jeopardy rather than affirmed.

Explicit instruction in Israelite oracles is much rarer than one would think, though one could easily claim that it is implied. The prophets occasionally call on the people to repent, seek the Lord, or turn from their wickedness, but in most cases it seems that the covenant is considered clear enough that they should know what to do. Repentance and resumed covenant faithfulness is the clear course of action. This instruction, however, bears little resemblance to that offered to the kings of Mari, and the Assyrian kings are not typically offered instruction or advice by the prophets. As with indictment, the Israelite prophets are calling the people to *covenant* accountability while the Mari prophets are occasionally calling the king to *ritual* accountability.

For all the differences in the other categories, the last category is so different that we must offer an alternative label. Even when the Israelite prophets do have hope to offer, it is generally not intended to indicate divine support for the king. The hope offered is for *after the judgment has come* (thus the label "aftermath"). The contrast then is clear: The "support" category in the ancient Near East focused hope primarily on *near-term* victory and protection, legitimizing the current regime; Israelite aftermath oracles generally focused on the *long term* because the near future held judgment and defeat for the current regime, which is consequently stigmatized. Ancient Near Eastern prophecies functioned in a context of immediacy and urgency[3] and had no long-term value. In contrast, the hope that is offered in Israelite prophecy is presented as part of a divine plan that is eschatological and covenant based.[4]

Though they sometimes make pronouncements about the future, the Israelite prophetic oracles are more interested in revealing God than in revealing the future. They are more interested in bringing the people back to the covenant than in making promises or predictions. Ancient Near Eastern prophecy focuses on the king and offers legitimation of the king. Israelite prophecy is addressed to the people of God and offers a vision of the person and plan of God on the basis of the covenant. We will discuss later in this chapter the extent to which these differences suggest a different epistemology and a different outcome in how the recipients would respond to the prophetic oracles.

Table 5. Types of Israelite and Ancient Near Eastern Prophetic Oracles

	Israel	Ancient Near East
Indictment	past and present— covenant accountability	past and present— cultic accountability
Judgment	future and occasionally present— prognostication or forecasting	future— forecasting
Instruction	present— covenant accountability	present— cultic accountability
Support	X	near future— legitimation
Aftermath	distant future— plan, vision casting	X

1. There may be a few arguable occasions where a Mari prophecy was motivated by an indictment.

2. DeJong Ellis, "Observations," 143, as a summary of M. Weippert, "Assyrische Prophetien der Zeit Asarhaddons und Assurbanipals," in *Assyrian Royal Inscriptions: New Horizons in Literary, Ideological and Historical Analysis*, ed. F. M. Fales, Oriens Antiqui Collectio 17 (Rome: Istituo per l'Oriente, 1981), 71–115.

3. DeJong Ellis, "Observations," 171.

4. Notice deJong Ellis's comment: "Not only is the 'Dynastic' aspect totally absent from Mesopotamian oracles, but so is the idea of a 'Covenant' with long-term implications" ("Observations," 175), and her discussion on 180–86.

omens from deductive divination.[18] In like manner, an interpretation gained strength if it found support in two realms—for instance, if celestial omens could be supported by terrestrial omens or by extispicy. Thus the Babylonian Diviner's Manual asserts: "The signs of the earth together with those of the sky produce a signal, heaven and earth both bring us portents, each separately but not different, since sky and earth are interconnected. A sign that is evil in the sky is evil on the earth, a sign that is evil on earth is evil in the sky."[19] Second, the interpretation of an omen gained strength if the omen could be repeated. For instance, the *exta* of several animals might be examined.[20] Third, if an omen were not repealed or contradicted by omens in other categories, it would stand as acceptable.[21] Finally, in Neo-Assyrian extispicy we find that in a given examination, all of the unfavorable signs are tallied against the favorable signs to arrive at an interpretation.[22]

18. Ibid., 25–26.

19. U. Koch-Westenholz, *Mesopotamian Astrology*, Carsten Niehbuhr Institue of Near Eastern Studies 19 (Copenhagen: Museum Tusculanum, University of Copenhagen, 1995), 138.

20. Kitz, "Prophecy," 25–26.

21. Ibid., 25.

22. E. Reiner, *Astral Magic in Babylonia* (Philadelphia: American Philosophical Society, 1995), 72.

Control. It was important to people that they gain access to those signs at every level possible so that they could try to exercise some minimal level of control over the events swirling around them. In our modern world, this might be comparable to the psychological benefits some find in financial forecasting provided by the Federal Reserve Board or even the weather forecasting on the nightly news. Though we understand that they do not offer certainty, we regularly base our decisions and actions on the information they provide. We take comfort in general information that gives us some confidence to act, as specialists read the signs associated with their profession. Through attention to the omens, the people felt that they could achieve at least a psychological relief from the dominion of the unknown and the forces that surrounded them.[23]

Speculative more than empirical. We should not make the mistake of thinking that the connections identified in the omen literature derived entirely from empirical observations.[24] Empirical observations were at least occasionally folded into the system as it developed, but it is clear that some of the omens could not have arisen in that way.[25] The system was the result of mystic speculation supplemented by observation.[26]

The level at which this mystic speculation played a role receives more recognition as scholarly work continues. Wordplays, numeric relationships, polar opposites, and metaphor all were used to multiply examples of omens.[27] D. Brown now argues that by the heyday of the late Neo-Assyrian period, the developments in celestial divination were due to internal literary expansion. Techniques of this expansion included *categorization* of phenomena and *codes* of association (e.g., days with countries).[28]

As a result we can conclude that the cognitive environment of divination in Mesopotamia could not be considered the forerunner of scientific empiricism and logic. It operated within a sphere that was both esoteric

23. S. M. Maul, "How the Babylonians Protected Themselves against Calamities Announced by Omens," in *Mesopotamian Magic*, ed. T. Abusch and K. van der Toorn, Ancient Magic and Divination 1 (Groningen: Styx, 1999), 123.

24. D. Brown, *Mesopotamian Planetary Astronomy-Astrology* (Groningen: Styx, 2000), 110–11.

25. Koch-Westenholz, *Mesopotamian Astrology*, 18. See also the discussion in F. Cryer, *Divination in Ancient Israel and Its Near Eastern Environment*, JSOTSup 142 (Sheffield: JSOT Press, 1994), 150–54.

26. Koch-Westenholz, *Mesopotamian Astrology*, 18–19.

27. Brown, *Mesopotamian Planetary Astronomy*, 126–39.

28. Ibid., 111; see also A. Guinan, "The Perils of High Living: Divinatory Rhetoric in *Šumma Ālu*," in *DUMU-E₂-DUB-BA-A: Studies in Honor of Åke W. Sjöberg*, ed. H. Behrens, D. Loding, and M. Roth (Philadelphia: Occasional Publications of the Samuel Noah Kramer Fund, 1989), 229.

and hypothetical as it expanded over the centuries to formulate more and more layers of imaginative elaboration, thus leading to A. Guinan's conclusion:

> The scribes were driven by a desire to be comprehensive and systematic; as they added omens to fill perceived classification gaps the scope of their inquiry expanded over the entire range of divinatory possibilities. The compendia became increasingly extensive as they developed over time. By the first millennium the scribes appear driven to record every possible permutation, to combine every sequence of signs with every available context. They follow contradictory lines of reasoning, recording omens that are observed and contrived, possible and impossible, real and surreal, historical and ahistorical, logical and patently absurd.[29]

Not only is divination not empirical, it has its own logic, which is not at all like what we today would call logic. Divinatory logic "achieves its effects through indirection, ambiguity, equivocation, contradiction, and subtle shifts from the logical to the figurative."[30]

Omen Approaches

Active/provoked

In this category of deductive divination, practitioners introduced a mechanism by which the gods could communicate and then performed appropriate rituals to entice them to do so. Answers to queries were found by observing patterns that would indicate the will of the gods.

Extispicy.[31] Extispicy was considered one of the most reliable forms of divination and was often used to verify omens from other sources.[32] This form of divination is observed as early as the late third millennium (Mari).[33] Sources are most numerous in the Old Babylonian period[34] and in

29. Guinan, "Severed Head," 10. Examples of the impossible are found in the omens for lunar eclipses on days of the month when lunar eclipses could not possibly occur (in the lunar calendar, the full moon is in the middle of the month and that is the only phase of the moon when it can be eclipsed).

30. Guinan, "Perils," 227.

31. Key resources include U. Jeyes, *Old Babylonian Extispicy*, Publication de l'Institut historique-archéologique néerlandais de Stamboul 64 (Istanbul: Nederlands Historisch-Archaeologisch Instituut, 1989); I. Starr, *The Rituals of the Diviner*, Bibliotheca Mesopotamica 12 (Malibu: Undena, 1983); idem, *Queries to the Sungod*, SAA 4 (Helsinki: University of Helsinki Press, 1990); U. Koch-Westenholz, *Babylonian Liver Omens* (Copenhagen: Museum Tusculanum, 2000).

32. Starr, *Rituals*, 4–5; Reiner, *Astral Magic*, 63, 74–79.

33. Starr, *Rituals*, 4.

34. See A. Goetze, *Old Babylonian Omen Texts*, YOS 10 (New Haven: Yale University Press, 1947); Jeyes, *Old Babylonian Extispicy*.

seventh-century Assyria.[35] Many omens are known from the Neo-Assyrian tabulation of the omen series into a handbook known as *Bārîtu*.[36]

The readings made from the internal organs had nothing to do with knowledge of the way the organ functioned or with any aspect of physiology or pathology. "To them, the insides of the animal had no functional significance; they were instead regarded as instruments of communication."[37] After the sheep was chosen and purified, the gods were asked questions and were requested to write their verdicts or instructions on the *exta* (entrails) of the animal. Those answers would then be read by the diviner in the process of autopsy.[38] Although the liver was the most important of the organs and drew the most attention,[39] all of the *exta* were examined in a set sequence established as early as the Old Babylonian period.[40] For example:

- If the base of the Presence[41] has a Branch and it (the Branch) has seized the Path[42] to the right of the gall bladder: the prince will expropriate a country which is not his.[43]
- If a Weapon[44] is placed between the Presence and the Path and it points to the Narrowing to the right: he who is not the occupant of the throne will seize the throne.[45]

Lots.[46] In the casting of lots, markers with designated meaning were put together in a container. The container was shaken up and down until one of the markers came out (thus drawn by deity rather than by human

35. See Starr, *Queries*.

36. Starr, *Rituals*, 6.

37. Cryer, *Divination*, 176. Compare palmistry or phrenology today.

38. W. Farber, "Witchcraft, Magic, and Divination in Ancient Mesopotamia," *CANE* 3:1904.

39. Cf. Koch-Westenholz, *Babylonian Liver Omens*.

40. Cryer, *Divination*, 175.

41. The "Presence" refers to the vertical groove on the left lobe of the liver and usually symbolized the god (Jeyes, *Old Babylonian Extispicy*, 93).

42. The "Path" is the horizontal groove and the surrounding area in the abomasal impression usually symbolizing a military campaign (Jeyes, *Old Babylonian Extispicy*, 93).

43. Ibid., 101.

44. The "Weapon" refers to a protrusion of flesh that is pointed and symbolizes armed forces (Jeyes, *Old Babylonian Extispicy*, 93).

45. Ibid., 145.

46. Key resources include A. M. Kitz "The Hebrew Terminology of Lot Casting and Its Ancient Near Eastern Context," *CBQ* 62 (2000): 207–14; C. Van Dam, *The Urim and Thummim* (Winona Lake, IN: Eisenbrauns, 1997), 39–79; W. Horowitz and V. Hurowitz, "Urim and Thummim in Light of a Psephomancy Ritual from Assur (LKA 137)," *JANES* 24 (1992): 95–115.

Comparative Exploration: Jeremiah 31:33

The metaphor of "writing on the heart" is a significant one in the understanding of the new covenant—a theological construct that is of central importance both in the development of the theology of the Hebrew Bible and in the development of New Testament and Christian theology. The metaphor has often been unpacked in relation to similar heart metaphors elsewhere in the biblical text. In these contexts, having something written on one's heart is a metaphor of memory or intimate familiarity.[1] The difficulty is that in these passages the individual is the one doing the writing on his/her own heart. Writing on the tablet of the heart evokes the image of a scribe's practice tablet on which something is written again and again. In the same way the law is to be practiced day in and day out and be part of one's regular lessons.

In contrast, Jeremiah 31 explicitly features *Yahweh* writing the law on the heart of Israel. The difference in who is doing the writing is significant in that the force of the metaphor inherent in the "tablets of the heart" passages is lost if someone else is doing the writing. It would be contrary to everything else in the prophets if the suggestion were being made that God was going to cause them to keep the law against their own desire or inclination. Instead, the terminology draws our attention to the divination texts in that here in Jeremiah we have several lines in which each element finds parallels in the omen literature.

1. Jeremiah uses the same sorts of verbs (*natan*, NIV "put"; and *katab*, NIV "write") as the extispicy texts.

2. The verbs are followed by a preposition that takes a word connected with the *exta* as its object (*qereb*, NIV "minds"; technically, the intestines;[2] *leb*, NIV "heart"). As I. Starr observes, "The metaphor of the entrails in general and the liver in particular as the 'writing pad' of the gods is well-attested."[3]

3. Jeremiah speaks of the torah being written on the heart, which is comparable to the diviners requesting that the deities write a verdict or judgment (*dinu*) or an oracle (*têrtu*). These are all ways of referring to the revelation that is expected from the deity.

Before we proceed, we must note some of the significant ways that Jeremiah 31 differs from the divination literature. Most importantly, Jeremiah in no sense seeks to reproduce the literary structure or ritual setting of an extispicy procedure. The comparative question concerns only whether the text is adapting the terminology/metaphor of revelation through the *exta* for its own theological expressions. Such a metaphor parallel would find support in the genre overlap between divination and prophecy.

If a comparison could be drawn on the basis of the overlap in terminology and genre functions, what would the resulting interpretation look like and how would it differ from the traditional consensus reading? In an extispicy context there are three parties: the client who is making inquiry (seeking to receive divine revelation), the deity, and the specialist who is mediating the procedure. Of course, there is also the animal, which is the mechanism. Since Jeremiah would only be using a metaphor rather than portraying an actual divination procedure, we need not attempt to identify the three parties.

Nevertheless, if the metaphor has its roots in the world of divination, there must be some basic correlation that makes the metaphor work. The client is the party seeking information (i.e., "knowledge of God")—in this case the client role would be played by the Israelites or even the larger world around them who observe them. The latter would be the case if the idea is something like Israel being a light to the nations. The possibility also exists that Israel should be thought of as comparable to the sacrificed animal since its heart is written on. Predictably, the second party is entirely absent—there is no mediating specialist. The text even makes the point that anyone would be able to read the information. Consequently Yahweh will communicate (place . . . write) his revelation on the *exta* of his people so that he would be known. The essence of the metaphor, rather than memory and internalization of the torah, would be revelation of the torah.

The revelation that is sought out in extispicy proceedings is for guidance in major decisions and understanding of the intentions and will of deity. If Yahweh were writing the torah on the heart of Israel, he would be providing the same sort of guidance. The torah on the heart would give Israel guidance in major decisions and in understanding the intentions and will of Yahweh.

How would this be any different from the revelation of the torah in the Pentateuch that also had knowledge of God as its objective? That is, how does having the torah written on the heart differ from having it written on stone tablets? If the metaphor is from the world of extispicy, the text indicates that with God's instructions/law written on the heart of his people, there would be no need for continuing guidance to teach God's law. This had been an essential element in the Sinaitic law. What would happen instead? God would be known through his people, who would be living out the law faithfully. People with the law written on their heart become a *medium of communication*. Writing on the heart replaces not the law, but the teaching of the law. The law on stone had to be taught and could be ignored. The law on the heart represents a medium of modeling, in which case it is not being ignored. In this interpretation of the metaphor, then, the heart is a medium, not a repository. The metaphor would be one of revelation, not of memory.

1. This denotation of the concept of writing on the heart is supported by Prov. 3:3 and 7:3. See also Exod. 28:29; Pss. 37:31; 40:8; Deut. 6:6; and Isa. 51:7. In the NT see Rom. 2:15; 2 Cor. 3:2–3.

2. J. Milgrom, *Leviticus 1–16*, AB (New York: Doubleday, 1991), 159, 207.

3. Starr, *Rituals*, 57–58; examples provided.

involvement[47]). Instead of observing a sign that deity was believed to have written of his/her own accord (such as celestial signs), this method gave the deity the opportunity to provide a sign (just as extispicy did). This oracular procedure operates in a context where communication by a sign is desired and requested. Lot casting is done before deity, just as extispicy is. In Israel this principle can be seen in the official operation of the Urim and Thummim by the priest and in the use of lots by the general population.[48]

Other. Various other mechanisms were used in the ancient world for oracular inquiry. Pouring oil[49] on water or drawing arrows from a quiver are two of the better known, but even these are not evidenced widely in the literature. Similarly in Israel a variety of ad hoc mechanisms are designated for use in oracular inquiry. Perhaps the most familiar is Gideon's fleece, though other examples would include the procedure used by Abraham's servant (Gen. 24) or by the Philistines seeking to return the ark (1 Sam. 6).

Passive/unprovoked

In this category the mechanism was not introduced by the practitioner, but was observed and interpreted. The observations could concern repeated regularities, but usually focused on anomalies. Unusual occurrences were considered to have been introduced into the system by the gods with a communicative purpose in mind.[50]

Celestial.[51] The important elements in celestial observation included risings and settings, stationary points, positions relative to other bodies, eclipses, and colors. Signs pertained to particular directions (four com-

47. Note how the lottery machines are set up today so that one of the balls pops up rather than being drawn, thus assuring the random nature of the selection.

48. Division of the land by Joshua (Josh. 18–19), selection of Saul as king (1 Sam. 10), determining the guilty party at Jericho (Josh. 7).

49. Cryer, *Divination*, 145–47.

50. Most of what is being discussed in this chapter focuses on Mesopotamia, from where most of the literature derives and where anomalies are given highest value. J. Assmann has noted that in Egypt it is rather the regularities that hold divinatory significance (*Mind of Egypt* [New York: Metropolitan, 2002], 205). Hittite divination follows many of the same ideas found in Mesopotamia, though it evidences some divinatory methods more prominently than found in Mesopotamia, such as lots and augury. See R. Beal, "Hittite Oracles," in *Magic and Divination*, ed. Ciraolo and Seidel, 57–81.

51. Key sources include Brown, *Mesopotamian Planetary Astronomy*; H. Hunger, *Astrological Reports to Assyrian Kings*, SAA 8 (Helsinki: University of Helsinki Press, 1992); H. Hunger and D. Pingree, *Astral Sciences in Mesopotamia* (Leiden: Brill, 1999); Reiner, *Astral Magic*; E. Reiner and D. Pingree, *Babylonian Planetary Omens, Part III* (Groningen: Styx, 1998); Koch-Westenholz, *Mesopotamian Astrology*; F. Rochberg, *Heavenly Writing* (Cambridge: Cambridge University Press, 2005).

pass points) and to particular time periods.[52] Brown has suggested that typically celestial divination indicated one of the four cardinal directions and portended either good or ill. It is therefore a complex binary system (i.e., numerous binary indicators are combined and weighed against one another with the specialist arriving at an interpretation based on the meaning signified by each of the indicators).[53] For example:

- If the moon is not seen with the sun on the 14th or the 15th day of Addaru: Destruction of Ur.[54]
- If on the 16th day the moon and sun are seen together: the king will be confined in his palace the whole month, the enemy will march against his land, the enemy will walk proudly in his land.[55]

The most significant period of celestial divination both in terms of its prominence and the sources related to it is the Neo-Assyrian period during the reigns of Sargon II, Sennacherib, Esarhaddon, and Ashurbanipal.[56] In that general time period the series of celestial omens, entitled *Enuma Anu Enlil*, was organized (approximately 70 tablets in the series contain nearly 7,000 omens concerning the moon, sun, weather, and stars/constellations/planets[57]). This series enjoyed continued popularity into the Hellenistic period. Celestial divination was based on the premise that the gods were directing the movement of the heavenly bodies and that they were communicating to humankind through those movements. Until the mid-eighth century, people believed that the gods caused all celestial events individually and arbitrarily. Any patterns they were aware of failed to suggest to them a predictable cycle.[58] Though astrology has never gone out of style, the prominence it enjoyed was significantly reduced once it was learned that the movements of celestial bodies is regular and can be calculated precisely. This knowledge was gained in the latter half of the first millennium. Thereafter it became difficult to think of the celestial phenomena as communication from the gods.[59]

52. Koch-Westenholz, *Mesopotamian Astrology*, 97–99; see details with regard to the planets in Brown, *Mesopotamian Planetary Astronomy*, 86–93.

53. Brown, *Mesopotamian Planetary Astronomy*, 151–52. Here he refers to the underlying code of the *Enuma Anu Enlil* paradigm.

54. Koch-Westenholz, *Mesopotamian Astrology*, 180.

55. Ibid.

56. Ibid., 51. This covers a span of a century from 721 to 627.

57. For the canonical status of this series see ibid., 74–76.

58. Brown, *Mesopotamian Planetary Astronomy*, 234.

59. Koch-Westenholz, *Mesopotamian Astrology*, 51. She observes that mathematical calculations thus replace divinatory lore.

Terrestrial. Terrestrial omens are compiled in the 113 tablets of the series known as *Šumma alu*.[60] They range over a wide variety of phenomena including features of cities, features of houses, appearances of supernatural beings, behavior of land animals, appearance of fire, actions of the king, occurrences in fields, gardens, rivers, and marshes, behavior of aquatic animals and birds, personal behavior when sleeping or waking, appearance of strange lights, occurrences on the way to prayer, human sexual behavior, and family relations.[61] For example:

- If there is a river and a wood in a city, that city's people will not be happy (I.26).[62]
- If a city's dump is situated upstream, that city will be abandoned (I.37).
- If idiots are numerous in a city, that city will be happy (I.87).
- If it rains frogs in a city, there will be plague in that city (II.79).
- If red ants are seen in the laid foundations [of a house], the owner of that house will die before his time (V.31).

This series also includes a few examples of "speech omens," in which an overheard comment (or even an animal noise) or a reported comment is seen as bearing significance to the hearer's situation, even though it was not directed to that situation.[63]

Physiognomic. The last series of omens to be presented, entitled *Šumma Izbu*,[64] contains 24 tablets connected with the birth of deformed animals (and includes stillborn or miscarriages), all designated as anomalies (= *izbu*). As with the other omen types in this category, these omens operate by means of a system derived from mystical speculation. For example:

- If an anomaly's right shoulder is raised—your enemy will carry off the power of your country; a palace official will die; birth of a moron in your land (XIV.10).
- If an anomaly has two heads, but (only) one neck—the king will conquer wherever he turns; he will conquer a land which does not belong to him (VII.A.1–2).

60. S. M. Freedman, *If a City Is Set on a Height* (Philadelphia: Occasional Publications of the Samuel Noah Kramer Fund, 1998); Guinan, "Perils."
61. List drawn from Freedman, *If a City Is Set*, 2.
62. Freedman's translations and numbering.
63. *CAD* E: 48 (*egirru*). This is often associated with the ominous Greek *klēdōn;* see intriguingly John 11:49–52.
64. E. Leichty, *The Omen Series Šumma Izbu*, TCS 4 (Locust Valley, NY: Augustin, 1970).

Comparative Exploration: Joshua 10:12–15

Many modern readers of the Bible have responded with incredulity at the apparent suggestion that the sun and moon stood still.[1] Unpersuaded that physics could be so tamed, they have offered alternative suggestions (e.g., that the army was protected from the heat of the sun), despite the problems that such suggestions posed for the text. Here I propose that Joshua 10 operates in the world of omens, not physics. Rather than ask what it would mean to us for the sun and moon to stop, we must ask what it would mean in the ancient context of celestial omens.

In the ancient Near East the months were not standardized in length, but varied according to the phases of the moon. The beginning of a month was calculated by the first appearance of the new moon. The full moon came in the middle of the month and was identified by the fact that the moon set just minutes after the sun rose. The day of the month on which the full moon occurred served as an indicator of how many days the month would have. It was considered a good omen if the full moon came on the 14th day of the month because then the month would be the "right" length and all would be in harmony. If "opposition" (moon and sun simultaneously on opposite horizons) occurred on the 14th, it was considered to

be a "full-length" month made up of full-length days (cf. Josh. 10:13). The horizon was observed very carefully in the middle section of the month in the hope that this opposition of sun and moon would come on the propitious day (14th). Opposition on the wrong day was believed to be an omen of all sorts of disaster, including military defeat and overthrow of cities. Thus great significance was attached to these omens. In Joshua 10, since the sun is over Gibeon (east) and the moon is over Aijalon (west), it is likely that it is near sunrise in the full moon phase.

The Mesopotamian celestial omens use verbs like "wait," "stand," and "stop" to record the relative movements and positions of the celestial bodies. When the moon and/or sun do not wait, the moon sinks over the horizon before the sun rises and no opposition occurs. When the moon and sun wait or stand, it indicates that the opposition occurs for the determination of the full moon day. For example:

- If on the 14th day the moon and sun are seen together: the speech of the land will become reliable; the land will become happy (517:6–7).[2]
- If on the 15th day the moon and sun are seen together: a strong enemy will raise his weapons against the

- If a ewe gives birth to a lion, and it has four horns on the right and left—the prince will rule the (four) quarters (V.29).

Terrestrial and physiognomic omens are more generally applicable to commoners, whereas extispicy and celestial divination are applied to the king and to matters of state. Protection by means of apotropaic rituals

land; the enemy will tear down the city gate (173:1–4).

- If the moon does not wait for the sun but sets: raging of lions and wolves (91:1–2; see also 174:4; 295:1; and 481:4).[3]
- If the moon is fast (= stands) in its course: business will diminish—on the 15th day it will be seen with the sun (295:7–8; see also 252:r.3).
- If the moon is hasty in its movements: business will diminish (173:7).
- Mars has entered Cancer, but it will not be regarded as an omen; it will not stand in it, it will not become stationary and not tarry; it will move out quickly (462:1–7).

In light of these omens, Joshua 10:12–15 could be translated as follows:

"O sun, wait over Gibeon and moon over the valley of Aijalon." So the sun waited and the moon stood before the nation took vengeance on its enemies. Is it not written in the book of Jashar, "The sun stood in the midst of the sky and did not hurry to set as on a day of full length?"

All of this language is familiar from the celestial omens. It should be noted that the biblical text does not suggest that the astronomical phenomena were unique; instead, Joshua 10:14 says plainly that what was unique was the Lord accepting a battle strategy from a man ("the Lord listened to a man"). Joshua's knowledge of the Amorites' dependence on omens may have led him to ask the Lord for one that he knew would deflate their morale—for the opposition to occur on an unpropitious day. This does not change the general idea that God fought on behalf of Israel, but it does give the interpreter a more accurate picture of the way in which God did so.

1. For more detail see J. H. Walton, "Joshua 10:12–15 and Mesopotamian Celestial Omen Texts," in *Faith, Tradition, and History*, ed. A. R. Millard, J. K. Hoffmeier, and D. W. Baker (Winona Lake, IN: Eisenbrauns, 1994), 181–90.

2. All taken from Hunger, *Astrological Reports*, and following the numbering system there.

3. Several texts speak of both the sun and moon not waiting (though Hunger does not translate them that way): 23:5; 24:6; 92:1–3; 173:9–10; 499:1–3.

(*namburbi*) that ward against evil are more often used in response to the terrestrial and physiognomic and rarely to extispicy and celestial omens.[65]

Practitioners

Baru

These diviners were considered the professional interpreters of omens and primarily engaged in extispicy.[66] Thus, though "diviner" or "divina-

65. Reiner, *Astral Magic*, 83–84.
66. On practioners in general see Brown, *Mesopotamian Planetary Astronomy*, 33. On the *baru* see Cryer, *Divination*, 194–205.

tion priest" might be acceptable, in practical terms "haruspex" (one who examines entrails of sacrificed animals for divination purposes) would accurately describe the major activity.

Tupšarru

Generically this term referred to scribes, but technically it is a label applied to celestial diviners.

Muḫḫu

This term occurs in the context of prophetic utterances and those so designated are generally considered "ecstatics." Contextual use suggests an altered state of mind.

Apilu

These specialists are "consultants" who provide divine communication in response to inquiries (cf. Balaam).[67]

Magic

We must understand from the beginning that magic in the ancient world cannot be dissociated from the category of religion. W. Farber defines "magic" as falling within the boundaries of religion in a way that orients it in relationship to the pursuit of self-interest.[68] G. Frantz-Szabó offers a definition that encompasses the whole range of magic and religion within the context of efficacious invocation of supernatural power.

[Magic] is a reasoned system of techniques for influencing the gods and other supernatural powers that can be taught and learned. . . . Magic is a praxis, indeed a science, that through established and for the most part empirical means seeks to alter or maintain earthly circumstances, or even call them forth anew. Magic not only manipulates occult forces but also endeavors to master the higher supernatural powers with which religion is concerned.[69]

67. Other terms are sometimes used for prophets; see the discussion in Nissinen, *Prophets and Prophecy*, 7.
68. W. Farber, "Witchcraft, Magic, and Divination in Ancient Mesopotamia," *CANE* 3:1896. See also J.-M. de Tarragon, "Witchcraft, Magic, and Divination in Canaan and Ancient Israel," *CANE* 3:2075.
69. G. Frantz-Szabó, "Hittite Witchcraft, Magic and Divination," *CANE* 3:2007.

Magic and Its Cognitive Environment

While divination is concerned with gaining knowledge, magic involves exercising power. "What divination reveals, magic can resolve."[70] Resolution is often sought by means of incantations, which consist of oral rituals, usually performed in association with manual rituals to accomplish protection (apotropaism), elimination (exorcism), or imposition of evil spells (hexing). These represent an attempt to manipulate cosmic forces in pursuit of self-interest. A major underlying concept in understanding the relationship between divination and magic is that contagion is attached to bad omens, which must be dealt with through incantations and rituals.[71]

The omen thus established a connective thread between the person and the portended evil that had to be cut to release the power of the omen. This was the role of the incantations and rituals. Maul identifies six aims of these *namburbi* rituals:

1. The anger of the gods who sent the omen must be placated.
2. The decision to send an evil fate must be revised or rescinded.
3. The impurity acquired from the omen must be removed.
4. The impurity of the surroundings must be removed.
5. The person must be returned to normal life.
6. The person should be provided with protection against renewed threat.[72]

Incantations operate as oral rites of transfer. They can transfer positive attributes such as purity, negative attributes such as illness, or identity attributes (usually to or from a representative item or object).[73] The underlying power of magic was built into the very cosmos.

Egyptian magic was a realm of legitimate action and a mode of understanding which, like conceptions of the cosmos, involved all of creation from the highest to the lowest. It was a force that had existed from the beginning and had been essential to the creation of the world. . . . [The] Instruction for Merikare says that the creator gave magic to humanity "as a weapon to ward off what might happen."[74]

70. Guinan, "Severed Head," 18.
71. Maul, "How the Babylonians," 124.
72. Ibid.
73. G. Cunningham, *Deliver Me from Evil: Mesopotamian Incantations 2500–1500 BC*, Studia Pohl: Series Maior 17 (Rome: Pontifical Biblical Institute, 1997), 2–3.
74. J. Baines, "Society, Morality and Religious Practice," in *Religion in Ancient Egypt*, ed. B. Shafer (Ithaca: Cornell University Press, 1991), 165.

In these roles magic was recognized as generally beneficial for society, although it could be abused for antisocial ends.[75] Thus the specialist in the performance of incantations was engaged in an honorable profession and was to be distinguished from the necromancers or those who cast spells.

Practitioners

Ašipu

This term describes the profession closest to the modern "physician,"[76] though we need to exercise care lest we think of them as physicians in the modern sense. They were concerned with symptoms, but viewed them as signs.[77] These practitioners engaged the realm of magic and served as exorcists. They received portions from the food offered to deities, which indicates that they were considered priestly personnel. They were experts in both magical and medical diagnosis and in the treatment of maladies.[78]

Asu

These experts often worked in close association with an *ašipu*. They specialize in drugs, herbs, and physical remedies, and as such combine the roles of nurse and pharmacist. Herbal remedies had to be administered at the propitious time (astronomy) and be accompanied by the appropriate incantations. The potency or effectiveness of herbs could sometimes be dictated by the times and conditions under which they were gathered as well as the astral conditions under which they were prepared and administered.[79]

Kaššapu/Kaššaptu

This is the most common Akkadian terminology to describe male and female sorcerers. This negative label designates those whose magic is detrimental to individuals and to society.

75. Ibid.
76. The distinction between *ašipu* and *asu* is treated in detail in J. Scurlock, "Physician, Exorcist, Conjurer, Magician: The Tale of Two Healing Professions," in *Mesopotamian Magic*, ed. Abusch and van der Toorn, 69–79; see also Cryer, *Divination*, 205–8.
77. Cryer, *Divination*, 206.
78. J. Scurlock and B. Andersen, *Diagnoses in Assyrian and Babylonian Medicine* (Urbana, IL: University of Illinois Press, 2005); J. Scurlock *Magico-Medical Means of Treating Ghost-Induced Illnesses in Ancient Mesopotamia* (Leiden: Brill/Styx, 2006).
79. Reiner, *Astral Magic*, 35–36, 48.

Epistemology and Semiotics

Divination produced the only divine revelation known in the ancient Near East. Through its mechanisms, the ancients believed not that they could know deity, but that they could get a glimpse of the designs and will of deity. In this section we will explore the underlying epistemology that supported their beliefs.

Epistemology deals with theories of knowing—how do people have confidence that what they "know" is worthwhile and meaningful? How is "true" knowledge derived and what is it based on? What makes it "true"? These are important questions as we try to understand divination. Why did divination make sense to the people of the ancient world? What sort of knowledge did they believe they received from the gods through divination? Of course, for them divination was vital and touched that which was real—they did not consider it farcical or contrived.[80]

Yet even as we acknowledge this fact, we recognize that since divination is so foreign to us in the Western world, our comprehension is at best superficial. As A. Guinan observed, "There are few genres whose conceptual structures remain so intransigently opaque."[81] It is like working with a language for which we know the alphabet, but recognize few of the words. Yet, as researchers seeking to understand a foreign culture, we must try to understand the credibility of the institution and its functions. We cannot allow our own assessments of its validity based on our own cognitive environment to interfere.[82]

Functions: Legitimation, Action, and Warning

It is important to recognize that there are differences between the function of divination as a practice and the ways that the literary collections of omens functioned. "An omen is a single cognitive construct which refers back to the event containing it; at the same time it looks forward to the future in order to serve as a warning."[83] Once an omen was committed to writing and organized with other omens to be used in future situations, it took on a life of its own. The preservation and formalization of the omen extended its meaning and expanded its potential for reuse.

Most forms of divination produce meaning that is singular and applicable to the situation at hand. However, the recording of omens produces meaning that appears fixed. By transforming a singular perception into

80. Cryer, *Divination*, 121.
81. Guinan, "Perils," 227.
82. Bottéro, *Religion*, 175.
83. Guinan, "Severed Head," 27.

an intelligible object whose meaning is applicable in other contexts, it suggests a process of abstraction and establishes a system of knowledge. Not only were the scribes adding new omens, they were also defining their meaning. When both signs and their meaning are envisioned in the human mind, divinatory inquiry seems to make an intellectual leap into new epistemological territory.[84]

Divination in Mesopotamia is founded on the observation of that which is anomalous, while incorporating omens into literary texts attempts systematization.[85] Our study must perforce focus on the literature and how it was used. We can perhaps at moments observe from the outside the actual experience of divination, but only through written sources, which is a handicap. The functions of divinatory literature can be classified into three general categories: legitimation, action, and warning. We will consider each briefly in turn.

First and foremost, divination in the ancient Near East was focused on the *legitimation* of the king and the current regime. That legitimation was found in the continual affirmation that the gods had put the king on the throne and supported his policies and activities. Positive omens validated the royal plan; negative omens warned of potential trouble spots or disastrous undertakings. Even these negative omens perpetuated the reign of the king by identifying what might jeopardize that reign. The king always desired to present his course of action as at least endorsed by the gods if not initiated and guided by them.[86]

Divination not only legitimized action that the king had already decided to undertake but also encouraged certain actions. When an omen indicated a favorable outcome or a prophet conveyed the message "I [the deity] am with you," the king could proceed under the conviction that he would succeed. In that sense divination was able to justify a course of *action*. The result of the divination was not a sure or specific knowledge of the future, but a confidence for the present. The omen apodoses then should not be considered predictions that would be assessed for their accuracy. They offered guidance in how to approach a situation.[87] Thus the king would also be careful to heed the *warnings* that divination offered. But just as a positive omen would not be understood as a guarantee of success, so a negative omen could often be reversed.[88] "The gods send the signs; but what these signs announce is not unavoidable fate. A sign in a Babylonian text is not an absolute cause of a coming event,

---

84. Ibid., 19.
85. Ibid., 20.
86. DeJong Ellis, "Observations," 178.
87. Guinan, "Severed Head," 19.
88. Ibid., 20.

but a warning. By appropriate actions one can prevent the predicted event from happening. The idea of determinism is not inherent in this concept of sign."[89] Consequently, the evidence suggests that the function of divination was to provide divine endorsement or warning concerning an action that the king had already undertaken or was contemplating in order to assure the king of the continuing support by the deity.

Certainty

In the wake of divination, of what could a person be certain? The problem with assuming that the intention of divination was the prediction of the future is that it poses an insurmountable hurdle. "To put it into cold rationalist terms, it cannot do what it claims. One would expect the inevitable accumulation of false predictions to undermine the process."[90] We find that the ancients suffered under no such cognitive dissonance, and that we therefore need to nuance our understanding more carefully to recognize that the apodoses are more forecast than prediction.[91]

If some proclamation of doom did not materialize, a variety of explanations would be easily available. One could conclude that the omens had been misread, other balancing omens had been missed, or apotropaic (protective) rituals had been successful.[92] But the system did not merely rely on such artificial means to sustain its viability. I. Starr suggests instead that what may appear to us to be predictions unveil the world of the potential: "Predictions embedded in apodoses of omens do not mirror reality but the fears and aspirations of the people of Mesopotamia. The unfavorable predictions, and these, understandably enough, are the majority, describe the calamities, both natural and man made, which may befall the king and country alike; the favorable ones describe the hopes of man for peace and prosperity."[93]

If this were indeed the case it would not be so much that the omens would be intended to predict as that because of a past correlation they would draw a particular issue to one's attention. The modern practices of reading tea leaves or using horoscopes have the same result but in our contemporary world are almost entirely secular. In the ancient world this drawing of one's attention was done by the gods, who were controlling the future, thus making the advice or warning much more compelling. Omens and at least some categories of prophecy tended to bring certain issues

---

89. Hunger and Pingree, *Astral Sciences*, 5; see also Maul, "How the Babylonians," 123: "A portent merely indicates one possibility."
90. Guinan, "Severed Head," 19.
91. Bottéro, *Religion*, 181.
92. Brown, *Mesopotamian Planetary Astronomy*, 231.
93. Starr, *Rituals*, 12.

to one's attention, and the intended result would be that this heightened awareness would lead to appropriate action. "The underlying tension of a personal situation kindles the signifying power of an omen."[94]

Divination therefore was not intended to provide certainty. Instead it provided some direction in choosing a course of action. It helped people to have a sense of what to do in the face of an uncertain future with a sense of divine guidance undergirding their decision. Forewarned is forearmed; or, alternatively, carpe diem.

Excursus: Deuteronomy 18:20–22

Before concluding this section it is important to pause to consider the epistemological implications for the test of a prophet in Deuteronomy 18:

> But a prophet who presumes to speak in my name anything I have not commanded him to say, or a prophet who speaks in the name of other gods, must be put to death. You may say to yourselves, "How can we know when a message has not been spoken by the Lord?" If what a prophet proclaims in the name of the Lord does not take place or come true, that is a message the Lord has not spoken. That prophet has spoken presumptuously. Do not be afraid of him. (Deut. 18:20–22)

Some observations are in order to discover how broad or narrow the offered epistemological test is.

- The question set forth is how they know when a word has *not* been spoken by Yahweh, not how they will know when a word *has* been spoken by him. Correspondingly, the text does *not* say that a prophet whose words *do* come true is a true prophet.[95]
- The final result is that they are not to be afraid of him (Heb. *gur* = dread), so the question concerns whose threats to fear. This suggests that the focus is on oracles of judgment because those are the only sort that would be feared.

The point is that the "false prophet" has no true knowledge of divine *judgment* decisions or activities. This would then logically deal specifically with the area of judgment prognostication rather than forecast-

94. Guinan, "Severed Head," 21.
95. Unlike the Sumerian statement about diviners: "A person who speaks a true word, the word (is) from his god; it is a favorable condition for existence and it is with him daily." See Kitz, "Prophecy," 34, from tablet 7352 in the Babylonian collection at Yale University.

Comparative Exploration: Why Was Deductive Divination Forbidden to Israel?

We have considered some of the continuing uncertainties regarding divination, including trying to understand how it signifies and establishes authenticity. Clarification of these issues should also help us to understand why deductive divination of most sorts would have been unacceptable in Yahwism, even though inspired divination was approved and used. In other words, what was different in the epistemology, theology, or semiotics of Israel that ruled out certain divinatory phenomena?

In order to understand why deductive divination was proscribed in Israel we need to look at four elements:

1. How they perceived the world around them, *semiotics* (do the omens signify?)
2. How the divine communication was interpreted, *hermeneutics* (including empirical assumptions, mystical development of the omen corpus, and the means by which the information was procured)
3. What they believed they could know and how they could know it, *epistemology*
4. How they perceived God, *theology*

Initial indications can be gained by considering why Israelites were permitted to use lots but were not permitted to do extispicy, when both are provoked forms of deductive divination. The two are simply variant mechanisms for placing an oracular request before deity. The major difference that exists between them is found in the basis of how the sign is read. Mystic speculation is not necessary for deriving meaning from lot casting—the answer is transparent. In contrast, the reading of the *exta* is entirely premised on such mystic speculation. Furthermore, the reading of the *exta* involves considerably more complexity, for there were numerous signs given in any liver reading, and these signs had to be balanced and figured in the interpretive reading of the divination expert. In other words, it appears that for provoked deductive divination to be acceptable in Israel, it had to be entirely binary, because with only two choices, the human interpreter had no role. Extispicy worked on binary principles, but it had to combine a number of binary readings and the hermeneutic was based in mystical speculation. Thus procedures such as oil on water were also prohibited in Israel. As a result, it was not the epistemology of divination that was at odds with Israelite theology, but the hermeneutics associated with the interpretation required of the haruspex. In other words, there was agreement between Israel and its neighbors in the belief that queries could be placed before deity. There was disagreement either in the semiotics (i.e., that the configuration of the liver carried no significance), or in the ability of the specialists to discern that which was signified (hermeneutics). This is similar to the distinction drawn earlier in the category of inspired divination. The semiotics behind both prophecies and dreams were believed to be legitimate—both were believed to offer information from deity. But the fact that dreams required the services of an interpreter made them more suspect, with the result that over time confidence in that form of communication declined (Jer. 23:25–28). No indications suggest that a difference in the perception of deity was at the heart of these distinctions, though to any extent that extispicy would be viewed as coercion, manipulation, or even somehow bypassing God, it would be unacceptable. None of these elements is clearly discernible in the way extispicy worked, and lots could be subject to the same abuses.

When we turn our attention to the other main category, passive/unprovoked deductive divination, we see that it was absolutely forbidden in Israel. Again the question is, for which reasons?

Semiotics

Biblical indications suggest that the Israelites did believe that celestial occurrences had significance (e.g., Joel 2:30). But there is never any indication that a suitable hermeneutic existed for gaining information from them aside from very general conclusions about God's control or that auspicious events were afoot. There is less reason to think that terrestrial phenomena had significance.

Hermeneutics

None of the interpretive means such as risings, settings, colors, and positional relationships are promoted in the biblical text. Both celestial and terrestrial interpretation used binary principles in complex combinations and the principles were developed by means of speculative expansion. We could infer that these elements are the most objectionable aspect.

Epistemology

Though the idea that people can gain information from deity through omens is not part of our modern cognitive environment, it was a belief that Israel shared with its neighbors. The differences then were not in the basic epistemology but in the semiotics (what has significance) and hermeneutics (how that significance is interpreted—both categories within epistemology) by which the divine communication was packaged and understood. According to ancient Near Eastern epistemology, the omens could give guidance for specific decisions. According to Israelite epistemology, divine communication was designed to help the people to know God and his plan.

Theology

Passive deductive divination does not intrinsically imply beliefs about deity that are contrary to Israelite theology. Communication by means of celestial or terrestrial omens is not beneath Yahweh's dignity nor do the Israelites assume the existence of other gods or powers. But, of course, the system does not stop there. In Mesopotamia they also believed that rituals and incantations could reverse the signs. This moves from the realm of knowledge being communicated to power being exercised. Here is where the theology breaks down and the differences emerge.

In passive deductive divination, then, the semiotic and hermeneutical principles mirror what we found for extispicy, and they provide the most likely explanation for why these divinatory practices were forbidden in Israel. Yahweh could speak (inspired divination), he could choose (provoked simple binary deductive divination), but he did not "write" his messages in the entrails of animals or in the movement of the heavenly bodies (provoked nonbinary or complex binary deductive divination, nonprovoked deductive divination). Israel believed that they could gain information about divine activity just as their ancient Near Eastern compatriots did, but the list of divinatory means they acknowledged as semiotically/hermeneutically acceptable was much more limited.

In Israel God "wrote" by means of the prophets, and the foundational repository from which the prophets operated was not omens or dreams but covenant. The ancient Near Eastern concept of a past correlation between an omen and the event connected to that omen has a role similar to what we can observe in the Israelite concept of a connection between the covenant and its correlative blessings and curses. As the recurrence of an omen stimulates awareness of the correlation, it motivates action in the portended area of behavior. Likewise prophecy stimulates awareness of the correlation and is expected to motivate appropriate action.

In both Israel and the ancient Near East, it was believed that deity controlled events and that deity communicated through events. Deity communicated and that communication could be read. True knowledge derived from the divine realm. Divination provided a means by which events and occurrences could be interpreted. Central to the interpretation of events offered by the prophets of Israel was the covenant. It was seen as the key to making sense of the experiences of the nation.

In contrast, central to the interpretation of events and occurrences in the ancient Near East was an artistic weaving together of omens, written and observed. Both systems have a human interpreter (prophet/diviner) who is believed to be in some sense directed by the deity, and both are based on past communication of the deity (covenant/omens). The difference is in the associations from which meaning is extracted. In Israel the covenant blessings and curses are associated with the behavior of the Israelites and the consequences they experience. In contrast, divination is based on circumstantial associations of omens that have no intrinsic relationship.[1]

1. Guinan, "Severed Head," 28.

ing or vision casting, which by definition did not offer the same type of knowledge and therefore would not be falsifiable in the same way.[96] Prognostication, forecasting, and vision casting all expect fulfillment, but in different ways. The criterion of Deuteronomy 18 would logically apply only to prognostication.

Certainly a prophet could also establish his credibility through prognostications that were not pronouncements of doom, with the result that

96. J. Tigay, *Deuteronomy*, JPS Torah Commentary (Philadelphia: Jewish Publication Society, 1996), 178.

when he made pronouncements of doom they would be taken seriously. The biblical text evidences a number of variations:

- Some prophets are incarcerated or threatened because of prophecies of doom that are suspect (Micaiah, 1 Kings 22; Jeremiah, Jer. 26).
- Some prophets offer prognostications that come true so as to establish their credibility (Jeremiah's pronouncement of death on Hananiah, Jer. 28:15–17; Ezekiel's prophecy that Jerusalem would fall, Ezek. 2:5; 33:33; in a similar way Moses performs signs to establish his credibility, Exod. 4:1–9).
- Some prophets enjoy credibility because of an established track record (cf. Samuel, 1 Sam. 3:19–20; 9:6).
- Jeremiah perhaps offers an expansion of Deuteronomy 18 when he indicates that it is not just prophecies of doom that serve as a basis for evaluation, but also prophecies of peace that come true (Jer. 28:7–9).

All of this suggests that the guideline offered is that of suspending judgment until a prophet has established a track record, though admittedly this would not always be practical.[97]

97. Ibid., 177–78.

12

Encountering the Present

Context of Life—Cities and Kingship

City

In Mesopotamia, and to a lesser extent in Egypt, the city was the ideal social context.[1] Nomadism was inferior and uncivilized. The order that characterized a city was parallel to and contributing to the order of the cosmos. Indeed, the cosmos found its ultimate ordered state in the city. The world could not exist at any meaningful level without cities.[2] We could delve into the history of urbanization to discover how and when cities developed in the ancient Near East, but our interest here is to try to understand how the *ancients* thought about cities and urbanization. There were certainly economic, technological, ecological, military, political, and, above all, religious aspects to the develop-

1. For more detail see the extensive and accessible work by M. van de Mieroop, *The Ancient Mesopotamian City* (Oxford: Oxford University Press, 1999), and his bibliography on 19–22.

2. For affirmations along these lines see H. Limet, "Ethnicity," in *Companion to the Ancient Near East*, ed. D. Snell (Oxford: Blackwell, 2005), 373; van de Mieroop, *Ancient Mesopotamian City*, 42; J. Assmann, *The Search for God in Ancient Egypt* (Ithaca: Cornell University Press, 2001), 25; P. Machinist, "On Self-Consciousness in Mesopotamia," in *The Origins and Diversity of Axial Age Civilizations*, ed. S. N. Eisenstadt (Albany: SUNY, 1986), 188–89.

ment of urbanization (which took place over the last half of the fourth millennium—in the preliterate period), but the ancients themselves considered all of this, as is to be expected, as reflexes of the activity of the gods.

Cities as Primordial

In both Mesopotamia and Egypt it was believed that cities existed before humans. Cities were the creations of the gods and were made for the gods.[3] This city of the gods is referred to by the personal name of one of Enlil's ancestors in the god lists: ^dEn-uru-ul-la, "Lord of the Ancient City." This city was believed to precede even the division of heavens and earth.[4]

The divine origin of cities resulted in their being considered sacred territory to some degree.

> The Mesopotamians' idea of their cities was thus tied to a respect for the past. Cities were monuments of the age-old culture; they were not new and modern, but old and respectable. They were not human creations but divine ones. When the walls of Uruk were praised, the fact that their foundations were laid by the seven primordial sages was stressed. When Sargon of Assyria—the only king who readily admitted to having built a new city—described his work on Dur-Sharrukin, he likened himself to one of these sages, Adapa. It was as if he re-enacted a primordial accomplishment.[5]

Eridu was considered the first city, but certainly the grandest, largest, and most significant in the earliest period was Uruk (where Gilgamesh was king at one time). A third important early urban center was Nippur, the early Sumerian religious center where Enlil was the patron deity.

Cosmic Identity of Cities (City = State = Cosmos)

In the early history of urbanization, government and political power were vested in the city-state. So, for instance, in the *Sumerian King List*, kingship descends from heaven, but it descends into a city. Rule is then passed from city to city. When something more like national states finally developed, they were still seen as extensions of cities. Whether

---

3. Limet, "Ethnicity," 375–76; Assmann, *Search for God*, 25.

4. F. Wiggermann, "Mythological Foundations of Nature," in *Natural Phenomena: Their Meaning, Depiction and Description in the Ancient Near East*, ed. D. J. W. Meijer (Amsterdam: Royal Netherlands Academy of Arts and Sciences, 1992), 279–306, quotation on 284.

5. Van de Mieroop, *Ancient Mesopotamian City*, 61.

early or late, the city stands for the state, whatever its size.[6] Just as the cosmos finds its ultimate fruition in the city, the state has its foundation in the city.

Cities outside Mesopotamia were not as central, were not as integrated into life and culture, and were not driven by the same concerns as in Mesopotamia.[7] For example, J. Assmann observes that in Egyptian religion the gods had withdrawn from their presence among humans to their habitation in the sky. There were important cities (e.g., Thebes or Memphis), but cities were not as central to the identity of the state—rather the state was more directly related to the cult. "The absence of deities made room for a specifically human sphere of activity and responsibility: the state, which—despite or because of its being a divine institution—kept the divine at a distance that had to be bridged by 'sacred signification.' The founding of the state amounted to the same thing as the founding of the cult."[8] Likewise in Syria-Palestine the role of the city in relation to the state and the cosmos never developed as it did in Mesopotamia, though cities such as Damascus or Samaria played a central role as the political centers of powerful states.

Sacred Identity of Cities (Gods-Temples-Cities)

The most important aspect of the role of cities is to be found in their relationship to the temples and the gods. The patron deity of a city was typically considered the one who founded, built, and sustained the city. So the prominence and prosperity of the city and its god were inextricably intertwined. "Each Mesopotamian city was the home of a god or goddess, and each prominent god or goddess was the patron deity of a city."[9] In Mesopotamia the gods were attached to cities, and temples were only in cities.[10] Worship as we know it therefore took place in cities. The archaeological record shows no evidence of sanctuaries in the mountains or plains, and no rivers or trees with cultic significance.[11] Likewise in Egypt there was an integral relationship between cities and gods. "The sum of landowning temples and deities embodied the state. . . . Just as the totality of deities embodied the political concept of 'Egypt,' the individual landowning local deity embodied the concept of 'city.' An Egyptian city was always the city of a deity."[12]

6. Machinist, "Self-Consciousness," 187.
7. Van de Mieroop, *Ancient Mesopotamian City*, 248–52.
8. Assmann, *Search for God*, 18.
9. Van de Mieroop, *Ancient Mesopotamian City*, 46.
10. Ibid., 217.
11. Ibid., 215.
12. Assmann, *Search for God*, 19.

Comparative Exploration: Jerusalem, the Holy City

In Israel there was only one authorized temple in one authorized location. Consequently, cities in general did not carry the same role or significance as is found particularly in Mesopotamia. Nevertheless, when we try to understand the status of Jerusalem as the location of the temple and the cult center for the worship of Yahweh, we find quite a bit of continuity with ancient Mesopotamian ideas. In relation to the categories listed above, no indicators suggest that Yahweh's ordered cosmos found its epitome in Jerusalem, nor was Jerusalem thought of as a primordial city. Nevertheless, Yahweh had made Jerusalem his dwelling place with the result that it was considered thereby to be the control center of the cosmos. Therefore, as Marduk was thought to rule the world from Babylon, Yahweh was understood to rule the world from Jerusalem as temple, city, state, and cosmos all related to Yahweh through Zion.

In Syria and Canaan cities often had their patron deities, but deities were not as dependent on cities. Sacred mountains and outdoor shrines attest to the greater diversity that existed in less urbanized cultures.

Kingship

What J. Baines observes about Egypt applies more or less generally across the ancient world: "Kingship was the central institution of society and civilization."[13] In the ancient world the king stood between the divine and human realms mediating the power of the deity in his city and beyond. He communed with the gods, was privy to their councils, and enjoyed their favor and protection. He was responsible for maintaining justice, for leading in battle, for initiating and accomplishing public building projects from canals to walls to temples, and had ultimate responsibility for the ongoing performance of the cult.[14] Beyond that, every aspect of order and balance in the cosmos was associated with the king's execution of his role, as is demonstrated in this list of the expected benefits from Esarhaddon's reign.

13. J. Baines, "Ancient Egyptian Kingship; Official Forms, Rhetoric, Context," in *King and Messiah in Israel and the Ancient Near East*, ed. J. Day, JSOTSup 270 (Sheffield: Sheffield Academic Press, 1998), 16.
14. For discussion on the Egyptian side, see the comments by Assmann, *Search for God*, 5.

A good reign—righteous days, years of justice, copious rains, huge floods, a fine rate of exchange! The gods are appeased, there is much fear of god, the temples abound; the great gods of heaven and earth have become exalted in the time of the king, my lord. The old men dance, the young men sing, the women and girls are merry and rejoice; women are married and provided with earrings; boys and girls are brought forth, the births thrive. The king, my lord, has revived the one who was guilty and condemned to death; you have released the one who was imprisoned for many years. Those who were sick for many days have got well, the hungry have been sated, the parched have been anointed with oil, the needy have been covered with garments.[15]

This basic profile is common throughout the ancient Near East, though it is articulated in many different forms from culture to culture, particularly in a variety of understandings concerning the extent to which the king shared the divine nature. The king in Egypt was, on the whole, divinized to a higher degree than kings in the other cultures,[16] though the Sargonic kings near the end of the third millennium in Mesopotamia approached the same level with cult statues of the king in temples and divine determinatives before their names.[17]

The various literatures describe the origins of kingship and in the process offer a profile of the king's role. An Egyptian hymn to Re provides a general description. "Re has placed the king in the land of the living forever and ever, judging humankind and satisfying the gods, realizing Maat and destroying Izfet. He (the king) gives offerings to the gods and mortuary offerings to the deceased."[18]

On the Mesopotamian side, a Neo-Babylonian account describes the creation of primitive humans in a very broken section, then proceeds to describe the creation of the king (clearly in archetypal fashion[19]). Ea commissions the mother goddess in the following speech:

> Belet-ili, you are the mistress of the great gods.
> You have created lullu-man:

---

15. S. Parpola, *Letters from Assyrian and Babylonian Scholars*, SAA 10 (Helsinki: University of Helsinki Press, 1993), #226, 177–78.

16. For fuller discussion of the divinity of the pharaoh see D. Silverman, "Divinity and Deities in Ancient Egypt," in *Religion in Ancient Egypt*, ed. B. Shafer (Ithaca: Cornell University Press, 1991), 58–73.

17. W. W. Hallo, "Texts, Statues and the Cult of the Divine King," in *Congress Volume: Jerusalem 1986*, VTSup 40 (Leiden: Brill, 1988), 54–66, esp. 58–59.

18. Text cited in Assmann, *Search for God*, 3.

19. Here it is not necessarily an individual king that is being created but the idea of the king, the job description and qualities of kingship. Returning to our ontological discussions, the functions are being created, and thus the reality exists. This is purely archetypal.

> Form now the king, the thinking-deciding man!
> With excellence cover his whole form,
> Form his features in harmony, make his whole body beautiful!

Then Belet-ili fulfilled her commission with the major gods contributing specific attributes.

> The great gods gave the king the battle.
> Anu gave him the crown, Ellil ga[ve him the throne],
> Nergal gave him the weapons, Ninurta ga[ve him shining splendor],
> Belet-ili gave [him a handsome appea]rance.
> Nusku gave instruction, imparted counsel *and sto[od by him in service]*.[20]

The common denominators concerning the role of the king are therefore evident throughout the various cultures of the ancient Near East across the span of time. We will look briefly at this profile below.

Origin of Kingship

The introduction to a disputation text entitled *Palm and Tamarisk* offers a mythological description of the origins of kingship in Mesopotamia. Several versions are extant from a variety of times and places. The scenario opens after the land had been founded and the gods had built cities for humans and had dug irrigation canals. As they sat together in council they decided to provide kingship. "Formerly kingship did not exist in the land, and rule was given to the gods. But the gods grew fond of the black-headed people and g[ave them a king. The people] of the land of Kish assembled around him so that he might protect (them)."[21]

The *Sumerian King List* opens with the line: "When kingship descended from heaven," representing the common idea that kingship was the creation of the gods given as a boon to humans. The Sumerian myth *Inanna and Enki* lists kingship among the control attributes (Sumerian ME) that define the cosmos.

All of this contrasts with Israelite concepts. The people request kingship, and Yahweh grants it somewhat grudgingly (1 Sam. 8). Deuter-

20. VAT 17019; R. J. Clifford, *Creation Accounts in the Ancient Near East and in the Bible*, CBQMS 26 (Washington, D.C.: Catholic Biblical Association, 1994), 70, where the translation is quoted from W. Mayer, "Ein Mythos von der Erschaffung des Menschen und des Königs," *Or* 56 (1987): 55–68.
21. Clifford, *Creation Accounts*, 66.

onomy 18 presents a negative view of kingship rather than lauding it as the highest form of humanity. In the early chapters of Genesis, kingship is noticeably absent. Archetypal humanity bears the image of God rather than this being a distinctive of the king. Likewise they are charged with subduing and ruling. When we first encounter individuals playing out the role of king in one form or another (without the title) they offer negative depictions—the violent arrogance of Lamech and the imperialism of Nimrod.[22]

Concern with the Divine Will

As individuals who stood between the divine and human worlds, kings were expected to discern the divine will and facilitate its execution. In Egypt the almost total immersion of the persona of the king into the divine realm led inexorably to the conclusion that the acts of Pharaoh were the acts of deity.[23]

In Mesopotamia there was significantly more fretting about this and more effort extended into the enterprise of learning the will of the gods. The gravity of the concern and the angst that surrounded it are reflected in the prominence of divination in the court and in the reports of the king's advisors as they attempted to help him discern the will of the gods. If kings lost touch with deity, divine sponsorship could be forfeit and divine authority withdrawn. This system was governed by an agreement that existed between the king and the sponsoring god(s)—a kingship covenant of sorts.

> A ruler's legitimate status was initially asserted at the time of his successful assumption of the throne, and was often phrased in terms of predetermined divine election. His destiny was then annually reaffirmed in the context of the New Year's ritual. A god's relationship with a ruler can in fact be shown at least once to involve specific covenant terminology, as illustrated in the case of the Neo-Assyrian oracle referred to as an *adû*. Similarly, we can demonstrate in Old Babylonian sources the expectation of quid-pro-quo behavior, honoring understood terms in a contractual agreement. It

22. This negative depiction would also include Gen. 6:1–4 if the "sons of God" are interpreted as kings. See discussion of this negative treatment and nonmention of kingship in Gen. 1–11 in J. Walton, *Genesis*, NIVAC (Grand Rapids: Zondervan, 2001), 277–78.

23. Egyptologists continue to discuss the purported divine character of the pharaoh. Many are uncomfortable with the simple popular equation of pharaoh as god, and seek a more careful and complex nuancing. See Baines, "Ancient Egyptian Kingship," 28–46.

Comparative Exploration: Examples of Kings Claiming Divine Sonship

Eannatum (Vulture Stele): "Ningirsu inserted the germ of Eannatum into the womb. Baba gave birth to him . . . Ninhursaga fed him at her right breast." (T. Jacobsen, "The Stele of Vultures, Col. I–X," *Kramer Anniversary Volume: Cuneiform Studies in Honor of Samuel Noah Kramer*, ed. B. Eichler, AOAT 25 [Neukirchen-Vluyn: Neukirchener Verlag, 1976], 247–59)

Ur-Nammu: "The son born of the goddess Ninsuna" (RIME 3/2, 37–38)

Gudea: "For me who has no mother, you are my mother; for me who has no father, you are my father. You implanted my semen in the womb, gave birth to me in the sanctuary, Gatumdug, sweet is your holy name." (J. Black, et al. *Literature of Ancient Sumer* [Oxford: Oxford University Press, 2004], 46)

Samsuiluna (Old Baylonian): "O Samsuiluna, eternal seed of the gods." (RIME 4, 386, line 64)

Tukulti-Ninurta Epic (Middle Assyrian): "Through the destiny of Nudimmud, he is reckoned as flesh godly in his limbs, by fiat of the lord of the world, he was cast sublimely from the womb of the gods." (*FDD*, 181, lines 63–64)

---

must be stressed that all these occurrences are found in contexts which emphasize the *ad hoc* quality of the covenant or treaty.[24]

Rule through Divine Sponsorship

The concept of divine sponsorship is the most important element in the ideology of kingship. It was reflected in a variety of ways and pervades the rhetoric of the royal inscriptions.

> The Neo-Assyrian royal titularies, narrative inscriptions, astrological prognostications and unctuously flattering correspondence hammer away at the theme of the unique proximity of the king to the divine realm and extol his god-like powers. The kings were summoned prenatally to kingship, suckled by goddesses, warned by eclipses and other portents of imminent personal hazards, and succored by upbeat, motherly prophecies uttered by goddesses. Kings, like the gods, strode into battle surrounded by the *melammu*, a radiant, terrifying nimbus devastating to foes . . . and kings embodied godlike wisdom and could be characterized as the very image of the gods. The kings were not members of the state pantheon, but they dwelt in closer physical and ontological proximity to the gods than any other mortals.[25]

24. M. deJong Ellis, "Observations on Mesopotamian Oracles and Prophetic Texts," *JCS* 41:2 (1989): 181.

25. S. Holloway, *Aššur Is King! Aššur Is King!* (Leiden: Brill, 2002), 181–82.

Kings were likewise eager to affirm at every opportunity the evidences that the gods supported their reign, claiming continuing good omens and favorable dreams and prophecies.[26] The kings themselves may not have been divine, but they were elected by the gods and adopted into sonship (see sidebar). As such, they are not portrayed as gods, but are sometimes treated as gods. S. Holloway thus notes that in the Neo-Assyrian period there are no temples to kings, no extant prayers to kings, no iconography portraying the king with divine garb, posture, or status. But statues of the king were produced and were placed in temples next to the divine image where they were worshiped.[27]

Responsible for Justice

The major responsibility of the king in the ancient world was to maintain order in the part of the cosmos that he could affect: his kingdom. In Egypt this is expressed in the goal of establishing *maat*.[28] Baines notes that in Egypt no other form of rule was an option—the choices were king or chaos.[29] In Mesopotamia the prologue to the stele of Hammurabi articulated the king's responsibility as he proclaimed, "I made the land speak with justice (*mišaru*) and truth (*kittu*), and improved the welfare of the people."[30] A millennium later Assyrian kings were making the same claim as Ashurbanipal asserts that the gods created him with these same qualities.[31] In Israel the mandate of the king was to establish justice (*mishpat*) and righteousness (*tsedeqah*, e.g., 1 Kings 10:9; Jer. 22:3, 15). Similar wording appears in the Phoenician inscription of Yahimilk, a tenth-century king of Byblos.[32]

This role involved administering a judicial system that protected the rights of the vulnerable. This task had been given to the king by the gods, and he carried it out as a representative of the divine authority with which he had been vested when he ascended to the throne.

26. M. Nissinen, *Prophets and Prophecy in the Ancient Near East*, SBLWAW 12 (Atlanta: Society of Biblical Literature, 2003), 98, p. 143.

27. Holloway, *Aššur*, 182–86. See also I. Winter, "'Idols of the King': Royal Images as Recipients of Ritual Action in Ancient Mesopotamia," *JRitSt* 6 (1992): 13–42.

28. This concept has already been treated in depth in chaps. 5 and 6.

29. Baines, "Ancient Egyptian Kingship,"17.

30. M. E. J. Richardson, *Hammurabi's Laws* (London: T & T Clark, 2000), 41.

31. M. Weinfeld, *Social Justice in Ancient Israel and in the Ancient Near East* (Jerusalem: Magnes, 1995), 30. Weinfeld presents a chapter on these terms (chap. 1) and another on the task of the king in relation to these ideals (chap. 2). See also K. Whitelam, *The Just King*, JSOTSup 12 (Sheffield: JSOT Press, 1979), 17–37.

32. *COS* 2.29.

Photo 20 Relief: Darius Seated, Xerxes Behind

Israelite Kingship

In Mesopotamia the chief god was king of the gods and ruled over the cosmos run by the gods. He was a king whom the human king represented and therefore, through the human king, he was king over the people. In Israel all of the same held true except, of course, that Yahweh was the only god, not king of the gods. This difference is important, however, in that the kingship of Marduk, for instance, over the gods served as one of the most significant analogies or metaphors describing the human king's rule over the people.[33] In Israel no such metaphor existed.

Many similarities between kingship ideas in Israel and in the rest of the ancient Near East emerge in almost every category considered above.[34] Divine sponsorship is noted in the historical literature and in Psalms. As in the ancient Near East, the Israelite king is the agent of the divine plan, concerned with the will of deity, and representative of divine authority (notice that authority was taken from Saul and would never be taken from David's son). The king was responsible for justice and accountable to Deity for protecting the vulnerable. The establishment of kingship by covenant agreement is not as prominent in the ancient Near East as in the Hebrew Bible, but the concept is evident in passing remarks, as noted above.

Despite this common core, the differences should be clearly noted. Cautious or negative assessment of present kingship is much more common in the biblical literature than in the ancient Near East. No divine origin for human kingship in the mythical realm is conveyed, and the

---

33. D. Launderville, *Piety and Politics* (Grand Rapids: Eerdmans, 2003), 188.
34. Most can be seen clearly in Ps. 2 and 2 Sam. 7, though many other passages could be mentioned.

Comparative Exploration: Messiah

"Messiah" in the context of the ancient world has been generically defined as "a royal person whose coming is the sign of national salvation following a crisis that is insurmountable from a human point of view."[1] By this definition many kings throughout history could have claimed this title. Some of the most obviously comparable material may be found in a category of Mesopotamian texts variously labeled "apocalypses,"[2] "Fictional Auto-biography,"[3] or *"naru* literature,"[4] which often concerns the coming of a future ideal king. As all interpreters recognize, however, these are actually produced *in* the time period of the so-called coming king as a means of legitimizing his rule by suggesting that he had been foreordained in the distant past. Despite the way these texts are framed, then, an important distinction is that their ideal king is to be found in the present ruler, not in some undetermined future king.[5]

In contrast, the ideal Israelite king was in part in the past (David), but primarily in the future (the future Davidic king, i.e., Messiah). The timing element aside, almost all of the main characteristics of the future ideal king and kingdom in the Hebrew Bible can also be found in Akkadian literature.[6] The royal psalms, often considered messianic psalms, are particularly rich with the rhetoric that is well known from Mesopotamian literature.[7] Not only is the rhetoric familiar

from the royal inscriptions, J. Hilber has recently demonstrated the similarities to the Neo-Assyrian prophecy texts.[8] These similarities suggest that the royal/messianic psalms do not represent a conceptual departure from the stream of tradition in the ancient Near East in the picture they offer of the king. Rather it is in the theological development regarding the interpretations of this material as time goes on that marks its distinctiveness.

1. J. G. Heintz, "Royal Traits and Messianic Figures: A Thematic and Iconographical Approach (Mesopotamian Elements)," in *The Messiah*, ed. J. H. Charlesworth (Minneapolis: Fortress, 1992), 52–66.
2. W. W. Hallo, "Akkadian Apocalypses," *IEJ* 16:4 (1966): 231–42. For early discussion of terminology see A. K. Grayson and W. G. Lambert, "Akkadian Prophecies," *JCS* 18 (1964): 7–30; S. A. Kaufman, "Prediction, Prophecy, and Apocalypse in the Light of New Akkadian Texts," in *Proceedings of the Sixth World Congress of Jewish Studies* (1973): 221–28; R. D. Biggs, "More Babylonian 'Prophecies,'" *Iraq* 29 (1967): 117–32; idem, "The Babylonian Prophecies and the Astrological Traditions of Mesopotamia," *JCS* 39 (1985): 86–90.
3. Tremper Longman III, *Fictional Akkadian Autobiography: A Generic and Comparative Study* (Winona Lake, IN: Eisenbrauns, 1991); see esp. 43–48 for discussion of terminology.
4. H. Güterbock, "Die historische Tradition und ihre literarische Gestaltung bei Babyloniern und Hethitern bis 1200," *ZA* 42 (1934): 1–191.
5. Launderville, *Piety*, 303.
6. Weinfeld, *Social Justice*, 67–69.
7. J. W. Hilber, "Psalm CX in the Light of Assyrian Prophecies," *VT* 53 (2003): 353–66.
8. J. W. Hilber, *Cultic Prophecy in the Psalms* (Berlin: Walter de Gruyter, 2005).

king has less obvious responsibility for the cult. Though the Israelite king is depicted as Yahweh's son and clearly enjoys divine sponsorship, overall he is situated less in the divine realm (i.e., the Egyptian king is almost entirely in the divine realm, the Mesopotamian king is firmly in the middle, the Israelite king is almost entirely in the human realm. This even applies to the Israelite ideal future king). Finally, as mentioned above, the kingship covenant in Israel came to be attached to an extended dynastic succession that stretched into the ideal future.

13

Encountering the Present

Guidelines for Life—Law and Wisdom

As we continue to consider how the ancients encountered the present in their day-to-day existence, we now turn our attention to the ways in which their lives and behavior were ordered. As in modern times, the ideal was to have law-abiding citizens who understood their roles and place within society and lived wisely so as to maintain the structures of society within the family and the town. The literature that is available to us approaches the issue from the institutional side of society from which we get legal collections, many court records, instructional literature, and lists of proverbs. These all help illumine the values that framed daily life.

Legal Treatises

Historically, the various collections have commonly been referred to as "codes" (e.g., the *Code of Hammurabi*).[1] J. Bottéro, joining many other

1. The bibliography on law is vast. A sampling of the most foundational and influential sources would include the following: J. Bottéro, "The 'Code' of Hammurabi," in *Mesopotamia* (Chicago: University of Chicago Press, 1992), 156–84; J. J. Finkelstein, *The Ox That Gored* (Philadelphia: American Philosophical Society, 1981); S. Greengus, "Legal and Social Insti-

Photo 21 Code of Hammurabi Stele

voices, explains that this is a misnomer. Codes are (1) comprehensive, and (2) prescriptive. Ancient collections are neither, but represent anthologies. Bottéro demonstrates that they are not comprehensive through his discussion of significant areas that are not addressed. He demonstrates that they are not prescriptive law by showing their "illogicality" and their "manifest inefficiency."[2] Closer to the mark is the approach that views this literature in the context of wisdom. We know that part of the wisdom enterprise in the ancient Near East focused on compilation—the ancients loved compiling lists. In place of "codes" Bottéro suggests that these pieces of literature be understood as belonging to the category of "treatise."

In the eyes of its author the "Code" [of Hammurabi] was not at all intended to exercise by itself a univocal normative value in the legislative order. But it did have value as a model; it was instructive and educative in the judicial order. A law applies to details; a model inspires—which is entirely different. In conclusion, we have here not a law code, nor the charter of a legal reform, but above all, in its own way, a treatise, with examples, on the exercise of judicial power.[3]

I have adopted this label of "treatise" to use in the remainder of this discussion. There are six major treatises currently extant (Ur-Nammu, Lipit-Ishtar, Eshnunna, Hammurabi, Middle Assyrian, Hittite) with a number of

---

tutions of Ancient Mesopotamia," *CANE* 1:469–84; C. Houtman, *Exodus*, 3 vols. (Kampen: Kok, 1993–2002), 3:78–98; B. S. Jackson, "The Ceremonial and the Judicial: Biblical Law as Sign and Symbol," *JSOT* 30 (1984): 25–50; idem, "Ideas of Law and Legal Administration," in *The World of Ancient Israel*, ed. R. E. Clements (Cambridge: Cambridge University Press, 1989), 185–202; S. Paul, *Studies in the Book of the Covenant in the Light of Cuneiform and Biblical Law*, VTSup 18 (Leiden: Brill, 1970); M. Roth, *Law Collections from Mesopotamia and Asia Minor*, SBLWAW 6 (Atlanta: Scholars Press, 1995); R. Westbrook, "Biblical and Cuneiform Law Codes," *RB* 92 (1985): 247–64; idem, *Studies in Biblical and Cuneiform Law* (Paris: Gabalda, 1988); idem, *History of Ancient Near Eastern Law* (Leiden: Brill, 2003).

2. Bottéro, "Code," 161–63.

3. Ibid., 167.

other fragments. Of the major treatises, three have prologues and epilogues,[4] and three do not. Those that include prologue and epilogue set the treatises in the context of royal inscriptions with legitimation objectives. Those that have no prologue or epilogue cannot be assumed to function in the same way. It is possible that all exemplars have a basic function (treatise), while a few of them have adapted the treatise to serve legitimation purposes.

Bottéro draws attention to the treatise form and provides a helpful understanding of its implications by comparing these legal treatises to other treatises, most notably the medical ones.[5] In these we find a series of related paragraphs identifying symptoms and then suggesting diagnosis, prognosis, or remedy. The paragraphs of the medical treatise, like those of the legal treatise, are introduced by an "if" statement. The paragraphs are arranged together in groupings that show a desire to address variations within a general area. A similar form is found in the divinatory treatises, where the observed or hypothesized omen is introduced in an "if" clause and then a prognostication or interpretation is offered.

As we consider these treatises as a group, we will notice certain similarities that will help us to understand each in light of the others. In the study of divination in chapter 11, we found that many of the omens in the treatises were developed theoretically or hypothetically rather than empirically. Bottéro suggests the same for the medical symptoms, and it is not impossible that we might find the same among the legal treatises. When we turn to the question of the purpose or function of the treatises, they find their common ground as a genre in that each offers practical and didactic principles. All three (medical, legal, divinatory) serve as manuals that are compiled to teach principles to practitioners through paradigms. Bottéro suggests that they learned these principles the way that we learn math or grammar.[6] The medical treatises teach medical practitioners about diagnosis, the divinatory treatises teach the practitioners about prognostication through omens, and the legal treatises teach practitioners (whether future kings or court personnel) about judicial wisdom, all through multiplying examples in patterns.[7]

The cuneiform treatises are nothing else but types of paradigms or tables. It was by repetition and the variation of particular cases, of models to be

4. Though included here, Ur-Nammu's treatise does not actually have an epilogue since only the beginning of the treatise is preserved—thus this is an assumption.

5. Bottéro, "Code," 169–79, labels all of this literature as "treatises" that constituted the "science" of the times. See also Westbrook (*History*, 17), who includes reference to divination treatises along with medical and legal as we have here.

6. Bottéro, "Code," 178.

7. By "patterns" I refer to the literary structuring that treats, for instance, the varying positions and colors of Jupiter all together, the appearances and behavior of the nose all together, and the theft of various types of property all together.

considered in a spirit of analogy, that the substance of the discipline in question was assimilated, that the habit of scientific judgment was formed, that the sense of correct reasoning was acquired at the same time as the capacity to extend these same judgments and reasoning to all the material objects of the science in question, according to their eventual presentation.[8]

Another observation that brings these three together is that in each, the protasis ("If . . .") introduces a situation that stands in contrast to order and normality. Each paragraph then offers information or a course of action designed to help resolve the situation or restore equilibrium. So medical conditions need to be recognized and treated, omens need to be responded to, crimes need to be punished, and social wrongs need to be righted. Table 6 indicates the categories that are represented in the legal remedies.

Table 6. Legal Remedies

	Physical Punishment	Financial Settlement, Penalty, or Restitution	Ordeal or Oath	Judicial Decision
Ur-Nammu	5	20	0	3
Lipit-Ishtar	1	22	0	15
Eshnunna	7	28	2	29
Hammurabi	52	114	6	104
Neo-Babylonian	1	9	0	3
Middle Assyrian	32	32	5	32
Hittite	16	127	2	77
Book of the Covenant	2	10	1	6
Deuteronomy	9	2	0	8

When consequences include two categories the entry is counted in both. This occurs a few times in Eshnunna and quite frequently in Middle Assyrian Laws (14 times).

When the legal treatises are viewed in this light, one can propose that these are not laws, but exemplary verdicts that can serve the intended didactic function.[9] It is in this sense that they offer model justice. To go

8. Bottéro, "Code," 178.
9. Ibid., 164. He points out that this is what Hammurabi himself considers them to be based on statements made in the epilogue.

the next step, one can infer that not only is what we find in documents such as Hammurabi's stele not a "code," it is not even "law." These are not legislative documents. They report verdicts, they do not prescribe laws.

> Rather than creating these laws like a legislator, Hammurapi was an executor who sustained them and made them effective. These laws were probably the decisions of verdicts of particular legal cases that were incorporated into the *Code* because of their exemplary character. These particular cases demonstrated how royal justice could positively intervene where customary ways no longer adequately addressed the social and political circumstances. It is important to note that the larger fabric of the social order was shaped by the traditional and customary ways of the land, which the *Code* presupposed but made no pretense of articulating.[10]

If this were the case, we would have to conclude that we have no evidence of written "laws" from ancient Mesopotamians—they simply did not approach the administration of justice in that way. The legal treatises administer justice by offering model decisions that were considered just.[11] Today we think of justice as that which conforms to the law. For them justice was that which conformed to traditions reflected in the paradigms. Bottéro concludes that the "Code" of Hammurabi "is clearly centered upon the establishment, not of a strict and literal justice, but of equity that inspires justice but also surpasses it."[12]

These model verdicts are in some cases then combined with prologue and epilogue in royal inscriptions as a means of legitimating the king, whose decisions inspire such justice and so admirably reflect this wisdom. These treatises are the evidence of his judicial wisdom. This is arguably a secondary literary context for the compiled treatise.[13]

Ontological Issues

R. Westbrook asserts that the ancient world shared a common legal ontology, but one that differs significantly from how we think today.[14] If we take what we have already learned about kings and kingship and combine it with what we have already learned about the cosmos and how it was perceived to run, we will be well on our way to understanding the administration of justice and the legal treatises. We know that for

10. D. Launderville, *Piety and Politics* (Grand Rapids: Eerdmans, 2003), 281.
11. Bottéro, "Code," 179.
12. Ibid., 183.
13. Ibid., 183–84.
14. Westbrook, *History*, 4.

Comparative Exploration: Literary Context of the Law in the Pentateuch

The collections of legal material in the Pentateuch evidence a variety of literary forms (internally) as well as a variety of literary contexts in which they are placed. Literary forms include both apodictic and casuistic examples and within each there are several possible formulations. These have long been recognized and are dealt with in detail in almost every work on biblical law. We can briefly summarize some of the biblical forms by attending to the vocabulary that is used.

Jethro advises Moses: "Teach[1] [the people] the decrees (*huqqim*) and laws (*torot*), and show them the way (*derek*) to live and the duties (*ma'aseh*, singular) they are to perform" (Exod. 18:20). One possibility is that Moses does this by publicizing (i.e., setting before them, Exod. 21:1) model decisions that he (inspired by Yahweh) had delivered in the past. In contrast to the Decalogue, which is introduced as the "words" (*debarim*) that Yahweh spoke (Exod. 20:1), the Book of the Covenant is introduced as the "judgments/decisions" (*mishpatim*) that Moses is instructed by God to set before the people. In Exodus 21:2–22:17 these decisions are presented as case law introduced by a protasis with the decision following, as in the ancient Near Eastern exemplars.[2] From Exodus 22:18–23:19 the text adopts the apodictic formula, which simply dictates what they are not to do.[3] At the conclusion of the Book of the Covenant both the "judgments/decisions" (*mishpatim*) and the "words" (*debarim*) are written down and the people agree to do all the words (*debarim*), perhaps suggesting that the "judgments/decisions" (*mishpatim*)

are not something one would do (Exod. 24:3). Alternatively, of course, all categories might be combined under the general rubric of Yahweh's words. What is written on the tablets (Exod. 24:12) are the laws (*torot*) and the commands (*mitswot*). The Deuteronomic laws are introduced as decrees (*huqqim*) and "judgments/decisions" (*mishpatim*) that must be followed (*shmr*). Most of the Deuteronomic law is framed in the second person, and casuistic formulation using a protasis is relatively rare:

- Seventeen entries that follow the normal casuistic formulation (introduced by *ki*) using third person forms in the protasis followed by a judicial course of action (Deut. 17:2–7; 18:6–8; 19:11–12, 16–19; 21:1–8, 15–17, 18–21; 22:13–21, 22, 23–24, 28–29; 23:10–11; 24:1–4, 5, 7; 25:5–6, 11–12)
- Seven examples of third person protasis followed by second person instruction (Deut. 13:1, 6, 12; 15:7, 12, 16; 21:22–23)
- Seven examples of second person protasis followed by a judicial decision concerning what *you* should do (Deut. 21:10–14; 22:1–3, 4, 6–7; 23:24–25; 24:10–13, 19–21)

When "judgments/decisions" (*mishpatim*) is used independently (i.e., not in a series with other near synonyms), it refers to the same sort of casuistic formulation found in the Mesopotamian juridical treatises (cf. Num. 35:24). In most contexts in Leviticus through Deuteronomy, at least two terms are referred to and often more.

At this point the observation that is most important to make is that there is very little in biblical law that reflects the treatise form most familiar in the ancient Near Eastern literature. It is primarily limited to the series found in the Book of the Covenant (Exod. 21:1–22:16) and scattered sections in Leviticus (e.g., Lev. 20:9–21) and Deuteronomy (e.g., through-

out Deut. 17–25). Consequently, only these could easily be characterized as model decisions representing wise verdicts.[4] These, as well as the other forms, are put in larger literary contexts including the covenant (where they serve as stipulations), Moses's sermons (in Deuteronomy, where they are accompanied by exhortations to obey), and instructions to priests (where they concern cultic observance and how to maintain sacred space).

Table 7. Literary Context of the Law in the Pentateuch and Ancient Near East

Pentateuch	Ancient Near East
Essentially a self-revelation of Deity	Essentially a self-glorification of the king
Covenant charter that synthesizes an entire detailed and organized vision of the "right" exercise of what it means to be a holy nation (Exod. 19:5–6; Deut. 26:19).*	Political charter that synthesizes an entire detailed and organized vision of the "right" exercise of justice
Stipulations of the covenant	Treatise on jurisprudence
Portrays the ideal covenant keeper	Portrays the ideal king
The prime purpose of the biblical compilation is sanctification.**	The prime purpose of the Mesopotamian compilations is justice

*Paul, *Studies*, 36.
**Paul, *Studies*, 41.

Deuteronomy collected legal materials around the Decalogue to begin to approximate the spirit of the law by which holiness and covenant adherence would be achieved. This is similar to the way that the ancient treatises organized verdicts around general topics to convey the spirit of justice. Deuteronomy accomplished it by using the Decalogue as the organizing principle. The treatises of the ancient Near East do it by using interior variable proliferation.[5]

Israelite distinctions in this area are then reflected in the concern with holiness, the insistence on obedience, and the

covenant context of the legal material. Similarities are found in the recognition that this is not legislation per se, having a larger role to play in the cognitive environment that transcends the formulation of law for society.

1. This is the relatively rare Hiphil stem of the root *zhr*, which carries the nuance of caution or warning, usually indicating impending danger or deviation from the right path.

2. There are 16 main casuistic entries (beginning with *ki*) with numerous subpoints (introduced by *'im*). In addition, four clauses offer generalized statements ("Anyone who . . .") in 21:12–17. This

form is also represented in the Neo-Babylonian collection.

3. There are 20 apodictic entries, but among them are 2 casuistic entries (Exod. 22:19–20). Several entries begin with a protasis (second person rather than third person, which is common for casuistic formulation), and rather than following up with the judge's ruling, the apodosis is instruction to the individual who is in the situation concerning what he ought to do (Exod. 22:25–27; 23:4–5). These are unparalleled in the ancient Near East and should not be counted as casuistic.

4. This might work particularly well in the Book of the Covenant if these *mishpatim* (judgments/decisions, Exod. 21:1) connect to Jethro's advice in Exod. 18:20; that is, that since the decisions given by Moses are presented as having derived from divine communication (cf. Exod. 18:19), God directs him to set some of these decisions before the people as a means of teaching them wisdom, justice, and holiness.

5. Example: Hammurabi §§196–205; the same procedure occurs occasionally in the Bible, e.g., Lev. 20. This phenomenon observable in the treatises involves stringing together entries that consider the same issue with variables switched in (What if the injured person were a slave, or a woman? What if the planet were to the left instead of the right? What if the eyes were red instead of yellow?).

the kings of the ancient Near East, the highest value was the legitimation of their reign (much in the same way that in American politics the highest value is often reelection[15]). Integrally related to this value was the concept of divine sponsorship, which in its turn was dependent on the king's demonstration of wisdom. The king demonstrated his wisdom by showing insight in judgments and, in general, by the way in which he administered justice. This is explicitly stated in the epilogue to Hammurabi's collection of laws where he indicates that in his *wisdom* he has administered *justice* for the vulnerable by inscribing his verdicts. So Westbrook concludes that the mode of thinking was that principles would be inferred from examples, not from abstractions.

> The "science" of the ancient Near East was by the standards of Aristotelian logic a proto-science. It lacked two vital factors: definition of abstract concepts and vertical categorization (i.e., into two or more all-embracing categories, which can then be broken down into subcategories). Instead it has been dubbed a "science of lists," the concatenation of endless examples, grouped suggestively in associated sequences but incapable of ever giving an exhaustive account of a subject.[16]

It would therefore be entirely logical that the king should sponsor the collection of lists of legal decisions that reflected insight and communicated a profound and penetrating sense of justice.[17] Then we add

15. G. Mendenhall, "The Conflict Between Value Systems and Social Control," in *Unity and Diversity: Essays in the History, Literature and Religion of the Ancient Near East,* ed. H. Goedicke and J. J. M. Roberts (Baltimore: Johns Hopkins University Press, 1975), 172.

16. Westbrook, *History,* 20.

17. For the connection to list making see the comments by Roth, *Law Collections,* 4, where she also cites other bibliography supporting this association.

to this what we know of the ancients' perception of the cosmos. In the ancient world what was most important about the cosmos was that it was stable. The order that characterized it was a product of the control attributes (the MES) that were built into the cosmos and were administered (but not created) by the gods. Aspects of law/justice and wisdom were among those control attributes that were the stewardship of the gods, the endowment from the gods on the king, and the obligation of the king to manifest.[18] Consequently, as the king compiled these lists of examples of "wise justice," he was legitimating his kingship,[19] not necessarily trying to impose legislation on society, but guiding lesser officials and future kings in maintaining stability and order in civilization. His examples of wise justice would serve a function not entirely dissimilar to the party platform of one of the political parties compiled prior to national elections—they gave shape to his values. In this way these kings desired to demonstrate their grasp of cosmic order and control attributes that framed the cosmos, and translate them into justice and order for society. This is what the gods required of them—in fact, it was the most fundamental expectation of the gods. This is expressed nowhere as plainly as in a prophet's words to Zimri-Lim of Mari from the god Adad as he communicates his desire to restore Zimri-Lim's family to the throne: "Now hear a single word of mine: If anyone cries out to you for judgment, saying: 'I have been wronged,' be there to decide his case; answer him fairly. This is what I desire from you."[20]

Role of King and Deity

Given the above discussion it now becomes clear that kings such as Hammurabi should in no sense be considered "lawgivers." The king was expounding his judicial wisdom by compiling sample verdicts. The scene at the top of the stele of Hammurabi portrays the sponsorship of Shamash, the sun god who administers justice. He is sitting on his throne holding the rod and ring symbol with Hammurabi standing before him.[21]

18. Related items from the list in *Inanna and Enki* include righteousness, truth, jurisdiction, decision making, understanding, knowledge, and deliberation, to name a few.

19. The relationship between the legal collections and royal legitimation was recognized as early as J. J. Finkelstein, "The Edict of *Ammiṣaduqa*: A New Text," *RA* 63 (1969): 45–64; idem, "The Laws of Ur-Nammu," *JCS* 22 (1968): 66–81.

20. A.1968, 6–11; translation from M. Nissinen, *Prophets and Prophecy in the Ancient Near East*, SBLWAW 12 (Atlanta: SBL, 2003), #2, pp. 21–22.

21. Some believe that Shamash is giving these articles to Hammurabi and that they are symbols of royal office (scepter and nose ring) enabling the king to guide the people and administer justice. See W. W. Hallo, "Sumerian History in Pictures: A New Look at the 'Stele of the Flying Angels,'" in *An Experienced Scribe Who Neglects Nothing*, ed. Y. Sefati et al. (Bethesda, MD: CDL, 2005), 142–62, discussion on 150–53. Others contend that Shamash

Comparative Exploration: Israelite Principles?

There is not much evidence to suggest that Israelites valued lists as highly as their Mesopotamian counterparts, though one can find list collections not only in the Pentateuch but in genealogies and in proverbs. The important question to consider at this juncture is whether the Israelites were simply using a variant literary form from which to infer principles, were stating principles explicitly, or were even making the jump to abstractions. In the category of principles being implied by literary organization, we have already noted that Deuteronomy works this way by organizing its material around the Decalogue.[1] This represents an organizing approach that suggests principles by its very organization. Another possible example may be found in the Book of the Covenant, if S. Paul is correct in his assessment that it is organized into re-

lated groupings similar to that found in the Mesopotamian treatises.[2] The Decalogue itself, however, along with other sections that use apodictic formulation, could be considered explicit statements of principles. This is not surprising if they are serving the purpose of covenant stipulations in that the ancient Near Eastern literature provides sayings much more like principles in the treaty literature. It is much more difficult to find examples of any of the literature moving to the level of abstractions.

1. Even the idea that the material in Deut. 12–26 is organized around the Decalogue is not explicit in the book and is not accepted by all. For the original case for the Decalogue as the organizing principle made in detail see S. A. Kaufman, "The Structure of the Deuteronomic Law," *Maarav* 1/2 (1978–79): 105–58.

2. Paul, *Studies*, 106–11 (Appendix 1).

It is thus implied that Shamash is the source of Hammurabi's wisdom as a judge who enables him to give wise verdicts.

From all of the above neither the king nor the deity is seen as law-giver (especially given the current consensus that these are not laws). No such abstraction as "law" exists in their minds, only the practical need to administer justice. Nevertheless, the king was the primary source for legislation, typically through decrees.[22] Subordinate officials operating in the judicial realm would offer their rulings in the

---

is regularly pictured with his arm extended and holding these insignia and that he is not giving them to anyone. In this view they are understood as measuring instruments. See T. Jacobsen, "Pictures and Pictorial Language (the Burney Relief)," in *Figurative Language in the Ancient Near East*, ed. M. Mindlen et al. (London: School of Oriental and African Studies, 1987), 1–11; C. E. Woods, "The Sun-God Tablet of Nabu-apla-iddina Revisited," *JCS* 56 (2004): 23–103. For a brief discussion of the rod and ring see J. Black and A. Green, *Gods, Demons and Symbols of Ancient Mesopotamia: An Illustrated Dictionary* (Austin: University of Texas Press, 1992), 156.

22. Westbrook, *History*, 26–27.

Comparative Exploration: What Are the Implications of the Fact That the Pentateuch Presents the Torah as Given by Yahweh?

In the ancient Near East we found that neither Shamash (the deity) nor Hammurabi (the king) could be considered a lawgiver. It has always been clear that Moses is not a lawgiver, but now we have to consider the question whether it is appropriate to consider Yahweh a lawgiver. On Sinai is Yahweh giving "Law" (the abstraction)?[1] Or perhaps should *torah* be translated differently, as "instruction/directives" (e.g., stipulations for the covenant) or "revelation" (of what is required for holiness; see Deut. 4:5–8)?[2] The idea that Yahweh was considered the source of materials given to Moses and Israel at Sinai does not necessarily suggest that Yahweh was considered the source of law.[3] If one considers what is given at Sinai to be covenant stipulations[4] related most closely to the treaty genre rather than to law per se, then one could argue whether "law" is even being discussed.[5] Just as Hammurabi's stele gives the secondary context of legitimation to the juridical lists, so the Pentateuch gives a secondary context of treaty stipulations to its catalog of legal clauses. This explains the apodictic style of some of the material and understandably posits Yahweh as the one issuing the *stipulations* in his role as the Great King entering into an agreement (treaty = covenant) with a vassal. In Exodus 24:3 it is the words (*debarim*) and the judgments (*mishpatim*) that Moses conveys to the people from the Lord (same terms used earlier to describe, respectively, the Decalogue and the Book of the Covenant). That the text portrays God as giving decrees, commands, and so on is unquestioned, but again we must continue to ask how these differ from the abstraction of "Law." These commands of Yahweh were obligatory, as were the stipulations of the covenant, but that does not make them the legislation of a legal system. Legislation probably worked in Israel similarly to how it worked in the ancient Near East. The difference would be that the covenant and its stipulations framed the cognitive environment of Israel and therefore would have penetrated the legislative process, whatever it looked like.

name of the king and at times with reference to the words or decrees of the king.[23] So it is that the king, with the sponsorship and endowment of wisdom from the deity, administers justice. He does so by perceiving the nature of the aspects of justice that are among the control attributes of the cosmos and doing what is necessary to establish them in society.[24] Though the gods do not give laws and the king does not make law, these documents are intended to reveal something about the king as sponsor of the document: his worthiness (legitimation), his wisdom (in giving verdicts), and his values (providing for order and protecting the vulnerable, etc.).

23. Bottéro, "Code," 163.
24. Paul, *Studies*, 6.

Is there evidence in any of the Israelite literature of a development in the perception of the ontology of law? Does it say anything at all about the ontology of law? As we have discussed previously (chap. 8 on cosmology), Israel views Yahweh not just as the steward and administrator of the control attributes of the cosmos but as the originator and shaper of those control attributes. It is not easy to see any such contrast in the Israelite understanding of law. Yahweh makes decrees, issues commands, and imposes stipulations upon a vassal as any king would do. The difference is that though kings regularly engage in these activities in the ancient Near East, the gods do not involve themselves in anything so programmatic. Nothing in the ancient Near East compares to the extent of revelation that Yahweh gives to his people and the depth of relationship that he desires with them.

1. The key passages to consider are Exod. 24:12 (Yahweh gave tablets of stone on which *torah* and *mitswah* were written); Deut. 4:44–45 (Moses sets the *torah* before the people, and speaks to them *'edut, huqqim, and mishpatim*); Ezra 7:6 (he was ex-pert in the *torah* of Moses that Yahweh had given); and Neh. 9:13 (on Sinai Yahweh gave *mishpatim, torot, huqqim,* and *mitswot*). But of course if technically speaking none of these Hebrew words is correctly rendered as "law(s)," then law is not what Yahweh is giving.

2. See the discussion in P. Enns, "Law of God," *NIDOTTE* 4:893–900, where it is defined generally as a "divine standard of conduct for God's people."

3. This does not suggest that anything or anyone else was the source of law; it rather recognizes the possibility that "law" was not an abstraction that they thought about.

4. See the objections that have been raised to the association of treaty stipulations and apodictic law in the Pentateuch in Paul, *Studies*, 120–24. Notice that the title of the material in Exodus is "Book of the Covenant." "Book of the *torah*" is used by Deuteronomy to refer to itself (Deut. 28:61), but Deuteronomy (i.e., the literary form of the book that we refer to as Deuteronomy) is not presented as itself having been given at Sinai, but as exhortation that is putting in a new context information that was given at Sinai with other materials. Notice, for instance, that Deut. 6:1 does not suggest that God gave this information on Sinai.

5. Cf. esp. Exod. 34, where Moses takes up two new tablets and Yahweh says specifically in 34:10 that he is making a covenant with them and proceeds to state stipulations. Moses then writes the terms of this covenant (v. 27), which in v. 28 is identified both as the words of the covenant and as the Ten Words.

Obligatory Force in Society

It follows from all of the above that material like Hammurabi's stele imposed no obligations on society or the courts. It did not represent at any level the "law of the land," and there is no call to obey. This assessment is confirmed by the fact that it does not serve as a reference in the judicial system, which is illuminated for us through thousands of court documents.

> In numerous studies of a range of legal situations, little correspondence has been found between the provisions in the law collections and contemporary practice. Furthermore, no court document or contract makes a direct reference to any of the formal law collections. From such an absence of

Comparative Exploration: Obligatory Force in Israel: What Does It Mean to Observe the Torah?

In Israel the sections of the Pentateuch that have in the past been considered as laws could now be considered as not carrying the obligatory force of legislation (if it is true that in conjunction with the literature from the ancient Near East these are not laws or legislation). They nevertheless do carry obligatory force for Israel as stipulations of the covenant.[1]

As stipulations they derive their binding character from the oath that is sworn by the gods.[2] Today this would be considered a rather weak enforcer because people today do not put much stock in oaths. Without other forms of enforcement, this would be considered a system without adequate restraints that could be remedied only by legislation. Although there may well have been oral or even written forms of legislation in Israel, we must also recognize that the absence of legislation does not suggest the lack of restraints. G. Mendenhall suggests instead that Israel has governance by value systems rather than by social control.[3] The biblical materials intend to offer the basis for the former, whereas interpreters have repeatedly tried to convert those same materials into the means for the latter. Whatever systems of social control existed in Israel, the covenant was more important as a value system, and as a value system it called for responses of various sorts, among them listening, observing, choosing the path of life, being holy, and obeying. The emphasis on the latter was much more prevalent in the Pentateuch than anywhere in the ancient Near East. We have noted that the verdict catalogs do not call for obedience at all. The treaties regularly indicate that there are repercussions to failing to observe or obey the stipulations, namely, that all the curses would come upon them.[4]

Table 8. Mendenhall's Chart Comparing Covenant and Law

	Covenant	Law
Purpose	Creates a community where none existed before, by establishing a common relationship to a common lord.	Presupposes a social order in which it serves as an instrument for maintaining an orderly freedom and security.
Basis	Gratitude: response to benefits already received = grace.	Social fear: attempts to protect society from disruption and attack by threat of force.
Enactment	By voluntary act in which each individual willingly accepts the obligations presented.	By competent social authority. It is binding upon each individual by virtue of his status as a member of the social organization, usually by birth.

	Covenant	Law
Validity	Binding upon each person without regard to social context. It is as universal as God himself and is, therefore, the real basis for the concept of the "omnipresence of God."	Entirely dependent upon social boundary lines. Completely irrelevant to one who has crossed the boundary of the social order.
Sanctions	Not under control of social organizations, unpredictable in specific cases, but connected with cause-and-effect concepts in human history. Both positive and negative sanctions included.	Enforced by social organization through its chosen authorities. Sanctions are largely negative, though nonpolitical organizations use economic and prestige motivations to obtain conformity.
Norms	Typically presented as verbal abstractions, the definition of which is an obligation of persons in concrete circumstances and the "fear of God" = conscience.	Defined by social authority in advance, usually with specific sanctions defined for specific violations. Arbitrary and formal in nature, since only forms of action can be witnessed to in a court of law.
Orientation	Toward the future: makes individual behavior reliable and therefore a basis for both private and public security. Prediction of consequences extends to four generations in case of violation.	Toward the past: attempts to punish violations of the public order in order to make that public order more secure. It is oriented toward the future only in the sense that it gives warning in advance of the penalties that the society has power to impose upon the violator. Very short attention span (statute of limitations).
Social Aspect	Obligations individual, but consequences (blessings and curses) are of necessity social, since they are "acts of God"—drought, epidemic, defeat in war, etc. Powerfully reinforces individual responsibility to society, and social responsibility to refrain from protection of the guilty.	Obligations defined by society are binding upon all members, but sanctions are imposed only upon guilty individual, in adversary procedure and rite. Is a form of warfare pitting society against the guilty person.
Evolution	Forms basis for social custom especially in early stages. As social control takes over, may degenerate into mere ritual reinforcement of a social solidarity.	Presupposes a customary morality that it attempts to protect, but cannot create. Tends to become increasingly rigid in formal definition, and increasingly devoid of real ethical content.

	Covenant	Law
Continuity	Since it is not produced by society, it cannot be guaranteed by society. Essentially private, individual, independent of roles. Prophets, the Christ, apostles. Destruction of a particular social control system, therefore, does not mean the end of the value system.	Cannot exist apart from social institutions—king, priest, political officers, legislative, executive, judicial. Ceases to exist when political structure falls.

From Mendenhall, "Conflict," 174–76.

Furthermore, besides the obligations that the individual items in the Pentateuch carry as stipulations, they are compelling as legal lists that point toward essential principles of holiness. Principles that are wise carry intrinsic weight and are ignored at one's peril. Both of these perspectives make clear that the biblical mandates cannot be ignored or taken lightly.[5]

1. For example, Deut 7:12 indicates that if you pay attention to these decisions (*mishpatim*), and do them, God will keep his covenant. In Deut. 6:24–25 being careful to observe every command (*mitswah*) "will be our righteousness." Observing the commandments is equated to revering the God who gave them (Deut. 8:6).

2. Westbrook, *History of Ancient Near Eastern Law*, 84.

3. Mendenhall, "Conflict."

4. For example, one of the Hittite treaties says: "If you do not observe these words which I have now placed under oath for you, then these oath gods shall thoroughly eradicate your persons" (+ lengthy list of relatives, possessions, and even the spirit from the netherworld); see G. Beckman, *Hittite Diplomatic Texts*, SBLWAW 7 (Atlanta: SBL, 1996), #3 §37 (p. 29). For additional examples see #5 §§17–18 (pp. 36–37), #6a §15 (pp. 43–44), #12 §§20–21 (p. 81), #13 §§21–22 (pp. 87–88), #18b §§9–10 (p. 107).

5. For those who consider the questions of the continuity of the "law" into the NT and the perspectives on the "law" by Jesus and Paul, many new possibilities open up when they think of the "law" in terms of covenant stipulations (note the new covenant with revised perspective on stipulations) and of principles for holiness. See J. Walton, *Covenant: God's Purpose, God's Plan* (Grand Rapids: Zondervan, 1994), 157–78.

linking evidence, some scholars have concluded that the law collections had little or no impact on the daily operation of legal affairs.[25]

Courts operated by wisdom, a sense of fairness, a knowledge of the traditions, a knowledge of the king's decrees, and experience in the administration of justice. Citizens understood their obligations by means of living in society and being taught customs and traditions in the home.[26]

This being the case, numerous other literary sources contributed to the understanding of how one ought to conduct oneself in society.

25. Roth, *Law*, 5.

26. Bottéro, "Code," 181. He goes on to observe that most modern people also have a detailed understanding of laws and their obligations both formal and informal without ever having read legislative documents.

Since we have understood the juridical treatises as being a form of wisdom, it is no surprise that we must turn our attention to other wisdom genres for more information.[27] Specifically we will look briefly at the instructional literature from Egypt and the collections of proverbs from Mesopotamia.

Wisdom Literature

The following brief treatment of a few of the categories of wisdom literature has a single purpose for the scope of this study. Both the instructions of Egypt and the proverbs of Mesopotamia stand as further examples of the idea that wisdom compilations were used widely in the ancient world as a means of offering principles that could serve as guides for living. These principles are in effect mandated in the pursuit of wisdom if order is to be maintained in society. Unlike the treatises considered above (judicial, medical, and divination), these wisdom literatures do not characteristically introduce situations that undermine order, though such situations are often addressed. Instead, they tend to anticipate situations that will be faced and offer advice so that order will *not* be undermined, and in so doing they frame the values of society. To the extent that these instructions seek to maintain order, teach practical wisdom, and provide legitimation, they overlap functionally with the judicial treatises of Mesopotamia. And like those legal treatises, principles for living and ruling are expected to be derived from this literature.

Instructional Literature (Egyptian)

Seven major works span the biblical period.[28] These are discourses that offer guidance concerning how to live according to *maat*.[29] *Maat*

27. Scholars are increasingly recognizing the close relationship of "law" and "wisdom." Note, for instance, the introduction in B. Alster, *Wisdom of Ancient Sumer* (Bethesda, MD: CDL, 2005), 21, where, interacting with J. Assmann's categorization of wisdom, he proposes Mesopotamian categories: (1) Law and Wisdom, (2) Magic and Wisdom, (3) Wisdom of the scribal schools, and (4) Wisdom of the ancient sages.

28. Old Kingdom: Hardjedef, Ptahhotep (*AEL* 1:61–80); First Intermediate period: Merikare (*COS* 1.35), Amenemhet (*COS* 1.36); New Kingdom: Any (*COS* 1.46), Amenemope (*COS* 1.47). It should be noted that there are also works of the instruction genre outside Egypt, for instance, the Sumerian Instructions of Shuruppak and the Aramaic Words of Ahiqar, ANET 427–30. See B. Alster, *Wisdom of Ancient Sumer* (Bethesda, MD: CDL, 2005), 31–220.

29. There are a number of extensive studies of this term. A few of the most helpful are M. V. Fox, "Two Decades of Research in Egyptian Wisdom Literature," in *Zeitschrift für Ägyptische Sprache und Altertumskunde* 107 (1980): 120–34, esp. 126–27; J. Assmann, *The Mind of Egypt* (New York: Metropolitan, 1996), 127–34. More discussion is in chap. 6 above.

is generally considered to be an abstraction. M. Fox associates it with "world-order," while J. Assmann expresses it similarly as the totality of all social norms. He translates it "connective justice" and identifies it as "the principle that forms individuals into communities and that gives their actions meaning and direction by ensuring that good is rewarded and evil punished."[30] This wisdom, passed from generation to generation, is expected to be heard, heeded, and acted upon.

Comparing the form of this literature to that found in the judicial treatises, the *Instruction of Ptahhotep* is comprised of prologue and epilogue with 37 maxims. Twenty-one of the maxims begin with the protasis "if" with second person forms introducing a variety of social situations, much like the judicial treatises. The apodosis in these cases may involve either instruction on how to behave or observations that take a proverbial tone. The remaining maxims take an apodictic form including, for instance, injunctions not to be greedy.

The instructions of both *Merikare* and *Amenemhet* represent royal wisdom passed from king to crown prince. Most of the entries take the form of exhortation or admonition with some wisdom observations sprinkled throughout. Some have considered them a type of legitimation literature since they are political tractates using the tomb autobiography form.[31] Again, as with *Hammurabi*, we may have multiple genre layers as the material was applied to different functions and embedded in different literary contexts.

Compilations of Proverbs (Mesopotamia)

Compilations of proverbial sayings are known already among the Sumerians at the close of the third millennium BC and continue into the first millennium.[32] Most of these are formulated as aphorisms rather than the second person direct address of the Egyptian instructions ("Marrying is human. Getting children is divine"[33]). In this way the proverbs convey principles more explicitly than the treatises do.

One of the principles that shows up often in the ancient Near East as well as in Israel, explicitly as well as implicitly, regarding both how God

30. Assmann, *Mind of Egypt*, 128.
31. See discussion in L. G. Perdue, "The Testament of Davidic and Egyptian Royal Instruction," in *Scripture in Context II: More Essays on the Comparative Method*, ed. W. W. Hallo, J. C. Moyer, and L. G. Perdue (Winona Lake, IN: Eisenbrauns, 1983), 86. Notice the explicit statements such as the one near the end of *Merikare*: "Do not neglect my speech, which lays down all the laws of kingship, which instructs you, that you may rule the land" (*COS* 1.66).
32. B. Alster, *Proverbs of Ancient Sumer*, 2 vols. (Bethesda, MD: CDL, 1997); idem, *Wisdom*; BWL.
33. Alster, *Proverbs*, 14.39.

Comparative Exploration: Israelite Proverbs: What Is Their Debt to the Ancient Near East?

As always, the issue does not concern literary borrowing but the commonalities and distinctions in the cognitive environment. Literature, in theory, can be borrowed or adapted at a variety of levels; cognitive environment is shared and can result in similarities in literature that are simply the outgrowth of that common cognitive environment, perhaps stimulated by occasional, vague, or indirect exposure to foreign literature. Our ability to measure literary debt is so limited as to make such speculation hazardous if not presumptuous. Nevertheless, we need not be in denial that some literature may have been more directly influenced by other literature and therefore retain a greater resemblance.

The Israelite sages of old, from Solomon through the postexilic period, had certainly imbibed of the wisdom tradition in the ancient world and were therefore heirs to some of its literary traditions. They had clearly embraced wholeheartedly the literary traditions of the ancient world and had readily accepted the responsibility to inculcate and propagate wisdom and its corollary, wise living. Much of what they believed to be wise living was also believed throughout the rest of the ancient world, making the literature of the ancient world adaptable should the Israelite sages choose to go about their task in that way.

Yet at the same time, based on their ontology they saw wisdom as deriving from God and wise living as intrinsically necessitating a relationship with God, specifically defined by the covenant. Consequently, even if they had borrowed literature directly from an Egyptian or Mesopotamian document, they would have considered it as representative of the wisdom from Yahweh, else it would not have been acceptable to them. One cannot therefore easily speak of debt, but must be content to speak of commonalities that reveal that Israel shared a stake in the cognitive environment of the ancient world.[1]

1. J. Assmann encompasses law and wisdom as he compares the book of Deuteronomy to the instruction literature in Egypt under the premise that both are texts that seek to codify norms. In the process he captures the tension between what Israel shares on the literary level, yet stands against on the cognitive level. See *Mind of Egypt*, 125.

acts and how society works, is the idea of just retribution. Speaking of the conceptual universe of ancient Egypt, Assmann says: "Justice is what holds the world together, and it does so by connecting consequences with deeds. This is what makes it 'connective.' Justice links human action to human destiny and welds individuals into a community. . . . When connective justice stops functioning, when evil goes unpunished and good no longer prospers, then the world is 'out of joint.'"[34] In this way we move from wisdom sayings that guide society toward order to

34. Assmann, *Mind of Egypt*, 132.

literature dealing with the concept of retribution that confronts the all too common experience of disorder.

Concepts of Retribution

Appropriate balance in response to social situations is in some ways at the core of wisdom. Crime, whether felony or misdemeanor, must be addressed in measured and approved terms. Excess in either direction is a perversion of justice. Social gaffes or breaches of etiquette must all be kept in proper perspective. If this is incumbent on society, how much more so is the divine realm under some sort of obligation? Yet for all the logic of such theorizing, the cold fact is that suffering and prosperity showed little evidence of being related to a person's goodness or wickedness. Thus arose a genre of wisdom literature to investigate philosophically the question of theodicy (questioning the justice of deity in the context of suffering: the problem of evil).[35]

Regardless of the literary similarities and differences between the variety of ancient Near Eastern exemplars and the biblical book of Job, we need to explore briefly the ways that the conclusions about theodicy might compare. The retribution principle has been investigated in comparative study as early as W. von Soden's 1965 study.[36] One resolution to the problem of theodicy may be found by positing the existence of competition in the divine realm (whether simply competing interests, or representing moral conflict). In such a circumstance, evil or suffering can be attributed to conflict between the gods that spills over into human experience. A second option is to conclude that the gods are not sufficiently powerful to deal with the problem of evil. J. de Moor concludes that this was the case in Ugarit.[37] A third option is simply to deny that the divine realm is characterized by justice. This is a more likely way of thinking in Mesopotamia, because

35. For studies considering this theme, see J. L. Crenshaw, ed., *Theodicy in the Old Testament* (Philadelphia: Fortress, 1983); A. Laato and J. C. de Moor eds., *Theodicy in the World of the Bible* (Leiden: Brill, 2003); R. G. Albertson, "Job and Ancient Near Eastern Wisdom Literature," in *Scripture in Context II*, ed. Hallo, Moyer, and Perdue, 213–30; D. P. Bricker, "Innocent Suffering in Mesopotamia," *TynBul* (2001): 121–42; G. L. Mattingly, "The Pious Sufferer: Mesopotamia's Traditional Theodicy and Job's Counselors," in *Scripture in Context III: The Bible in the Light of Cuneiform Literature*, ed. W. W. Hallo, B. W. Jones, and G. L. Mattingly (Lewiston, NY: Mellen, 1990), 305–48.

36. W. von Soden, "Das Fragen nach der Gerichtigkeit Gottes im Alten Orient," *Mitteilungen der deutschen Orient-Gesellschaft* 96 (1965): 41–59. For an English summary and assessment see H. W. F. Saggs, *The Encounter with the Divine in Mesopotamia and Israel* (London: Athlone, 1978), 115–17.

37. J. C. de Moor, "Theodicy in the Texts of Ugarit," in *Theodicy in the World of the Bible*, ed. A. Laato and J. C. de Moor (Leiden: Brill, 2003), 149.

while there were many deities, we do not often find them squabbling over worshipers or punishing those who chose another member of the pantheon to worship. Likewise, evil was associated with demons rather than with other gods. The gods could be vengeful or malicious (e.g., Ishtar's response to Gilgamesh's rejection of her; Erra's destructive behavior), but the gods were not generally characterized in that way. The gods were interested in justice being maintained in the human realm, but they were not necessarily committed to doing justice themselves.[38] Even so, the retribution principle goes beyond a god doing justice, because it also involves how righteous and wicked behavior that would merit the deity's response is defined. For the gods of the ancient Near East, social order was important, but a person's ethical or moral goodness was not as highly valued by the deity as their cultic conscientiousness.[39]

This last element is what distinguishes the theodicy literature in the Hebrew Bible from that in the ancient Near East. The sufferer in the ancient Near East, lacking revelation of the nature of deity, would have little way of knowing what his/her offense might have been.[40] A few examples will suffice to demonstrate the point.

Prayer to Every God

The transgression I have committed I do not know;
The sin I have done I do not know;
The forbidden thing I have eaten I do not know;
The prohibited place on which I have set foot I do not know;
The god whom I know or do not know has oppressed me;
I am troubled, I am overwhelmed, I cannot see.

Man is dumb; he knows nothing;
Mankind, everyone that exists—what does he know?
Whether he is committing sin or doing good, he does not even
    know.[41]

38. See the discussion of the justice of the gods in chap. 4.
39. See chap. 6, "The Role of Ethics and Morality."
40. In the ancient Near East the gods reveal answers to questions (in the divination process, which revealed to a limited extent the plans and purposes of deity; see K. van der Toorn, "Theodicy in Akkadian Literature," in *Theodicy in the World of the Bible*, ed. Laato and de Moor, 87), their support of the king (through prophecies), and, at one time in the past, the principles of divination (to the antediluvian king of Sippar, Enmeduranki, see W. G. Lambert, "Enmeduranki and Related Matters," *JCS* 21 [1967]: 126–38, esp. 132); in Israel Yahweh revealed himself—his attributes, his plan, his character, and his expectations.
41. *ANET*, 391–92.

Ludlul bel nemeqi:

> I wish I knew that these things were pleasing to one's god!
> What is proper to oneself is an offence to one's god,
> What in one's own heart seems despicable is proper to one's god.
> Who can learn the reasoning of the gods in heaven?
> Who could understand the intentions of the god of the depths?
> Where might human beings have learned the way of a god?[42]

Texts such as these lead van der Toorn to conclude concerning the core values of the Mesopotamian gods: "What the gods love by instinct is a respectful attitude and acts of philanthropy; what they abhor is anti-social behaviour. Pleasure and repulsion, the two principles that move the gods to action, correspond with the human appraisal of right and wrong."[43]

Since primary obligation to the gods was seen to be in the cultic realm, the logical conclusion would have been that those who suffered for no apparent reason were guilty of cultic negligence or desecration through ignorance of something sacred. Ethical crimes or violation of social norms would be possible, but difficult to identify specifically.[44] The minds of the gods were not easily penetrated.[45]

Since the ancients typically believed that their suffering was the result of the god's anger, they naturally sought to appease that anger. Appeasement could theoretically be accomplished by the identification of the offense and the offering of an appropriate sacrifice. A clear example of this procedure is found in the *Hittite Plague Prayers of Murshili II*. In response to the severe plague that decimated his kingdom over several decades, he queried the gods to discover the reason for the disastrous conditions. The results of divinations eventually allowed him to identify offenses both in the cultic realm and in treaty violations by his father. His plea to the gods shows the appeasement mentality.

> If the servant has incurred a guilt, but confesses his guilt to his master, his master may do with him as he likes. But because he has confessed . . . , his master's heart is satisfied, and he will not punish that servant. I have now confessed . . . the sin; . . . restitution has been made twenty fold. . . . If you demand additional restitution from me, just tell me about it in a dream, and I will give it.[46]

---

42. *BWL* II:33–38, p. 41.
43. Van der Toorn, "Theodicy," 61.
44. Van der Toorn identifies several categories of sin including "sins of the youth, sins unconsciously committed, hidden sins and a vague notion of pervasive sinfulness common to all humankind" ("Theodicy," 62).
45. Ibid., 72–74.
46. H. Hoffner, "Theodicy in Hittite Texts," in *Theodicy in the World of the Bible*, ed. Laato and de Moor, 100.

Alternatively, appeasement could be accomplished even if the precise crime were a mystery simply by using blanket confessions and generic offerings as advised by the cultic personnel.[47] Perhaps most suggestive of this approach is the instruction found in the incantation series *Shurpu*. This collection of spells compiles numerous types of possible misconduct (cultic, domestic, social, ritual) for the sufferer to confess.[48]

The procedure that Job's friends were suggesting, rather than advising discovery divination, urges Job to appease God through a procedure of blanket confession, thus more in line with *Shurpu* than with Murshili's procedure, though all show the importance of appeasement. In this aspect Job's friends were representatives of a revered ancient Near Eastern wisdom tradition, and also, unbeknown to them, the representatives for the case that the adversary was pressing. That is, if they had persuaded Job to follow their advice and make a blanket confession just to appease Deity and be restored to favor, the adversary's contention would have been confirmed: righteousness was not the issue, only reward. Instead, the integrity that Job maintained (Job 27:1–6) was one that insisted that his righteous standing be considered rather than just his favor being restored. If this interpretation is accurate, the book of Job argues pointedly against the theodicy philosophies in the ancient world and represents an Israelite modification. This modification, rather than offering a revised theodicy, seeks to reinterpret the justice of God from something that may be debated to something that is a given. In Yahweh's speech it is not his justice that is defended, it is his wisdom. The inference that should be drawn from this is that if it is determined that God is wise, then it can be accepted that he is just, even if not all the information to evaluate his justice is available.[49]

Cognitive Environment

What do all of these legal and practical maxims tell us about the cognitive environment of the ancient Near East? Did Israelites have the same approach to life in their daily routines as Egyptians or Babylonians? It is not my intention here to offer a reconstruction of daily life in the an-

47. W. Farber, "Witchcraft, Magic, and Divination in Ancient Mesopotamia," *CANE* 3:1898–99.

48. Ibid., 1899.

49. This is sometimes referred to as "Educative Theodicy," see Laato and de Moor, *Theodicy*, xxxix–xlii. For a more detailed presentation of this view, though still on an introductory level, see J. Walton and A. Hill, *Old Testament Today* (Grand Rapids: Zondervan, 2004), 306–12.

cient Near East.[50] It is obvious that similarities exist on many levels as we observe the commonalities that emerge in this literature. Relatively few sayings could be found in ancient Near Eastern literature that would be contrary or unacceptable to biblical wisdom, and vice versa.[51] We should pause for a moment, however, to consider where differences emerge.

Social protocol, etiquette, and the norms of social life show little difference. Similar cautions and commonsense advice can be found across the board. As always, the main differences emerge when we consider the aspect of the influence of religion—covenant observance and the nature of Yahweh. In the proverbial literature of the ancient Near East, virtually nothing can be found regarding understanding or relating to deity. The instruction literature has more, but not of the same sort as that found in Israelite literature. Consider the following example from *Any*:

> Offer to your god,
> Beware of offending him.
> Do not question his images,
> Do not accost him when he appears.
> Do not jostle him in order to carry him,
> Do not disturb the oracles.
> Be careful, help to protect him,
> Let your eye watch out for his wrath,
> And kiss the ground in his name.
> He gives power in a million forms,
> He who magnifies him is magnified.
> God of this earth is the sun in the sky,
> While his images are on earth;
> When incense is given them as daily food,
> The lord of risings is satisfied.[52]

Perhaps closer to biblical sentiments is the section from the *Instructions of Ur-Ninurta*:

50. That has been done, e.g., by K. R. Nemet-Nejat, *Daily Life in Ancient Mesopotamia* (Westport, CT: Greenwood, 1998); R. Averbeck, M. Chavalas, and D. Weisberg, *Life and Culture in the Ancient Near East* (Bethesda, MD: CDL, 2003); D. Snell, *Life in the Ancient Near East* (New Haven: Yale University Press, 1997).

51. A few examples will suffice to illustrate the types of exceptions that can be found. "The man who does not sacrifice to his god can make the god run after him like a dog" *Dialogue of Pessimism*; "Who is wealthy? Who is rich? For whom shall I reserve my intimacy?" "When you have seen for yourself the profit of reverencing god, You will praise god and bless the king"; "Do the wish of the one present, Slander the one not present" (B. Foster, *Before the Muses*, 3rd ed. [Bethesda, MD: CDL, 2005], 423–24, 431); "Do not open your heart to your wife; what you have said to her goes into the street"; "Let your wife see your wealth, do not trust her with it" (*AEL* 3:169; 12.13 and 13.16).

52. *COS* 1.46:113.

He who knows how to respect religious affairs,
Who voluntarily [pleases his god],
Who performs the rites,
To whom the name of his god is dear,
Who keeps away from swearing,
He goes straight to the place of worship,
What he has lost is restored (to him).
Days will be added to his days.
Years will be plenty in addition to the years he (already) has.
His descendants will experience good health.
His heir will pour water libations
His god will look favorably upon him.[53]

A similar list with all of the items negated then opens with: "But the man who does not fear the affairs of his god."[54] Both the wording and the elements included in the list bear a sharp resemblance to the results of fearing Yahweh in the book of Proverbs (10:27; 11:19; 12:2; 13:22; 14:26–27).

So what answer would be given in the ancient world to the question, "How then should we live?" In the world outside Israel, the salient points would include:

- Know your proper place within your clan and family and honor the traditions
- Conform your behavior to the expectations of society devised to protect and maintain order and security
- Fulfill scrupulously your cultic duty before the local and ancestral gods
- Honor god and king as those responsible for administering justice for the good of society
- When life becomes miserable, (1) examine your recent behavior for negligence or malfeasance; (2) inquire of the gods for identification of offense; (3) perform incantations with appropriate confessions for purification; (4) recognize that the gods are ultimately inscrutable
- Live a life of conformity to custom and tradition augmented by the cultic demand of deity

In Israelite thinking many of the same points would carry importance, but significant differences in orientation are clear.

53. Alster, *Wisdom*, 228–30.
54. Alster, *Wisdom*, 230.

- Know your proper place within your clan and family and honor the traditions *as defined in relationship to the fear of Yahweh*
- Conform your behavior to the expectations of society devised to protect and maintain order and security *and to reflect positively your status as a holy nation in covenant with Yahweh*
- Fulfill scrupulously your cultic duty before Yahweh
- Honor Yahweh as the embodiment of justice
- When life becomes miserable, (1) examine recent behavior for *violations of the covenant*; (2) recognize that Yahweh's purposes are not necessarily transparent, but he is wise
- Live a life of obedience to the covenant informed by the demands of holiness, in imitation of your holy God

14

Pondering the Future on Earth and after Death

The Future on Earth

On a personal level, the hope for the future on this earth was tied to making a name, either through exploits of renown, building projects that would endure, or, most importantly, by siring the next generation. "The aim of every family was to perpetuate itself forever, it being necessary to the dead that their descendants not die out. Conversely, everyone had a paramount concern in leaving a son after him, in self-interest and as a duty towards the ancestors."[1]

On the national level, the ideal future in the ancient Near East was not comprised of some utopian dream. It appears rather to exist only as an extension of the present status quo. Though there were undoubtedly times when tyrants, warfare, plague, or famine made life anything but good, the inevitable hope for better conditions never seems to have coalesced into an eschatological vision or hope. The idea of looking forward to a better time is represented in a few pieces of literature,[2] but the consen-

1. H. C. Brichto, "Kin, Cult, Land and Afterlife—A Biblical Complex," *HUCA* 44 (1973): 1–54; see 22–27 for the connection between "name" and descendants. See also D. Sheriffs, "The Human Need for Continuity: Some ANE and OT Perspectives," *TynBul* 55 (2004): 1–16.

2. Often termed apocalypses or fictional autobiographies; see footnotes in the sidebar on "Messiah" (p. 285)."

sus is that these have been written as if from the past in the time of the "ideal" king who now just happens to be on the throne. When people of the ancient Near East thought about the future on earth, they thought of it as unchanging—there is no better world coming, even though they would have hoped for more comfortable conditions.

In contrast, Israel has an expectation for a future that has never before existed, even in the time of the prototypical messiah, David. In their theology, something better was coming (though sometimes only after something terrifying).[3] This was not simply an unfocused hope—it was integrated into the covenant and was derived from it.[4]

The Future after Death

We need to focus more attention on the ancient concepts of the afterlife.[5] Egyptian concepts of the afterlife were far different from those found in Mesopotamia, so here we will have to treat each separately. Beliefs in the Levant had their distinctives, but generally followed the Mesopotamian model more than the Egyptian model. One should note that on a topic like this, it is very difficult to synthesize a consistent picture and hazardous to do so given the nature of the sources.[6]

3. See particularly the description of the new heaven and new earth in Isa. 65–66.

4. Unlike Christian theology, whose eschatology is realized after history has come to a close and judgment and resurrection have taken place, Israelite eschatology represented a new stage within history.

5. Key sources include T. Abusch, "Ghost and God: Some Observations on a Babylonian Understanding of Human Nature," in *Self, Soul and Body in Religious Experience*, ed. A. I. Baumgarten, J. Assmann, and G. G. Stroumsa (Leiden: Brill, 1998), 363–83; J. Assmann, "A Dialogue Between Self and Soul: Papyrus Berlin 3024," in *Self, Soul and Body*, ed. Baumgarten, Assmann, and Stroumsa, 384–403; J. Bottéro, *Religion in Ancient Mesopotamia* (Chicago: University of Chicago Press, 2001); Brichto, "Kin, Cult"; E. Hornung, *The Ancient Egyptian Books of the Afterlife* (Ithaca: Cornell University Press, 1999); P. Johnston, *Shades of Sheol* (Downers Grove, IL: InterVarsity Press, 2002); D. Katz, *The Image of the Netherworld in Sumerian Sources* (Bethesda, MD: CDL, 2003); N. Tromp, *Primitive Conceptions of Death and the Nether World in the Old Testament*, BibOr 21 (Rome: Pontifical Biblical Institute, 1969). See also the helpful summaries on death and afterlife in *CANE* 3: in Egypt (L. Lesko, "Death and Afterlife in Ancient Egyptian Thought," 1763–74), in Mesopotamia (J. Scurlock, "Death and Afterlife in Ancient Mesopotamian Thought," 1883–93), in Hittite Thought (V. Haas, "Death and Afterlife in Hittite Thought," 2021–30), and in Canaanite and Hebrew Thought (P. Xella, "Death and Afterlife in Canaanite and Hebrew Thought," 2059–70), and numerous articles in *Death in Mesopotamia*, ed. B. Alster, Mesopotamia 8, RAI 26 (Copenhagen: Akademisk Forlag, 1980).

6. For instance, Lesko notes that the Egyptian material "favors the later periods, the southern part of the country, and the upper classes of society" ("Death and Afterlife in Ancient Egyptian Thought," *CANE* 3:1763).

Egyptian sources include four major corpora of literature:[7]

1. The *Pyramid Texts* consist of spells that were found carved in the pyramid sarcophagus chambers, so that they would be available to the deceased trying to make his way to the afterlife. They date to the end of the third millennium BC (the Old Kingdom period).
2. The *Coffin Texts* superseded the *Pyramid Texts* at end of the Old Kingdom and continued through the Middle Kingdom. These texts show that the afterlife was now available to common folk (unlike the earlier period when only pharaohs had any hope). These texts conceptualize afterlife more concretely and portray the dangers more dramatically.
3. The *Book of the Dead* superseded the *Coffin Texts* in the 17th Dynasty. It includes spells to teach a person how to pass the guardians and gain entrance to Duat. They also provide important information concerning how to avoid all the serpents that waylaid those who traveled the road to the netherworld (particularly serpents that were winged, fire-breathing, or had human legs).
4. The *Books of the Netherworld* (Amduat) are New Kingdom descriptions of the netherworld (the earliest, from Thutmose I, in the 15th century BC). These were arranged around and focused on the nightly journey of the sun god's barque.

In contrast, few remnants of afterlife literature per se are extant for Mesopotamia and the Levant.[8] Instead, we are dependent on various statements made incidentally in the literature, though occasionally an extended comment may be found. If the nature of the literature is any indication, people in the Levant and Mesopotamia did not profess near as much knowledge of the afterlife as did the Egyptians, and their hopes are much more vague. Much of their thinking was less philosophical or theological, and more based on extrapolation from their observations and experiences.[9] We will therefore turn our attention initially to the issues of death and burial.

Death and Burial

In chapter 9, concerning human origins, we learned that in the mythological texts from Mesopotamia people were presented as having been created from various components (e.g., clay, blood of slain deity). We

---

7. Hornung, *Ancient Egyptian Books*.

8. Some funerary ritual texts; for a couple of examples see Katz, *Image of the Netherworld*, 202–10; and a few mythological texts that offer more extensive treatments (sections of *Gilgamesh*, *Descent of Inanna/Ishtar*, *Ningishzida's Journey to the Netherworld*, to name a few).

9. Scurlock, "Death and Afterlife in Ancient Mesopotamian Thought," *CANE* 3:1883.

find that these components are also understood as setting the course for the nature and destiny of each human being.[10] The *Epic of Atrahasis* informs us both of the introduction of mortality to the human world and the "creation of an afterlife."[11]

Egyptian literature offers no such information about the origins of human mortality or of the concept of afterlife. Despite the absence of such ontologies, all of the Egyptian concepts concerning what death is and the procedures for interment are nevertheless linked, as in Mesopotamia, to their understanding of the constituent parts of the person. Besides the body, each individual Egyptian was believed to possess a *ba* and a *ka*. These concepts cannot easily be equated with English terms or concepts in Greek or Western anthropology, such as soul or spirit. Suggestions would equate them, respectively, with "mind/self" and "essence/personality/vital force."[12] What is important here is to recognize that at death the *ba* and *ka* were separated from the body. This separation defines death for Egyptians and poses the problem of death, as they sought understanding of how these aspects of a person that survived into the afterlife were to be reunited.

> In normal life, the unity or unanimous cooperation of these different components [*ba*, *ka*, body, etc.] is no problem. Death, however, dissolves this interior community. Yet there are ritual means to overcome this critical situation and to achieve a new and even more powerful state of personality where the different constituents or aspects of the person are brought into new forms of interaction and cooperation. The Egyptian concepts of death and immortality are based on this idea of the person as a community that is threatened with dissolution but is capable of reintegration.[13]

All of the complexities of mummification are designed to achieve this end. Duat is the place where this reintegration took place. Here the individual received a new body that was the counterpart of the earthly body.

In contrast, in Mesopotamia and the Levant there is much more interest in preserving the *social* community rather than the *interior* community. Death threatens to isolate one from the community of the family (comprised of the dead and the living, ancestors and descendants

10. Abusch, "Ghost and God," 366–67.

11. Ibid., 376.

12. Many books on ancient Egypt contain some discussion of these terms. See Lesko, "Death and Afterlife in Ancient Egyptian Thought," *CANE* 3:1763–64; S. Morenz, *Egyptian Religion* (Ithaca: Cornell University Press, 1973), esp. chap. 9 on "Death and the Dead"; and the articles in *OEAE* on "ba" (J. Allen, 1:161–62) and "ka" (A. Bolshakov, 2:215–17).

13. Assmann, "Dialogue," 384.

alike). Burial and mourning practices are designed to secure the *eṭemmu* ("ghost") of the deceased an ongoing place in that community.[14]

> In Mesopotamian thought, what remains after death is the lifeless body and some form of intangible, but visible and audible *eṭemmu*. The body must be buried; otherwise, the ghost will have no rest and will not find its place in the community of the dead, usually associated with the netherworld. In addition, burial is crucial for future care, for the dead are to be the recipients of ongoing mortuary rites, which include invocations of the name of the deceased, presentation of food, and libation of water. In this way, the dead are cared for and kept (alive) in memory. The dead may be remembered as individuals up to several generations and then become part of the ancestral family.[15]

In Mesopotamia the dead ancestors were given some status of divinity, by terminology if nothing else.[16] In Ugarit these deceased ancestors are identified as the *Rapiuma*.[17] The deceased ancestors were generally believed to eat and sleep in the family house, and they were considered the source of some nightmares.[18] At times this interaction centered on an icon, an image of the ancestor that mediated between the departed spirit and the living family.[19] All of these aspects surrounding death emphasize the central importance in being remembered. As Bottéro observes, true death is being forgotten.[20]

Geography and Nature of the Netherworld

In Egypt the netherworld was referred to by terms that are related to the sky, such as Rosetau (the heavens and also the necropolis), Imhet (the west), and Duat (the east).[21] This reflects a largely horizontal model

---

14. Bottéro believes Hebrew *nephesh* and Akkadian *eṭemmu* to be functionally equivalent (*Religion*, 204). See Abusch, "Ghost and God," 373 n. 23. One key difference, however, is that there is no indication in the OT that the *nephesh* continues to exist after death.

15. Abusch, "Ghost and God," 373.

16. K. van der Toorn, *Family Religion in Babylonia, Syria and Israel: Continuity and Change in the Forms of Religious Life* (Leiden: Brill, 1996), 55–58.

17. Controversy concerning all of the possible meanings and nuances of this word continue, though few detractors would deny that one of its possible meanings is the denizens of the netherworld. For summary discussions see W. Pitard, "The *Rpum* Texts," in *Handbook of Ugaritic Studies*, ed. W. G. E. Watson and N. Wyatt (Leiden: Brill, 1999), 259–69; and H. Rouillard, "Rephaim," *DDD* 692–700; Johnston, *Shades*, 128–42.

18. Van der Toorn, *Family Religion*, 59–61. This was especially true when the burial plots were under the house.

19. Katz, *Image*, 201.

20. Bottéro, *Religion*, 110.

21. L. Lesko, "Ancient Egyptian Cosmogonies and Cosmology," in *Religion in Ancient Egypt*, ed. B. Shafer (Ithaca: Cornell University Press, 1991), 119–20.

of the cosmos. The Egyptians were purified in the Field of Reeds (at the eastern horizon), then took up their permanent dwelling in the Field of Hetep, associated with the western horizon: a paradise of abundance and the fulfillment of desires.[22] For Egyptians, then, the afterlife was entered by ascending to the sky to join the gods, particularly the sun god in his journey across the sky.[23]

Early Sumerian thought placed the netherworld to the west in their horizontal perception of the cosmos (modeled on the movement of the sun). But this was gradually replaced in the third millennium by a vertical model that became the norm (though exceptions persisted).[24]

In Mesopotamia the netherworld was ruled by the gods, particularly the queen, Ereshkigal, and her consort, Nergal. The Anunnaki gods also helped administer the netherworld. Both politically and architecturally it was construed as a city.[25] Seven walls, each with its own gate, surrounded the city. Before passing through these, the deceased had to cross the demon-infested steppe land and the river Hubur.[26] After enduring all of these trials, what one encountered hardly made it seem worth the effort.

> To the house whose entrants are bereft of light,
> Where dust is their sustenance and clay their food.
> They see no light but dwell in darkness,
> They are clothed like birds in wings for garments,
> And dust has gathered on the door and bolt.[27]

This description and others like it are based on observations concerning the grave and the corpse. After death, while the body decayed, the phantom "joined the countless multitude of other specters, assembled there since the beginning of time and forever to lead a gloomy and mournful existence that was suggested by the rigid and pensive cadaver, as well as the fabulous image of a Below of black night, of heavy silence, and of endless, weighty sleep."[28]

22. See *Coffin Text* spells 464–68 and chap. 110 of the *Book of the Dead*; Lesko, "Ancient Egyptian Cosmogonies," 120.

23. For alternative means of ascent see Lesko, "Ancient Egyptian Cosmogonies," 121.

24. Katz, *Image*, 54.

25. One Akkadian term for the netherworld is *irkallu*, from Sumerian IRI.GAL, the "great city." For other Sumerian terminology see Katz, *Image*. Other Akkadian terms include *arallu*.

26. Scurlock, "Death and Afterlife in Ancient Mesopotamian Thought," *CANE* 3:1886.

27. *Descent of Ishtar*, translation from B. Foster, *Before the Muses*. 2nd ed. (Potomac, MD: CDL, 1996), 499. This work, along with sections of the *Gilgamesh Epic* and a work called *The Death of Ur-Nammu*, offer the most evidence concerning this view of the netherworld.

28. Bottéro, *Religion*, 107.

Many texts parallel the existence of the dead in the netherworld to those that sleep,[29] which suggests that in a semiconscious state their discomforts are set aside. By other accounts, however, the aura of despair is somewhat mitigated as the afterlife is characterized as in some ways parallel to life on earth. For example, the sun is said to pass through the netherworld after it sets in the land of the living as it moves back to the east to rise again the next morning. This suggests that the darkness of the netherworld is therefore dispelled, if only briefly, in regular intervals.[30] The barely tolerable conditions could be mitigated by continued attention from those who remained in the land of the living. This premise was the foundation of the cult of the dead, to which we now turn our attention.

Cult of the Dead and Communication with the Dead

The cult of the dead can include a number of different elements: from the initial funeral rituals through regularly occurring mortuary rituals, and from ancestor veneration to ancestor deification (at various levels) to ancestor worship.[31] It is not always easy to discern which of these is involved in any given text or practiced in any given culture. Especially controversial is the extent to which the cult of the dead was practiced in Israel, and the related but different question concerning the extent to which it was tolerated in normative, biblical Yahwism.

The study of the cult of the dead is important in relation to the Hebrew Bible at two levels. First, if we are to understand how Israelites thought about their prospects in the afterlife, we have to discern the extent to which the cult of the dead was practiced and what impact they believed such practices had on the conditions of their existence in the afterlife. Second, once we understand the dimensions of how the cult of the dead was practiced in the ancient world, we will inevitably find numerous passages in the Hebrew Bible that reflect some points of contact with those practices that we would not have otherwise noticed.

In most of the ancient Near East the dead were cared for through occasional water libations and food scraps from regular family meals left

29. Cf. the texts cited by J. Scurlock, "Ghosts in the Ancient Near East," *HUCA* 68 (1997): 81–82.

30. W. Heimpel, "The Sun at Night and the Doors of Heaven in Babylonian Texts," *JCS* 38 (1986): 127–51, discusses at length the contradictory information concerning this issue in the primary texts. He concludes that a significantly muted sun brings light to the netherworld below the western horizon only briefly before retiring to his quarters for the night.

31. T. J. Lewis, *Cults of the Dead in Ancient Israel and Ugarit* (Atlanta: Scholars Press, 1989); van der Toorn, *Family Religion*, 42–65, 154–68, 206–35; Scurlock, "Ghosts," 77–96.

Comparative Exploration: Sheol

Did Israel have any revelation about the afterlife that would lead them to reject their native cognitive environment? The main element of the cognitive environment that was rejected in the biblical text, though not always by the Israelites struggling with syncretism, was the fully articulated cult of the dead, though certainly Israel still venerated ancestors in some of the same ways that are found in the larger cultural context.

Sheol is the Hebrew term used to designate the place where the dead go. The term has no known antecedent in other cultures or religions of the ancient world, and the etymology of the word is uncertain and therefore unable to contribute to the discussion.[1] The most extensive Old Testament passage concerning Sheol is Isaiah 14:9–11. There the spirits of the dead are portrayed as coming to meet the recently deceased king of Babylon. The spirits of other deceased kings commiserate with him about their loss of power. They observe that his former pomp has procured no status in Sheol where he has only a maggot mattress and worm blankets. The figurative nature of this passage makes it difficult to make any conclusive statements about the details of life in Sheol, but the author is quite successful in conveying the idea that it is not particularly pleasant. In this sense it is very similar to the picture of the netherworld in Mesopotamian literature, though there the kings are believed to retain some of their earthly status.[2]

One of the complicating issues when trying to develop an understanding of Sheol as the netherworld is that the term is often used metaphorically to refer to death or the grave (e.g., Isa. 28:15). As a result it is spoken of as a place of decay (Ps. 16:10) to which someone would dig down (Amos 9:2). The consequence of the metaphorical usage is that many passages become ambiguous. When Jacob speaks of going to Sheol (Gen. 37:35; 42:38; 44:29, 31) is he speaking of the netherworld or the grave? Some have maintained that the term never refers to the netherworld, but always to the grave.[3] Difficulties with this view include:

- In Psalm 55:15 the psalmist prays: "Let death take my enemies by surprise; let them go down alive to Sheol, for evil finds lodging among them." The contrast between "death" in the first stich and "alive" in the second warns us that death and Sheol are not synonymous. It would be difficult to imagine that the psalmist hopes for his enemy to be buried alive.
- In Psalm 139:8 the psalmist observes: "If I make my bed in Sheol, you are there," as he speaks of the impossibility of fleeing from God. One could hardly contend that God is in the grave, while his access to the netherworld is of appropriate significance (see also Amos 9:2; Prov. 15:11).

These suggest that the concept of Sheol as the netherworld must be considered central to the understanding of the Israelite concept of afterlife.

Observations from the text that contribute to our understanding of the theology related to Sheol are as follows:

1. Those in Sheol are viewed as separated from God (Pss. 6:6; 88:3, 10–12; Isa. 38:18), though as previously mentioned, God has access to Sheol.
2. Sheol is never referred to as the abode of the wicked alone.
3. While Sheol is never identified as the place where all go, the burden of proof rests on those who suggest that there was an alternative.[4]
4. Sheol is a place of negation: no possessions, memory, knowledge, joy.[5]
5. It is not viewed as a place where judgment or punishment takes place, though it is considered an act of God's judgment to be sent there rather than remaining alive. Thus it is inaccurate to translate *sheol* as "hell," for the latter is by definition a place of punishment.[6]
6. There is no reference that suggests varying compartments in Sheol. "Deepest" Sheol (e.g., Deut. 32:22) refers only to its location ("beneath") rather than a lower compartment.[7]

There is little in this profile that would be foreign to or incompatible with the ancient Near Eastern cognitive environment, though it should also be noted that there are many additional elements within ancient Near Eastern thinking that would be incompatible with Israelite theology. We might say then that the Israelite thoughts on the matter would be a smaller circle of ideas nearly entirely encompassed within the larger ancient Near Eastern circle.

1. For the most complete discussion and critique of etymological suggestions, see T. Lewis, *ABD* 2:101–2. Add to his list the more recent suggestion that a precursor form of Sheol occurs as the proper name of a netherworld deity (*šu-wa-la*) in the late-second-millennium texts from Emar. For discussion and citations see Johnston, *Shades*, 78.

2. Compare, for instance, the description of the death of King Urnammu; see discussion in Katz, *Image*, 121–22, and pertinent sections in transliteration, translation, and commentary in appendix 5, 329–36.

3. R. L. Harris, "The Meaning of the Word Sheol as Shown by Parallels in Poetic Texts," *Bulletin of the Evangelical Theological Society* 4 (1961): 129–35.

4. R. Rosenberg contends that Sheol and "the pit" are places for the "wicked dead"—those who suffer untimely or unnatural death. She sees the alternative as being gathered to one's ancestors ("The Concept of Biblical Sheol Within the Context of Ancient Near Eastern Beliefs" [diss., Harvard, 1981], 174–93). Nonetheless, her evidence is not able to rule out that the untimely/unnatural death itself is the punishment of God, or that going down to the pit simply refers to improper burial. Additionally, verses like 1 Kings 2:6 suggest that one could go down to Sheol "in peace." Her explanation of this passage (240–41) is unconvincing.

5. Tromp, *Primitive Conceptions*, 187–90. Tromp has the most thorough treatment of Sheol and other netherworld concepts.

6. Ibid., 190–94, this notwithstanding Rosenberg's etymological analysis. She offers a sound defense of Sheol as derived from the root *sh'l* meaning "to conduct an investigation" (found with this meaning also in Ugaritic, Akkadian, and Aramaic) and thus conveying a forensic concept of "call to account (= punish)" ("Concept," 9–12). She does not succeed, however, in demonstrating that the etymology has carried over into the concepts attached to the meaning of the term in Israelite usage.

7. E. F. Sutcliffe, *The Old Testament and the Future Life* (London: Burns Oates and Washbourne, 1947), 57–59.

at the grave. More importantly they were honored through a monthly family meal of remembrance (*kispu*) to which the dead were invited. This meal usually took place during the "interluniam" when the moon was invisible before its reappearance in the new moon phase.[32] In this way the sustenance needs of the dead were met, easing their existence in the netherworld, and at the same time their status in the community of the family was reaffirmed.[33]

The dependence of the dead on the living suggests, as do the texts, that they are inherently weak. Yet they should not be underestimated. "If, then, ancient Mesopotamian ghosts were pitiably weak, helpless, and silent, and if they required offerings to keep them literally from eating mud in the Netherworld, it by no means followed that there was no point in seeking their assistance or that there was no reason to fear their wrath."[34]

In contrast to the normal interaction with the dead that involved caring for them in the netherworld, unusual circumstances occasionally brought other interaction with the dead as they made their presence known in the land of the living. The earlier discussion of the cult of the dead concerned the goals and values of the cult of the dead. Community was preserved and the dead were fondly remembered and cared for. In return for the efforts of the living on behalf of the dead, occasion arose when the dead were consulted for their aid on behalf of the living. This was possible because the deceased continued to exist—simply in another sphere and another form. The difficulty was making contact, and that was the specialty of the necromancer. The objective of seeking communication from the dead was to gain information about the future.[35] Shamash, the sun god who travels nightly through the netherworld, is requested (through magical incantations) to bring up the ghost of a particular person. Considerable caution is exercised lest a demonic or malevolent entity be mistakenly summoned. The ghost of the dead manifests its presence in a specially prepared skull. Then the ghost may be consulted. The ghost can be both seen and heard by the participants. All of this was very dangerous in that contact with a ghost was believed to jeopardize one's own life. Incantations were then used to reduce the risk of fatality.[36] The following

32. Van der Toorn, *Family Religion*, 50.
33. Abusch, "Ghost and God," 373.
34. Scurlock, "Ghosts," 83.
35. I. Finkel, "Necromancy in Ancient Mesopotamia," *AfO* 29 (1983): 1–17. I should stress that this quest for information is entirely separate from the care and feeding practices, in other words, that necromancy is a separate phenomenon from the cult of the dead; see B. Schmidt, *Israel's Beneficent Dead* (Winona Lake, IN: Eisenbrauns, 1994), 280–81 n. 21.
36. These incantations are of the *namburbi* genre, a genre designed to protect from the portended consequences of ill omens, particularly those omens cataloged in the omen series *šumma alu*.

text illustrates the various aspects of care and expectation between the living and the dead.

> You all are my family ghost(s), creators of everything . . . I have made for you a *kispu*-offering; I have poured you (a libation of) water. I have honored you; I have made you proud; I have shown you respect. On this day, before Šamaš (and) Gilgameš stand forth and judge my case, make a decision about me. The evil which is in my body, my flesh (and) my sinews, entrust it into the care of Namtar, the *sukkallu*-official of the Netherworld. [May] Ningizzida, chair bearer of the "broad earth," strengthen the watch over them. [May] Nedu, great keeper of the Netherworld [lock] (the gate) in their faces. Seize it and take it down to the "land of no return." May I, your servant, live; may I get well. Yet, on account of magical practices, I want to be cleared in your name. Let me give (you) cold water to drink via your water pipe. Keep me alive that I may praise you.[37]

Ghosts that were provided for and incorporated into the community engendered no cause for fear. Such ghosts were insipidly weak and innocuous. But then there were the others: those who had had no community even in life or whose lives and relationships were troubled; those who had none to remember them or were quickly forgotten or neglected; those who had not been able to receive proper burial; these were terrifyingly virulent and malevolent, and could become quite troublesome for the living. A considerable amount of literature from Mesopotamia is devoted to incantations to protect one from them or to exorcise or bind them.

Although it is clear that the Israelites knew of such practices and that they engaged in some level of activity that venerated the ancestors, one can still argue the extent to which they were involved in any sort of ancestor cult. The clearest biblical references to the recognizable cultic practices are negative (cf. Deut. 26:14; Jer. 16:6–8; Isa. 8:19–20).[38] Yet, at the same time, that Josiah had to purge many elements connected with the cult of the dead and necromancy in his reform (2 Kings 23:24) suggests that these practices had some currency in Israel even throughout much of the monarchy period.

Some contend that since the Israelite literature consistently presents the dead as weak, it would be contradictory to consider them as having the power to terrorize the living.

---

37. Scurlock, "Ghosts," 92.

38. The interpretation of the biblical passages is open to constant discussion. Van der Toorn (*Family Religion*) is largely in agreement with Spronk (*Beatific Afterlife*), whose interpretations are debated point by point by M. and E. Bloch-Smith, "Death and Afterlife in Ugarit and Israel," *JAOS* 108.2 (1988): 277–84. See also the extensive treatment in Lewis, *Cults*, 99–170.

The Old Testament, unlike Mesopotamian religious literature, contains no evidence of a highly developed demonology. Nor is it suggested anywhere that the spirits of the dead have power to harm the living. There is none of the dread, so graphically expressed in Babylonian incantations, of the unburied and untended spirit wreaking revenge on the living. In the few verses where 'ob does mean unequivocally the spirit of the dead, the usual impression is one of pathetic weakness rather than demonic strength.[39]

As pointed out by Scurlock, however, the weakness of the dead does not contradict the potential power of the spirits of the dead to terrify the living.[40] Nonetheless, neither is there sufficient evidence to provide a full profile of how the Israelites imagined the dead and their role. As many have commented, necromancy was not forbidden in Israel on the premise that it did not work, but because its efficacy was recognized and deemed illicit and contradictory to normative Yahwistic theology.

Reward, Punishment, and Eternal Hope

Throughout most of the ancient world, "eternal hope" was a foreign concept, for the ancients' thinking was framed by a bleak hope at best. "A common, unpleasant, equal, and sad destiny awaits everyone who leaves this world."[41] Here we get to the crux of the issue and begin to address the most important questions, toward which all of the above discussion has been leading. The question in the ancient world was *not*: "Is there life after death?" It was universally affirmed that there was. The questions were two: (1) What were the conditions in the afterlife? (2) What courses of action could improve one's condition or achieve desired conditions in the afterlife?

Conditions

The worst possible conditions imagined were either to be destroyed (only found in Egypt if one failed the weighing of the heart)[42] or to be a homeless spirit. Few hints can be found of torment as punishment. Philosophers today think of misery in the afterlife as a result of choice

39. Johnston, *Shades*, 166, quoting J. B. Burns, "Necromancy and the Spirit of the Dead in the Old Testament," *Transactions of Glasgow University Oriental Society* 26 (1979): 1–14, quotation on 11.

40. Scurlock, "Ghosts," 77–96.

41. Xella, "Death and Afterlife in Canaanite and Hebrew Thought," *CANE* 3:2063.

42. Other depictions of Egyptian "hell" indicate that the one who failed was bound, burned, stood upside down, and beheaded, or had his heart torn out by demons and was thrown into fiery pits or cauldrons.

Comparative Exploration: 1 Samuel 28

Ever since the publication of a number of Hittite texts dealing with rituals for consulting the spirits of the dead,[1] the details of Saul's encounter with the woman at Endor have been the focus of much attention. Of particular interest has been whether the Hebrew and cognate term *'ob* refers to a ritual pit used by the necromancer or to the spirit of the dead that is called up by the necromancer by means of a ritual pit (or something else).[2] The current consensus has swung in favor of the latter, but whatever the outcome of the semantic discussion, the ritual reflected in 1 Samuel 28 and the details of the encounter between Saul and the spirit of Samuel can be recognized as fitting quite comfortably in the cognitive environment of the ancient world.

The silence of the biblical text on a pit being dug or on the rituals that were performed by the woman is easily explained by the illicit nature of the practices. Of particular interest is that the woman describes what she sees as *'elohim*, which in the Old Testament is usually translated "God." The testimony of texts throughout the ancient Near East, however, confirms that spirits of the dead are referred to by such terms (cf. Akkadian cognate, *ilu*).[3]

1. H. Hoffner, "Second Millennium Antecedents to the Hebrew *'ôb*," *JBL* 86 (1967): 385–401; cf. also his article on *'ob* in *TDOT* 1:130–34.
2. See discussion and critique of major positions in Johnston, *Shades*, 161–66.
3. See, for instance, Lewis, *Cults*, 115–16. This point is contested by Schmidt (*Israel's Beneficent Dead*, 210–20). He suggests alternatively that the *'elohim* the woman refers to is the deity who has retrieved Samuel's spirit from the netherworld, as in necromancy the god Shamash was considered the one who would make sure that the spirit that was summoned was the one who came. Regardless of which interpretation of *'elohim* is correct, it is evident that knowledge of the ancient Near East is essential for understanding the biblical text.

or punishment. In the ancient world neither applied: the netherworld was not construed as a place of punishment, nor did one's choices in either life or death have an impact on one's eternal destiny.

Fundamentally people hoped that they would at the very least receive sustenance and that they would experience a peaceful rest with a continuing sense of community with both ancestors and descendants who were still living. A second tier of possibility would be that life would continue on in similar fashion to what they had experienced on earth. Specifically for kings this would include an extension of their status and prerogatives. As early as the third millennium Sumerians imagined a full spectrum of societal relationships in the netherworld. "The inhabitants of the netherworld are divided into three groups: human spirits, deities, and evil spirits that are neither human nor divine but a kind of demonic creature. The role of each group in the community of the netherworld, the offices they occupied, and their images build up a vision of a governmental system and social organization."[43] At this level, reward is to be found in the granting of status or prestige in the community of the netherworld.[44]

In a third tier of expectation we find the hope for a beatific life with deity, either in his presence or merging into him (e.g., in Egyptian thinking). Vague allusions in Mesopotamian sources also attest to the possibility that some might ascend to heaven, though typically only gods and occasionally kings are so honored.[45]

Methods to Achieve or Improve Conditions

Proper burial and the performance of funerary rites were always the first step and absolutely essential. These assured that the deceased would not wander or be excluded from family meals. The core fear was of becoming an outcast experiencing only a disconnected loneliness, for these cultures found their identity in community. Ongoing rituals performed by the survivors would continue to sustain the deceased both with food and drink and with remembrance (invoking the name of the deceased).[46] These elements were common across the ancient world, though the forms varied. At this level the conscientiousness of one's descendants determined one's experience of the afterlife, as community was preserved in a continuing symbiosis between the living and the dead.

> For both parties involved the manifestation of mutual acceptance was important. "The word of the living is precious to the dead, the word of the dead is precious to the living," as the Sumerian Hymn to the sun god says. The central moment in this contact between the dead and the living was the *kispum*. It constituted the rite by which the family proclaimed and, by the same token, reaffirmed and reinforced its identity. Outside the family, there was no such identity. Only under the roof of the family home would there be kin to call you by your name after death; out on the street one died nameless.[47]

The second tier of possibility, continuation of life as they knew it, had no requirements attached to it. It was simply the reflection of the natural hope that there was more than dust and desiccation after death. Not able to believe that death was the great equalizer, they came to accept first that kings had special status in the netherworld, "their fate in the netherworld depending more or less, not on their behavior, but on the conditions of life

43. Katz, *Image*, 113. Even priests are included in this social structure; see 122–23.
44. Ibid., 247.
45. P. Lapinkivi, *The Sumerian Sacred Marriage in Light of Comparative Evidence*, SAAS 15 (Helsinki: Neo-Assyrian Text Corpus Project, 2004), 148–54.
46. Van der Toorn, *Family Religion*, 52. In the Bible, notice Absalom's concern that he has no son to invoke his name (2 Sam. 18:18).
47. Ibid., 65.

on earth."[48] This was at times democratized so that social status and/or conditions of one's life or death (e.g., the number of sons, the nature of one's death, women who did not give birth, couples who did not consummate their marriage, the leper, the one who died in a fire) became the factors dictating one's experience of the afterlife. This is reflected in Enkidu's description of the netherworld to Gilgamesh.[49]

In Egypt the burial practices (for royal and wealthy patrons at least) were much more extensive than in the rest of the ancient Near East. Along with spells and incantations, they

Photo 22 Gilgamesh Tablet

provided a magical means of improving the lot of the deceased in the afterlife. In the *Book of the Dead* ethical behavior has a role, but only as part of the spells that magically accomplish their aim. Chapter 125 in the *Book of the Dead* entails a declaration of innocence to be made before the tribunal of Osiris by the person seeking to ascend into the presence of the gods.[50] The forty-two declarations listed there claim that the person is innocent of a variety of offenses from murder to lying, bringing lawsuits, being hot-tempered, and even not using a loud voice. Included in the numeration are a few sexual offenses as well as a few ritual offenses. This latter category is further clarified in the *Instruction of Merikare* (§65).

> Make ample the daily offerings, it profits him who does it.
> Endow your monuments according to your wealth,
> Even one day gives to eternity, an hour contributes to the future,
> God recognizes him who works for him.

The "weighing of the heart" ceremony comes in this context. Anubis weighed the heart of the deceased against the feather of Maat. As he does so, Amamet ("Gobbler") stood by to devour those who failed (who then

48. Bottéro, *Religion*, 109.
49. Tablet XII. See discussion in Katz, *Image*, 213–15.
50. R. O. Faulkner, *The Egyptian Book of the Dead: The Going Forth by Day* (San Francisco: Chronicle, 1998).

became evil spirits or ceased to exist). Passing opened the door to the fields of Yalu to live with Osiris. In this way ethical and cultic behavior during one's life were woven into a magical context to improve one's lot. This Egyptian scenario is the only one known from the ancient world to feature judgment of the deceased by the gods.

In Mesopotamia there was no judgment that would affect one's experience in the afterlife,[51] though there were three judgment halls in the netherworld. The first was ruled by the Anunnaki, deities who consulted the lists to make sure that only those who belonged (i.e., were dead and buried) came in and that they were advised of the rules. The second was ruled by Gilgamesh, who, from what can be determined from the limited data, adjudicated cases among the demons. The third, administered by the sun god Shamash, dealt with claims of the living against the dead (for haunting them) and to assure that the dead received their entitlements from offerings.[52]

In Israel the role of funerary offerings is downplayed in the biblical text and is rarely mentioned. Proper burial continued to be important. The biblical text includes no suggestion of judgment in the afterlife.[53] Psalmists at times express the hope of being delivered from Sheol, seeing the face of God, or enjoying his presence forever, but these can all also be interpreted as experiences in continuing life rather than referring to afterlife conditions.[54] When psalms speak in terms of awakening and seeing God's face (e.g., Pss. 11:7; 17:15), contextually speaking this is an anticipation not of heaven, but of an experience in the temple, as Psalms 27:4 and 63:3 make clear. This phrase occurs with the same meaning in Akkadian, where, for instance, Ashurbanipal longs to look at the face of his god, Ashur, (in the temple) and bow before him.[55] In a *Hymn to Ishtar* it is said that the sick man who sees her face revives.[56] In more general terms, the Babylonian sufferer in *Ludlul bel Nemeqi* says that he calls to his god, who does not show his face,[57] yet he hopes that the morning will bring him good things.[58] The psalmist also expects his deliverance to come when he awakes in the morning (Ps. 139:18).

---

51. Bottéro, *Religion*, 107.

52. Scurlock, "Death and Afterlife in Ancient Mesopotamian Thought," *CANE* 3:1887–88.

53. The barest hints of punishment for the wicked are found by some interpreters in places such as Isa. 66:24, though others would contend that these do not pertain to afterlife experience.

54. J. Walton, V. Matthews, and M. Chavalas, *IVP Bible Background Commentary: Old Testament* (Downers Grove, IL: InterVarsity Press, 2000), 512. For the interpretation that these refer to some hope in the afterlife, see Johnston, *Shades*, 200–207.

55. *CAD* B: 320.

56. *FDD* 245:5.

57. *BWL* 39, line 4.

58. E. Reiner, *Poetry from Babylonia and Assyria* (Ann Arbor: University of Michigan Press, 1985), 103.

A second expression concerns being redeemed from Sheol (e.g., Ps. 49:15). This only means that the psalmist has been spared from death for the moment, not that he will go to heaven instead of Sheol (compare the wording and contexts in Pss. 18:16–19; 30:2–3). Again comparable wording occurs in Mesopotamian literature where Marduk is considered one who restores life from the grave or gives life to the dead.[59] Gula, the goddess of healing, states that she can return the dead from the netherworld.[60] These are expressions not of resurrection but of healing.

Some contend that the way that Israelites could improve their lot in the afterlife was directly connected to covenant faithfulness and tied closely to the land. This would be no surprise given the pervasive impact of the covenant on Israel's identity and cognitive environment in virtually every area that we have investigated.

> By their sepulture in the family land, it was clear that the ancestors owned that land. Their offspring had received it from them; in a sense, the children lived off their forebears. By forsaking the cult of the ancestors (i.e., by not offering the libations due to the dead, and by failing to invoke their names), the living would lose the moral right to their land. Family estate, ancestral graves, and ancestor cult were closely intertwined realities; they could not very well be disentangled.[61]

H. C. Brichto, agreeing with this assessment of the pivotal role of the land, suggests that it is not the deceased's own covenant adherence (e.g., one's observance of torah or one's faith in Yahweh alone) that secured one's felicity in the afterlife, but rather one's success at passing the covenant on to the next generation. If continuity of covenant faithfulness were not vouchsafed to the next generation, then they would lose the land and could no longer sustain with their offerings and libations the deceased who were buried in the land.[62] In this way Brichto sees the Israelite perspective departing from the standard ancient Near Eastern viewpoints.

The difficulty with this view is the extent to which it understands Israel as fully involved in the care of the ancestors through funerary or mortuary cult. The ontology of the cults of the dead in the cognitive environment was at odds with normative Yahwistic theology. These cults were motivated by the desire either to placate the dead or to gain protection or information from them. In Yahwistic theology such practice encroached on Yahweh's domain.[63]

59. *CAD* B: 47; M/2: 141.
60. *CAD* M/2: 142.
61. Van der Toorn, *Family Religion*, 211.
62. Brichto, "Kin, Cult," 50.
63. Lewis, *Cults*, 177.

Postscript

Generalizations are always misleading (including that one). As hazardous as generalizations can be, they also can provide a helpful educational tool if used in a careful, nuanced way. Many of the specialists in the field of ancient Near Eastern studies have steadfastly eschewed the sort of synthesis that has been presented in this book, preferring instead the safe and reliable harbors of description. Their caution is to be commended and the integrity they bring to their discipline has made their work a tremendous resource.

The synthesis that I have offered is undoubtedly characterized by assessments that some scholars will judge to be misleading, premature, or even wrongheaded. But my intention was not to provide a failsafe guide to crawl inside the mind of someone from the ancient Near East. This is not possible and will never be possible. Instead, I desired to sift through the information provided by the specialists who have diligently made the literatures and cultures of the ancient Near East available to us, to perceive some of the important basics of that ancient cognitive environment. I attempted this specifically with the intention of demonstrating that Israel was indeed a partaker of this cognitive environment and shared many of the basics in some degree with its neighbors.

As we have studied the cognitive environments of the ancient Near East, the similarities across a broad spectrum of issues have emerged. The foundations, at least, show significant homogeneity. Where there are differences, they emerge due to a number of factors. Some could be the result of the physical environment (e.g., climate, topography): Egypt with its Nile, the Levant with its forbidding mountains, or southern Mesopotamia with its alluvial basin. Others are the result of sociopolitical realities or developments (e.g., the cities of Mesopotamia). Perhaps more significant are the driving forces that come to inhabit individual cultures and serve as catalysts that shape the unique characteristics of each. Egypt had its sense of afterlife that was fueled by the idea of a divinized king. In life he spoke as a god, and the only acceptable change of status after death was promotion. Mesopotamia had its divination, an institution fueled by a king whose divine sponsorship legitimated his rule. As son of the god, he was the one to whom the gods spoke. Israel had its covenant with its one God, Yahweh, who spoke through his covenant and the prophets, who were its guardians and champions.

The common cognitive environment was not borrowed from one culture to another. A cognitive environment is a cultural heritage shaped by infinite forces and influences generation by generation, through complexities that cannot be traced or identified. Even today when one culture decides to imbibe deeply of the cognitive environment of another (e.g., the Japanese adoption of Western culture), the result is a complex mix of that which is adopted wholesale, that which is adapted, that which is taken at one level without really being understood, that which is utterly rejected, and on and on in innumerable variations.

The literature of a culture reflects its own cognitive environment with all of the subtleties and nuances that have been forged both in continuity and discontinuity with the general culture. The extent to which the cultural environment expressed in any piece of literature derives from the commonalities is the extent to which one may detect familiarity, allusion, intertextuality, polemics, interaction, or even mimicry or adaptation. But it is never straightforward or simple. Our analysis of any literature will be more significant when we move beyond the forces and processes that shaped it to an understanding of how it functions and what it reflects in its new environment. This is true whether we are considering the intracultural use of the *Atrahasis Epic* in the *Gilgamesh Epic*, or of the motifs of the *Tale of Anzu* in *Enuma Elish*; or the intercultural use of El mythology by the Hittites or the treaty formula by the Israelites. It is the understanding of the cognitive environment that contributes most to the interpretation. Literary sources and history of composition have their place, but their significance pales in comparison. Interior literary analysis, whether structuralist or rhetorical, is important, but must be informed by knowledge of the cognitive environment lest the issues of modernity or postmodernity fuel the effort.

A brief review of some of the main findings of our study of the cognitive environment will serve to summarize the salient points of continuity and discontinuity between Israel and its neighbors.

Ontology in Israel differed little from that of the rest of the ancient Near East. Existence was perceived in terms of order and function, which were in turn determined by deity. The difference for Israel was that Yahweh had ultimate and ongoing responsibility for this ordered system from the outside, while in the ancient Near East the gods were administering it from the inside.

Epistemology in Israel was heavily influenced by the conviction that God had spoken. Everyone in the ancient world believed that much of what they knew, they knew because of the communication of the gods. The differences concerned how deity spoke and how that communication could be interpreted and known. Israel's unique convictions are represented in the communication of the covenant to Abraham and David, through Moses, in the direct communication of the prophets, and in the eventual canonization of literature accepted as divine revelation.

Anthropology in Israel, as everywhere else, understood that humanity derived from divine actions, and that human dignity was the product of the relationship to deity. The foundation of Israel's understanding of human dignity was the democratized image of God passed on generation by generation, beginning from a pair of primordial ancestors. In the larger ancient Near East, human dignity was located in the service to the gods as their needs were addressed.

Historiography in Israel was driven by the covenant, not by the king. In the rest of the ancient Near East, historiography had the function of promoting and legitimating the king. Divine sponsorship of the king was revealed in the activities of the gods in the human world, and historiography gave voice to that reality. Israelite historiography was more often negative toward the king and focused on divine faithfulness to the covenant (its blessings and curses). Historiography gave voice to that reality as it offered a divinely revealed interpretation of Yahweh's activities.

Sociology, at least in terms of major forces in society that dictated how life was lived, found its common ground in the way that very similar traditions and customs shaped daily life. The distinguishing element in Israelite thinking here was provided in the goal of imitating Yahweh. The understanding of both justice and wisdom were founded on this principle, which in turn became the keystone of ethics and influenced what might be called the development of interiority and morality. The knowledge of God required in such an enterprise was available only to the extent that the Israelites were persuaded that God did not reveal simply answers or commands but his character. Human interiority was linked to divine interiority and produced a value system rather than a social control system.

Theology in Israel expresses several major distinctives from the rest of the ancient world: God was one (and their worship of him was aniconic), God had made a covenant with a select people, God worked from outside the cosmos, God had no needs, and God had spoken in ways and to an extent not evident in other cultures. These distinctives were at the core

333

of Israelite identity and had a significant influence on their cognitive environment. Nevertheless, many aspects of their cognitive environment remained in continuity with the rest of the ancient world.

These points of continuity and discontinuity should have an important role in our interpretation of the Bible, and knowledge of them should guard against a facile or uninformed imposition of our own cognitive environment on the texts of ancient Israel, which is all too typical in confessional circles. This recognition should also create a more level playing ground as critical scholarship continues to evaluate the literature of the ancient world.

Appendix

Individual Gods[1]

Mesopotamian

Anu

This god is the earliest head of the pantheon known in the literature.[2] He is a sky god and, as the patriarch of the gods, is most often connected with authority. He has the status of one of the chief gods, but is not commonly the object of worship after the third millennium. He grants kingship in the human realm and elevates deities to higher ranks in the pantheon. He is responsible for the calendar, and in the natural world, he engenders vegetation. His main temple was in Uruk. He is the deity who summons Adapa, the first sage, to appear before him.

Enlil

Enlil succeeds his father Anu to the position at the head of the pantheon, which office he holds in the *Tale of Anzu* and in the epics of *Gil-*

---

1. Major sources of information on the various deities include the following: *DDD;* S. Bertman, *Handbook to Life in Ancient Mesopotamia* (New York: Facts on File, 2003); G. Leick, *A Dictionary of Ancient Near Eastern Mythology* (London: Routledge, 1991); P. Bienkowski and A. R. Millard, *Dictionary of the Ancient Near East* (Philadelphia: University of Pennsylvania Press, 2000); J. Black and A. Green, *Gods, Demons and Symbols of Ancient Mesopotamia: An Illustrated Dictionary* (Austin: University of Texas Press, 1992); T. Jacobsen, *Treasures of Darkness* (New Haven: Yale University Press, 1976); E. Hornung, *Conceptions of God in Ancient Egypt* (Ithaca: Cornell University Press, 1982); S. Morenz, *Egyptian Religion* (Ithaca: Cornell University Press, 1973); L. K. Handy, *Among the Host of Heaven* (Winona Lake, IN: Eisenbrauns, 1994); *CANE; OEAE.*
2. H. Wohlstein, *The Sky-God An-Anu* (Jericho: Stroock, 1976).

gamesh and *Atrahasis*. He was patron of the city of Nippur, the religious center in Sumerian religion. Under his father's authority, he also grants kingship and appoints the gods to their positions. His cosmic association is with the winds and the weather. Jacobsen contrasts Anu's identification with authority to Enlil's identification with force.[3] In flood stories and laments over fallen cities, that force is destructive.

Ea *(Sumerian Enki)*

This deity is known for his cunning.[4] He often takes on the role of advocate for humankind, but is not consistently benevolent. He is the god of wisdom and therefore of magic, omens, and divination. He is the third of the significant triad along with Anu and Enlil. His cosmic realm is the Apsu, the freshwater springs and underground rivers, and therefore he is seen as controlling fecundity. He is the patron god of Eridu, known as the first city. He plays a prominent role in a number of myths and epics, including *Inanna and Enki, Atrahasis, Gilgamesh, Enuma Elish,* and Adapa. He is often portrayed as involved in the creation of humans. His role as administrator of civilization is portrayed in *Enki and World Order*.

Shamash *(Sumerian Utu)*

As the sun god, Shamash was also the god of justice, and as such, was associated with law. He is the source of omens and the defender of the vulnerable and disenfranchised. The principal locations of his cult were in Sippar and Larsa. He is not a significant character in mythology, but has a number of major hymns in his honor. Gilgamesh relies on Shamash as he undertakes his quest for immortality.

Ishtar *(Sumerian Inanna)*

This goddess, the most popular of Mesopotamian deities, is characterized by paradox and conflict within her personality.[5] As both virgin and prostitute she embodies within herself order and disorder. She is ambiguous, at times androgynous, and aggressive. She disrupts values

---

3. Jacobsen, *Treasures*, 98–104.

4. S. N. Kramer and J. Maier, *Myths of Enki, the Crafty God* (New York: Oxford University Press, 1989).

5. In general see B. De Shong Meador, *Inanna: Lady of the Largest Heart* (Austin: University of Texas Press, 2000); D. Wolkstein and S. N. Kramer, *Inanna: Queen of Heaven and Earth* (New York: Harper & Row, 1983); P. Lapinkivi, *The Sumerian Sacred Marriage in Light of Comparative Evidence*, SAAS 15 (Helsinki: Neo-Assyrian Text Corpus Project, 2004), 155–66. On her personality see R. Harris, "Inanna-Ishtar as Paradox and a Coincidence of Opposites," in *Gender and Aging in Mesopotamia* (Norman: University of Oklahoma, 2000), 158–71.

and obscures the lines between gender roles. Sex, violence, storm, and fertility are all associated with her. Jacobsen calls her the goddess of "infinite variety."[6] T. Abusch emphasizes her foundational associations with life and death.[7] She is the patron deity of Uruk, identified with the planet Venus, and her emblem animal is the lion. She is featured in a variety of literature, including *Inanna and Enki*, *Gilgamesh Epic*, *Descent of Inanna/Ishtar*, *Exaltation of Inanna*, the *Dumuzi Cycle*, and a number of major hymns by the high priestess Enheduanna.[8]

Nergal

Though he is known as the lord of the netherworld, he is often subordinated to his spouse, Ereshkigal, who outranks him. Originally an astral deity (associated with Mars), he finds himself in the netherworld and is taken as husband by Ereshkigal and is thereby elevated to his throne. This account is found in the myth *Nergal and Ereshkigal*. Hymns honoring him associate him with disease and pestilence. He is referred to as Erra in *Erra and Ishum* and his cult is centered in the town of Cutha.

Ninurta

Initially a god of fertility, Ninurta came to be viewed as a warrior as his persona developed.[9] The former is seen in the instructions for farming given in the Sumerian work often referred to as the *Farmer's Almanac*. The latter is evident in his role as the heroic god who served as the champion of the gods in the *Tale of Anzu* and whose adventures are recorded in the *Exploits of Ninurta* (Lugal-e). Kings identified themselves with Ninurta, and he was the keeper of their royal insignia. He was a particular favorite of the Neo-Assyrian kings. As the son of Enlil the center of his cult was at Nippur, but he is also identified with Ningirsu, the god of Lagash.

Marduk

Enuma Elish recounts Marduk's emergence as the head of the Babylonian pantheon. He is patron of the city of Babylon and begins his rise to prominence early in the second millennium. He is considered the son of Ea and is a creator god. As a heroic god, he follows in the footsteps of Ninurta. Whatever cosmic associations Marduk may have had, they were subordinate to his political role, which did not reach its climax

6. Jacobsen, *Treasures*, 135–43.

7. T. Abusch, "Ishtar," *DDD* 454–55.

8. *COS* 1.161; Dalley, *MFM* 39–153; *ANET* 52–57; *COS* 1.160; *HTO* 1–84; Meador, *Innana*, note 5.

9. A. Annus, *The God Ninurta*, SAAS 14 (Helsinki: Neo-Assyrian Text Corpus Project, 2002).

until the Kassite period or the second dynasty of Isin (12th century). As king of the gods, he played the major role in the *Akitu* festivals. He was invoked in incantations and praised in hymns.[10]

Canaanite

El

El holds the highest position in the Syro-Palestinian pantheon.[11] He is king and father of the gods, specifically the father of Baal. He is wise and benevolent and is generally thought of as a creator god from whose place of residence the fertile waters flow. He is described as having seniority among the gods, but some scholars have considered him to be impotent and no longer of any real consequence in the biblical period.

Baal/Hadad

The best-known god of the ancient Near East by readers of the Bible, Baal was the storm god par excellence in the religious perception of the inhabitants of Syria-Palestine during the biblical period.[12] It has long been recognized that "Ba'al" is a title for Hadad rather than a proper name, though it is used as a proper name would be used in the Ugaritic texts. Though subordinate to El in the divine assembly, he is more active than El. As the storm god, he is the source of vitalizing rains. This connection, as well as his connection to the agricultural cycle, associates him with fertility. The other important aspect of the storm god is that armed with thunder, lightning, and flood he is a divine warrior. In the Ugaritic mythology he does battle against Yamm (a god of the sea) and Mot (a god of death) and has a house built for himself.

Dagan

Perhaps a grain/corn god,[13] Dagan is attested as a major god in Ebla and is associated with Emar and especially Mari in the area of the middle Euphrates.[14] There was also a major temple to Dagan in Ugarit. He is familiar in the Bible as the principal deity of the Philistines, who adopted him when they settled in Canaan. There are no extant myths

10. T. Abusch, *DDD* 543–49.

11. On the whole topic of Canaanite gods see C. L'Heureux, *Rank Among the Canaanite Gods: El, Ba'al, and the Repha'im*, HSM 21 (Missoula, MT: Scholars Press, 1979); M. Smith, *The Origins of Biblical Monotheism* (New York: Oxford University Press, 2001).

12. A. R. W. Green, *The Storm-God in the Ancient Near East* (Winona Lake, IN: Eisenbrauns, 2003), 153–218.

13. For discussion see J. F. Healey, "Dagon," *DDD* 216–19.

14. L. Feliu, *The God Dagan in Bronze Age Syria* (Leiden: Brill, 2003).

about him, so he is known only through passing references, offering lists, and the onomastica. In the Bronze Age he had the same status in the mid-Euphrates region as El had on the coast and Enlil had in southern Mesopotamia.[15]

Asherah

Consort of El, this goddess is often connected with fertility.[16] She is the queen mother of the gods. In syncretistic Israelite practice she may have been viewed as a consort to Yahweh.[17]

Anat

This goddess is the (adolescent?) sister, and by some accounts the consort, of Baal and is preeminently portrayed as a war goddess.[18] She is violent and temperamental, defying typical social and gender roles.

Egyptian

Amun-Re

A syncretistic formulation that depicts a relationship between the primeval creator god and wind god Amun and the sun god Re.[19] Amun was honored in Thebes by the temples of Karnak and Luxor and was associated with the ram. The priesthood of Amun-Re was politically powerful in the 18th Dynasty.

Osiris

Portrayed in mummified, anthropomorphic form, Osiris is the judge and king in the realm of the dead. His main cult center is in Abydos. In the mythology he was murdered by his brother, Seth. His rebirth and resurrection in the western land of Duat is the premise for the hope of afterlife in Egyptian religion. In the *Book of the Dead* he receives the vindicated individuals into the next life as he is portrayed sitting on his throne and flanked by his wife/sister, Isis, and her sister, Nephthys.

15. Ibid., 302.
16. J. Hadley, *The Cult of Asherah in Ancient Israel and Judah: Evidence for a Hebrew Goddess* (Cambridge: Cambridge University Press, 2000); W. A. Maier, *'Asherah: Extrabiblical Evidence* (Atlanta: Scholars Press, 1986); S. M. Olyan, *Asherah and the Cult of Yahweh in Israel* (Atlanta: Scholars Press, 1988).
17. Z. Zevit, *The Religions of Ancient Israel* (New York: Continuum, 2001), 359–405.
18. N. H. Walls, *The Goddess Anat in Ugaritic Myth* (Atlanta: Scholars Press, 1992).
19. Sources for information about the Egyptian gods include Hornung, *Conceptions of God*; Morenz, *Egyptian Religion*.

Isis

This goddess of magic is the wife of Osiris and the mother of Horus. In the latter role she is portrayed as suckling the child Horus and becomes the picture of motherly nurture and protection. By the New Kingdom she is joined to Hathor and connected to the inundation of the Nile.

Horus

Horus is most closely connected with the pharaoh, who was considered an incarnation of the deity. He is portrayed as a bird of prey (falcon), which befits his identity as a sky god.

Seth

The antithesis of Horus, Seth is the villain among the Egyptian gods. He represents disorder and darkness, and is the murderer of Osiris in the mythology. He was considered the lord of foreign lands. His emblem animal is zoologically unidentifiable.

Thoth

The ibis-headed deity is the scribe among the gods and the patron of scribes. He is depicted as the record keeper in the judgment scene from the *Book of the Dead*. His principal cult center was Hermopolis. He is also a moon god and in addition to the ibis was from the second millennium associated with a baboon.

Aten

Not a sun god per se, but a representation of the sun disk and its rays, this god became the focus of Akhenaten's move toward monotheism in the fourteenth century. According to Assmann, Aten is a cosmic power that "manifests itself in the form of the sun, of light, of time, of radiance and motion."[20] The worship of Aten was antimythical and antianthropomorphic. Other gods were demoted and cults eliminated or disenfranchised.[21]

Ptah

This god was associated with artisans and craftsmen and was typically represented in human form. His primary role in the literature is as a primordial creator deity, particularly dominating the tradition in Memphis, where he was patron deity. He created by the spoken word,

20. J. Assmann, *The Mind of Egypt* (New York: Metropolitan, 1996), 216.
21. Ibid., 216–17.

an act that eventuated in the creation of the hieroglyph for that which was created.[22]

Others

Kemosh

As Yahweh was the national God of Israel, Kemosh (Chemosh) was the national god of Moab. He is known as early as the third millennium BC among the gods of Ebla (under the name Kamish), hence he is an ancient West Semitic deity. He is mentioned prominently in the Mesha Stele, the major Moabite royal inscription from the mid-ninth century.

Yahweh

The God of Israel is a cosmic deity, a covenant deity, a national deity, and a family deity.[23] He is the patron of Jerusalem, where his temple was located. Both the Elephantine texts and the excavation of what is probably a temple of Yahweh at Arad suggest that other shrines to Yahweh existed despite official policy.[24] Texts indicate that he had identity both as a sun god and a storm/fertility god.[25] Only tantalizing hints suggest an early history outside Israel.

22. Ibid., 353.

23. T. Mettinger, *In Search of God* (Philadelphia: Fortress, 1988); M. Smith, *The Early History of God* (San Francisco: Harper & Row, 1990); idem, *Origins*; J. de Moor, *The Rise of Yahwism* (Leuven: Peeters, 1997); B. Lang, *The Hebrew God: Portrait of an Ancient Deity* (New Haven: Yale University Press, 2002).

24. *ABD* 2:445–55.

25. J. G. Taylor, *Yahweh and the Sun*, JSOTSup 111 (Sheffield: Sheffield Academic Press, 1993); A. R. W. Green, *The Storm-God in the Ancient Near East* (Winona Lake, IN: Eisenbrauns, 2003), 219–80.

Bibliography

Ackerman, Susan. *Under Every Green Tree: Popular Religion in Sixth-Century Judah.* HSM 46. Atlanta: Scholars Press, 1992.

Archi, A. "Hittite and Hurrian Literatures: An Overview," *CANE* 4:2367–78.

Assmann, Jan. *The Search for God in Ancient Egypt.* Ithaca: Cornell University Press, 2001.

Batto, B., W. W. Hallo, and K. L. Younger. *Scripture in Context IV: The Biblical Canon in Comparative Perspective.* Lewiston, NY: Mellen, 1991.

Beckman, G. *Hittite Diplomatic Texts.* SBLWAW 7. Atlanta: SBL, 1996.

Bertman, Stephen. *Handbook to Life in Ancient Mesopotamia.* New York: Facts on File, 2003.

Bienkowski, P., and A. R. Millard, eds. *Dictionary of the Ancient Near East.* Philadelphia: University of Pennsylvania Press, 2000.

Black, J. A., and W. J. Tait. "Archives and Libraries in the Ancient Near East," *CANE* 4:2197–2210.

Block, Daniel I. *The Gods of the Nations.* Rev. ed. Evangelical Theological Society Studies. Grand Rapids: Baker, 2000.

Boardman, J., et al., eds. *Cambridge Ancient History.* Cambridge: Cambridge University Press, 1970–.

Bottéro, J. "Akkadian Literature: An Overview," *CANE* 4:2293–2304.

———. *Everyday Life in Ancient Mesopotamia.* Baltimore: Johns Hopkins University Press, 2001.

Braun, Joachim. *Music in Ancient Israel/Palestine.* Grand Rapids: Eerdmans, 2002.

Brody, Aaron. *Each Man Cried out to His God.* HSM 58. Atlanta: Scholars Press, 1998.

Bryce, Glendon. *The Legacy of Wisdom.* Cranbury, NJ: Assoc. Universities, 1979.

Carr, G. L. "The Love Poetry Genre in the Old Testament and the Ancient Near East." *JETS* 25 (1982): 489–98.

Cartledge, Tony W. *Vows in the Hebrew Bible and the Ancient Near East.* JSOTSup 147. Sheffield: JSOT Press, 1992.

Chavalas, Mark, and K. Lawson Younger, eds. *Mesopotamia and the Bible*. Grand Rapids: Baker, 2002.

Chirichigno, Gregory. *Debt-Slavery in Israel and the Ancient Near East*. JSOTSup 141. Sheffield: JSOT Press, 1993.

Clifford, Richard J. *The Cosmic Mountain in Canaan and the Old Testament*. HSM 4. Cambridge: Harvard University Press, 1972.

Crenshaw, James C. *Education in Ancient Israel*. New York: Doubleday, 1998.

Cross, F. M. *Canaanite Myth and Hebrew Epic*. Cambridge: Harvard University Press, 1971.

Currid, John. *Ancient Egypt and the Old Testament*. Grand Rapids: Baker, 1997.

Dalglish, Edward R. *Psalm Fifty-One in the Light of Near Eastern Patternism*. Leiden: Brill, 1962.

Damrosch, David. *The Narrative Covenant*. San Francisco: Harper & Row, 1987.

Day, John. *Yahweh and the Gods and Goddesses of Canaan*. JSOTSup 265. Sheffield: JSOT Press, 2000.

Dearman, Andrew. *Religion and Culture in Ancient Israel*. Peabody, MA: Hendrickson, 1992.

de Vaux, Roland. *Early History of Israel*. Philadelphia: Westminster, 1978.

Evans, Carl D., W. W. Hallo, and John B. White. *Scripture in Context: Essays on the Comparative Method*. Pittsburgh: Pickwick, 1980.

Ferguson, P. "Who Was the 'King of Nineveh' in Jonah 3:6?" *TynBul* 47.2 (1996): 301–14.

Ferris, Paul Wayne. *The Genre of Communal Lament in the Bible and the Ancient Near East*. SBLDS 127. Atlanta: Scholars Press, 1992.

Finkelstein, J. J. "Bible and Babel: A Comparative Study of the Hebrew and Babylonian Religious Spirit." Pages 355–80 in *Essential Papers on Israel and the Ancient Near East*. Ed. F. E. Greenspahn. New York: New York University Press, 1991.

Fisher, Loren R., ed. *Ras Shamra Parallels, Vol. II*. Analecta Orientalia 50. Rome: Pontifical Biblical Institute, 1975.

Fox, Michael V. *The Song of Songs and the Ancient Egyptian Love Songs*. Madison: University of Wisconsin Press, 1985.

Frankfort, Henri, et al. *Intellectual Adventure of Ancient Man*. Chicago: University of Chicago Press, 1946.

Freedman, D. N., ed. *The Anchor Bible Dictionary*. 6 vols. New York: Doubleday, 1992.

Fritz, Volkmar. *The City in Ancient Israel*. Sheffield: Sheffield Academic Press, 1995.

Gammie, J., and L. G. Perdue, eds. *The Sage in Israel and the Ancient Near East*. Winona Lake, IN: Eisenbrauns, 1990.

Green, Alberto R. W. *The Role of Human Sacrifice in the Ancient Near East*. ASOR Dissertation 1. Missoula, MT: Scholars Press, 1975.

——. *The Storm-God in the Ancient Near East*. Winona Lake, IN: Eisenbrauns, 2003.

Greengus, S. "Sisterhood Adoption at Nuzi and the 'Wife-Sister' in Genesis." *HUCA* 46 (1975): 5–31.

Greenspahn, Frederick. *Essential Papers on Israel and the Ancient Near East*. New York: New York University Press, 1991.

Greenspoon, L. J. "The Origin of the Idea of Resurrection." Pages 247–322 in *Traditions in Transformation*. Ed. B. Halpern and J. D. Levenson. Winona Lake, IN: Eisenbrauns, 1981.

Hallo, W. W. "Biblical History in Its Near Eastern Setting: The Contextual Approach." Pages 1–26 in *Scripture in Context: Essays on the Comparative Method*. Ed. Carl D. Evans et al. Pittsburgh: Pickwick, 1980.

———. "Compare and Contrast: The Contextual Approach to Biblical Literature." Pages 1–19 in *Scripture in Context III: The Bible in Light of Cuneiform Literature*. Ed. W. W. Hallo, B. Jones, and G. Mattingly. Lewiston, NY: Mellen, 1990.

———. "New Moons and Sabbaths: A Case Study in the Contrastive Approach." *HUCA* 48 (1977): 1–18. Repr. pp. 313–32 in *Essential Papers on Israel and the Ancient Near East*. Ed. F. E. Greenspahn. New York: New York University Press, 1991.

———. "The Origins of the Sacrificial Cult: New Evidence from Mesopotamia and Israel." Pages 3–14 in *Ancient Israelite Religion: Essays in Honor of Frank Moore Cross*. Ed. P. D. Miller, P. D. Hanson, and S. D. McBride. Philadelphia: Fortress, 1987.

Hallo, W. W., Bruce Jones, and Gerald Mattingly. *Scripture in Context III: The Bible in Light of Cuneiform Literature*. Lewiston, NY: Mellen, 1990.

Hallo, W. W., James Moyer, and Leo Perdue. *Scripture in Context II: More Essays on the Comparative Method*. Winona Lake, IN: Eisenbrauns, 1983.

Hallo, W. W., and K. L. Younger, eds. *Context of Scripture*. 3 vols. Leiden: Brill, 1997–2002.

Halpern, B. "The Ritual Background of Zechariah's Temple Song." *CBQ* 40 (1978): 167–90.

Haran, Menahem. *Temples and Temple Service in Ancient Israel*. Winona Lake, IN: Eisenbrauns, 1985.

Harris, Rivkah. *Gender and Aging in Mesopotamia*. Norman, OK: University of Oklahoma Press, 2000.

Hasel, Michael. *Military Practice and Polemic: Israel's Laws of Warfare in Near Eastern Perspective*. Berrien Springs, MI: Andrews University Press, 2005.

Hess, Richard S., and D. T. Tsumura, eds. *I Studied Inscriptions from Before the Flood*. SBTS 4. Winona Lake, IN: Eisenbrauns, 1994.

Hilber, J. W. "Psalm CX in the Light of Assyrian Prophecies." *VT* 53 (2003): 353–66.

Hill, Andrew. *Enter His Courts with Praise*. Grand Rapids: Baker, 1993.

Hoerth, A. *Archaeology and the Old Testament*. Grand Rapids: Baker, 1998.

Hoerth, A., G. Mattingly, and E. Yamauchi, eds. *Peoples of the Old Testament World*. Grand Rapids: Baker, 1994.

Hoffmeier, James K. *Ancient Israel in Sinai*. Oxford: Oxford University Press, 2005.

———. "The Arm of God versus the Arm of Pharaoh in the Exodus Narratives." *Bib* 67 (1986): 378–87.

———. *Israel in Egypt*. Oxford: Oxford University Press, 1997.

Hoffner, H. *Hittite Myths*. SBLWAW 2. Atlanta: SBL, 1990.

———. "Some Thoughts on Genesis 1 and 2 and Egyptian Cosmology." *JANES* 15 (1983): 39–49.

Holladay, J. S. "Assyrian Statecraft and the Prophets of Israel." *HTR* 63 (1970): 29–51.

Horowitz, Wayne, and Victor (Avigdor) Hurowitz. "Urim and Thummim in Light of a Psephomancy Ritual from Assur (LKA 137)." *JANES* 24 (1992): 95–115.

Hurowitz, V. "The Golden Calf: Made by Man or God?" *BRev* 20.2 (2004): 28–32, 47.

———. "Isaiah's Impure Lips and Their Purification in Light of Mouth Purification and Mouth Purity in Akkadian Sources." *HUCA* 60 (1989): 39–89.

Izre'el, Shlomo. *Adapa and the South Wind*. Winona Lake, IN: Eisenbrauns, 2001.

Jacobsen, Thorkild. *Treasures of Darkness*. New Haven: Yale University Press, 1976.

Johnston, S. I., ed. *Religions of the Ancient World*. Cambridge, MA: Belknap, 2004.

Kalluveettil, Paul. *Declaration and Covenant*. Rome: Pontifical Biblical Institute, 1982.

Keel, Othmar. *The Symbolism of the Biblical World*. New York: Seabury, 1978.

Keel, Othmar, and Christoph Uehlinger. *Gods, Goddesses and Images of God in Ancient Israel*. Minneapolis: Fortress, 1998.

King, Philip. *Amos, Hosea, Micah: An Archaeological Commentary*. Philadelphia: Westminster, 1988.

King, Philip, and Lawrence Stager. *Life in Biblical Israel*. Louisville: Westminster John Knox, 2002.

Kitchen, Kenneth A. *On the Reliability of the Old Testament*. Grand Rapids: Eerdmans, 2003.

———. "Proverbs and Wisdom Books of the Ancient Near East: The Factual History of a Literary Form." *TynBul* 28 (1977): 69–114.

———. "The Tabernacle—A Bronze Age Artifact." *EI* 24 (1993): 121–29.

———. *The Third Intermediate Period in Egypt*. Warminster: Aris & Phillips, 1986.

Kitz, A. M. "The Hebrew Terminology of Lot Casting and Its Ancient Near Eastern Context." *CBQ* 62 (2000): 207–14.

Kloos, Carola. *Yhwh's Combat with the Sea*. Leiden: Brill, 1986.

Korpel, M. C. A. *A Rift in the Clouds: Ugaritic and Hebrew Descriptions of the Divine*. UBL 8. Münster: Ugarit-Verlag, 1990.

Kuhrt, Amélie. *The Ancient Near East, 3000–330 BC*. 2 vols. London: Routledge, 1997.

Lambert, W. G. "Destiny and Divine Intervention in Babylon and Israel." *OtSt* 17 (1972): 65–72.

Launderville, Dale. *Piety and Politics*. Grand Rapids: Eerdmans, 2003.

Levenson, J. D. "The Temple and the World." *JR* 64 (1984): 275–98.

Lichtheim, Miriam. *Ancient Egyptian Literature*. 3 vols. Berkeley: University of California Press, 1973–80.

Lindenberger, James M. *Ancient Aramaic and Hebrew Letters*. Atlanta: SBL, 2003.

Lipiński, Edward. *The Aramaeans: Their Ancient History, Culture, Religion*. Leuven: Peeters, 2000.

Loewenstamm, S. E. "Biblical Studies in the Light of Akkadian Texts." Pages 256–67 in *From Babylon to Canaan*. Jerusalem: Magnes, 1992.

Longman, Tremper, III. *Fictional Akkadian Autobiography: A Generic and Comparative Study*. Winona Lake, IN: Eisenbrauns, 1991.

Machinist, P. "The Question of Distinctiveness in Ancient Israel." Pages 196–212 in *Ah, Assyria*, ed. M. Cogan and I. Eph'al, Scripta Hierosolymitana 33. Jerusalem: Magnes, 1991. Repr. pp. 420–42 in *Essential Papers on Israel and the Ancient Near East*. Ed. F. E. Greenspahn. New York: New York University Press, 1991.

Malamat, A. "Mari and the Bible: A Comparative Perspective." Pages 1–10 in *Mari and the Bible*. Leiden: Brill, 1998.

———. *Mari and the Early Israelite Experience*. New York: Oxford University Press, 1989.

———. "The Proto-History of Israel: A Study in Method." Pages 303–13 in *The Word of the Lord Shall Go Forth: Essays in Honor of David Noel Freedman*. Ed. C. L. Meyers and M. O'Connor. Winona Lake, IN: Eisenbrauns, 1983.

Malul, M. *The Comparative Method in Ancient Near Eastern and Biblical Legal Studies*. AOAT 227. Kevelaer: Butzon & Bercker; Neukirchen-Vluyn: Neukirchener Verlag, 1990.

———. *Knowledge, Control and Sex*. Jaffa: Archaeological Center, 2002.

Marsman, Hennie J. *Women in Ugarit and Israel*. Leiden: Brill, 2003.

Matthews, Victor. *Manners and Customs in the Bible*. Peabody, MA: Hendrickson, 1988.

Matthews, Victor, and D. Benjamin. *The Social World of Ancient Israel, 1250–587 BCE*. Peabody, MA: Hendrickson, 1993.

Mattingly, G. L. "The Pious Sufferer: Mesopotamia's Traditional Theodicy and Job's Counselors." Pages 305–48 in *Scripture in Context III: The Bible in Light of Cuneiform Literature*. Ed. W. W. Hallo, B. Jones, and G. Mattingly. Lewiston, NY: Mellen, 1990.

Mazar, Amihai. *Archaeology of the Land of the Bible, 10,000–586 B.C.E.* New York: Doubleday, 1990.

Mazar, Benjamin, ed. *Views of the Biblical World*. 5 vols. Jerusalem: International, 1956–61.

McCarthy, D. J. *Treaty and Covenant*. Rev. ed. AnBib 21A. Rome: Pontifical Biblical Institute, 1978.

McComiskey, T. E. "The Seventy 'Weeks' of Daniel Against the Background of Ancient Near Eastern Literature." *WTJ* 47 (1985): 18–45.

McNutt, P. M. *The Forging of Israel: Iron Technology, Symbolism, and Tradition in Ancient Society*. Sheffield: Almond Press, 1990.

Mettinger, Tryggve. *No Graven Image?* ConBOT 42. Stockholm: Almqvist & Wiksell, 1995.

Michalowski, P. "Sumerian Literature: An Overview," *CANE* 4:2279–92.

Middleton, J. Richard. *The Liberating Image*. Grand Rapids: Baker, 2005.

Millard, A. R. "Methods of Studying the Patriarchal Narratives as Ancient Texts." Pages 35–51 in *Essays on the Patriarchal Narratives*. Ed. A. R. Millard and D. J. Wiseman. Winona Lake, IN: Eisenbrauns, 1983.

Millard, A. R., and D. J. Wiseman, eds. *Essays on the Patriarchal Narratives*. Winona Lake, IN: Eisenbrauns, 1983.

Miller, J. Maxwell, and John H. Hayes. *A History of Ancient Israel and Judah*. Philadelphia: Westminster, 1986.

Miller, Patrick D. *The Religion of Ancient Israel*. Louisville: Westminster John Knox, 2000.

———. *They Cried to the Lord*. Minneapolis: Fortress, 1994.

Moorey, P. R. S. *Ancient Mesopotamian Materials and Industries*. Winona Lake, IN: Eisenbrauns, 1999.

Moran, William L. *The Amarna Letters*. Baltimore: Johns Hopkins University Press, 1992.

Morenz, Siegfried. *Egyptian Religion*. Ithaca: Cornell University Press, 1973.

Nakhai, Beth Alpert. *Archaeology and the Religions of Canaan and Israel*. Boston: ASOR, 2001.

Nemet-Nejat, Karen Rhea. *Daily Life in Ancient Mesopotamia*. Westport, CT: Greenwood, 1998.

Netanyahu, B., et al., eds. *World History of the Jewish People, First Series*. 8 vols. Jerusalem: Masada, 1963–77.

Nissen, Hans J. *Early History of the Ancient Near East*. Chicago: University of Chicago Press, 1988.

Nissinen, M. *Prophets and Prophecy in the Ancient Near East*. SBLWAW 12. Atlanta: SBL, 2003.

Noegel, S. E. "Moses and Magic: Notes on the Book of Exodus." *JANES* 24 (1992): 45–59.

Noll, K. L. *Canaan and Israel in Antiquity*. London: Sheffield, 2001.

Olyan, Saul. *Biblical Mourning*. Oxford: Oxford University Press, 2004.

Oppenheim, A. L. *Ancient Mesopotamia: Portrait of a Dead Civilization*. Chicago: University of Chicago Press, 1964.

Pagolu, Augustine. *The Religion of the Patriarchs*. JSOTSup 277. Sheffield: JSOT Press, 1998.

Parker, S. B. "The Literatures of Canaan, Ancient Israel, and Phoenicia: An Overview," *CANE* 4:2399–2410.

Parker, S. B., ed. *Ugaritic Narrative Poetry*. Atlanta: Scholars Press, 1997.

Pedersén, O. *Archives and Libraries in the Ancient Near East. 1500–300 B.C.* Bethesda, MD: CDL, 1998.

Perdue, Leo G., et al., eds. *Families in Ancient Israel*. Louisville: Westminster John Knox, 1997.

Petersen, Allan Rosengren. *The Royal God: Enthronement Festivals in Ancient Israel and Ugarit*. JSOTSup 259. Sheffield: JSOT Press, 1998.

Pham, Xuan Huong Thi. *Mourning in the Ancient Near East and the Hebrew Bible*. JSOTSup 302. Sheffield: JSOT Press, 1999.

Pitard, Wayne. *Ancient Damascus*. Winona Lake, IN: Eisenbrauns, 1987.

Pollock, Susan. *Ancient Mesopotamia*. Cambridge: Cambridge University Press, 1999.

Porter, Barbara Nevling. *One God or Many? Concepts of Divinity in the Ancient World*. Bethesda, MD: CDL, 2000.

Porter, Paul A. *Metaphors and Monsters*. ConBOT 20. Lund: Gleerup, 1983.

Postgate, J. N. *Early Mesopotamia: Society and Economy at the Dawn of History*. London: Routledge, 1992.

Pritchard, James B., ed. *Ancient Near Eastern Texts*. 3rd ed. with supplement. Princeton: Princeton University Press, 1969.

———, ed. *Ancient Near East in Pictures*. Princeton: Princeton University Press, 1954.

Redford, D. B. "Ancient Egyptian Literature: An Overview," *CANE* 4:2223–42.

———. *Egypt, Canaan, and Israel in Ancient Times*. Princeton: Princeton University Press, 1992.

———, ed. *Oxford Encyclopedia of Ancient Egypt*. 3 vols. New York: Oxford University Press, 2001.

Reviv, H. *The Elders in Ancient Israel*. Jerusalem: Magnes, 1989.

Ringgren, H. "The Impact of the Ancient Near East on the Israelite Tradition." Pages 3–43 in *Tradition and Theology in the Old Testament*. Ed. Douglas A. Knight. 1977. Repr. Sheffield: JSOT Press, 1990.

———. "Remarks on the Method of Comparative Mythology." Pages 407–11 in *Near Eastern Studies in Honor of William Foxwell Albright*. Ed. H. Goedicke. Baltimore: Johns Hopkins University Press, 1971.

Roberts, J. J. M. "The Ancient Near Eastern Environment." Pages 3–43 in *The Bible and the Ancient Near East*. Winona Lake, IN: Eisenbrauns, 2002.

———. "The Bible and the Literature of the Ancient Near East." Pages 44–58 in *The Bible and the Ancient Near East*. Winona Lake, IN: Eisenbrauns, 2002.

———. "Myth versus History: Relaying the Comparative Foundations." *CBQ* 38 (1976): 1–13.

Roth, M. *Law Collections from Mesopotamia and Asia Minor.* SBLWAW 6. Atlanta: Scholars Press, 1995.

Ruffle, J. "The Teaching of Amenemope and Its Connection with the Book of Proverbs." *TynBul* 28 (1977): 29–68.

Saggs, H. W. F. *The Encounter with the Divine in Mesopotamia and Israel.* London: Athlone, 1978.

———. *The Greatness That Was Babylon.* New York: Mentor, 1962.

———. *The Might That Was Assyria.* London: Sidgwick & Jackson, 1984.

Sasson, Jack, ed. *Civilizations of the Ancient Near East.* 4 vols. New York: Scribner's, 1995.

Schmidt, Brian B. *Israel's Beneficent Dead.* Winona Lake, IN: Eisenbrauns, 1996.

Selman, M. J. "Comparative Customs and the Patriarchal Age." Pages 93–138 in *Essays on the Patriarchal Narratives.* Ed. A. R. Millard and D. J. Wiseman. Winona Lake, IN: Eisenbrauns, 1983.

Selms, A. van. *Marriage and Family Life in Ugaritic Literature.* London: Luzac, 1954.

Shafer, Byron E., ed. *Religion in Ancient Egypt.* Ithaca: Cornell University Press, 1991.

Snell, Daniel, ed. *Companion to the Ancient Near East.* Oxford: Blackwell, 2005.

———. *Life in the Ancient Near East.* New Haven: Yale University Press, 1997.

Sparks, Kenton L. *Ancient Texts for the Study of the Hebrew Bible.* Peabody, MA: Hendrickson, 2005.

Stern, Ephraim. *Archaeology of the Land of the Bible*, Vol. 2: The Assyrian, Babylonian, and Persian Periods, 732–332 BCE. New York: Doubleday, 2001.

Talmon, S. "The Comparative Method in Biblical Interpretation: Principles and Problems." Pages 320–56 in *Congress Volume, Göttingen 1977.* VTSup 29 (1977). Repr. pp. 381–419 in *Essential Papers on Israel and the Ancient Near East.* Ed. F. E. Greenspahn. New York: New York University Press, 1991.

Thompson, Thomas L. *Historicity of the Patriarchal Narratives.* BZAW 133. Berlin: de Gruyter, 1974.

Tigay, Jeffrey. *The Evolution of the Gilgamesh Epic.* Philadelphia: University of Pennsylvania Press, 1982.

Tsumura, David. *Creation and Destruction.* Winona Lake, IN: Eisenbrauns, 2005.

Van de Mieroop, M. *Cuneiform Texts and the Writing of History.* London: Routledge, 1999.

———. *A History of the Ancient Near East: ca. 3000–323 BC.* London: Blackwell, 2003.

van der Toorn, K. *Family Religion in Babylonia, Syria and Israel: Continuity and Change in the Forms of Religious Life.* Leiden: Brill, 1996.

———. *From Her Cradle to Her Grave.* Sheffield: JSOT Press, 1994.

———. *The Image and the Book.* Leuven: Peeters, 1997.

———. "The Significance of the Veil in the Ancient Near East." Pages 327–40 in *Pomegranates and Golden Bells: Studies in Biblical, Jewish, and Near Eastern Ritual, Law, and Literature in Honor of Jacob Milgrom.* Ed. D. P. Wright, D. N. Freedman, and A. Hurvitz. Winona Lake, IN: Eisenbrauns, 1995.

———. *Sin and Sanction in Israel and Mesopotamia.* Assen: Van Gorcum, 1985.

van der Toorn, K., Bob Becking, and Pieter W. van der Horst, eds. *Dictionary of Deities and Demons in the Bible.* 2nd ed. Leiden: Brill, 1999.

Van Seters, John. *Abraham in History and Tradition.* New Haven: Yale University Press, 1975.

Vanstiphout, H. *Epics of Sumerian Kings.* SBLWAW 20. Atlanta: SBL, 2003.

Vaux, Roland de. *Ancient Israel.* New York: McGraw-Hill, 1961.

Walton, John H. *Ancient Israelite Literature in Its Cultural Context.* Grand Rapids: Zondervan, 1989.

Walton, John, Victor Matthews, and Mark Chavalas. *IVP Bible Background Commentary: Old Testament.* Downers Grove, IL: InterVarsity Press, 2000.

Wasilewska, Ewa. *Creation Stories of the Middle East.* London: Jessica Kingsley, 2000.

Watanabe, Kazuko. *Priests and Officials in the Ancient Near East.* Heidelberg: C. Winter, 1999.

Weinfeld, M. "The Covenant of Grant in the Old Testament and the Ancient Near East." *JAOS* 90 (1970): 184–203.

———. *Social Justice in Ancient Israel.* Minneapolis: Fortress, 1995.

Westbrook, R. "Biblical and Cuneiform Law Codes." *RB* 92 (1985): 247–64.

———. *History of the Ancient Near Eastern Law.* Leiden: Brill, 2003.

Westenholz, Joan Goodnick. *Legends of the Kings of Akkade.* Winona Lake, IN: Eisenbrauns, 1997.

Wilson, Robert R. *Genealogy and History in the Biblical World.* New Haven: Yale University Press, 1977.

———. *Prophecy and Society in Ancient Israel.* Philadelphia: Fortress, 1980.

Wiseman, D. J. *Nebuchadrezzar and Babylon.* Oxford: Oxford University Press, 1985.

Wolters, A. "The Riddle of the Scales in Daniel 5." *HUCA* 62 (1991): 155–77.

Wyatt, Nicholas. *Space and Time in the Religious Life of the Ancient Near East.* Sheffield: Sheffield Academic Press, 2001.

Yadin, Y. *The Art of Warfare in Biblical Lands.* 2 vols. London: Weidenfeld & Nicolson, 1963.

Yamauchi, Edwin. *Persia and the Bible.* Grand Rapids: Baker, 1990.

Younger, K. Lawson, William W. Hallo, and Bernard F. Batto. *The Biblical Canon in Comparative Perspective.* Lewiston, NY: Mellen, 1991.

Zevit, Ziony. *Religions of Ancient Israel.* New York: Continuum, 2001.

Scripture Index

Genesis

1 30, 98, 183, 187, 190–91, 194–95, 197–99, 212–13
1–5 207n20
1–11 31, 34, 281n22
1:1 186n15
1:2 187–88
1:3–5 180
1:5 180
1:17 171
1:21 183
1:26 95
1:26–27 212–13
1:29–30 125
2 124–25, 198, 208–9
2:1 198
2:5–6 187n1
2:7 213
2:15 198
2:18 187
2:24 208
3:22 95
5 108
5:2 183
6:1–4 281n22
6:17 177
7:4 177
7:10 170
7:11 170n27
7:11–12 177
8:2 170n27
8:21 195n1
8:22 190
11:1–9 25, 120–21

11:7 95
12–50 34
20 243
24 259
25:20 150
28 118n23, 243
28:5 150
31 150
35:2–4 150
35:18 213
37 243
37:35 320
41 243
41:16 243
42:38 320
44:29 320
44:31 320

Exodus

1–12 34–35
3:13 92
4:1–9 274
6:2–3 92
18:19 294
18:20 292, 294
19:3–6 93
19:5–6 93, 293
20:1 292, 294
20:1–8 155–60
21:1 292
21:1–22:16 293
21:2–22:17 292
21:12–17 293n2

22:18–23:19 292
22:19–20 294
22:25–27 294
23:4–5 294
24:3 292, 297
24:10 169, 174, 169n12
24:12 292, 298n1
25:9 113n3
25:14 209n1
28:29 258n1
34 298n5
34:10 183
36:31–32 209n1

Leviticus

16 313–32
17:11 214
20 294n5
20:9–21 293
26:12 93

Numbers

16:30 183
22–25 83
35:24 292

Deuteronomy

4:5–8 297
4:44–45 298n1
6:1 298n4
6:6 258n1
6:24–25 301n1

Foreign Words Index

Akkadian

abubu, 177
adû, 281
akitu, 57, 57n21, 132n5, 194, 194n38, 197, 221, 338
apilu, 264
apkallu, 52, 108n60
apsu, 47, 47n8, 90, 157, 158, 186, 188, 188n21, 336
arallu, 176, 318n25
arik-din-ili, 128
ašipu, 266, 266n76
asu, 266, 266n76
awilu, 207
banu, 93
baru, 243, 263, 263n66
bašāmu, 182
bit-rimki, 58
burumu, 182
damu, 210
dinu, 257
du₆-kù, 186
ebbu, 111n73
ehursaggula, 126
ekur, 51, 72, 119n28
ellu, 111, 111n74
eninnu, 126, 196
ṭetemmu, 210, 211, 212, 317
ilu, 207, 325
irkallu, 318n25

kaššaptu, 266
kaššapu, 266
kinu, 109n68
kispu, 322, 323
kispum, 326
kittu, 109n68, 283
ki-tuš ni-dub-bu-da-ni, 158
kudurru, 108n59, 168, 178
lamassu, 81
limmu, 67
marratu, 173
meḫu, 177, 177n59
melammu, 282
mesu, 176
mišaru, 107n56, 283
muḫḫu, 264
nagu, 172
namburbi, 58, 58n26, 263, 265, 322n36
napištu, 148, 214n36
naru, 285
palah ilim, 153
parṣu, 98–99, 191, 193
qâpu, 153n65
radu, 177, 177n58
saggilmud, 169
salmu, 212
ṣelu, 208
šertu, 108n59
shuilla, 73
šimati, 191
šīmtu, 98, 193
sukkallu, 323

šuklulu, 99n37
šumma alu, 261, 322n36
šumma izbu, 61n34, 243, 243n2, 261, 261n64
šurpu, 60n31, 145n30
šu-wa-la, 321
ṭemu, 147, 210, 211
têrtu, 257
tupšarru, 264
ubašimu parṣišu, 193
uṣurtu, 99
utu, 72, 126, 191, 336

Egyptian

akh, 210, 211, 212
ba, 211, 211n30, 316, 316n12
djet, 210
duat, 172, 178, 184, 315, 316, 317, 339
ha'u, 210
ḫpr, 182
írí, 182
izfet, 154n70, 279
ka, 210, 211, 211n29, 316, 316n12
ḳbḥw-Ḥr, 170
ḳm3, 182
maat, 107, 130, 152, 154, 125, 279, 283, 302, 327
msì, 182
rmtn, 206n14

354

Modern Author Index

356

Ancient Literature Index

Book of the Dead (Negative Confession) E, 59, 96n28, 111n70, 315, 327, 339, 340
Coffin Texts E, 204, 206, 315, 318n22
Daily Ritual of Amun-Re E, 59
Execration Texts E, 59
Hittite Priests H, 59
Menologies/Hemerologies A, 57
Mistress of the Pit H, 59
Namburbi Incantations A, 58
Substitute King A, 57, 138–39
Washing of the Mouth A, 58, 114–15
Zukru Festival at Emar A, 58

Royal Inscriptions

Azatiwada Inscription from Karatepe P, 65
Behistun Inscription P, 66
Black Obelisk of Shalmaneser III A, 7, 63
Cyrus Cylinder P, 7, 66
Edict of Hattushili H, 64
Gudea Temple Cylinders S, 63, 126n43, 127, 128n48, 196n43, 198, 199n5
Merneptah Stele E, 64

Mesha Inscription Moabite, 65, 236n2
Ramesses II—Battle of Qadesh E, 64
Sennacherib Prism A, 7, 64
Tel Dan Inscription Aramaic, 65, 236n2
Zakkur Inscription Aramaic, 65

Wisdom Literature

Admonitions of Ipuwer E, 77
Babylonian Theodicy A, 76
Dialogue of Pessimism A, 76, 309n51
Farmer's Almanac S, 337
Instruction of Amenemope E, 35, 77
Instruction of Any E, 77
Instruction of Merikare E, 77, 153, 204, 206, 212, 327
Instruction of Ptahhotep E, 76, 303
Ludlul bel Nemeqi A, 75, 145n29, 307, 328
Man and His Ba E, 76
Man and His God S, 75
Satire on the Trades E, 77
Sumerian Proverbs S, 75
Words of Ahiqar Aramaean, 78, 302n28

Subject Index